EDGEHILL

The Campaign and the Battle

THE AUTHOR

Peter Young was born in 1915, and educated at Monmouth School and Trinity College, Oxford. He was commissioned as a Second Lieutenant in the Bedfordshire and Hertfordshire Regiment in 1939. He saw frequent action throughout the Second World War, principally in Europe, and took command of the Number 3 Commando Brigade in 1945. In 1959, after post-war service in the Arab Legion, he became Reader of Military History at the Royal Military Academy, Sandhurst. He has published and edited numerous books on military history and taken part in many television and radio programmes. In 1968 he became 'Captain-Generall' of The Sealed Knot Society of Cavaliers and Roundheads. He died in 1988.

Titles in the GREAT BATTLES series

Agincourt by Christopher Hibbert
Hastings by Peter Poyntz-Wright
Marston Moor: 1644 by Peter Young
The Boyne and Aughrim by John Kinross
Corunna by Christopher Hibbert
Wellington's Peninsular Victories by Michael Glover
Trafalgar: The Nelson Touch by David Howarth
Waterloo: A Near Run Thing by David Howarth
Arnhem by Christopher Hibbert

Military Memoirs published by The Windrush Press

The Recollections of Rifleman Harris
   Edited and Introduced by Christopher Hibbert
The Letters of Private Wheeler
   Edited and with a Foreword by B.H. Liddell Hart
The Diaries of a Napoleonic Foot Soldier
   Edited and Introduced by Mark Raeff
A Soldier of the 71ˢᵗ
   Edited and Introduced by Christopher Hibbert
The Wheatley Diary
   Edited and Introduced by Christopher Hibbert
The Recollections of Sergeant Morris
   Edited by John Selby

EDGEHILL 1642

The Campaign and the Battle

BRIGADIER

PETER YOUNG

DSO, MC, MA, FSA, F.R.HIST.S.

Introduction by C.V. Wedgwood

THE WINDRUSH PRESS · GLOUCESTERSHIRE

First published in Great Britain by The Roundwood Press Ltd, 1967
Reprinted by The Windrush Press, 1995 and 1998
Little Window, High Street
Moreton-in-Marsh
Gloucestershire GL56 0LL
Tel: 01608 652012
Fax: 01608 652125

British Library Cataloguing in Publication Data
A catalogue record for this book is available from the British Library

ISBN 0 900075 34 1

Typeset by Archetype, Stow-on-the-Wold
Printed and bound in Great Britain by Bell & Bain Ltd., Glasgow

The front cover shows a detail from *Battle of Edgehill, 1642* by Harry
Payne by courtesy of Peter Newark's Military Pictures.
Cover design by Miranda Harvey.

To Cicely Veronica Wedgwood

Contents

PART THREE

APPENDICES

List of Illustrations, Maps and Diagrams

Plate section between pages 206 and 207

Photographs of the battlefield taken from the air
Photographs by John Wright

Ford of the Dene River
Photograph by John Wright

Mediaeval Round Tower on Beacon Hill
Photograph by John Wright

De Gomme's Plan
The Royal Collection © Her Majesty the Queen

Edgehill: Then and Now
Photograph by John Wright

The Monument at Edgehill
Photograph by Roger Dowdeswell

MAPS AND DIAGRAMS

Author's Acknowledgements
from First Edition

Sir Bernard de Gomme's plan showing the Order of Battle of the Royalist Army is reproduced by gracious permission of Her Majesty the Queen from the original in Windsor Castle.

The portrait of Colonel Nathaniel Fiennes is reproduced by kind permission of Lord Saye and Sele, who also allowed photographs of Broughton Castle to be taken.

My special thanks are due to Miss Margaret Toynbee for reading the proofs. Her diligence, only rivalled by her erudition, has steered me past many pitfalls. The blemishes that remain are all my own.

To Major G. Tylden, VD, author of *Horses and Saddlery*, for contributing the 'Notes on Horseflesh' in Chapter Three (pp. 29–31).

Dr. Ian Roy has placed his specialist knowledge of Royalist administration at my disposal. His edition of the Royalist Ordnance Papers is of the greatest value to students of the military history of the period and I am most grateful for permission to quote a number of these interesting documents in full.

Major Michael Terry, RAOC, who made extensive researches into the history of the battle during his time at the C.A.D., Kineton. He placed the results of this work at my disposal. His topographical knowledge was particularly valuable.

A very great number of individuals, public bodies and firms have placed me in their debt by helping me in a variety of ways. I offer them my grateful thanks. Their ready cooperation has greatly lightened my task, besides making it more pleasant.

For permission to reproduce pictures:

The Armouries, H.M. Tower of London, George Bell & Co. Ltd., The Bodleian Library, Dunedin Public Art Gallery Society Inc., New Zealand, The Mansell Collection, The National Army Museum, The National Gallery of Canada, The National Portrait Gallery, The National Portrait Gallery of Scotland, Newark Corporation, The Parker Gallery, The Royal Commission on Historic Monuments (England), The Stadtische Galerie in Landesmuseum, Hanover, The Trustees of Dr. Williams' Library, London, The Victoria and Albert Musum, Lieut. Colonel J. L. B. Leicester-Warren, T.D., H. J. Lloyd-Johnes, Esq., T.D., F.S.A., J. D.

H. Pennant, Esq., Major Sir Charles Shuckburgh, T.D., D.L., J.P.

For original pictures and drawings:
W. Y. Carman, Esq., F.S.A., Francois Caron Delion, Miss J. Desfontaines, H. R. Hosking, Esq., John Vale, Esq.

For his assistance in collecting the illustrations:
Captain R. G. Hollies-Smith, F.R.G.S.

For permission to reconnoitre and explore on their land or on land in their charge:
Henry Boswell, Esq., T. T. Jeffes, Esq., Colonel R. F. Stretch, the Commandant of the C.A.D., Kineton.

For assistance in searching the battlefield for relics:
Major M. G. H. Little, RE(V) and the ranks of 225 (City of Birmingham) Field Squadron RE (T & AVR) devoted several weekends to the project. Jack Greenhill, Esq., whose skill as a diviner was placed at our disposal. David Fisher and Gerard Lewis.

For the generous gift of three musket bullets picked up on the battlefield by her grandfather: Miss M. Fell.

For permission to use documents in their possession:
Anthony W. G. Lowther, Esq., ARIBA, FSA, for allowing me to reproduce the Royalist pay warrant in his collection.

Bickham Sweet-Escott, Esq., was good enough to place his researches into the career of William Beaw at my disposal.

D. W. King, Esq., OBE, FLA, Chief Librarian of the Ministry of Defence Library (Central and Army) gave me much assistance, as so often in the past, especially assembling material on the organization of Essex's army.

For information regarding the supernatural:
T. Perry, Esq., Miss B. M. Seaton, Michael Howard Romney-Wollard, Esq., and The Society for Psychical Research.

For cartography: P. Vaughan Williams.

For photography:
Roger Dowdeswell, The National Army Museum, Alan Palmer of Dunedin, New Zealand, John Wright, and The Ravenna Studies, Putney.

For compiling the index – no light task: Bruce Stevenson, Esq., FLA.

P. W. Dix, by arousing local interest in the work, has brought me much information which would otherwise have been denied me.

Captain G. C. Blundell, R.N. (retd.) besides much other assistance, lent me his handsome steed, Misty, for my initial reconnaissance. I am grateful to the one for mounting me, and the other for permitting me to remain in the saddle.

Mrs. G. Marion Norwood Callam for information on the Norwoods who fought in the Royalist Army.

I must here mention an old friend, the late Rev. Percy Sumner, a leading expert on uniforms. It was he that discovered de Gomme's Plan during the course of researches in the Royal Library, and, knowing of my interest in the battle, brought it to my notice.

Gordon Norwood, who first conceived this project, has been generous and helpful at every stage. It was his declared intention that only the best would do, maps, pictures or what you will. To him and his wife, Ruth, whose hospitality I have so often enjoyed, I owe a real debt of gratitude.

My wife, Joan, in addition to typing the MSS has read and checked all the proofs, a work of great self-sacrifice since (as I suspect) the Civil Wars is not her favourite subject.

Abbreviations

ADD.	Additional.
BM.	British Museum.
BOD. LIB.	Bodleian Library.
CAM.	Calendar of the Committee for the Advance of Money.
CCC.	Calendar of the Committee for Compounding.
CSPD.	Calendar of State Papers, Domestic.
D.	Dragoons.
DNB.	Dictionary of National Biography.
EHR.	English Historical Review.
F.	Foot.
H.	Horse.
HMC.	Historical Manuscripts Commission.
IO.	Indigent Officer.
JSAHR.	Journal of the Society for Army Historical Research.
K.	Killed.
L of C.	Lines of Communications.
L & T.	Life and Times.
MS.	Manuscript.
MW.	Mortally wounded.
NLW.	National Library of Wales.
ORD.	Ordnance.
POA.	Parliamentary Official Account.
PRO.	Public Record Office.
PW.	Prisoner of War.
QMG.	Quartermaster General.
QSR.	Quarter Sessions Records.
Rawl.	Rawlinson.
Regt.	Regiment.
ROA.	Royalist Official Account.
SP.	State Papers.
W.	Wounded.
WO.	War Office.

Introduction

As a life-long devotee of the English Civil War I welcome this comprehensive and absorbing book on the Battle of Edgehill. Brigadier Young enjoys an unrivalled position as the leading authority on the military history of the Civil War. He knows seventeenth century warfare and armies through and through, but he brings to all he writes something more than can be gained from even the most careful study of contemporary sources: a practical understanding and experience such as few historians of this epoch have been able to apply to the subject. He sees the significant material points that are by no means always apparent to the scholar at his desk, and he is as scrupulous as the scholar in emphasising the doubts and difficulties which limit the historian's powers of imaginative reconstruction. Thus he writes:

> 'For a variety of reasons it is extremely difficult to piece together the sequence of events in a battle that took place three centuries ago. The officers did not have watches, or if they did, failed to synchronise them. Hardly anyone had a map and certainly not one of a scale to show tactical dispositions . . . After a few vollies, black powder smoke obscured the scene, and eye-witnesses tended to improve their personal observations with hearsay picked up afterwards around the camp fire. Many regiments whose doings were of real importance have no chronicler . . . One is left clutching at straws and the name of a fallen officer or the device on a captured colour may have real significance.'

The problems of the military historian could not be better put. His writing is always clear, practical and to the point and enlivened by a nice touch of humour. I for one shall never henceforward forget the military shortcomings of the Earl of Essex, thus succinctly put: 'As a strategist he must be considered distinctly suspect. What other general fought three of his major battles with the enemy between his army and his base?'

For this study of the Battle of Edgehill, Brigadier Young has submitted all the available evidence to the light of his experience and judgment, and has most carefully worked out the Order of Battle on the opposing sides. By this means he lays the foundation for his reconstruction of the battle itself. No picturesque flourishes or imaginative alarums and excursions, but a straightforward account of the action as it probably happened.

The interest of his book is not confined to this single memorable encounter on October 23rd 1642 and the campaign of which it was the most important event. Here, built up from a variety of sources, is a picture of the recruiting, character, organization and equipment of the two armies at the outset of the Civil War together with useful character sketches of their leaders. In later chapters he follows out the results of the battle and the fate of many of the combatants. His chapter 'On Veterans' rescues many names from oblivion and will spring the imagination of anyone interested in what became of the individual men who fought on that day.

The rich documentation of his text, the important assemblage of accounts by contemporaries that he has gathered together and published in the appendix, and the many valuable lists of officers make this book an essential possession for serious students of the armies in the Civil War. It is also fascinating reading for lovers of English history in the seventeenth century. We know much of the thoughts and theories of the men involved in this great conflict within the nation. But in these pages we see the process of physical conflict in close-up, meet our ancestors face to face in action and hear in their own words what they had to say about it.

Peter Young has written and compiled a work invaluable to the military historian and enthralling to all who seek through history to know more about the actions and characters of men.

C. V. WEDGWOOD

Foreword

And there went out another horse that was red, and power was given to
him that sat thereon to take peace from the earth, and that they should kill
one another: and there was given unto him a great sword.

Revelations, Chapter 6, Verses 3 & 4

JOHN VICARS, the Puritan chronicler, found it very remarkable 'that God
did so order it,' that the battle of Edgehill was fought in The Vale of the
Red Horse. He conceived that this had 'fit reference and resemblance to
that Red Horse, mentioned by the Spirit of God in the Revelations'. He
interprets the passage thus:

'The *Rider* is Truth, the *Red-Horse, Gods vindicative-wrath*, the *Great-Sword,*
the *great destruction* to be made, Peace taken from the Earth, that is, from
the wicked and Idolaters of the Earth. Thus Mr Brightman, and thus say
I, here was Truth in our Parliaments Army riding on the *Red-Horse*, this
Meadow so called, with a great Sword or slaughter of just revenge, taking
peace and comfort from those wicked Earthen-Cavaliers, and Romish
Idolaters, there combined and banded together against God and his Truth.
And was not here a most remarkable mistery, thus made clear unto us in
this *Meadow?* let the judicious and godly judge.'[1]

The causes of the war between King Charles and his Parliament are no
part of this story. The reader who seeks information on this subject will
do well to turn to the pages of Miss Wedgwood.[2] The causes of the
struggle were complex, and affected different men in different ways. The
Parliamentarians could claim that they fought for freedom of religion and
for justice, though political power was at least as powerful a cause. To
Oliver Cromwell the first may have been the strongest motive and to
John Hampden, the second. Unquestionably it was the third which
carried most weight with John Pym.

Englishmen have not greatly changed in 300 years. It demands no great
imaginative powers to see one's friends and neighbours as Cavaliers and
Roundheads. The rights and wrongs of the struggle are still capable of
rousing passions, and it is difficult for the historian to achieve absolute

impartiality. Believing this to be so I feel compelled to say at the outset that my personal sympathies are with the Royalists. I trust that I am sufficiently aware of my bias to prevent its destroying my critical faculties.

The significance of great events is often concealed from contemporaries. It may be doubted, for example, whether in 1643 the French or the Spaniards regarded the battle of Rocroi as being a landmark. But now it seems to mark the end of the long Spanish supremacy in the Art of War. Edgehill on the other hand was seen from the first to be an event of decisive importance. Before the battle it still seemed possible that a peace might be negotiated. Thereafter, there could be no real question of sheathing the sword until one side or the other had been fought to a standstill. The news of Edgehill told men all over the country that it was to be war in earnest.

The battle must be seen in its setting of the campaign, but in planning this book I have deliberately avoided detailed descriptions of minor operations such as Southam, Powick Bridge and Brentford, which, though they do not lack interest, would in my judgment throw the story out of balance.

The authorities for the battle are far from comprehensive, and some are difficult to obtain. For this reason I have included transcripts and précis of some of them in Part III, where the general reader will have no difficulty in ignoring them.

The armies of 1642, consisting almost entirely of volunteers, differed in character from those of 1643 and after. As the war dragged on its temper grew more bitter. Early enthusiasms waned and both sides were compelled to recruit their foot by impressment. In describing the solder of 1642 one is compelled to some extent to draw illustrations from the later years of the war, but I have endeavoured to avoid this.

Admirers of Cromwell may find it strange that he scarcely figures in this story. The evidence of Nathaniel Fiennes seems to show conclusively that Cromwell's troop was not one of those actually engaged in the battle.

It testifies to the urgency of the issue between them that the armies should have taken the field so late in the year – practically beyond the end of the campaigning season.

1   Vicars, Jehova-Jireh, p. 201.
2   Wedgwood, The King's Peace, & The King's War.

PART ONE

The English Soldier of 1642

CHRONOLOGY

1

Experience

> This Kingdom hath been too long in peace – our old commanders both
> by sea and by land are worn out, and few men are bred in their places, for
> the knowledge of war and almost the thought of war is extinguished.
>
> Sir Edward Cecil, 1628

HISTORIANS HAVE NOT spared their criticisms of the military system of the
later Tudors and the early Stuarts, and Sir Charles Firth goes so far as to
assert that the 'history of the Civil War is the history of the evolution of
an efficient army out of a chaos'. He is referring, of course, to the New
Model Army. But though Bosworth and Flodden lay far in the past, the
Englishmen of 1642 were not altogether lacking either in military virtues
or military experience. For if England had long enjoyed a profound peace,
all Europe had long been at war, and English soldiers had not lacked
employment and the chance to learn their trade. Most of the Englishmen
and Scots who served on the continent did so in the pay of the States of
Holland or the King of Sweden, but others fought under French or
Danish colours, or even as far afield as Austria and Russia.

It was the Dutch service that had most influence on the warriors of our
Civil Wars for the States had long employed four English and four Scots
foot regiments. But there were also English regiments in the service of
Spain and France, and the successes of Gustavus Adolphus had given
British soldiers a high regard for Swedish innovations in the art of war.

The officers and men who had sailed with Mansfield or had taken part
in the Cadiz expedition or the attempt to relieve La Rochelle, had no
reason to applaud the administrative arrangements made by King Charles'
government, but it cannot be denied that it was military experience of a
sort.

The failure to subdue the Scots rebellion of 1639 may be attributed to
the disaffection of Charles' English subjects as well as an empty treasury.
Even so he was able to put some 20,000 men from the northern counties
into the field. According to Sir Edmund Verney, who was to carry the
Banner Royal at Edgehill, the men were very raw and ill-provided: 'I
daresay there was never so raw, so unskilful, and so unwilling an army,

brought to fight'. Next year the King raised about 25,000 men from the southern counties, who showed themselves, at first, extremely ill-disciplined – even murdering two of their officers. Routed at Newburn in August 1640, they were compelled to retreat into Yorkshire. Here their officers gradually got the upper hand and men like Sir Jacob Astley, the Sergeant-Major-General, were able not only to reduce them to discipline, but to instil into them the rudiments of military skill. On 10 September the King reviewed 2,000 horse and 16,000 foot at York and 'they looked very well to the unpractised eyes of civilian observers. Secretary Vane ventured the opinion that Gustavus Adolphus had never had better. With these, and Strafford's boasted army from Ireland, the Scots were as good as dead men!'[1] The longer the men were kept together under experienced officers, the better they were bound to become. How many of these soldiers fought in the armies of 1642–1646 none can say. At least one Royalist colonel, Sir Thomas Lunsford, attempted with some success to levy his former soldiers again in 1642.

Both sides were naturally anxious not only to obtain the services of such professional soldiers as were available, but if possible to prevent the other side doing so. The Parliament went to the length of giving half pay to unemployed officers on the pretext that they would be given commands in Ireland. In July 1642 a broadsheet was published in London entitled 'A List of The Names Of Such Persons Who are thought fit for their Accommodation, and the furtherance of the Service in Ireland, to be entertained as Reformadoes; And to receive the halfe Pay due to the severall Officers here under named, untill opportunity be offered, according to their merit, further to prefer them; or that Order by given to the contrary . . .'

This measure of the Committee at Guildhall was not unsuccessful, though it is unlikely that many of these officers ever went to Ireland, or were even intended for that service.

There are in the list 30 officers of horse and 138 of foot, a total of 168. Of these, no less that 63 had before long found employment in the army under the Earl of Essex, while more than 30 became officers in the Royalist armies, including several who fought at Edgehill. Lieutenant Troilus Turbervile, though discharged as a Papist in December 1640, succeeded in persuading the Guildhall Committee to give him his half-pay, though he probably did not draw it for long, as he became Captain-Lieutenant of the King's Lifeguard, H. One of these reformado captains, who certainly fought at Edgehill, was James Usher, soon to be colonel of a Royalist dragoon regiment.

By no means all these officers were men who had been in the army raised to fight the Scots. Of the 138 foot officers only 40 figure in the

1640 list. It must be assumed, therefore, that many others had returned from service with the Dutch, the Germans and the Swedes.

The Reformadoes included:

	Horse	Foot
Colonel	–	1
Lt. Colonels	–	3
Sergeant-Majors	–	3
Captains	4	40
Captain-Lieutenants	–	8
Lieutenants	7	30
Cornets	9	–
Ensigns	–	53
Quartermasters	10	–
	30	138 = 168

Then, as later, bloody war meant quick promotion, and though Colonel Henry Billingsley, soon to be stigmatized by one of his puritan sergeants as 'a Godamme blade and doubtlesse hatche in hell'[2] could only obtain the lieutenant-colonelcy of Denzil Holles' Regiment, more junior officers often obtained a step in rank if not two.

DISCIPLINE

I remember what a sober friend of mine told me that he replied to an old acquaintance of his engaged with Fairfax vaunting of the sanctity of their army and the negligence of ours. 'Faith,' says he, 'thou sayest true; for in our army we have the sins of men (drinking and wenching) but in yours you have those of devils, spiritual pride and rebellion'.

Sir Philip Warwick[3]

The Royalist army gained a reputation, not altogether undeserved, for plundering and licentiousness. Nor were its officers always as exact in the performance of their duties as could be wished. As time went by and money grew short the soldiers were compelled to maraud in order to subsist, and discipline was undermined.

But the young Royalist soldiers of 1642 do not seem to have been particularly badly behaved. Clarendon, no lover of the soldiery, may be cited in support of this view.

'And this must be confessed, that, either by the care and diligence of the officers, or by the good inclinations and temper of the soldiers themselves, the army was in so good order and discipline, that, during the King's stay at Shrewsbury, there was not a disorder of name, the country being kind to the soldiers, and the soldiers just and regardful to the country. And by

the free loans and contributions of the gentlemen and substantial
inhabitants, but especially by the assistance of the nobility who attended,
the army was so well paid that there was not the least mutiny or discontent
for want of pay; nor was there any cause; for they seldom failed every
week, never went above a fortnight unpaid.'[4]

At Birmingham, a town notoriously hostile to him, the King had two
men executed for stealing from the house of a Rebel soldier.[4]

This is not to say that there was no indiscipline at all in 1642. One
smiles when Mrs Hutchinson speaks of the Royalist soldiers at
Nottingham 'plundering all the honest men of their arms'. No doubt she
would have preferred to see them left in the hands of the King's enemies.
A little later (August) she mentions that Sir Lewis Dyve's troop searched
the house of a noted Puritan, Colonel Needham, the Governor of
Leicester. She says his house was 'lightly plundered'. A few days after,
another company came to look for her husband, who was a well-known
Parliamentarian. They searched for arms and plate 'of which finding none,
they took nothing else'.[5]

It cannot be denied that at Edgehill troops, who would have been better
employed in action, busied themselves with plundering the Parliamentarian baggage train – though there is evidence that men of both sides
engaged in this.

Sir John Byron's men quartered on a Roundhead, Bulstrode
Whitelocke, in November took horses and provender, which could be
regarded as fair booty, and necessary to the 'war effort'. But they also did
malicious damage, lighting their pipes with leaves from his books and so
on. But on the whole the Royalist officers managed to control their men
reasonably well during the campaign of 1642. No doubt they were helped
to some extent by the fact that there were a large number of gentlemen
in the ranks. This is certainly true of the horse regiments and, according
to one authority, of the Lifeguard of Foot. It may have been true of other
regiments, for the tradition that a gentleman might with honour 'trail the
puissant pike' lingered on, and as recently as the siege of Breda (1637)
many gentlemen had fought as volunteers in the ranks of the English foot
regiments of the Dutch service.[6]

The Royalist Army was subject to Martial Law at least as early as 19
September 1642. On that day the King made a speech 'in the Head of
his Army', between Stafford and Wellington, after 'the Reading of his
Orders of War'.

'Gentlemen,
You have heard these Orders read, it is your part, in your several places,

to observe them exactly; The time cannot be long before we come to Action, therefore you have the more reason to be careful. And I must tell you, I shall be very severe in the punishing of those, of what Condition soever, who transgress these Instructions. I cannot suspect your Courage and Resolution; your Conscience and your Loyalty hath brought you hither to fight for your Religion, your King, and the Laws of your Land. You shall meet with no Enemies but Traytors, most of them Brownists, Anabaptists and Atheists, such who desire to destroy both Church and State, and who have already Condemned you to Ruin, for being Loyal to us. That you may see what use I mean to make of your Valour, if it please God to bless it with Success, I have thought fit to publish my Resolution in a Protestation, which when you have heard me make, you will believe you cannot fight in a better Quarrel, in which I promise to Live and Dye with you.'[7]

Turning to the Parliamentarian Army we find a different story, not only in the letters of Sergeant Nehemiah Wharton of Denzil Holles' Regiment,[8] but in the notes which Brian Twyne kept of happenings at Oxford.[9]

Essex and his senior officers made some attempts to impose discipline, but as they were extremely reluctant to punish in order to see that they were obeyed, their efforts were in vain. There was a strong feeling in the ranks of the Roundhead Army that they were all rebels together, commanders and common soldiers alike. This must have made the officers feel uncertain of themselves. Indeed one feels that the chaplains and preachers, with Hell and Damnation to back them, had more power over the men than the other leaders. Not that all these soldiers were in fact zealous Puritans. Quite the contrary. Wharton makes it clear that many took the field from base motives, while others, more innocent perhaps, seem to have embarked on the campaign as a pleasant holiday from the daily life of a London apprentice or a Buckinghamshire ploughboy.

The favourite pastimes of this army, all amply attested by Wharton, were tormenting priests, burning altar rails, breaking stained glass windows, killing deer and plundering papists and malignants.

More serious from a strictly military point of view were their mutinous spirit, the ill feeling between horse and foot and the murderous brawling between one infantry regiment and another. Holles' Regiment got rid of its lieutenant-colonel, the reformado Henry Billingsley, by simply refusing to march when he ordered them to. In this two captains, Francis and Beacon, were implicated. Billingsley probably owed his unpopularity to his efforts, in the absence of a colonel who was also a member of Parliament, to instil some discipline into the unit. Wharton writes of him as 'a Godamme blade, and doubtlesse hatche in hell, and we all desire that ether the Parliament would depose him, or God convert him, or the Devill fetch him away quick.' (10 August). Four days later at Aylesbury Billingsley, 'upon an ungrounded whimsey', ordered Captains Francis and Beacon to march out of the town, 'but they went not'. Less than a week later the lieutenant-colonel was cashiered. Evidently the generals were somewhat afraid of their own men, for, one would think, it was the two captains rather than Billingsley that merited dismissal.

Wharton could attest the ill-will between horse and foot from personal experience. On 4 September he was robbed by a troop of horse belonging to Colonel Foynes (Captain Nathaniel Fiennes?) and lost goods to the value of about £3. He would have lost his sword as well had he not threatened to order his men to open fire on these pillagers.

On the same day he had prevented some of Colonel Cholmley's Regiment pillaging the house of a J.P.

Even more serious was the drunken brawl that took place in the High Street at Oxford around Carfax and about the Starre Inn on 30 September.

'The quarrell was betwixt the blewe coates & russett coates[10] and their captaines,' . . . They fell out, 'some of them beinge in drinke' and saying that 'when they came to fight, if it were against the Kinge, they would take his part rather than fight against him,' . . . They fought 'with their naked swordes', some having their thumbs cut off and some their fingers. One of these regiments was that of Colonel Thomas Grantham, which since at least ten of its officers had previous military experience, should have been among the best in Essex's army.

When (2 and 3 October) the two regiments marched to join Essex at Worcester many of the men were missing, 'the captaines & constables goinge up & downe the towne to seeke them: many of them having flunge awaye their armes, and ran awaye.'

It must not be supposed that Parliament and its commanders did nothing to repress these acts of indiscipline. As early as 18 August 1642 complaints had reached Parliament 'of many disorders committed by the soldiers in their marching, and in such places wherever they have been quartered or billeted . . . ' These disorders were attributed to 'the neglect of their officers to go along with them,'[11] – a neglect which is in part explained by the fact that a number of them were members of Parliament and had not yet left for the front, while others, being colonels of foot as well as captains of troops of horse, found it difficult to be in two places at once.

A further proclamation published soon afterwards (27 August) sets forth that 'divers soldiers have in a tumultuous and violent manner broken into divers of the King's subject's houses, pillaged and ransacked them, under colour that they are papists' houses or the houses of person's disaffected'.

That these complaints were not groundless is amply proven by Wharton's candid letters.

At Coventry the pillaging of the house of 'a malignant fellowe' provoked Lord Brooke. In an attempt to assert discipline he 'immediately proclaimed that whosoever should for the future offend in that kind should have martiall law'. This seems to have made little impression on the soldiery.

At Oxford Lord Saye made similar efforts, doing his best to pacify the soldiers when they said they had been promised 5/- a month as a reward over and above their daily pay, and announced that if they did not get it 'they would doe no more service nor muster'. Saye could do little with them and eventually told them 'he cared not for their helpe, and bid them begone'. And so, having failed to get the upper hand, he took coach and went home to Broughton (24 September).[12]

Meanwhile, somewhat belatedly, Essex himself had taken the field. He had the Laws and Ordinances of War read to the troops who, it would seem, were unimpressed. Wharton records, not without sarcasm (15 September), 'Thursday our regiment met again, when those famous lawes for our army were read and expounded. This day we received and accepted Serjt. Major Neale.' This officer had been sent to the regiment to take the place of Quarles, promoted *vice* Billingsley.

On 24 September at Worcester 'his Excellency proclaimed that no soldier should plunder either church or private house, upon pain of death'. But only three days later the soldiers went 'by commission from his Excellency' and plundered Sir William Russell's house at Strensham 'to the bare walls'. If Essex himself was so inconsistent he had only himself to thank if his men failed to respond to his lightest command.

In the weeks leading up to Edgehill one finds only two examples of punishment in the Parliamentarian army. At Oxford on 23 September Lord Saye actually sent some of the mutineers to prison.[13]

The only other sufferer was a whore who had followed the camp from London. On 27 August at Coventry she 'was taken by the soldiers, and first led about the city, then set in the pillory, after in the cage, then duckt in a river, and at the last banisht the City'.

Already in September Hampden and five other colonels had complained that their soldiers plundered everywhere. 'The truth is unless we were able to execute some exemplary punishment upon the principal malefactors, we have no hope to redress this horrid enormity.' They pointed out that 'if this go on awhile, the army will grow as odious to the country as the Cavaliers'. In their view the army 'without martial law (to extend to soldiers only) . . . may prove a ruin as likely as a remedy to this distracted kingdom'.

Parliament was slow to act but at last on 9 November 1642 it issued a declaration saying:

'Whereas it is found, that great inconveniences have ensued for want of a strict and severe discipline to have been observed in the army now raised by authority of Parliament, under the command of Robert Earl of Essex, and for that the laws and ordinances of war by him set forth for the government of the said army, have not been put in execution it is now ordained and declared by the Lords and Commons in Parliament assembled, that from henceforth the officers and soldiers of the said army may not expect any further forbearance of such punishments to be inflicted on them for any their offences, as shall be due unto them by the said ordinances. But that the Lord General may and ought to punish them by death or otherwise, according to their demerits.'[14]

'The Laws and Ordinances of War established for the better conduct of the Army'[15] were comprehensive and the penalties laid down severe. A great number of the crimes listed were forbidden upon pain of death. Perhaps this threatened severity defeated its own ends in an army in which the men, whatever their motives, were nevertheless volunteers.

Before we leave the subject of discipline it may be as well to discuss the duties of the Provost of a regiment. According to Venn[16] it was his duty to see that all Proclamations, Orders, and Decrees published by the Provost-Marshal of the Army were promulgated in his regiment. Once a week he was to let the Provost-Marshal-General know what prisoners he had in his charge, and the causes of their commital. To him fell the task of overseeing the victuallers of the regiment, seeing that they did not charge any unreasonable prices, nor do so at unlawful hours. In order that no wrong should be done he was to go about the quarters thrice daily: once in the morning, once in the afternoon, and 'once in the dead time in the night, if it may be conveniently performed'.

The victualler was to let him know each night what victuals were in the quarter, and he was to take notes of them to the Provost-Marshal-General. The division of booty between the several companies was another of his tasks. He was to see the quarters kept clean and sweet and all garbage and filth buried. He was to lodge in the midst of the victuallers of the regiment.

The Provost was to go to the Carriage-Master for directions as to where the baggage should march, where it should assemble, and what way it should go. And 'after he hath given the first place to the Colonels baggage' he was to lay down the order of march of that of the other companies. He was to see that the carriages were accompanied by sufficient men and instruments to 'amend every thing that is amiss' in the ways, or carriages. If any carriage was unable to go he was 'to provide that it may be no hindrance to the rest'.

As the war went on commanders on each side gradually asserted their authority. The Royalists at Oxford erected gallows and a wooden-horse. Murderers and deserters were punished with death, though one who had been a double turncoat and had sold his arms was only 'put uppon the woodden horse over against Gild hall,' . . .[17] Flogging was not so much in use as in the eighteenth century though Symonds records one strange example:

' . . . This day (24 May 1645) a foot soldjer was tyed (with his sholders and breast naked) to a tree, and every carter of the trayne and carriages was to have a lash; for ravishing two women. *Secundum usum Hispaniarum.*'[18]

The execution (3 May 1645) of the unfortunate Colonel Windebanke, a veteran of Edgehill and Cheriton, for the surrender of Bletchingdon House was an unusual example of severity on the part of King Charles, who, if anything, was too lenient. With an inconsistency typical of his vacillating nature he granted the colonel's widow a pension. Ordinarily he reserved his wrath for crimes such as kirkrapine, which really stirred his soul. On Thursday 28 August 1645, for example, a soldier was 'hang'd on the tree in Wing towne, for stealing the communion plate there'.[19]

Neither Charles nor Essex can be said to have had an army which was in the highest state of discipline. The Royalists it may be claimed were reasonably well-behaved – neither mutiny nor armed brawls had marked their progress. The discipline of the Roundheads on the evidence alike of their best officers and of a singularly candid N.C.O. was decidedly brittle. It remained to be seen whether religious zeal and natural courage would prove adequate substitutes.

An officer who does not mean to see his orders punctually obeyed is useless. On this important point the Earl of Essex seems to have been in two minds.

TRAINING

'It is well scited out of Vegetius,
That knowledge in all things
belonging to Warr, giveth Courage; . . .
No man feareth to do that which
he hath well learned how to do: . . . '
Captain Thomas Venn, 1672

The Earl of Essex received his commission as Captain-General on 13 July 1642, but he did not leave London to join his army until nearly two months later (9 September). By that time his army was already strong in numbers, greatly outnumbering the troops so far assembled by the King. But there had been little time for training. The Earl may be condemned for not attacking while the Royalists were at Nottingham, and were still weak, when, as Sir Jacob Astley told the King, 'he could not give any assurance against his majesty's being taken out of his bed if the rebels should make a brisk attempt . . . '[20] Still it is quite understandable that a general should not wish to operate with untrained men. In addition Essex's somewhat lethargic nature predisposed him to inactivity. More important, the Earl, being in rebellion, was perhaps hesitant to strike the first blow.

Essex certainly attempted to train his men. At a review at Worcester on 24 September he held forth upon the causes of the war and gave his officers good advice. They were to be careful in the exercising of their men and 'to bring them to use their arms readily and expertly.' . . . They were 'not to busy them in practising the ceremonious forms of military discipline'. Rather he wished the men to 'be well instructed in the necessary rudiments of war, that they may know to fall on with discretion and retreat with care'.[21]

Quaintly put though this is it is sensible. Essex's horse had been roughly handled by Rupert at Powick Bridge on the previous day. He was not to know that he had another month before his army would find itself face to face with the King's. When time is short a commander must concentrate on teaching his men to march, to shoot, to handle their weapons and to obey their orders. A little tactical training was also desirable. The men were getting plenty of marching; their discipline, as we have seen, was poor, and on this occasion Essex reminded them of the code already laid down. Very sensibly he confined himself to nine main articles.[22]

We have little evidence as to the detail of the training in Essex's Army. No doubt the company officers had with them such books as John Raynford's *The Yong Soulldier* (London: 1642) or William Barriffe's *Militarie Discipline, or the Young Artillery-man, wherein is discoursed and showne the postures both of musket and pike* (London: 1635, 3rd ed. 1643). Both these officers seem to have served in Essex's army, Raynford probably as captain-lieutenant to Essex's own regiment[23] and, since Bariffe is a most unusual name, it is evident that the author and the major of Hampden's Regiment are one and the same man.

Wharton's account of the doings of Holles' Regiment begins on 8 August. Not until 17 September, when they were at Aylesbury, is there any mention of training: 'After noone our regiment marched into the feild and skirmished'. On arrival at Coventry an attempt was made to put things on a more regular footing. On 25 August 'command was given that all soldiers should attend their colours every morne by sixe of the clock to march into the feilde to practise, which is done acordingly'. Since their drill was done so early in the morning the soldiers still had plenty of time for their more popular pastimes; marauding and listening to sermons.

These drill parades were not always a success. At Northampton (7 September) 'being drawne into the fields to exercise, many of them discovered their base ends in undertaking this designe, and demaunded five shillings a man, which, they say, was promised them monthly by the (Guildhall) Committee, or they would surrender their armes. Whereupon Colonell Hamden, and other commaunders, laboured to appease them, but could not: . . . '

A bluecoat regiment, some 450 strong, 'from London and beyond', entered Oxford on 22 September. Its commanders struck Twyne as 'very likely and proper men', the soldiers for the most part very young and 'but meanely apperreled and very unexpert in their armes'. Mustered next day in New Parks they were 'very untractable & undocile in their postures'. They too became mutinous and demanded the promised 5/- gratuity.

Wharton gives us two examples of the men's lack of weapon training. At Wendover (13 August) one of Captain Francis' company 'forgettinge he was charged with a bullet' shot a maid through the head, killing her instantly. After this accident the 'soldiers marched very sadlye two miles . . . ' At Worcester (2 October) one of the Lord General's soldiers 'shot at randum, and, with a brace of bullets', killed one of his fellows.

One must not be too critical of Essex's raw levies. Officers visiting their sentries at night, and soldiers hit when a comrade was cleaning his rifle, are generally the first casualties of a modern campaign.

Essex first saw the main body of his army at Northampton on 14 September when 'both foot and horse, marched into the field, and the Lord General viewed us, both front, rear, and flank, when the drums beating and the trumpets sounding made a harmony delectable to our friends, but terrible to our enemies.' To new units, five weeks drilling can make a great deal of difference. Unfortunately Wharton's letters end on 7 October and we have no direct evidence of the progress made in the weeks immediately before the battle. But in the nature of things one would expect a considerable improvement by the time of Edgehill.

On the face of it the Parliamentarians had a considerable advantage over the Royalists simply because they concentrated sooner. There were only 500 horse, five regiments of foot, and 12 guns with the King when

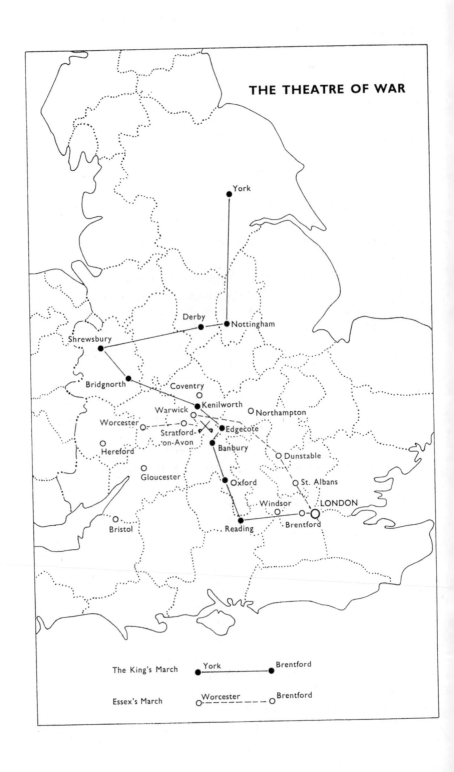

THE THEATRE OF WAR

York

Derby ● Nottingham

Shrewsbury

Bridgnorth Coventry
○
Warwick ●Kenilworth ○Northampton
Worcester ○
○ Stratford- ●Edgecote
·on-Avon
Hereford ●Banbury
○
Gloucester ●Dunstable
○ ○
●Oxford ○St. Albans
Windsor
LONDON
○
Bristol ●Reading Brentford
○

The King's March York ●————● Brentford

Essex's March Worcester ○– – – – –○ Brentford

he marched from Nottingham on 13 September. It was only after his arrival at Shrewsbury that his levies came pouring in.

It was on the march from Nottingham to Derby that the King first reviewed his army – the day before Essex's review at Northampton. Lord Paget's Regiment (Colonel Richard Bolle) joined that day and according to Clarendon 'the whole made so good an appearance that all men were even wishing for the earl of Essex, and all fears were vanished'. But six regiments of foot do not make an army.

No doubt the 2,000–3,000 arms that had come over in *The Providence* had been distributed to the oldest regiments and in the nature of things these would be the best trained – Pennyman's, Dutton's, Belasyse's, the Lifeguard and the Lord General's. But some of the others had smelt powder. Lunsford's, which joined after the King left Shrewsbury, built up on a cadre of officers and men of the 1640 army, had been the backbone of the successful Royalist defence of Sherborne Castle, and was later to achieve distinction as Prince Rupert's bluecoats. Some of the Lancashire men of Lord Molyneux and Sir Gilbert Gerard had had a baptism of fire in the abortive siege of Manchester.

The ultimate responsibility for the training of the Royalist foot lay with Sir Jacob Astley, who had been made sergeant-major-general, 'a command he was very equal to, and had exercised before, and executed after with great approbation'. Such a man would not neglect the drilling and training of the regiments assembling at Shrewsbury. But some came very late and time was short, while others were led, not by soldiers of experience, but by loyal squires and county potentates. Still of the five brigade commanders only one, Belasyse, was not a soldier.

Rupert lost no time in exercising the horse. He gave them a victory at Powick Bridge, and was quick to correct mistaken tactics. On that occasion Sir Lewis Dyve's troop had received that of Captain Nathaniel Fiennes with a discharge of pistols and carbines instead of falling on with their swords.[24] In consequence they had lost their cornet, Strangewayes, and would have been routed had not the Parliamentarian troops on either flank melted away. The Prince was not slow to check such tactical errors.

During the time he was at Shrewsbury Rupert took pains to exercise his men and one observer, 'an eminent Cavalier', who saw them at work, commended the King's troop, the Prince of Wales', Lord Willoughby (d'Eresby's), Prince Rupert's and Sir William Pennyman's as being 'very well set off'. But a handsome equipage is not everything. Cavalry, and especially English cavalry, have shown throughout their history, that proficiency in outpost duties and the ability to rally after a charge, are the marks of well-trained horse. In these respects both armies were still notably deficient. But the Cavaliers had at least shown that they would fight. The Parliamentarians had yet to live down Powick Bridge.

1 Wedgwood, The King's Peace, p. 352
2 Archaeologia, Vol. XXXV, p. 313.
3 Memoirs, p. 253.
4 Clarendon, Vol. II, p. 346 & p. 359
5 Hutchinson, Vol. I, pp. 173, 174.
6 See Hexham's account of the Siege of Breda.
7 Clarendon, Vol. II, p. 312.
8 Archaeologia, Vol. XXXV, p. 313.
9 Wood's Life and Times.
10 One of these regiments must have been Colonel Thomas Grantham's, which was then in Oxford. The men may have worn russet coats.
11 Firth, p. 279, quoting Husband's *Ordinances*.
12 Wood's Life and Times, p. 65.
13 *Ibid*, p. 64.
14 Firth, p. 281.
15 Essex ordered their publication on 8 September 1642. See C.S.P.D. 1641–3, pp. 387 & 391.
16 Venn, pp. 188–189.
17 Wood's Life and Times, pp. 83, 91 & 93.
18 Symond's Diary, p. 176.
19 *Ibid.*, p. 231.
20 Clarendon, Vol. II, p. 293.
21 Davies, Parliamentarian Army, p. 35.
22 *Ibid.*, p. 36.
23 Though possibly as captain-lieutenant to Lord Saye, whose regiment became Sir John Meldrum's.
24 Firth, p. 134.

2

Organization

'Organization is a necessary evil'.
Clausewitz

THE EXPERIENCE ON which the Englishmen of 1642 based their organization was common to both sides. The staffs of the two armies will be discussed later, since they differed somewhat, but in general both sides were organized in much the same way.

THE HORSE

In the Royalist Army colonels were usually commissioned 'to raise and entertayne a Regiment of 500 horse voluntiers'.[1] But in practice a normal regiment had six troops of about 70 officers and men, a total of 420. Royalist regiments were seldom at full strength, especially during the later stages of the war. When Wilmot's brigade, which consisted of some of the best regiments, mustered at Aldbourne Chase on 10 April 1644, units varied greatly in strength. The four strongest each numbered 300, while the two weakest were only 100 strong. Troops seem by then to have averaged about 40.[2] Certain commanders, notably Prince Rupert, managed to keep their regiments up to strength, but this was rare, and may be attributed to his powers of leadership. Some regimental commanders proved unable to raise the full number of troops, and at Edgehill several of the regiments were as yet incomplete.

Royalist regiments generally had three field officers: colonel, lieutenant-colonel and major. The Roundhead regiments only had a colonel and a major. Field officers were also troop commanders, the colonel's troop being commanded by his captain-lieutenant.

The theoretical strength of a troop was:—

Field officer or Captain	1
Capt.-Lieut. or Lieutenant	1
Cornet	1
Quartermaster	1
Corporals	3
Trumpeters	2

Sadler	1
Farrier	1
Troopers	60
	71[3]

The quartermaster was a commissioned officer.

Judging by a muster taken at Tiverton in the summer of 1644 the regiments in Essex's army managed to keep well up to strength. Thirty-nine troops, including one of dragoons, totalled 3,205 officers and men, an average of nearly 85 per troop. Two troops, Sir Philip Stapleton's and Sir William Balfour's, actually numbered 100 and the very weakest had 44 officers and men.[4] But at Edgehill the troops were probably not up to strength and, as we shall see, the process of regimenting them was apparently incomplete.

In battle troops were often grouped in pairs to form squadrons, or 'divisions'.

THE FOOT

In theory a regiment consisted of ten companies, each commanded by a field-officer or a captain. The companies were not equal in size, for the colonel had 200 men, the lieutenant-colonel 160, the major 140, and each captain 100. This made 1,200 soldiers besides officers.[5]

The officers of a normal company were:–

Captain	1
Lieutenant	1
Ensign	1
Gentlemen of the arms	1
Sergeants	2
Corporals	3
Drummers	2
	11[6]

Thus a full regiment would be just over 1,300 strong.

At the beginning of the war several regiments on each side were well up to strength – for example the Lifeguard and Salusbury's on the Royalist side; the Earl of Essex's and Lord Brooke's in the Parliament's army. But in both armies the strength of regiments tended to dwindle as the war went on. Variations in strength, particularly in the King's army, can also be accounted for by some regiments having less than the standard 10 companies. In May 1643 a number of Royalist regiments that had fought at Edgehill were in camp at Culham, near Abingdon. Of these only three had 10 companies, one had nine, six had eight, and one had seven.[7]

It must have been extremely difficult for a commanding officer to control 10 companies, and so we may suppose that it was actually an improvement when the number was somewhat reduced.

The common soldiers of a regiment consisted partly of pikemen and partly of musketeers. In theory there were two musketeers to one pikeman, though in the Royalist army at Edgehill, the numbers of each seem to have been about equal. Pikemen and musketeers were not organized in separate companies, but each company had its proportion of each.

The staff of a Roundhead regiment included a quartermaster, a chaplain, a provost-marshal, a 'chirurgion,' and his mate, a carriage-master and a drum-major. Royalist regiments usually had quartermasters, though one sometimes finds the waggoner doing his duties, as well as surgeons and chaplains. They do not appear to have had provost-marshals. On the other hand the appointment of gentlemen-of-the-arms, which was introduced in their army before April 1644,[6] may have been peculiar to them. The care of arms was of more than ordinary importance, when expensive weapons had to be imported from abroad, and brought down to Oxford from the North.

No modern British regiment would be complete without its Adjutant and its R.S.M. In the Civil Wars the Sergeant-Major, or Major as he was now often called, combined the functions of both. By about 1720 one begins to find the senior sergeant of a regiment described as 'sergeant-major'. The increase of literacy among the non-commissioned officers may account for the wider delegation of duties to them. The Adjutant comes in during the reign of King Charles II. The Holland Regiment had one in June 1665, when it was placed on the English Establishment.[8]

THE DRAGOONS

'Rascals, did I not know you at first to be three tattered musketeers, and by plundering a malt-mill of three blind horses, you then turned dragooners'.

John Lacy[9]

Dragoons were still nearer to infantry than cavalry. They usually moved about on their nags, which were cheaper than those of the horse, and fought on foot. According to Sir James Turner: 'They ought to be taught to give fire on horse back,' . . . but . . . 'their service is on foot, and is no other than that of musketeers.'[10]

At Edgehill the Royalists had three regiments of dragoons and the Roundheads two. Their precise organization is obscure, but may be deduced from that of the single dragoon regiment in the New Model Army. This had an establishment of 1,000 and was organized in ten companies.[11]

These mounted infantry, so much less expensive to mount and arm than cavalry, had been much used on the continent where, according to the Duc de Rohan, 'they ruined the infantry, every man desiring to have a nag so that he might be the fitter to rob and to pillage'.[12] According to Captain Edward Kightley the Roundhead dragoons distinguished themselves in this fashion during the battle of Edgehill.

The organization of the two Trains of Artillery is discussed later.

1   W.H. Black, Docquets of Letters Patent . . . passed at Oxford. Printed 1838, but never published.
2   Richard Symonds' unpublished notebook (B.M. Harleian MS. 986).
3   Peacock, p. 47.
4   Symonds' Diary, p. 73.
5   Peacock, p. 46.
6   See Muster of the Royalist garrison of Reading, April 1644, in Symonds' notebook (B.M. Harleian MS. 986).
7   PRO WO 55. 1661 'Arms delivery at the Camp'.
8   C. Dalton, English Army Lists and Commission Registers, Vol. I, p. 50.
9   The Old Troop, Act. i, Scene i.
    John Lacey, the actor and dramatist (d. 1681), had been a Royalist officer. He served as a quartermaster in Charles Gerard's Regiment of Horse.
10 Quoted by C. H. Firth in Cromwell's Army, p. 125.
11 Joshua Sprigge, *Anglia Rediviva*, p. 331.
12 Firth, *op, cit.*, p. 124.

3

Clothing and Equipment, Arms, Armour and Horseflesh

A 'plain russet-coated captain . . . '
Oliver Cromwell 1643

ONE OF THE HOARIER myths about the Civil War is that soldiers in those days did not wear uniform. Another is that the traditional British red coat came in with the New Model Army. At Edgehill foot regiments on either side wore red coats, notably the King's Lifeguard and the Roundhead regiments of Lord Robartes and Denzil Holles. If the mid-seventeenth century warrior did not have the lace, the facings and the powdered hair, which gave sartorial sustenance to the soldiers of Dettingen or Minden, at least he was issued sufficient articles of clothing and equipment to present an appearance uniform with the rest of his company. One of the services of Thomas Bushell, 'Warden of our Mint and Mr Worker of our Mynes Royall', was his 'cloathing our liefe Guard and three regiments more, with suites, stockings, shoes, and mounteroes when we were readie to march in(to) the ffield: . . . "[1] Nearly a year later (15 July 1643) there was an issue when 'all the common soldiers then at Oxford were newe apparelled, some all in red, coates, breeches, & mounteers; & some all in blewe'.[2] The regiments then at Oxford included the King's Lifeguard and the Queen's Regiment, both being redcoats, Charles Gerard's, bluecoats, and Sir William Pennyman's, who, we may suppose, perhaps were also bluecoats. It is evident that only the common soldiers benefited by these general issues. Officers and sergeants provided their own raiment not so much because they were compelled to, but because they were allowed a certain latitude in the matter of dress. Their rank was known because, instead of pike or musket, they carried a partisan or a halbert. We find the Roundhead Sergeant Nehemiah Wharton writing gratefully (13 September) to acknowledge the receipt of 'my mistresses' scarfe and Mr Molloyne's hatband, both of which came very seasonably, for I had gathered a little money together, and had this day made me a soldier's sute for winter, edged with gold and silver lace'.[3] In the same letter he complains that he had been robbed by a troop of Parliamentarian horse,[4] and lost 'a scarlet coate lined with plush,' which he had been given for saving a Justice from pillage by 'the base blew coats of Colonell Cholmley's regiment'.[3]

But if officers and sergeants might wear what they chose the private soldiers, at least among the foot, were fairly uniform in appearance. Indeed the lace embellishments, so dear to the eighteenth century soldier, were already creeping in.

On 30 August 1643 John Malet writes to his 'assured loving friend' Captain George Trevelyan:

> 'I understand . . . of a desire you had to put your colours upon your coats for the better knowing of your men, which if you do, in mine opinion would much wrong the coat. The differences that Captains use in the wars is in the arming of his pikes for the pikemen, which is to be of his colours, and likewise the fringe of the headpiece of the shot for the shot. The daubing of a coat with lace of sundry colours, as some do use them, I do neither take to be soldierlike nor profitable for the coat. If a Captain miscarry, he that cometh in his room, his colours being contrary, tears off the former and puts in his own, and by this means often times tears coat and all. Myself have resolved for my company in such sort as I have written unto you, which I desire might be to all your good likings.'[5]

At the siege of York (1644) the Roundheads took some men of Newcastle's army who had crosses embroidered on their sleeves. According to a contemporary account by a Parliamentarian chaplain on 8 June 1644, during the siege of York, a soldier of the Marquis of Newcastle's garrison was taken prisoner in the Earl of Manchester's camp. He wore a red suit and had with him pitch, flax and other materials for setting fire to the suburbs. Other prisoners had white coats 'with crosses on the sleeves, wrought with red and blew silk'. This their captors took to be the 'ensigne', or badge of some Popish regiment.[6]

In the Army of the Eastern Association, if no other, it was customary to issue coats with linings of a different colour, the origin of regimental facings. On 2 October 1643 Manchester ordered coats of 'green cloth lined with red' for the soldiers of his own regiment, and in 1645 the Committee of Both Kingdoms ordered the county of Essex to send its recruits to the New Model 'commodiously provided, as hath formerly been practised, with 1000 red coats lined with blue'.[7]

It seems that the New Model wore red from the start. *Perfect Passages* (7 May 1645) says:

> 'The men are Redcoats all, the whole army only are distinguished by several facings of their coats.'

The breeches may have been of other colours, coats ordered for the army in Ireland (October 1649) were to be of 'Venice colour red', with breeches 'of grey or other good colour'.

The besiegers of Worcester according to a Royalist's Diary (entry of 9 July 1646) were 'Most Red coats', but the New Model troops were supported by local forces from Worcestershire, Shropshire and elsewhere.[8]

The infantry soldiers of the Civil Wars are usually pictured in a broad-brimmed hat or a steel helmet. Yet they certainly had caps also. In 1642 Parliament paid 23/- a dozen for 'Monmouth caps' for the troops serving in Ulster.[9] Symonds, writing at Bewdley in 1644, says:

> ' . . . The only manufacture of this town is making of caps called Monmouth caps, knitted by poor people for twopence apiece, ordinary ones sold for two shillings, three shillings, and four shillings. First they are knit, then they mill them, then block them, then they work them with tassels, then they sheer them.'[10]

Colonel Richard Bagot bought caps for the 300 foot he raised in April 1643 to garrison Lichfield Close for the King.[11] But he paid only 6d. each for them so it seems unlikely that they were Monmouth caps, but they can scarcely have been monteroes. It is evident that senior officers did not scorn the montero. At Naseby a cavalier, 'who we have since heard was Rupert', led up a party of horse to attack Fairfax's baggage train. A Roundhead described him as 'being a person somewhat in habit like our General, in a red montero as the General had, . . . '[12] One cannot imagine the Prince or Fairfax sporting a Monmouth cap. Indeed one would suppose that if they were not wearing helmets, at least they would have a steel cap under their headgear.

One description of this mysterious cap is given by a certain Thomas Ellwood, who describes himself as wearing 'a large montero cap of black velvet, the skirt of which being turned up in folds, looked, it seems, somewhat above the then common garb of a Quaker . . . ' Corporal Trim, veteran of the siege of Namur (1695), was given a montero cap, which is thus described in *Tristram Shandy*: 'The montero cap was scarlet, of a superfine Spanish cloth, dyed in grain, and mounted all round with fur, except about four inches in the front, which was faced with a light blue, slightly embroidered; . . . ' Of course the cap may have changed somewhat between 1642 and 1695, but it is evident that the Monmouth cap, which by 1724 was 'sold chiefly to Dutch seamen',[13] and the montero were quite different. Whatever Bagot may have given his regiment, the King's Lifeguard and other regiments of the main

Royalist army received a much more handsome head-dress than a sailor's woollen cap.

Perhaps the soldiers, like their commanders, preferred the broad-brimmed felt, or beaver, hat. When about 1653 Tom Verney enlisted as a pikeman in Colonel Ingoldsby's Regiment he asked his brother's agent for 'a grey Dutch felt', a pair or grey worsted stockings, a pair of strong buck's leather gloves and a black leather sword belt.[14]

As early as 1587–8 according to Norwich Accounts, quoted by W. Y. Carman in his *British Military Uniforms*, a drummer's coat of green kersey was embellished with 11 yards of lace and six yards of 'pointing'. Not only the coats, but the sleeves must, therefore, have been ornamented with lace. Probably there were bars of lace all the way up the sleeves. The Royalist drummer in the window of the church at Farndon, Cheshire, carries on this style of ornamentation, and though the figure is copied from one of the Gardes Françaises, it is some evidence of the uniform worn in England. A drum, probably of the Lifeguard, is shown in the painting of King Charles I dictating to Sir Edward Walker (1644).

Beyond doubt the Parliamentarian foot were completely equipped, and well armed. Clarendon paints a rather gloomy picture of the Royalists' armament. He says that only 800 muskets, 500 pairs of pistols and 200 swords had been landed in Yorkshire, and the King had been compelled 'to borrow the arms from the train-bands'. Noblemen and gentlemen of quality sent the contents of their own armouries 'which were very mean'. Eventually 'the foot, (all but three or four hundred who marched without any weapon but a cudgel,) were armed with muskets, and bags for their powder, and pikes; but in the whole body there was not one pikeman had a corslet, and very few musketeers who had swords'.[15]

This almost certainly gives a false impression to modern eyes for by our standards the private armouries of those days were far from mean. At the beginning of the war Captain Robert Millington, who commanded a foot company at Edgehill, presented the King with 80 muskets,[16] while an ordinary Oxford citizen, the father of Antony Wood the antiquary, 'had then armour or furniture for one man, viz. a helmet, a back and breast piece, a pyke and a musquet, and other appurtenances, . . .'[17]

In addition to their clothing the soldiers received 'snapsacks' of leather or canvas, and the musketeers were issued with bags for their powder and bandoleers, from which dangled their cartridges – a most inconvenient, not to say dangerous, method of carrying one's ammunition. It seems that water bottles were not supplied.

The Royalist cavalry, being for the most part gentlemen and their outdoor servants, doubtless took the field in the dress they normally wore when out riding. To this they added, if they could, a buff coat, over which 'back and breast' were worn by those that had them. The normal 'harquebusier' of the day wore a 'pot' helmet, but in the Royalist army these were by no means a general issue. At Powick Bridge Bulstrode wore a hat which, 'being upon an unruly horse', he lost. Clarendon tells us that

' . . . Amongst the horse, the officers had their full desire if they were able to procure old backs and breasts and pots, with pistols or carbines for their two or three first ranks, and swords for the rest; themselves (and some soldiers by their examples) having gotten, besides their pistols and swords, a short pole-axe.'[15]

Captain Richard Atkyns, who raised his troop early in 1643, says:

' . . . within one month, I mustered 60 men besides officers, and almost all of them well armed; Master (John) Dutton giving me 30 steel backs, breasts and head pieces, and two men and horses completely armed . . .'[18]

Perhaps these last were cuirassiers, 'Lobsters' as they were called, with armour to the knee. If so they were something of a rarity in the Royalist army, though the Earl of Northampton was certainly equipped in this fashion when he was killed at Hopton Heath (19 March 1643). Captain Edward St. John, who probably served with Sir John Byron at Edgehill, wears this armour in his monument in the church at Lydiard Tregoze.

Back, breast, pot and scarves were sufficient in themselves to lend a troop a certain air of uniformity, and some of the Royalist troops were evidently very well turned-out – so much so indeed that the Lifeguard was called the 'Troop of Show'. The basic equipment of the Lifeguard is given in a warrant in the Royalist Ordnance Papers. On 27 January 1643, Dr. Edmund Peirce, 'beinge of the Kings garde', received 'an horse armor layde a side formerly for him'. He signed for:

Backe	1
Breast	1
Headpeece	1
Gorgett	1

and the document is endorsed 'Mr Peirce his Receipt for one Corslett.'[19]

Another troop which joined the King at Beverley in July is thus described:

They rode ' . . . fifty great horses all of a darke Bay, handsomely set out with ash-colour'd ribbins, every man gentilely accoutred, and armed. They were presented to His Majesty, but it was not knowne from whom certainly, but supposed from the Earle of Newcastle, by the bravery of their accoutrements.'[20]

If these were indeed Newcastle's men they went into the Prince of Wales' Regiment.

Cavalry troopers evidently received coats or cloaks. On 4 August 1644, Sir Thomas Dallison, who was commanding Rupert's Regiment, wrote to the Prince that he had 'three or four hundred yards of cloth, which may serve to make coats or cloaks for your Highness' regiment of horse'.[21] On the Parliamentarian side, before Edgehill, Whitelock met Mr. Francis Russell, of Essex's Lifeguard, with 'twelve of his servants in scarlet cloaks well horsed and armed'.[22]

In May 1644, a Captain Roper's quartermaster was issued with 8½ yards of grey cloth. This officer seems to have belonged to the regiment of the Earl of Denbigh, which was based on the Parliamentarian garrison of Stafford. No doubt this cloth also was intended for coats and cloaks[23]. Denbigh had fought at Edgehill as Lord Feilding, and it seems likely that he had dressed his men in clothing of this sober hue from the first.

The Parliamentarian troop commanders received mounting money to purchase horses, arms and saddlery for their men. They received orange-tawny scarves which cost 10/- apiece, and in general were fully equipped 'harquebusiers'. A few troops, Stapleton's and probably Hesilrige's, wore the full cuirassier's armour, a much heavier kit than that worn by the cuirassier of later days. The French heavy cavalry at Waterloo were equipped much more like the 'harquebusier' of 1642 than the cuirassier. Many, if not all, of the Roundhead cavalry, had carbines as well as a pair of pistols.

The Provost-Marshal's 20 men were distinguished by a badge of crossed swords embroidered on their sleeves.

At the coronation of King Charles II the Lifeguard had a kettle-drummer, but one finds no mention of them in the Civil Wars. The trumpeters, judging from the monument to Sir Richard Astley at Patshull, were dressed quite differently to the troop, having a distinctive form of hanging sleeve, and no defensive armour. Whether they rode white horses, as became customary later, is uncertain. In 1643 one Parliamentarian troop, according to Dugdale, had silver trumpets, which was evidently exceptional.

The dragoons seem to have been dressed and armed like infantry. Firth considered that in the New Model they did not have buff coats, but wore the red coat of the foot soldier. Lt. Colonel John Lilburne is described in 1648 as wearing a 'short red coat'. The men were armed with a sword and a musket. Firelocks were preferred to matchlocks, since with them the men could fire from the saddle.[24]

The artillerymen on either side probably wore much the same dress as the foot. The carters, being hired or pressed civilians, would wear their everyday clothing. When on 28 March 1643 a bye train was organized for Prince Rupert's siege of Lichfield it was noted that long pole-axes had been delivered to the five gunners and 12 matrosses and swords to the two wheelwrights.[25]

In general the appearance of the senior officers can be seen in their portraits. On the day of Edgehill the King wore a black velvet coat lined with ermine, and a steel cap covered with velvet.[26]

The Prince of Wales' 'battle dress' can be seen in a portrait by William Dobson in the Scottish National Portrait Gallery. He is described when at York, just before the siege of Hull (July), as commanding 'as brave a Troope as ever came into field . . . ' On his coming into the field and leaving his coach, the knights and gentry who formed it presented him 'with a very goodly white horse, trapped most richly to the ground with velvet all studded with burning waves of gold' as well as a rich tent. The Prince 'put on a very curious guilt armour, and straight away mounted his gallant present, with general acclamations through the field . . . '[27] Perhaps this was the mount he rode at Edgehill.

At Brentford, later in the campaign, according to the report of a London merchant:

> ' . . . Prince Rupert took off his scarlet coat, which was very rich, and gave it to his man, and buckled on his arms, and put a gray coate over it, that he might not be discovered.'[28]

Mrs Hutchinson describes the Roundheads of 1642 who 'marched out so as if they had been only sent out till their hair was grown', but adds that 'two or three years after, any stranger that had seen them, would have inquired the reason of that name'.[29] Their senior officers, as their portraits show, were seldom if ever 'cropheads'. Colonel Thomas Harrison who commanded the King's escort, when he was on his way to his trial wore 'a velvet montero on his head, a new buff coat upon his back, and a crimson silk scarf about his waist, richly fringed'. In 1650 the disapproving Mrs Hutchinson saw him in a 'scarlet coat and cloak both laden with gold and silver lace, and the coat so covered with clinquant, that scarcely could one discern the ground'.[30]

Earlier in the war a Parliamentarian officer would not have worn a crimson scarf. In 1642 the orange-tawny colours of the Earl of Essex were universally adopted by the Roundheads, and crimson scarves were the mark of a Royalist. The King's supporters also sometimes wore hatbands of that colour.

In the Royalist army, thanks to the initiative of Thomas Bushell, an early form of gallantry medal was introduced. One of the services particularized in the Royal letter of 12 June (Section I, Document 28) was 'your invention for our better knowinge and rewardinge the Forlorn Hope with Badges of Silver at your own charge when the soldiers were ready to run away through the instigation of some disaffected persons'. Nor were medals confined to other ranks, for Sir Thomas Tyldesley wears one in his portrait and Sir Robert Walsh also had one (Section I, Document 13).

The Parliament did not, it seems, reward its soldiers with medals until after Dunbar (1650) when one was given to all officers and soldiers 'that were in this service in Scotland'. This was the first general service medal given to a British army. There was not another until the great Duke of Wellington obtained one for his whole army after Waterloo.

If both sides resorted to field-signs, sprigs of oak, white bands or pieces of paper stuck in their hats, it was not entirely because uniform was lacking, but because both sides had their regiments of redcoats and bluecoats, and naturally wished to avoid falling foul of their own side.

The martinets of later days would no doubt have seen much to find fault with in the appearance of the rival armies of 1642. Yet in their new suits of red and blue, green, white and russet they must have made a brave sight – but the imagination boggles at the thought of Lord Brooke's Regiment clad in those purple coats.

Uniforms of Foot Regiments in the Edgehill Campaign

ROYALIST

	Coats
Charles Gerard	Blue
Sir Ralph Dutton	White
Sir William Pennyman	Blue?
Sir Thomas Lunsford	Blue
Lifeguard	Red
Earl of Northampton	Green?

PARLIAMENT

Earl of Essex	Orange
Sir John Merrick	Grey
Earl of Stamford	Blue
Lord Brooke	Purple
Lord Robartes	Red
Colonel Sir Henry Cholmley	Blue
Colonel Denzil Holles	Red
Colonel Thomas Grantham	Russet?
Colonel Sir William Constable	Blue

Colonel Thomas Ballard	Grey
Colonel John Hampden	Green
Colonel Lord Saye and Sele	Blue

HORSE

Lord Feilding	Grey?
Earl of Essex, Lifeguard	Grey

Ordnance in use in the Civil wars.[31]

	Calibre of piece	Weight of piece	Length of piece	Weight of shot
Cannon Royal	8 in.	8000 lb.	8 ft.	63 lb.
Cannon	7	7000	10	47
Demi-cannon	6	6000	12	27
Culverin	5	4000	11	15
Demi-culverin	4½	3600	10	9
Saker	3½	2500	9½	5¼
Minion	3	1500	8	4
Falcon	2¾	700	6	2¼
Falconet	2	210	4	1¼
Robinet	1¼	120	3	¾

Ranges in yards

	Point-blank	At 10° elevation
Culverin	460	2650
Demi-culverin	400	2400
Saker	360	2170
Falcon	320	1920

A warrant of 27 October 1642 shows that in the Royalist Army a demi-cannon had a team of three gunners and six matrosses, while the crew for a culverin was two gunners and four matrosses.[32]

Notes on Horseflesh as used by the Armed Forces operating in England during the early stages of the Civil Wars, 1642

At this period the only mounted troops in Great Britain were small militia units of horse, presumably medium cavalry. They would have provided their own mounts and saddlery. There was no official pattern of the latter, but there were sufficient deep seating heavy saddles to equip one regiment of cuirassiers, wearing armour, in London. A moiety of the horse on both sides wore back and breast but as no 'luggage', except a pair of heavy pistols, was carried on the saddle the latter were not very heavy. Besides the 'English' saddle, practically the hunting saddle of modern times, and two other types of civilian saddle there was in use a medium weight military saddle derived from the French with a high cantle, a fairly high pommel, padded supports for the thighs and a padded and ribbed seat: the pistols usually had the end of the holsters attached to the breastplate. As far as is known this saddle was fairly common. Very full details and plates showing this saddle can be studied in *Horses and Saddlery*[33] and there is an illustration in another recently published book, *Hastings to Culloden*[34], which gives a useful all round view of a mounted officer of the period and his charger. His saddle is as described above. He is riding with a single curb bit and one rein, as used by all cavalry at this date.

With the exception of small units like Rupert's Lifeguard, which would have had a proportion of continental trained men in the ranks and would be as well mounted as possible, there would be little uniformity in horseflesh and very few trained men in the ranks. There were no thoroughbreds as we know them and not a very large proportion of well bred horses with the much prized Eastern blood in them. It is unlikely that any except very senior officers would have ridden the now fast disappearing Great Horse of the days of armour; by this time only used in the manége. Probably such a horse might have been ridden as a parade or first charger. But the average cavalry officer would have ridden, if possible, a well bred horse up to weight, showing a dash of Eastern blood, 'Barbary' or 'Turk' were usual terms, standing about 15 hands. The English horse of the period would not have been any bigger, as a general rule, and was described as 'very well made and for endurance able to suffer and execute as much and more than ever noted of any foreign creation'. Thus Gervase Markham, slightly modified, a well known contemporary writer on military matters. Judged by their performances the troops' horses were very good indeed, but it is likely that at the beginning of hostilities the general appearance of most units would be rather ragged with mounts of varying sizes next to each other. Also there would have been little time or opportunity to teach the horses their drill so, as a horse works mainly by memory, there would be a certain amount of confusion in the ranks and how the raw units were ever rallied after a charge – we know Prince Rupert rallied a few at Edgehill – is a thing that none who has worked with undrilled remounts will ever understand. The illustration already referred to gives a good idea of a useful type of remount of the period.

Dragoons were mounted infantry and rode what we should call ponies of about 14 hands. These would soon pick up what little drill they needed.

Draught horses were simply farm or carter's heavy animals, impressed with farm harness, almost all with collars, much as may still be seen today here and there. There were no limbers to the guns so the strongest cart horse of a team – of any number up to six or eight for field pieces – had to go in shafts fastened on the very heavy trail of the gun itself. There was no real mobility except in a few cases when very light pieces were equipped as horse artillery, probably a rarity, and with oxen even less. Oxen with the wooden ox bow pull well enough but the one idea was always to sell them and buy horses. They are much slower than horses.

The Edgehill campaign would put a great deal of regularity into the Horse of both sides and in another year the improvement would have been incredible by most standards. At this date and for long afterwards a very large number of men of all classes rode as a matter of course. It would be fair to class a large proportion of the men in the ranks as yeomen. And right through the centuries the yeomen could ride and made excellent cavalrymen once they had learnt their drill. They would have ridden with a slightly bent leg, not with the straight leg of the manége, and would have picked up sword drill as they went along. The lance was not used in England but all who could get them carried pistols and wore buff coats which should turn a sword cut.

Good cavalry were not difficult to raise in the England of 1642.

1 Sir Henry Ellis, 'Original Letters' . . . 2nd Series, Vol. 3, p. 309.
2 Wood's Life and Times, p. 103.
3 Archaeologia, Vol. XXXV. p. 322 & 323.
4 They belonged to 'Colonel Foynes', which presumably means one of the three Fiennes brothers, sons of Lord Saye and Sele.
5 Trevelyan Papers, Vol. III, p. 242. Camden Society. 1872. Malet's odd spelling has been modernized. Shot = musketeers.
6 I am grateful to L.P. Wenham, Esq., of York, for this information.
7 Firth, p. 234.
8 Diary of Henry Townsend, Vol. I, p. 170.
9 Firth, p. 237.
10 Symonds' Diary. p. 14.
11 Lichfield Cathedral MS.
12 Firth, p. 241.
13 Firth, p. 237, quoting Defoe.
14 Firth, p. 237, quoting Memoirs of the Verney Family, Vol. III, p. 160.
15 Clarendon, Vol. II, p. 347.
16 Petition, Bod. Lib. Rawl. MS.D.18.f.27.
17 Wood's Life & Times, p. 53.
18 Atkyns/Gwyn, p. 7.
19 Roy, p. 193.
20 Reckitt, Charles the First and Hull, p. 55.
21 J.R. Phillips. Memoirs of the Civil War in Wales . . ., Vol. II, p. 195.
22 Memorials, Vol. I, p. 183.
23 D.H. Pennington and I.A. Roots, The Committee at Stafford, 1642–1645, p. 315.
24 Firth, p. 125.
25 Roy, pp. 212, 213.
26 Bulstrode, pp. 77 & 78.
27 Reckitt, p. 54.

28 Warburton, Vol. II, p. 62.
29 Firth, p. 231, quoting the Life of Colonel Hutchinson, Vol. I, p. 170.
30 Firth, p. 240.
31 From William Eldred, *The Gunners' Glass*, 1646.
32 Roy, Ord., p. 156.
33 Horses and Saddlery, by G. Tylden, 1965. J.A. Allen & Co.
34 Hastings to Culloden, by P. Young & J. Adair, 1964. Bell: facing page 162.

4

Standards and Colours

'And indeed a greater Act of Cowardice cannot be found, than to suffer the Colours to be lost.'

Captain Thomas Venn

THE SIMILARITY OF the military heritage of both sides is illustrated by the fact that each used the same system for their colours of horse and foot.

Throughout the Civil Wars, and at least as late as the reign of King James II, every company and troop had its own colour, guidon or standard.

The system in vogue in 1642 is well described by Captain Thomas Venn, whose military experience, though his book was published in 1672, went back to 1641 and 1642.[1] As to the foot he tells us:

' . . . The Colonels Colours in the first place is of a pure and clean colour, without any mixture. The Lieutenant Colonels only with Saint Georges Armes in the upper corner next the staff, the Majors the same, but in the lower and outmost corner with a little stream Blazant, And every Captain with Saint Goerges Armes alone, but with so many spots or several Devices as pertain to the dignity of their respective places.'

The colours that exemplify this system belonged to regiments that fought at Edgehill.[2] Six colours were actually captured from the Royalists at Edgehill.[3]

The devices displayed on the captain's colours were often taken from the Colonel's armorial bearings. Thus Sir Edward Stradling's colours bore the cinquefoil of his house, and a Colonel Talbot (not at Edgehill) had dogs for his devices. Very occasionally one comes across colours that do not conform to this system. Perhaps the explanation is that they are of an earlier pattern that for some reason was still in use. But in general, both sides employed the system described by Venn. This occasionally led to confusion. Major Will. Legge at Southam (23 August 1642) and Lt. Colonel Sir Francis Butler at Nantwich (25 January 1644) both fell into the hands of the Parliamentarians through mistaking their colours for those of their own side![4]

The colours, which were of painted taffeta, were larger than those now in use, measuring 6½ feet by 6½ feet.

The devices on the guidons of the dragoons followed the same system as the foot. They are well exemplified by those of Colonel James Wardlaw's Regiment[5], which belonged to the army under the Earl of Essex. Guidons were much the same size as cavalry standards.

At least two cavalry standards from the Civil War period are still in existence, preserved in the Church at Bromsberrow. They measure 2 feet by 2 feet. Neither was carried at Edgehill, but details of many that were have survived. Except that generally speaking the field was the same for the standards of every troop in the regiment, the system in the horse was quite different from that used by the foot, although the colonel's standards were often of plain damask. Most of the standards on each side bore mottoes and devices of a political, religious or even derisive character.

Cavalier standards included:

Lifeguard. A lion passant, crowned or, with DIEU ET MON DROIT for motto.

Earl of Carnarvon. A lion, and six dogs baiting or baying at him. One of the dogs was bigger than the others and from his mouth issued a little scroll, wherein was written KIMBOLTON. From the other five issued scrolls with PYM, PYM, written on them. From the lion's mouth came the words TANDEM ABUTERIS PATIENTA NOSTRA?

The Earl had yet another cornet showing five hands reaching at a crown, and an armed hand with a sword issuing out of a cloud defending it, with the motto REDDITE CÆSARI. The five hands symbolized the five members.[6]

Charles Gerard's Lifeguard (1645) had a standard with a sphere painted on it, and the motto 'At all that's round' beneath it.[7]

Another Cavalier had a picture of a trooper holding his sword in his right hand and a less martial instrument in the other. *Ready with either weapon* was his motto.[8]

Lord Hopton when he was General of the Ordnance in 1644, had for the standard of his Lifeguard a standard gules, bearing for device a cannon discharging or, above this the motto 'ET SACRIS COMPESCUIT IGNIBUS IGNES'.[9]

Venn, quoting Gervase Markham's *Souldiers Accidence* (1625) (p. 31) explains the meaning of the metals, colours and furs represented in colours. As in heraldry 'no mettal is to be carried upon mettal: . . .'

Yellow (Gold): 'betokeneth honour, or height of Spirit.'

White (Silver): 'signifieth Innocencie, or purity of conscience, Truth, and upright integrity without blemish.'

Black: 'signifieth Wisdome, and sobriety, together with a severe correction of too much Ambition, being mixed with Yellow, or with too much belief or lenity being mixed with White.'

Blue: 'Faith, constancy or truth in affection.'

Red: 'Justice, or Noble worthy Anger in defence of Religion or the oppressed.'

Green: 'good hope, or the accomplishment of holy and honourable actions.'

Purple: 'fortitude with discretion, or a most true discharge of any trust reposed.'

'Tunnis or Tawny, signifieth merit, or desert, and a foe to Ingratitude.'

'Ermine, which is only a rich Furr, with curious spots, signifieth Religion, or holiness, and that all names are not divine objects.'

Venn mentions certain other considerations. A commander should not put his full Coat-Armour in his ensign. Nor should he bear a single black spot therein for 'it sheweth some blemish in the owner.'

He should not carry words in his colours without a device, or vice versa, and the words should not exceed four in number.

Lastly he should not carry more than two colours in his ensign 'except it be for some special note, or the Ensign of several Kingdoms, it is surcharge and esteemed folly.'[10]

In addition there are many rules to be observed too numerous to name, in the 'Postures and Flourishes' belonging to colours. For example, the ensign

> ' . . . If he shall enter into any City or great Town; then he shall unfold or open his Colours, and let them fly at full length . . . This is a marching in Triumph; but if the wind blow stiff . . . then he may set the butt against his waste and not otherwise; and is to have but one hand upon his staff in any march whatever.'
>
> 'When the Company is drawn up into a Body, the Colours must be flying; and . . . in case the General . . . or any Noble Stranger worthy of respect, do come, immediately upon his or their approach, the Ensign-bearer in all humility is to bow the head of his Colours, waving them with the bow of his body, and to raise both it and himself up again: And as the said person shall pass away, the Drum shall beat, and the Colours shall be displayed: . . . '

This ceremony says Venn 'is no more but as the vailing of your hat, or giving your friend a courtesie.'

More important was the ensign's behaviour

> ' . . . when the Body is drawn up into Battalia and the Enemy within view thereof, then every man being in his place is to express all the Gallantry he can, and especially the Ensign-bearer either in displaying his Colours standing, marching, charging and retreiting (or retiring;) . . . '

Venn goes on to detail eleven 'Postures' which the ensign should be taught, as elaborate in their way as those practised by Drum-Majors to this day. For example

> '5. With turns or flourishes you bring the butt end of the staff to your left hand turning the palm of your left hand outwards . . . and with the same hand only throw it off upon its turn with a flourish to deliver it unto the left hand, and to perform the same with the left hand, and deliver the Colours into the right hand, as at first.'

Truly the authors of military manuals have changed but little in 300 years![11]

One 'Dignity' that every ensign or cornet had was 'to have a Guard ever about it, which no other Officer hath, neither is it . . . unlodged, without a special Guard attending upon it both of Musqueteers and Pikes; (And so for a Cornet with his own Squadron of Horse.)'

In the field an ensign was never to

> 'lay his Colours upon the ground, or put them in unworthy or base hands, but he shall first furle and fold them up and set the butt end on the ground supported with the Serjeants Holbearts, and the Ensign himself shall not go from the view thereof, unless he shall leave sufficient guard for them.'[12]

The lodging of the colours was another occasion of ceremony.

> 'The Captain leading them out of the field, and coming near the place intended to lodge his Colours, Converts the ranks of Musqueteers of both divisions to the right and left outwards and joyns them; and being so fixed, the body of Pikes stand in the reer, and the Ensign in the head of them, the Captain before the Colours, with the Drums and Serjants guarding the Colours on each side, and the Lieutenant behind, the Ensign bearer, and all being advanced, shall troop up with the Colours furl'd to his lodging or quarters; and as he approacheth thereto, he shall with a bow to his Captain carry in his Colours; then the word shall be given to all the Musquetteers to make ready; that being done, they shall all present, and upon the beat of Drum, or other word of command give one intire Volley; and then command every Officer to go to their quarters, and to be in readiness upon the next summons, either by Drum or Command.'[13]

In the days when the great majority of the soldiers up to the rank of sergeant were unlettered, much depended on their recognizing, following and rallying to their colours, whether on the march or in action. The post of cornet or ensign could not easily be filled by the captain's son fresh from school, but was one for a stout-hearted, athletic man, such as that valiant Welshman John Gwyn who writing of the storming of Brentford says 'for my farther encouragement, I had the Colours conferred upon me, to go on as I had begun'. He was in Salusbury's Regiment. He describes how at First Newbury he saved his ensign when Essex's horse compelled his regiment to retreat – 'with my colours in my hand, I jumped over hedge and ditch, or I had died by multitude of hands'.[14]

One last tradition deserves mention. By the Law of Arms a troop or company that lost its colour was not permitted to carry another until it had captured one from the enemy in action. Thus the Prince of Wales' Troop lost its cornet at Hopton Heath (19 March 1643), but the major of the regiment, Thomas Daniel, restored its honour by taking one from the Roundheads at Chalgrove Field (18 June 1643).[15]

1 *Military Observations or the Tacticks put into Practice*, London, 1672, see p. 186.
2 Richard Symonds the antiquary, who served in King Charles' Lifeguard, H., noted many colours, especially at the rendezvous at Aldbourne Chase, 10 April 1644. See his unpublished notebook in the British Museum (Harleian MS. 986) and his interesting Diary (Camden Society, 1859).
3 Dr. Williams' Library. MS Modern, folio 7. This book shows Parliamentarian standards and guidons, and Royalist colours taken by Essex's army and the New Model. It was painted by Jonathan Turmile, belonged to Thomas Hollis (1720–1774) and was bequeathed to Dr. Williams' Library by his heir in 1803.
4 J.R. Phillips: *Memoirs of the Civil War in Wales*, Volume II, p. 130.
5 'Colonell Worleys Regement of Dragoners'. Dr. Williams' MS, f. 103.
6 Thomas Blount, The art of making devises . . . London, 1650.
7 Symonds' Diary, p. 242.
8 Thomas Blount, op.cit., The motto was in latin: IN UTRUMQUE PARATUS.
9 Symonds' Diary, p. 93.
10 Venn, p. 182.
11 Venn, p. 185.
12 Venn, p. 181.
13 Venn, p. 186.
14 Military Memoirs. Richard Atkyns and John Gwyn, pp. 47 and 53.
15 Anon (? (Sir) Bernard de Gomme): 'His Highness Prince Rupert's late beating up the Rebels' quarters at Postcombe and Chinnor'. Leonard Lichfield, Oxford, 1643.

5

Pay

'Moneys are the Nerves of War.'
King Charles to the Oxford Parliament, 1644

'Nervos belli, pecuniam infinitam.'
Cicero

'Truly my bowels yearn for the poor soldiers, who have run so many hazards and fought so many famous battles, stormed so many towns, waded through so many rivers with the loss of limbs and blood; besides all the hunger and cold and lodging on the ground, which they have gone through during the summer service in winter season; . . . '[1]

THUS WROTE A pamphleteer of 1656 and indeed, then as now, the old campaigner usually had little to show for long service but his scars. It was not only in the Royalist armies that pay was often in arrears. In the West in 1645 the New Model, so often extolled as a triumph of Parliamentarian organization, actually came to a halt for want of pay. But in 1642 the Royalists certainly paid their foot (see Section I, Document 17) and the Parliamentarian army not only received its pay but a gift of half-a-crown a man (11 November).

The rates of pay varied somewhat at different stages in the war but in December 1642 the Royalists were offering 6/- a week to musketeers, 12/10d. to dragooners and 17/6d. to harquebusiers, or troopers. It was hoped that the men would provide their own arms and equipment.[2]

In April 1644 Symonds calculated the weekly pay of 200 Royalist foot at £40.[3] The pay of individuals was:

		£	s.	d.
Captain	1	2	12	6
Lieutenant	1	1	8	0
Ensign	1	1	1	0
Gentlemen of the arms	1	0	10	6
Sergeants	2	0	10	6 each
Corporals	3	0	7	0 each
Drummers	2	0	7	0 each
Soldiers	100	0	4	0 each

In April 1644, the foot soldier was only receiving 4/- a week, but it is evident from a comparison of the warrants of 16 and 24 November that in 1642 he was still on the higher rate of 6/- a week. It follows that a captain's company (111 officers and men) should then have been getting £40.8.0 a week. This gives us a fairly accurate idea of the strength of the Royalist infantry in mid-November, for we may calculate as a guide that each £5 of pay represents 14 officers and men. The value of this guide to the strength of the Royalist infantry brigades and regiments will be apparent.

As to the horse, their pay was soon in arrears and by November 1642 they were living at free quarters.

On 27 November the King gave orders to Prince Rupert authorizing him to order the colonels of horse and dragoons

> ' . . . to quarter and billet their respective regiments in such places as we have assigned, and there to take up such necessary provision of diet, lodging, hay, oats, and straw, as shall be necessary for them. And if there shall not be sufficient for such their supply in their quarters, they they are to send out their warrants to the several hundreds and parishes adjacent, requiring the inhabitants to bring in all fitting provisions for their daily supply. For all which, as for that taken up in their quarters, they [are] to give their respective tickets, and not to presume, upon pain of our high displeasure, to send for greater quantities than will suffice for their numbers of men and horses, and such as may be proportionable to half of each officer's pay by the day, for all manner of diet, lodging, and horse-meat, and half of every ordinary horsemans' pay by day for diet only, their horse-meat being to be supplied by the counties adjacent to each quarter. In this manner we will that you proceed and continue until such time as the counties wherein they are quartered shall agree of, and settle some other course for their constant and daily supply.'[4]

It needs no great imaginative powers to picture the difficulties of this system. Living at free quarters, even in the most loyal areas, a troop of horse would soon outstay its welcome.

Oxfordshire which in January 1643 agreed to maintain 27 troops of horse and a company of dragoons had to provide for each trooper at the rate of 10/6d. a week: 3/6d. for the man, and 7/- for the horse.[5]

Rates of pay in the Royalist army were not ungenerous and when money was available senior officers did well enough. A general officer might receive £10 a day and the governor of a fortress, £3.[6]

Turning to the Parliamentarians we find that in March 1644 the monthly cost of maintaining Essex's army, then reduced to an establishment of 10,500 men, was calculated at £30,504. But in 1642 his 20 infantry regiments alone should, at full strength, have mustered 29,180 officers and men.[7]

Among the uncalendared State Papers in the Public Record Office[8] is an order from the Earl of Essex to Henry, Earl of Stamford, Colonel of a Regiment of 1,200 men, which tells us the monthly pay of all the officers of a regiment of foot.

	£	s.	d.
Colonel	63	0	0
Lt. Colonel	42	0	0
Major	33	10	0
Captain	7	0	0
Lieutenant	5	12	0
Ensign	4	4	0
Sergeant	2	2	0
Corporal	1	17	4
Drum Major	2	2	0
Drum	1	7	0
Preacher	5	12	0
Quartermaster	7	0	0
Provost	7	0	0
Chirurgion	5	12	0
Mate	2	16	0
Wagon Master	4	4	0

The private soldier is omitted, but it may be assumed that he was not paid less than his Royalist opponent, that is 6/- per week.

It is interesting to see that the Quartermaster and the Provost-Marshal were paid as captains, but the Preacher and the Surgeon only as lieutenants. The Wagon Master rated as an ensign, while the Surgeons's mate's pay was more than that of a Sergeant. It will be observed that, generally speaking, the rates of pay were the same in both armies, which is by no means surprising when one considers that both armies were working on the same War Establishment, that laid down for the recent Scots Wars. But while the Royalist foot were still in constant pay it is extremely unlikely that the field officers were getting the high rates of pay to which they were entitled.[9]

1 Firth, Cromwell's Army, p. 187 quoting *The Picture of a New Courtier*.
2 Proclamation of 3 December 1642. R. Steele, Tudor and Stuart Proclamations 1485–1714, Vol. I, No. 2316.
3 Unpublished notebook. BM. Harleian MS. 986, f. 96.
4 Warburton, Vol. II, p. 70.
5 An Explanation of the Agreement, 16 January, 1642/3. Madan, Vol. II, No. 1187.
6 Roy, Royalist Army, p. 225.

7   Essex's own regiment had a higher establishment than the others, being allowed 1,500 soldiers.

8   SP 28.

9   See Part Three, Section III for the rates of pay of the Royalist Artillery.

6

Victuals

'Since money is generally scarce in the wars, in so much that soldiers cannot receive their wages duly, let us see what allowance of meat and drink . . . princes allow their soldiery;'

Sir James Turner (1615–1686?)

TURNER, WHO AFTER serving under Gustavus Adolphus, fought with the Scots Army in England in 1645, with Hamilton in 1648 and under Charles II at Worcester (1651) tells us much about the commissariat system of his day.[1] He emphasizes the importance of the commissary whose duty is

' . . . to provide victuals, corn, flesh, wine, bread, and beer; he hath the inspection of them, and should see them equally and proportionably divided to the regiments, according to their several strengths; for which purpose he should have all the rolls and lists by him, which his secretaries should carefully keep. He hath no power to sell any proviant under what pretence soever, without the general's express warrant. All mills where the army comes are under his protection, and he is obliged to protect them. He hath the ordering of all the magazines for victuals, and to him belongs the care of seeing the garrisons and fortified places sufficiently provided with such meats and drinks as are most fit to preserve; these are, corn, grain and meal of several kinds, stock-fish, herrings, and all other salted fishes; salted and hung fleshes, especially beef and bacon, cheese, butter, almonds, chesnuts and hazel nuts, wine, beer, malt, honey, vinegar, oil, tobacco, wood and coal for firing, and as many living oxen, cows, sheep and swine, hens and turkeys, as can be conveniently fed; for which purpose, as also for horses, he is to provide straw, hay and oats . . . '[2]

According to Turner 'The ordinary allowance for a soldier in the field is daily, two pounds of bread, one pound of flesh, or in lieu of it, one pound of cheese, one pottle of wine, or in lieu of it, two bottles of beer.' In the French army we are told that the soldier's ration was two loaves of bread a day, of ten ounce weight apiece, and one pint of wine Paris measure. Firth explains that this 'ammunition bread' was composed two parts of wheat and a third part of rye, and that the bran and meal were mixed together in making it.[3]

It was very common during the English Civil War for the armies, especially the horse, to live 'at free quarter'. Lord Hopton, writing of the Royalist advance into Somerset in 1643, laments:

> 'There began the disorder of the horse visibly to break in upon all the prosperity of the publique proceedings. The Towne [Taunton] agreing willingly to rayse and pay 8000li. composition, (which would have suffized for some weekes necessarie paye for the whole Army;) The Countrye being then full, and not relucting at free-quarter soberly taken, And the Generalls being verie fully advertized of the opportunity to begin a discipline in the Army, and being of themselves verie desirous of it, were yet never able to represse the extravagant disorder of the horse to the ruine and discomposure of all.'[4]

Turner, practical as ever, enlarges on this difficulty pointing out that

> ' . . . withal it is very hard to get soldiers and horsemen kept within the limits of their duty in these quarters after they have endured hunger, thirst, and other hardships in the field. It is true, all Princes who for preservation of their armies from extream ruin, and for want of treasure, are necessitated too often to make use of this free quarter, do not only make strict laws and ordinances, how many times a day officers and soldiers are to eat, and how many dishes every one according to his quality is to call for, but likewise set down the precise rates, and values of the dishes, that the host be not obliged to do beyond those limitations, yet the grievance continues heavy and great.'[5]

Royalist and Roundhead, Clarendon and Ludlow alike, attest the shortage of provisions at Edgehill. Clarendon attributes this to the hostility of the country people in an area

> ' . . . so disaffected to the King's party that they had carried away or hid all their provisions, insomuch as there was neither meat for man or horse; and the very smiths hid themselves, that they might not be compelled to shoe the horses, of which in those stony ways there was great need.'

Clarendon points out that the 'circuit' in which Edgehill was fought lying between 'the dominions' of Lord Saye and Lord Brooke was 'the most eminently corrupted of any country in England'. He omits to mention, however, that the Royalist Earl of Northampton derived his strength from the same area. Clarendon asserts that 'there were very many companies of the common soldiers who had scarce eaten bread in eight and forty hours before', while on the other side Ludlow, who eventually got some food on the night of the 24th, complains 'I could scarce eat it my jaws for want of use having almost lost their natural faculty'.

During the Edgehill campaign the supply of provisions to both armies was evidently very haphazard. Thereafter, things were put on a more regular footing. The Royalists established magazines and stores at Oxford, and made serious efforts to provision their army in a methodical fashion. Oats and corn were collected and stored in the Schools; wheat was laid up in the Guildhall.[7] Bread or biscuit was baked under the supervision of the Wagon-Master-General,[8] and forwarded to the army as occasion demanded. Country carts were normally employed, but it was suggested, probably in October 1643, that a train of 30 covered wagons should be formed for the carriage of victuals.[9]

Even when 'the Oxford Army' was as far away as Gloucester provisions were forwarded to it from the Royalist capital. But to a very great extent the armies, especially the horse, lived 'at free quarters'. In theory the men had to pay the country people with tickets, whose issue could only be authorized by a commissary, but in practice much pillage and waste resulted. When pay and subsistence is not assured marauding is bound to follow, with a consequent loss of discipline.

Sir Charles Firth is justly critical of the administration of Essex's army.

'To supply an army operating in England was a comparatively easy task, and yet the army which fought under the Earl of Essex was never well supplied. His commissariat was under the charge of a "commissary for the provisions" and his train under a "carriage-master-general". The train must have been extremely small. Two waggons per regiment for the sutlers appears to have been the official allowance, and forty were apparently held enough for the whole army. Others were hired with their teams as wanted, or, if necessary, were impressed . . . '[10]

On at least one occasion Essex's soldiers found unexpected plenty. After the Royalists stormed Brentford (11 November 1642) the citizens of London, thoroughly alarmed, were generous with victuals.

' . . . The ministers therefore were moved by a motion from the said ever to be honoured, pious, and prudent Lord Mayor, on the said Lord's day in their morning sermon in their pulpits, to encourage and incite the people to spare some part of their diet, ready dressed for that present dinner, and to bestow it upon the soldiers aforesaid. Whereupon after the sermon was done, carts being ordered to stand ready in the streets in every parish throughout the City, to carry presently away what was sent, there were sent at least an hundred loads of all manner of good provision of victuals, bottles of wine, and barrels of beer instantly carried to them, and accompanied by honest and religious gentlemen, who went to see it faithfully distributed to them. And this was done so freely and with such willingness and cheerfulness, that not only the liberal contribution itself, but the forwardness therein, deserves a perpetual memory.'[11]

But this was an altogether exceptional state of affairs.

The normal subsistence of Essex's unfortunate men emerges from Sergeant Henry Foster's account of the relief of Gloucester (1643).[12]

'At Chesham we were well accomodated for beer, having great plenty; at Aynhoe we were very much scanted of victuals; at Chipping Norton our regiment stood in the open field all night having neither bread nor water to refresh ourselves, having also marched the day before without any sustenance.'

For six days they marched with very little provision. On the march back he complains 'we had no provision but what little every one had in his snapsack'. They had a windfall when they surprised Cirencester (16 September) and found 40 cartloads of victuals provided by the diligent Royalist commissaries for their own side. Near Swindon they rounded up about 1000 sheep and 60 head of cattle, which, curiously enough, belonged to 'malignants and papists'! The 87 sheep issued to the Red Regiment were all lost when they came to fight.

It would be idle to deny that the Royalist army suffered grievous shortages from time to time. These may be traced to the chronic shortage of money. The Parliamentarians, thanks to Pym's Excise Ordinance, suffered no such disadvantage. Yet it would seem that King Charles' Council of War administered their main army a great deal better than the Earl of Essex did his.

To end on a cheerful note, it seems that the tradition of 'wetting' the stripes, pips, or crowns on promotion is rooted deep in the past – as one might expect. On 30 August Nehemiah Wharton and his fellows honoured this custom. 'Tuesday morning we officers [sergeants] wet our halberts with a barrel of strong beere, called ould Hum, which we gave our soldiers.'

1 *Pallas Armata*, 1683.
2 Firth, p. 210.
3 Firth, p. 212.
4 Hopton, p. 47.
5 Firth, p. 211.

 6 Clarendon, Vol. II, p. 358 *et seq.*

 7 Wood, L. & T. p. 74.

 8 Stevens, pp. 32–33.

 9 British Museum, Harleian MS, 6804, f.216

10 Firth, p. 214.

11 Vicars, Parliamentary Chronicle, Vol. I, p. 216.

12 Sergeant Henry Foster was in the Red Regiment of the London Trained Bands. His 'True and Exact Relation' is printed in John Washbourne's *Bibliotheca Gloucestrensis*, two volumes. Gloucester, 1823.

7

Raising the Royalist Army

Recruit me Lancashire and Cheshire both,
And Derbyshire Hills that are so free,
But no married man, nor no widow's son,
For no woman's curse shall go with me.
Ballad of Agincourt

THE RAISING OF the two armies is treated separately, for though in many respects so alike, they were raised in different ways.

We will deal first with the Royalists. King Charles had virtually no military establishment in 1642. It is true that he had his Gentlemen Pensioners, who amounted to a troop of horse, and his Yeomen of the Guard. Some of these last were certainly present with the army at Shrewsbury, and may have been absorbed in the Lifeguard of Foot. The garrisons of the various castles and forts, which guarded our shores, played little part in building up the forces of either side except perhaps in the Western Royalist Army. The already ancient Board of Ordnance, though its headquarters was in the Tower of London, was to render invaluable service to the King, thanks to the loyalty of some of its officers.

Historians have poured scorn on the trained bands, as the militia were called, and even such a learned and fair-minded writer as the late Sir Charles Firth opined that 'London was the only part of the kingdom in which any attempt was made really to drill and exercise the trained bands'.[1] Certainly in point of numbers the London trained bands, who served as a strategic reserve to the Parliamentarians throughout the war, were more formidable than those of the rest of the Kingdom. But it was the Yorkshire trained bands that gave the King his first body of foot, besides providing a nucleus for the regiments of Pennyman and Belasyse, while it was the *Posse Comitatus*, led by Sir Ralph Hopton and Cornish gentlemen like Sir Bevil Grenvile and Sir Nicholas Slanning, that drove the Roundheads back across the Tamar at the beginning of the war.

The nucleus of the Royalist Horse was the troop raised at York for the defence of the King's person. As early as 24 May 1642 Lord Fairfax and others wrote to the Speaker:

'We do not as yet hear of any resolution to lay down these guards. The foot are here still in the same number as they were, and the horse as we hear do increase, so likewise do mens' apprehensions and fears. The Prince [of Wales] is made captain of these horse, a brother of Sir John Byron's their lieutenant, and one of Sir Ingleby Daniel's sons, a gentleman of this county, is made cornet.'[2]

On 21 June a Newsletter from York reported that the gentlemen of these northern parts were very forward in offering their service. The King's guard was already 1,000 foot and 200 horse.[3]

The Parliament, though busy raising its own army under cover of subduing Ireland, was quick to resent these Royalist levies. On 9 June it made a declaration setting forth that:

'It appears that the King, seduced by wicked counsel, intends to make war against his Parliament; and in pursuance thereof, under pretence of a guard for his person, has actually begun to levy forces both of horse and foot, and sent out summons throughout Yorkshire and other counties for calling together greater numbers; and some ill-affected persons have been employed in other parts to raise troops under colour of the King's service . . .'[4]

It may be that the King had already given out a few commissions, but it seems that the majority of his officers received theirs considerably later. Stephen Hawkins, lieutenant-colonel of the second regiment raised, did not get his until 28 July 1642.[5] The officers of Dyve's Regiment were not commissioned until 13 August.[6] In theory the Royalist army was raised by the mediaeval process of issuing Commissions of Array. King Charles, who arrived at York in March 1642, began in June to issue Commissions of Array to his powerful supporters in every county. It required them to hold musters, view arms and report their findings to the King.

The Commission of Array was valuable as giving the King's levies a cloak of genuine legal respectability. But in fact the individual officers of the various regiments were given commissions, not so very different to those that modern officers receive today. An example will be found in Section I, Document 16. Armed with this an officer would raise volunteers by beat of drum. On 19 September, Lieutenant John Roane, Yeoman Pricker to the King, was examined by the Parliamentarians at Northampton. It was found that 'he was employed by Lt. Colonel (Richard) d'Ewes in a regiment assigned by Lord Paget to Colonel Bolls (Richard Bolle) with a commission . . . to raise volunteers, which he showed to the Mayor of Walsall, who refused to let him beat up his drum and apprehended him'.[7]

It may be that the raising of the Standard at Nottingham (22 August) was somewhat premature, since it was difficult for a man commissioned on 28 July to raise 160 men in less than three weeks. Even so some managed very well. Gervase Holles, commissioned as a captain (13 August), and major (16 September), brought 117 men to Nottingham,[8] while Dutton's Regiment, to which Lt. Colonel Stephen Hawkins belonged, 'was the 2^d raised, and came in to His Mat^{ie} (complete 800 with flying Colours) at the setting up of his Royal Standard at Nottingham'.[5]

Other colonels were not unsuccessful. Colonel John Belasyse, a son of Lord Fauconberg, 'raised a regiment of foot (at his father's charge), with which he advanced to the King at Nottingham, his being one of the first regiments that came into His Majesty's service, which was soon after armed and recruited to the number of 1,000 men from Nottingham'.[9] This regiment was partly raised in Yorkshire, like Sir William Penny-man's, the oldest of the army.[10] Clarendon puts the strength of these two regiments at 600 apiece, and says each brought a troop of horse. Pennyman certainly did.[11]

The Earl of Lindsey and his son Lord Willoughby d'Eresby, who had been a captain in Holland, both raised their regiments in Lincolnshire. Clarendon says that both were 'near one thousand', that the Lord General's was 'very well officered' and that Willoughby's, the Lifeguard, was also 'under officers of good experience'.

There is quite a lot of evidence that experienced officers were joining the King. Rupert, who joined at Nottingham, brought a number, including the engineer, Bernard de Gomme, and the fireworker, Bartholomew La Roche, as well as Richard Crane, who was to command his Lifeguard, and Somerset Fox, his cornet.[12] Patrick Ruthven, Lord Forth, brought a score of Scots officers with him.[13]

On 12 August 1642 a list was published in London giving the names of 77 English and Scots commanders who had left their commands under the Prince of Orange. It is endorsed 'These are for the King's service'.

	English	Scots	Totals
Captains	11	7	18
Lieutenants	12	9	21
Ensigns	11	8	19
Sergeants	11	7	18
Quartermaster	–	1	1
	45	32	77[14]

Even so there were regiments that had little background of experience. On 6 August Colonel Sir Thomas Salusbury of Lleweny wrote to Thomas Bulkeley describing how his regiment came into being. A meeting had been held at Flint, when the gentlemen of Denbighshire and Flint had

THE RECRUITING AREAS

Counties supplying a Regiment or more to the Royalist Army

Counties supplying some troops to the Royalist Army

Counties supplying a Regiment or more to the Parliamentarian Army.

Counties supplying some troops to the Parliamentarian Army

NOTE: Troops not at Edgehill omitted, but there were, for example five regiments of Royalist Foot being raised in Cornwall.

agreed to levy the sum of £1,500 to raise a regiment of foot in the King's defence. Salusbury had been elected colonel, and was in hopes that the greater part of his men would be levied by the end of the week, for many of the companies were nearly full. He desired Bulkeley 'to spare half a score of lusty fellows' from Anglesey for it fell to the colonel to raise 350 men, for his own company (200) and that of his sergeant-major (George Boncle), 'a stranger' (150).[15]

Beyond question the Royalists depended to a great extent upon their cavalry. These were not very numerous in 1642, mustering less than a quarter of the foot, but they were good horsemen, well-mounted and reasonably well armed.

The Prince of Wales' Regiment, based on the troop raised at York, could perhaps claim to be the oldest regiment, though it was said that Sir John Byron's was the first completed, the Marquis of Worcester having lent him £5,000 for mounting money.[16] But it is unlikely that Byron's regiment was complete by the time of Edgehill, for the indications are that it was well short of the 420 men that six troops should have totalled. Indeed, with the exception of the Prince of Wales' Regiment all the Royalist cavalry units at Edgehill were probably under strength. That they were ready at all was due to the loyal peers and ministers who had subscribed to levy horse. They had undertaken to pay horse for three months at 2/6s. per diem.[17] Of these a number took the field in person. The Earl of Northampton only subscribed for 40 horse, but according to Bulstrode his troop mustered 100 gentlemen. Presumably a number of these were gentlemen volunteers, who brought their own horses and equipment, and served at their own or their fathers' expense.

Judging from the subscriptions from the troop commanders the Prince of Wales' Regiment for one was well backed.

	Horse
The Prince	200
The Duke of York	120
Lord Great Chamberlain (Earl of Lindsey)	30
Lord Willoughby d'Eresby	30
Earl of Northampton	40
Earl of Westmorland	20
	440

In all, the peers and officials guaranteed 2,015 horse. Since the Lifeguard, Northampton's troop and Wilmot's troop and no doubt many others, contained a great number of gentlemen, the Royalist cavalry that fought at Edgehill cannot have lacked for pay, good horses and saddlery. If arms and armour were lacking it was not because there was no money to buy it, but because the main sources of supply were the continent and London; the one remote, the other in hostile hands.

King Charles made it clear to his followers that he went to fight Atheists and Brownists. His enemies made much of the Popish character of his following. Clarendon was at pains to deny that the King employed Roman Catholics and in his anxiety to make propaganda for the Royalist cause told what can only be described as a black lie when he wrote that the King had 'in his whole army not one officer of the field who was a Papist, except Sir Arthur Aston, if he were one; and very few common soldiers of that religion'.[18] Besides Aston, who was well known to be a Catholic, Charles Gerard, John Belasyse, Lord Dillon, Lord Taafe, Thomas Tyldesley, and Sir John Beaumont were all of that religion, to name but a few.

The classic view is that the less developed parts of the country, the North and the West, supported the King, and that the more populous and industrially developed South-East supported the Parliament. It is a view that certainly seems to be supported by the Order of Battle of the 1642 armies. The King began his southward march with the Yorkshire-men of the Prince's troop and the regiments of Pennyman and Belasyse. He was joined at Nottingham by the Lincolnshiremen of the Lifeguard and Lord General. Belasyse added Nottinghamshire men to his unit, and the Byron brothers, whose home was at Strelley, began to raise their horse. Marching West, Derbyshire miners recruit the Lifeguard and a Staffordshire regiment joins. The Cheshiremen of Lord Rivers, Sir Edward Fitton and Sir Thomas Aston swell the numbers at Shrewsbury, as do the men of North Wales under Sir Thomas Salusbury. Dyve, though himself a Bedfordshire man, and with a major, Gervase Holles, from Lincolnshire, evidently levied soldiers at Shrewsbury and these no doubt included Welshmen as well as the local men. It is odd that the Edgehill army contained no unit which one can specifically associate with Shropshire, Worcestershire, or Herefordshire. Certainly the two Conyngsbys who commanded companies in Feilding's Regiment must have raised their men in the latter county, but in general the men of those counties, all notably well disposed to the Royal cause, must have enlisted in existing regiments. One would imagine that the Lifeguard was well up to strength after the Derbyshiremen joined it, but it seems to have absorbed as many as three companies of Cheshiremen, probably while the army was at Shrewsbury.

The Lancashiremen of Lord Molyneux and Sir Gilbert Gerard do not figure in the list of quarters for 12 October and must have joined after the advance began. So did Sir Thomas Lunsford's Somersetshire Regiment, Sir Edward Stradling's from South Wales and Sir John

Beaumont's from Staffordshire. The first two made their junction with the King at Kenilworth (19 October). How they managed to get through from South Wales when Essex's main body was at Worcester is something of a mystery. They probably crossed the Severn at Upton.

Historians believe the ranks of the Royalist foot to have been full of Welshmen. This may be so. But the fact remains that except for the two regiments of Salusbury and Stradling there were no specifically Welsh regiments in the Edgehill army, though others like Sir John Owen's and Richard Herbert's were already raising.

On 18 October there was a rendezvous of the whole army on Meriden Heath where, according to the anonymous author of the *Journal of Prince Rupert's Marches*,[19] 'we had the first appearance of an Army'. Its first ordeal lay only five days ahead.

 1 Firth, p. 10.
 2 CSPD, 1641–3, p. 330.
 3 CSPD, 1641–3, p. 340
 4 CSPD, 1641–3, p. 337.
 5 BM, Harleian MS.
 6 Memorials of the Holles Family, p. 186.
 7 HMC Portland, Vol. I, p. 63.
 8 HMC Buccleuch, Vol. I, p. 527.
 9 HMC Ormonde. Life of Lord John Belasyse by his Secretary, Joshua Moone.
10 Symonds' Diary, p. 160.
11 Clarendon, Vol. II, p. 335.
12 Warburton, Vol. I.
13 Slingsby.
14 Two of these 'English' were evidently Dutch – Captain Vanhuish and Ensign Vandowse. Peacock, p. 92.
15 National Library of Wales. Calendar of Wynn Papers, p. 277. No. 1711.
16 Warburton, Vol. III, Appendix I.
17 Peacock, p. 7.
18 Clarendon, Vol. II, p. 348.
19 EHR, Vol. XIII, 1898.

8

Raising the Parliamentarian Army

'Curse ye Meroz, said the angel of the Lord, curse ye bitterly the inhabitants thereof, because they came not to the help of the Lord, to the help of the Lord against the mighty.'

Judges, Chapter 5, Verse 23

THE FINAL BREACH between King Charles and the Commons came when on 5 March 1642 the House passed the Militia Ordinance. By this act Pym and his colleagues took over the defence of the Kingdom, and proclaimed their power to act independently of the King. The Ordinance was intended, it was announced, to protect the country from those 'Papists and other ill-affected persons who have already raised a rebellion in the Kingdom of Ireland'. In future the Lords Lieutenants of counties, who were responsible for recruiting, were to be appointed by Parliament.

About the beginning of June Parliament started to levy troops. Anyone able to 'find and maintain' horse and horseman was to be paid 2/6d. a day. Volunteers were to leave their addresses at the Guildhall in London. A committee of five noblemen was set up, which as soon as 60 men had been enrolled, appointed officers.

The list published in Peacock shows that 77 troops were raised in this way, but it is certainly incomplete. In addition there were several regiments of dragoons, and in theory Essex should have had more than 5,000 horse at his command. The troops were eventually organized in regiments but this sensible measure seems to have been taken belatedly.

Twenty regiments of foot were raised, the colonels being given levy money for their men.

On 13 July 1642 the Earl of Essex was commissioned as captain-general, and given power to raise horse and foot, to grant commissions to officers, and to appoint a provost-marshal.[1] Lord Brooke was commissioned by Essex as captain of a company of 200 men in his regiment on 30 July 1642.

London and the eastern counties supplied many of the men. The Lord General's own regiment was raised in Essex; Denzil Holles' in London; those of John Hampden and Thomas Ballard in Buckinghamshire; and

Lord Saye's in North Oxfordshire. It is said that Lord Brooke raised his men in London, but it seems likely that he drew some of them from Warwickshire, for Warwick Castle belonged to him. Many of the cavalrymen were doubtless Londoners, but captains like Oliver Cromwell of Ely and Sir Samuel Luke of Woodend, Bedfordshire, must have levied their men around their own homes. Ireton commanded a Nottingham troop.

Cromwell got good men from the first according to Richard Baxter.

> ' . . . he had special care to get religious men into his troop. These men were of greater understanding than common soldiers and therefore more apprehensive of the importance and consequence of war and making not money but that which they took for the public felicity to be their end, they were the more engaged to be valiant . . . These things it's probable Cromwell understood, . . . But yet I conjecture that . . . it was the very esteem and love of religious men that principally moved him; and the avoiding of those disorders, mutinies, plunderings and grievances of the country which deboist [debauched] men in armies are commonly guilty of. By this means he indeed sped better than he expected. Aires, Desborough, Berry, Evanson and the rest of that troop did prove so valiant that as far as I can learn they never once ran away before an enemy.'[2]

That all the troop commanders were not so judicious or so fortunate, is evident not only from the indiscipline which prevailed, but from the misconduct of many of them in action. Cromwell's own words are the best commentary upon this.

> 'At my first going into this engagement, I saw our men were beaten at every hand . . . and I told him [John Hampden] I would be serviceable to him in bringing such men in as I thought had a spirit that would do something in the work . . . "Your troopers", said I, "are most of them old decayed servingmen and tapsters and such kind of fellows; and", said I, "their troopers are gentlemen's sons, younger sons and persons of quality; do you think that the spirits of such base and mean fellows will be ever able to encounter gentlemen that have honour and courage and resolution in them? . . . You must get men . . . of a spirit that is likely to go on as far as gentlemen will go, or else I am sure you will be beaten still" . . . He was a wise and worthy person, and he did think that I talked a good notion but an impracticable one.'[3]

It would be quite wrong, however, to suppose that in 1642 none of the Parliamentarian horse were good. The cuirassiers of Essex's own lifeguard, mostly gentlemen, after a panic on 23 September, when they fled at the mere sight of the runaways from Powick Bridge, fought valiantly at Edgehill. So indeed did the rest of Sir Philip Stapleton's Regiment. Sir William Balfour, an excellent soldier, had an effective unit from the outset. The fact is that the Roundhead troops varied in quality from a large number which were not worth their mounting money, to a much smaller number who could hold their own with the bravest of the Cavaliers.

The foot were equally uneven in quality. To some their religious ardour was their strength. Nehemiah Wharton's company marched in rank and file to hear worthy Mr. Obadiah Sedgewick give a sermon (9 September), but he does not scruple to condemn 'the ruder sort of soldiers, whose society, blessed be God, I hate and avoide' (7 October). In other words the men were the usual mixture of every sort that has composed every British Army from 1642 onwards. Villains and saints soldiered side by side, influencing by their example the great mass of their comrades who were neither. The lively Londoners of Holles, the stalwart Buckinghamshire peasants who followed Hampden, were fundamentally good material. All they needed was discipline, or at least officers they were prepared to obey and to follow.

There seems to have been a serious shortage of good officers in Essex's army. This is not to say that there were insufficient professional soldiers, though this too seems to have been the case. The trouble was that too many of the officers lacked the personal qualities that make a man a leader.

Part of the trouble was that those members of both Houses, who had taken commissions, in their anxiety to set a good example took on too much. Each of the lords who commanded a foot regiment also had his troop of horse. If their regiments had their colonels at their head, their troops lacked a captain. Nor were they the only 'pluralists'. Sir Faithfull Fortescue, who led a troop at Edgehill, was also a lieutenant-colonel of foot.

Units that had MPs as their commanders lacked their example during the time they were forming. Sir Samuel Luke did not obtain leave to attend his charge until 15 September.[4] As late as the 30th Wharton writes 'Wee should bee very glad to see our colonell'. The Royalists, too, had their pluralists, but by no means as many as there were in the ranks of their foes.

On 9 September 1642 the Earl of Essex 'in much state', accompanied by many members of both Houses of Parliament, set out from London and went to his headquarters at St. Albans. From thence he went on to Northampton, 'where his Forces met him; and they were together above 15000 Men'.

Rushworth prints the Directions the Earl received from his employers.

I

'YOU shall carefully Restrain all Impieties, Prophaneness, and Disorders, Violence, Insolence, and Plundering in your Souldiers as well by strict and severe Punishment of such Offences, as by all other means, which you in your Wisdom shall think fit.

II

Your Lordship is to march with such Forces as you think fit, towards the Army raised in his Majesties Name against the Parliament and Kingdom. And you shall use your utmost Endeavours, by Battel or otherwise, to rescue his Majesty's Person, and the Persons of the Prince and the Duke of *York*, out of the hands of those desperate persons who are now about them.

III

You shall take an Opportunity, in some safe and honourable way, to cause the Petition of both Houses of Parliament herewith sent unto you to be presented unto his Majesty: And if his Majesty shall thereupon please to withdraw himself from the Forces now about him, and to resort to the Parliament, you shall cause all those Forces to Disband, and shall serve and defend his Majesty with a sufficient strength in his Return.'[5]

An ordinance issued by parliament on 23 September casts much light on the formation of Essex's army.

'*An* Ordinance or *Declaration of the Lords and Commons Assembled in Parliament, That all the Regiments of Foot and Troops of Horse in* London, *and all Parts of* England, *shall within* 48 *Hours after Publication hereof, March to his Excellence* Robert *Earl of* Essex, *to be employed for the Defence of his Majesty and Kingdom, the Priviledges of Parliament, and the Liberty of the Subject.*

Whereas divers Regiments of Foot and Troops of Horse, have long since been listed in the Army raised by the Parliament for the Defence of the King and Kingdom, under the Command of *Robert* Earl of *Essex*, of which some are not marched away to their Rendezvous, according to their Duty, and others are not of fitting Numbers for Service, yet all receive pay, to the great Charge of the Kingdom, and by this their Neglect do great prejudice to the publick Cause, in which Religion, Laws, and Liberty are so much concerned. It is therefore Ordained and Declared by the Lords and Commons in Parliament Assembled, That such Regiments of Foot as consist of Four hundred Men or more, and Troops of Horse that consist of Forty or more, shall within Forty eight hours after publication hereof March towards the place where they shall understand the Lord General to be, except by special Order they be directed to any other place; and they shall not stay by the way longer than for their necessary Refreshment: And such Regiments or Troops, as shall fail herein, or shall not consist of such

Numbers as is before specified; that is to say, a Regiment of Foot of Four hundred, and a Troop of Horse of Forty shall be cashiered, and also liable to such further punishment, as upon Examination of the Cause of their failing and neglect, shall be found that they have deserved. And the common Soldiers of such Regiment or Troop so cashiered, shall be disposed of for the filling up and recruiting of others.

Yet in regard the Captains of some Regiments, which have not the Number of Four hundred, may have been careful to raise and compleat their own Companies, and that there is no reason they should suffer for the Defaults of others, either the Colonels or other Captains, that have not been so careful, it is thought fit that such Captain of any Regiment now to be cashiered, as shall have his Company compleat, shall be continued together with his Company, and shall march unto the place where the Lord General shall be, to be disposed of by him in any other Regiment, or otherwise employed, as his Lordship shall think fit.

And it is further declared, That the Regiments of Colonel [Charles] *Essex* and Colonel [Thomas] *Ballard*, shall not be understood to be within this Order, in regard both those Colonels have been, and yet are imployed in the Service of the State, and their Absence may be a cause that their Regiments are not in that forwardness that otherwise they would have been; but they are hereby enjoyned with all possible speed to March unto the Army.'

Die Veneris, Septemb. 28. 1642[5]

In the ranks of this army fought Sir William Balfour, John Hampden, Denzil Holles, Sir William Waller, Oliver Cromwell, Henry Ireton, John Lilburne, Edmund Ludlow and Charles Fleetwood. Many of them were as yet young soldiers, but no army which numbered such stalwarts in its ranks is to be despised. Of the 130 officers serving with the cavalry of the 1641 Army, only 13 seem to have turned Roundhead and, of those, only 11 were probably at Edgehill.

It remained to be seen what 'old Robin' could do with it.

1 Davies, Parliamentary Army, p. 33.
2 Young, Oliver Cromwell and his Times, p. 36.
3 *Ibid*, p. 37.
4 Commons Journals, p. 768.
5 Rushworth, Vol. III, Pt. II, pp. 19 & 20.

9

The Generals and their Staff

'If the art of war consisted merely in not taking risks glory would be at the mercy of very mediocre talent.'

Napoleon

ROYALIST

KING CHARLES, as Captain-General, exercised his command of the Royalist army with the assistance of a permanent Council of War. This body, which sat frequently, consisted of generals, peers, ministers and field officers. These last were chosen from among those who had seen service abroad. The names of the Council are printed in a list, first published at York and then at London, which was obtained by Thomason on 9 August.[1] Not all of those named were at Edgehill, but those marked with an asterisk★ certainly were.

	Remarks
Duke of Richmond★	In attendance on the King at Edgehill.
Marquis of Hertford	May have been at Edgehill as Lunsford's Regiment, which had been with him in Somerset, was present.
Earl of Lindsey★	Lord General.
Earl of Cumberland	In command at York.
Earl of Bath	
Earl of Southampton★	
Earl of Dorset★	In attendance on the King at Edgehill.
Earl of Bristol★	
Earl of Carnarvon★	Colonel, H.
Lord Sackville	
Lord Falkland★	Volunteer, H.
Lord Grandison★	Colonel, H.
Lord Willoughby d'Eresby★	Colonel, F. Lifeguard.
Lord Seymour	Had been with Hertford in Somerset.
Secretary Nicholas	
Sir John Colepeper★	Chancellor of the Exchequer. Volunteer, H.
Master Comptroller	
Colonel (Henry) Wilmot★	Commissary-General, H.
Colonel William Vavasour★	Lt. Colonel, F. Lifeguard.
Colonel Richard Feilding★	Tertia, F.
Colonel Sir Thomas Lunsford★	F.
Sir William Uvedale	Treasurer of the Army.

59

Sir Jacob Astley★	Sergeant-Major-General, F.
Sir Thomas Glemham	Governor of York, and later Colonel-General of Newcastle's Army.
Colonel Sir Nicholas Byron★	Tertia, F.

Other officers were added to the Council from time to time, as is shown by the composition of two Councils of War held at Reading on 22 November[2] and at Oxford on 14 December.

			22 Nov.	14 Dec.
His Majesty		Captain-General	+	+
Prince Rupert	★	General, H.	+	+
Prince Maurice	★	Colonel, H.	+	–
Lord General	★	Now Patrick Ruthven, Lord Forth	+	+
Earl of Northampton	★	Colonel, F.	+	–
Lord Digby	★	Colonel, H.	+	–
Lord Dunsmore	★		+	+
Earl of Southampton			+	+
Lord Capel	★		+	–
Secretary Nicholas			+	+
Sir Jacob Astley		Sergeant-Major-General, F.	+	+
Sir Arthur Aston	★	Sergeant-Major-General, D.	+	–
Chancellor of the Exchequer		Sir John Colepeper	+	+
Colonel Henry Wentworth	★	Tertia, F.	+	–
Colonel Richard Fielding		Tertia, F.	+	–
(Lt.) Colonel John Innis	★	D.	+	+
Lord Mowbray	★		–	+
Lord Grey	★		–	+
Lord Newark	★		–	+
Lord Andover	★	Colonel, H.	–	+
Lt. Colonel (Will) Legge	★	Major, Prince Rupert, H.	–	+

Of these, those whose names are marked with an asterisk★ had not been in the Council of War at York. Officers of experience, such as Prince Rupert, Lord Forth and Sir Arthur Aston, were evidently added to the Council as soon as they joined the army. The minutes of some 70 Councils held throughout the war have been preserved. It is significant that nobody attended more frequently than the King himself.

It is impossible to understand the relationship of the senior Royalist commanders if it is not appreciated from the outset that, like England's mediaeval kings, Charles I commanded his Army in person. The Lord General and the General of the Horse, both had direct access to the King in his role of captain-general, and Prince Rupert was not obliged to take orders from the Earl of Lindsey. The last British king to take the field in person was King George II, who, it will be recalled, fought at Dettingen a hundred years after Edgehill. Having no capital, the King had no alternative but to accompany his Army during the campaign of 1642.

Charles' qualifications for command were not very remarkable. At the age of 42 he had never been in battle, although his two Scots Wars must have afforded him some experience of the problems of military organization and administration. It is well-known that he possessed personal courage, though of a somewhat passive kind. His main disqualification for high military command was that he had been sheltered by a ceremonious court from that contact with ordinary men which has given great generals their insight into the human heart. Charles was a poor judge of character, and his habit of listening to the advice of the last councillor he spoke to, encouraged intrigue amongst his entourage. Even so he was to have his successes in the field, particularly in the campaign of 1644, when his main army was to defeat Waller at Cropredy Bridge and Essex at Lostwithiel.

Robert Bertie, first Earl of Lindsey (1582–1642), was a warrior of good, though not very recent, experience. He had been in the Spanish expedition as long ago as 1597; at the siege of Amiens in 1598, and then after more than 20 years living on his Lincolnshire estates, he had served as a colonel in the Low Countries, and in Buckingham's naval expeditions. He was made admiral for the relief of La Rochelle (1628). In 1639 he had been Governor of Berwick, and now at 60 he found himself Lord Lieutenant-General of the main Royalist army. He was to have little opportunity to prove his worth, though he seems to have been a man of spirit and good sense.

The General of the Horse, the Prince Palatine Rupert (1619–1682), was to prove the outstanding Royalist leader of the First Civil War. Three centuries have failed to dim his vivid personality. *Le Prince estoit toujours soldat*, wrote Sir Philip Warwick, one who rode with him at Edgehill, and though only 22 years old, he was already an officer of experience, who had studied his profession. He had first seen service when the Prince of Orange invaded Brabant in 1635 and from the first he had distinguished himself by his daring valour. After a visit to his uncle's court (1636) he had been at that famous siege of Breda in 1637, where so many of his Civil War companions in arms had played a part. Captured at Lemgo in his brother's disastrous campaign in Westphalia, he had used his three year imprisonment to improve his theoretical knowledge of the Military Art. Released through the intervention of his uncle, he devoted all his blazing energy to the Royalist cause. To say that he comprehended the quarrel in which he now drew sword would be going too far. For Rupert, loyalty was enough; sufficient for him that the enemy were rebels and traitors. He did not seek the rewards of the statesman, but the laurels of the soldier.

Without a leader of Rupert's calibre the squires, gentlemen, and indeed noblemen, who formed the front ranks of the Royalist cavalry, would have been nothing more than the 'rabble of gentility', which Monck once called them. From the first he gave them positive leadership of a sort they could understand. As time went by he turned his own command into that 'iron wall' of which even an enemy could speak with respect.[3] Men of spirit are not easily disciplined, and if Rupert managed to impose his personality on friend and foe alike, it was because both were to some extent afraid of the tall, dark, saturnine young foreigner[4], who was so expert with sword and pistol, such an accomplished horseman. In appearance Rupert – 'very sparkish in his dress' – was the arch-type of Cavalier, but notably abstemious; he was never one to enjoy the carousals which occupied the leisure moments of men like George Goring, Thomas Wentworth and George Porter.

Rupert was not merely a dashing cavalry officer. He was proficient in gunnery and engineering. To him the Royalists owed the introduction of the galloping guns[5], a rudimentary form of horse artillery; it was he who first introduced mining to siege warfare in England[6]. In future years he was to show his versatility in the role of a hard-fighting admiral.

Next in the Royalist hierarchy must come Patrick Ruthven, Earl of Forth (1573?–1651), who was to be Lindsey's successor, and to act as Charles' 'Chief of Staff', if the term may be permitted at a period when that appointment had not yet been invented. He was an officer with long experience in the Swedish army under the great Gustavus. He had recently distinguished himself by his resolute defence of Berwick Castle against the Covenanters (1640). Nearly 70 years of age and decidedly fond of the bottle, he was still a brave and knowing officer, though somewhat past his best.

Command of the foot from 1642 to 1645 was entrusted to Sergeant-Major-General Sir Jacob Astley (1579–1652), a little, silver-haired old veteran of the Dutch Service, whom Rupert's mother, Elizabeth of Bohemia, had once called her monkey. A man of few words, what he did have to say was much to the point. A thorough master of the art of training and leading infantry, he had the advantage that he could get on with Prince Rupert, whose tutor he had once been.

Second in command to Rupert was the commissary-general of the Horse, Henry Wilmot (1612?–1658), shortly to be promoted lieutenant-general. He had been captain of a troop of horse in the Dutch army (1635), and had been wounded at Breda (1637). He had served in the second Scots War. Despite his victory at Roundway Down (13 July 1643) and his part in the escape of King Charles II after Worcester (1651), he was too much the sly politician to make a good soldier. He had the dubious distinction of sireing the foremost libertine of his age, John Wilmot, second Earl of Rochester.

The dragoons were entrusted to Sir Arthur Aston (k. 1649), a testy and imperious Roman Catholic veteran who had seen more service in outlandish parts than most. After serving in Russia (c. 1613–18) and fighting with the Poles against the Turks (1618–31), he had been with Gustavus Adolphus in the Lützen campaign (1632), returning home at the beginning of the Scots War. Rupert commissioned him as Sergeant-Major-General of Dragoons on 20th October 1642. He later became an extremely unpopular Governor of Oxford, lost both his leg and his appointment in consequence of a riding accident (1644) and came to a bad end when Drogheda was stormed by Cromwell. It is said that his brains were dashed out with his own wooden leg.

The tertia commanders of foot were:

Colonel Charles Gerard (d. 1694), who after serving as a captain in the Dutch army and in the Scots war, was to rise rapidly, being valued by Rupert, and to command the Royalist forces in South Wales.

Colonel John Belasyse (1614–1689), son of a Yorkshire magnate, Lord Fauconberg, had no previous military service. He saw a good deal of fighting during the war, with rather mixed success, though his resolute defence of Newark in the last stages was extremely creditable. He was afterwards Governor of Tangier (1664–1666).

Colonel Richard Feilding (d. 1650) served in foreign parts and returned to Endland as a captain (1639). He was colonel of a foot regiment in 1640. Disgraced for the surrender of Reading, he lost his regiment and narrowly escaped being executed. Perhaps he was wronged. At any rate he got the Royalist guns away after the defeat at Cheriton, and later commanded *The Constant Reformation* in Prince Rupert's fleet, until he died at Lisbon.

Colonel Sir Nicholas Byron (b. 1600), was uncle of Sir John Byron. In 1638 he was captain of a company in the Low Countries and was a colonel, F., in the Scots War (1640). He distinguished himself at First Newbury, and later became Colonel-General in Shropshire and the adjacent counties.

Colonel Henry Wentworth (b. 1594), brother of the Earl of Cleveland, was a colonel, F., in the Scots War (1640). He fought at Cirencester (2 February) and commanded a tertia at the storming of Bristol (26 July 1643). Thereafter he disappears from view.

Sir John Heydon (d. 1653), the Lieutenant-General of the Ordnance, will be discussed when we come to the Train of Artillery. Suffice it to say here that he was an excellent organizer and a noted mathematician.

Sir John Byron (d. 1652) led the second line of Rupert's wing, consisting of his own regiment of horse. He had served in the Low Countries. He was a doughty fighter as he showed at Roundway Down (13 July 1643) and First Newbury. He hung on to Chester with the greatest tenacity at the end of the war. His record at Nantwich, Marston Moor and Montgomery Castle reveals, however, that he was an indifferent tactician.

Lord Digby (1612–1677), eldest son of the Earl of Bristol, led Wilmot's second line. He had been in action once before, at Powick Bridge, where he had been wounded. He was no soldier, though his gallantry in action is attested by wounds received at Lichfield and Aldbourne. He was to succeed Lord Falkland as Secretary of State, when the latter fell at First Newbury. It may be said without exaggeration that his counsels did as much to lose King Charles his crown as any other single factor.

The Royalist High Command had its weak points. The King, Belasyse and Digby lacked experience. Lindsey, Ruthven and Astley were rather too elderly by modern standards – though the last named was still perfectly competent. Others, notably Rupert and Gerard, were rather young, even by seventeenth century standards, for high command. But on the whole the Royalist army had competent commanders, capable, given time, of turning a mass of raw levies into a professional marching army. But they had all too little time for training when they set out on their autumn campaign.

Officers General of the Field

Captain-General	King Charles
Lord Lieutenant-General	The Earl of Lindsey, then Lord Forth, w.e.f. 23 October 1642.
Sergeant-Major-General, F.	Sir Jacob Astley
Provost-Marshal-General	Captain William Smith
Treasurer at Wars	Sir William Uvedale, then John Ashburnham
Paymaster-General	Mathew Brodley, Esq.
Muster-Master-General	Sir William Brouncker?
Advocate of the Army	
Secretary at War	(Sir) Edward Walker
Auditor of the Army	
Commisary	Leonard Pinkney

PARLIAMENTARIAN

Robert Devereux, third Earl of Essex (1591–1646), was handicapped throughout the time of his command by a dearth of competent general officers.

Although an officer of some experience – he had been a colonel of foot in the Dutch service – the Earl was no military genius. As a strategist he must be considered distinctly suspect. What other general fought three of his major battles with the enemy between his army and his base? Though his relief of Gloucester in the summer of 1643 was an enterprising piece of work, he was generally lethargic. His successes at Gloucester and

First Newbury were balanced by the amazing excursion into Cornwall the following year, when his army was hemmed in and, with the exception of the Horse, compelled to surrender.

Essex showed himself an uncooperative general and was never prepared to work with his more active colleague, Sir William Waller, but he did lend him Balfour and his cavalry for Cheriton. As to tactics, the Earl knew how to draw up his army in a plain order that he and they could comprehend. Lastly, as an administrator he was decidedly indifferent.

The Earls of Bedford (1613–1700) and of Peterborough (d. 1642), who were generals respectively of the Horse and the Ordnance, were grandees who lacked any military experience prior to 1642. Bedford is praised for his courage at Edgehill, but he was soon to quit the Parliament service.

The Lt. General of the Horse, Sir William Balfour (d. 1660), the Scot who, after being in the Dutch service, had been Governor of the Tower of London when Strafford was imprisoned there, was to prove himself an excellent officer. He distinguished himself at Edgehill and in Cornwall (1644).

The list of Essex's army shows Philip Skippon (d. 1660) – 'stout Skippon' of Macauley's poem on Naseby – as Sergeant-Major-General and President of the Council of War. Well for Essex had he indeed been with him, but at this time he was commanding the London Trained Bands. He had risen from humble origins: starting his military life as a pikeman under Sir Horace Vere in the Dutch service, he had been at both sieges of Breda (1625 and 1637). He was to distinguish himself at both battles of Newbury, to become Sergeant-Major-General of the Foot in the New Model Army, and to survive a terrible wound in the belly at Naseby. It seems that Colonel Thomas Ballard exercised this office for a time, for on 21 September Nehemiah Wharton complains 'we can get no carriage for officers, so that my trunk is more slighted than any other, which is occasioned, as I conceive, partly by the false informations of Lieut.-Col. Briddeman (Billingsley) and our late Serjeant Major General Ballard, prophane wretches; . . . '

Sir James Ramsey, who commanded the left wing of horse, was another Scots soldier of fortune. His conduct at Edgehill, as we shall see, was to be the subject of an enquiry, which it would be wrong to pre-judge.

The three infantry brigade commanders, Sir John Meldrum (d. 1645), Charles Essex and Thomas Ballard, were all, it seems, competent professional soldiers. Charles Essex fell at Edgehill and the other two soon left Essex's army. Ballard soon fell out with his employers, and Meldrum, despite a respectable fighting record, was to suffer a resounding defeat at the hands of Prince Rupert at Newark (19 March 1644). He was mortally wounded at the siege of Scarborough Castle (1645).

The lieutenant-general of the Ordnance, Philibert Emanuel Du-Bois, was, as will appear, useless.

There was as yet no Scoutmaster-General, which accounts for the fact that Essex only discovered his opponents' movements by accident. On 14 January 1643 Sir Samuel Luke was commissioned as Scoutmaster-General and his interesting papers are a valuable source for the history of the war.[7]

The Staff of the Parliamentarian army were:

Officers General of the Field

Captain-General	The Earl of Essex
Sergeant-Major-General and President of the Council of War	Philip Skippon. Absent.
Provost-Marshal-General	Captain James Seigneur
Carriage-Master-General	Captain Thomas Richardson

Officers of the Lord General's Train

Treasurer at Wars	Sir Gilbert Gerrard, Kt.
Muster-Master General	Lionel Copley, Esq.
Advocate of the Army	Doctor Isaac Dorislaus
Secretary of the Army	Henry Parker, Esq.
Auditor of the Army	Robert Chambers

1 British Museum. Thomason Tracts, E.669.f.6.64. For twenty years George Thomason, Bookseller of the Rose and Crown in St. Paul's Church Yard, collected the ephemeral literature pouring daily from the press.
2 Roy, pp. 167 & 179.
3 Lord Saye.
4 Though his father was German, his mother was half Scots and half Danish.
5 Royalist Ordnance Papers.
6 The first mine was sprung in England at Lichfield in April 1643. Mine and countermine had, however, been employed at the siege of St. Andrews Castle in 1546. Mining was, of course, a feature of mediaeval siege warfare, but without gunpowder.
7 See The Letter Books 1644–45 of Sir Samuel Luke, ed. H. G. Tibbutt, F.S.A.

PART TWO

The Campaign

10

Approach March

There cannot be too often mention of the wonderful providence of God, that, from that low despised condition the King was in at Nottingham after the setting up his standard, he should be able to get men, money, or arms, and yet within twenty days after his coming to Shrewsbury he resolved to march in despite of the enemy even towards London . . .

Clarendon[1]

THE TACTICS OF 1642 can be reconstructed from the works of men like Hexham, Ward, Barriffe, Norton and Venn, none of whom ever reached a higher rank than major. Strategy, one might almost say, had not yet been invented. With Jomini and Clausewitz to guide them the generals of our day do not always manage their affairs with exemplary skill. How much more difficult was it for the generals of the Civil Wars, ignorant of the Principles of War by which modern generals may, or may not, conduct their operations, and unable to justify their 'hunches' by quoting learned authorities to the rest of the Council of War.

The officers who formed the headquarters of the two armies may have had experience, but they had no common body of staff training, and at best only a rule of thumb grounding in logistics – the art of moving and supplying an army in the field.

Maps were woefully defective – John Speed's survey of 1610, though it covers the whole country, has little military value – and it is doubtful whether any but the most senior officers had them. The value of local guides must have been most marked. The synchronization of movements was difficult when few officers had watches. A modern officer would do better to go into action unarmed than without his field-glasses, but in 1642 very few 'perspective' glasses, or telescopes, were to be had. One may criticise the generals of either side, but one should bear in mind the factors that handicapped them.

When, on 12 October 1642, King Charles I set out from Shrewsbury to march on London, the war was already some three months old. Although the Standard had not been raised until 22 August, first blood had probably been shed at Hull in July.

The Royalist forces now amounted to 13 regiments of foot, ten[2] regiments of horse, three of dragoons, and the Train of Artillery of 20 guns. More infantry regiments were on the march and others raising.

It is not likely that Charles knew precisely what Essex had at Worcester, but at least he knew that the Earl was not directly in his path to London.

Essex, according to *Speciall Passages*,[3] had 18 regiments of foot, excluding two that were to be left to guard Worcester and Hereford. He had also 61 troops of horse and 46 pieces of ordnance. This is not quite accurate for it takes no account of the two regiments of dragoons, and it has not got the dispositions of the infantry quite right. Even so the estimate of the strength of the cavalry and the artillery is worth attention, for it fits in well with what is known from other contemporary sources.

The news of the King's advance does not seem to have reached Essex very quickly. This is odd for there was as yet but little restriction on the movements of travellers. On 12 September Wharton at Northampton received a letter from London of 8 September, brought by Thomas Weedon, the 'post that serveth our army at the Saracen's Head, in Carter Lane'. Yet the Captain-General was so ill-served by his intelligence that it was not until 18 October that he could make the decision to move, and rendezvous the main body of his army next day.[4] His army was not at full strength for he had already garrisoned a number of towns, and he meant also to hold Worcester.

	Regiment
Hereford	Earl of Stamford
Worcester	{ Lord St. John Sir John Merrick
Coventry	Lord Rochford
Northampton?	Colonel William Bamfield
Banbury	Earl of Peterborough

These were very considerable detachments, and besides the foot there were troops of horse in at least some of these places. There was one at Banbury, and Stamford, when he went to Hereford, took three troops of horse and two guns with him.[5] In addition Warwick Castle was held by a garrison of horse and foot under Captain John Bridges[6] of Lord Brooke's Regiment.

Could Essex afford these detachments? His base was London and it was, of course, reasonable that he should guard his L. of C. by detachments at Banbury and Warwick castles. It is certain that had he kept these regiments with him he would have outnumbered the King at Edgehill. This would have given him some chance of ending the war at a blow. But in the long term, places like Warwick Castle, and Gloucester, to which Stamford's Regiment shortly removed itself, were of great value to the Parliamentarians. The men at Banbury on the other hand proved an easy prey to their enemies. Mediocre generals love to lock up men in fortresses, hoping to be strong everywhere and, which is impossible in war, to ensure against every eventuality. The surest way to victory is to begin by destroying the enemy's main forces in the field. That done, even the strongest fortresses are bound to fall in the long run.

Since Essex, largely for political reasons, felt it best to let the King take the initiative in 'this war without an enemy', he may be criticised for not posting his army to bar the road to London. Had he deployed his main body in the vicinity of Warwick he might have been in a more favourable strategic position. Commentators have failed to discern any reasonable motive for his placing himself at Worcester. It may be, however, that his idea was to prevent a Royalist advance on Bristol, which was then the second city and seaport in the Kingdom and might have made them a valuable base. Moreover at Worcester Essex was between Charles and his numerous supporters in Monmouthshire, Herefordshire and South Wales.

There had been much debate in the Royalist camp as to the direction their march should take. Some of the Council were for marching against Essex at Worcester, knowing the population thereabouts to be well-affected to the King, and willing to supply him with provisions and recruits. These urged that no time should be lost 'in coming to a battle, because the longer it was deferred the stronger the earl would grow by the supplies which were every day sent to him from London; . . . ' However it was decided eventually 'to march directly towards London, it being morally sure that the earl of Essex would put himself in their way'. In the country round Worcester the Royalist cavalry, in which the King had much confidence, would have become 'entangled in the enclosures' . . . 'whereas there were many great *campanias* near the other way, much fitter for an engagement'.[7]

The Royalist army advanced slowly through the Midlands, quartering at night in a wide circle of villages for it had few tents. The October nights were cold and it was essential to get the men under cover, though this dispersal meant that much time was consumed each morning getting the soldiers to the rendezvous.

It may be some consolation to modern Englishmen to observe that our weather even in those days left something to be desired. Denzil Holles' Regiment was unable to exercise on 18 August 'by reason of foule weather'. On 23 September Wharton notes 'such foul weather that before I had marched one mile I was wet to the skin'. The next day near Worcester he speaks of 'the rain continuing the whole day, and the way so base that we went up to the ancles in thick clay; . . . ' On the march

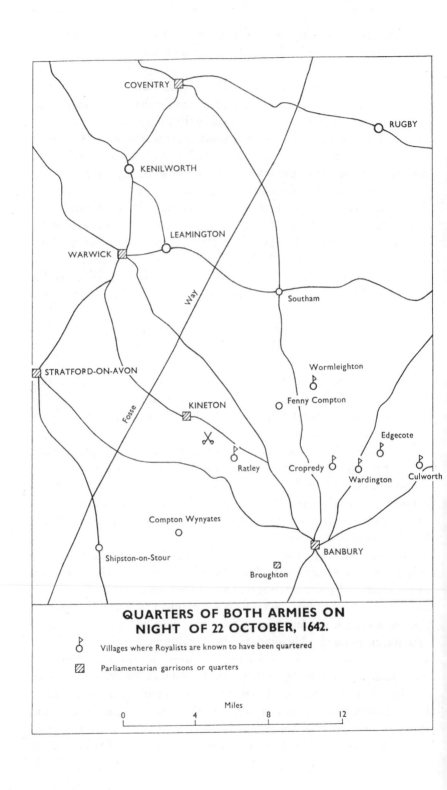

COVENTRY

RUGBY

KENILWORTH

LEAMINGTON

WARWICK

Way

Southam

STRATFORD-ON-AVON

Wormleighton

Fosse

KINETON

Fenny Compton

Edgecote

Ratley

Cropredy

Wardington

Culworth

Compton Wynyates

Shipston-on-Stour

BANBURY

Broughton

QUARTERS OF BOTH ARMIES ON
NIGHT OF 22 OCTOBER, 1642.

Villages where Royalists are known to have been quartered

Parliamentarian garrisons or quarters

Miles

0   4   8   12

to Hereford (30 September) a soldier actually died 'by reason of the raine and snow, and extremity of cold'.

Progress was bound to be slow on the unmetalled roads, and the Royalist pikemen must have been glad they had not got corslets. If the King's army did not thunder forward at the pace of the *Blitzkrieg* this was partly because it would have been dangerous to get ahead of the Train of Artillery, which might then have fallen a prey to the Roundheads of Coventry or Warwick Castle.

The Artillery, all its vehicles harnessed tandem, must have occupied plenty of road space. The carts and guns marched in three Divisions in this order:

1st Division.	The Captain and his Pioneers
	Materials. (Shovels, spades, hatchets, pickaxes &c).
	Horse harness.
	Hurdles.
	The Ordnance.
	Budge barrels, cartouches, &c.
	Gynns, and miches &c.
	The Lord General's waggon.
	The Lt.-General's waggon.
	Principal officers' waggons.
	Iron shot, & caseshot.
	Match.
	Powder.
	Materials. (Smith's tools &c, tents).
2nd Division.	For the Foot and Horse.
	Powder.
	Match.
	Musket, carbine and pistol shot.
3rd Division	The Standing Magazine.[8]

Nobody can imagine that this procession was fast moving, and, of course, the army, accompanied as it was by the Court, had much other baggage besides. Generals and cavalry officers had spare horses, even the infantry officers had an astonishing number of horses, either for riding or for carrying their 'sumpter'. No doubt there were victuallers as well, and one can scarcely picture a seventeenth-century army without a host of other camp followers. If a whore had the temerity to follow the psalm-singing Roundheads to Coventry, it is scarcely to be supposed that the Royalists did not have the company of other ladies than the wives of officers and soldiers.

It took the Royalists 10 days to move from Shrewsbury to the neighbourhood of Banbury, a distance of less than 100 miles. And even so some of the baggage straggled and was snapped up by Bridges' men from Warwick Castle.[6] By the standards of the Civil War 10 miles a day was fair marching. The roads were little better than broad, rutted, tracks of mud, and the cart-horses, harnessed tandem to their heavy clumsy vehicles, could scarcely keep up with the foot soldiers.

The Earl of Essex's army was probably even less mobile than the King's. According to Clarendon 'his train was so very great that he could move but in slow marches'.[9]

As the war progressed both sides raised a great deal of cavalry. In 1642 neither side had a very high proportion of mounted troops. The Royalists foot out-numbered their horse by 4 to 1, and although the Parliament had raised many troops, only some 60 seems to have been with Essex at Worcester.

The horsemen on either side were being trained as heavy rather than light cavalry. The armies of the Civil Wars had nothing like the hussars or chasseurs of later days. The commanders of these newly-raised troops were concerned with training them to take their place in the line of battle, to keep their horses straight in the ranks, and to advance to the charge without losing their order. It follows that what we nowadays call 'forward recce' suffered. 'So that the two armies,' as Clarendon puts it, 'though they were but twenty miles asunder when they first set forth, and both marched the same way, they gave not the least disquiet in ten day's march to each other; and in truth, as it appeared afterwards, neither army knew where the other was'.[9] Shrewsbury is in fact 49 miles from Worcester, not 20, and it is scarcely accurate to describe the armies as marching the same way for the King had moved down in a south-easterly direction, threading his way, somewhat hazardously perhaps, between Parliamentarian garrisons – Kenilworth lies half way from Coventry to Warwick, 6 miles from the one and only 5 miles from the other. Essex's march was almost due east. Starting from Worcester only on the 19th, he made the 35 miles to Kineton in 4 days, for his men arrived between about 9 or 10 at night on the 22nd, an average of $8\frac{3}{4}$ miles a day. Even at this slow rate much of the artillery, with a strong escort, was left a day's march behind.

Marching from Southam to Edgecote on the 22nd, the Royalists held a rendezvous of their army. We do not know precisely where, but one might hazard a guess that it was not far from Fenny Compton. Lord Digby was sent with a party of 400 horse 'to find out' the enemy and brought word there was no news of him. The implication of the entry in 'Prince Rupert's Diary' is that Digby failed in his duty, a conclusion all too easy to accept for he was no soldier. But on this occasion he must be exonerated for it seems that it was already night when the Parliamentarians marched into Kineton.

On arrival at Edgecote a Council of War was held, 'and having no intelligence that the earl of Essex was within any distance, it was resolved the King and the army should rest in those quarters the next day, only that sir Nicholas Byron should march with his brigade and attempt the taking in of Banbury'.[9] The King signed a warrant for 'A Proporcon of Ordennce, Carriages, Powder, Shott, Match, &c to attend a Bye Trayne of 4 Peeces of Ordennce, & 4000 ffoote.' Two brass demi-cannons and 2 brass culverins, with 50 'Round shott of yron' per gun, were allotted for the service. In addition 24 'Cases of tynn wth Muskett shott, or Cartouches' were to be sent. No less than 57 waggons and carts supported this 'Bye Trayne'. The four guns were the biggest the Royalists had.[10] *En passant* it may be remarked that Sir Nicholas Byron's brigade can scarcely have numbered so many as 4,000 foot, but it may have been augmented.

These matters settled, the Royalists marched off to their quarters, which, as on 12 October, were widely scattered. The King had five more regiments than he had had on the 12th and so the army must have taken up a good deal of room. Charles himself was at Sir William Chancie's house at Edgecote, Rupert was five miles away staying at Lord Spencer's house at Wormleighton. The Earl of Lindsey was at Culworth, and the army generally was spread out between Cropredy and Edgecote. The Prince of Wales's Regiment of Horse was in some villages 'under Wormington Hills',[11] and the Train of Artillery was probably at Wardington.[12]

The Prince rode into Wormleighton, his quartermasters arriving there just as those of the Earl of Essex put in an appearance. In this sudden encounter the Royalists seem to have been the more alert, for they took the Roundheads prisoner, 'by which meanes we had intelligence where ye Enemy was'.[13]

The Prince very properly followed up this success by sending a patrol of 24 troopers under Lieutenant Clement Martin, of his own regiment, to Kineton to investigate. Martin returned to report that the Parliamentarians were indeed there. Characteristically Rupert was for falling on them without delay, but, as the Diary put it, 'others thought fit to send first to ye K'. Certainly the Captain-General was entitled to be kept informed and consulted.

It is possible that a sudden onslaught would have thrown Essex's men into confusion, but it would have been a raid by cavalry alone, for there could hardly have been time to reassemble the foot and the train. It is likely, too, that the late autumn day was drawing to a close.

According to Clarendon it was 'about 12 of the clock' that Rupert sent the King word that Essex had his headquarters at Kineton.[14] The Royalist Official Account's version is that intelligence came in on the evening of the 22nd that 'the Rebels had a Resolution' to relieve Banbury, 'but it was not so certain, as to make any Change of the former Orders; . . . '

Not until 3 a.m. did certain information come that the enemy were marching 'with all Expedition' to Banbury, whereupon the King gave orders to march to Edgehill. Presumably Charles was getting intelligence from various sources. It seems that Rupert's message was accompanied by the suggestion that the army should rendezvous at Edgehill as soon as possible, for very early in the morning the King penned him this brief message:

> Nepheu,
>   I have given order as you have desyred; so I dout not but all the foot and canon will bee at Eggehill betymes this morning, where you will also find
>   Your loving oncle &
>   Faithful frend, Charles R.[15]
> 4 o'clock this Sunday morning.

Did some trooper from the quartermasters' party taken at Worm-leighton escape to give the alarm? Did no sentry challenge Lieutenant Martin's patrol? According to Lord Wharton's speech, 'all that night there was news came that the King was going to Banbury'. Although Essex had a spy, one Blake, in the Royalist camp, and may have had information of the King's original orders for the 23rd, he evidently knew nothing of the change of plan. It may be that the Earl received no intelligence of any value until his army had already dispersed to its quarters. Still one would have expected him to have given orders for a rendezvous at Kineton early next day. The Parliamentarian staff work was certainly defective. Captain John Fiennes' troop was at Evesham, some 20 miles from Kineton, Captain Kightley's was 5 miles away, and Cromwell's was another which was in some outlying village and seems to have had no orders as to what to do next day. The absence, already mentioned, of many of the guns, is further evidence of indifferent staff work.

It is likely that Essex held a Council of War in Kineton that night. With little information to act upon he decided, not unreasonably, to march next day to the relief of Banbury. It may be imagined that swift messengers were sent to warn Colonel John Hampden and Lord Rochford to march on Kineton without delay on the 23rd. Whether Essex made any attempt to get in touch with the garrison of Banbury Castle cannot be said. It seems a reasonable precaution.

Captain Bridges at Warwick castle was not unaware of what was going forward, for there is evidence that his men took 11 carts,[6] which had evidently failed to keep up with the main body of the Royalists army.

Both armies were short of provisions, and both, no doubt, had orders to parade at an early hour. The Royalists may have had a few hours more sleep than their enemies, and *qui dort dine.*

Drums beating in the dark of a frosty dawn, drowsy, breakfastless soldiers emerging from barn and cottage, buckling on their equipment, and stamping about to keep warm. As the trumpets sounded 'Butta Sella' many a soldier of either army must have wondered what had induced him to follow his squire from some North Wales valley, or to listen to eloquent Stephen Marshall fulminating from the pulpit of St. Margaret's Westminster. 'Curse ye Meroz', had been his text. Soldiers have changed very much in 300 years if, thinking back, a Londoner or two did not mutter: 'And curse you too Master Marshall.'

1 Clarendon, Vol. II, p. 346.
2 Counting the Lifeguard, for although it only had two troops, it was some 300 strong, and certainly out-numbered several of the regiments.
3 Number 11. (BM. E. 124/4.)
4 *Ibid.* This says that Essex hoped to rendezvous near Ancester (Alcester), but as that place is 17 miles from Worcester that seems rather optimistic.
5 Nehemiah Wharton, Archaeologia, Vol. XXXV, p. 331.
6 CSPD. 1645–1647, p. 552.
7 Clarendon, Vol. II, p. 349.
8 Roy, Ordnance Papers, p. 154.
9 Clarendon, Vol. II, p. 356.
10 Roy, Ordnance Papers, p. 153.
11 Bulstrode.
12 It was there on 25 October, when the army seems to have returned to quarters occupied before the battle. Roy, Ordnance Papers, p. 155.
13 'Prince Rupert's Diary'.
14 Clarendon, Vol. II, p. 357.
15 Warburton, Vol. II, p. 12.

Near Edgecote on 22nd the King saw a gentleman hunting with a very good pack of hounds, and, fetching a heavy sigh, asked who the gentleman was that hunted so merrily that morning when he was going to fight for his crown and dignity. Told that it was one Richard Shuckburgh of Shuckburgh, Charles graciously ordered him to be called to him, and received him very graciously. Thereupon Shuckburgh went home immediately, armed all his tenants and attended the King in the field next day in the battle.
(Walford, p. 10, quoting Thomas's Edition of Dugdale's Warwickshire. Shuckburgh was knighted at Edgecote on the 22nd. After the capture of Banbury Castle, he is said to have gone home and fortified himself on the top of Shuckburgh Hill, where he was attacked and defended himself till he fell, with most of his tenants about him. He was taken prisoner and after a long time in Kenilworth Castle was forced to purchase his liberty at a dear rate.)

11

The Royalist Order of Battle

'Their forces came down the Hill; and drew likewise into Battel in the
Bottom; a great broad Company.'

Letter of six Parliamentarian commanders

IT WAS STILL dark when Prince Rupert's troops assembled, in response to
the 'points of war'[1] sounded upon the trumpet, for the Cavaliers made
little secret of their doings. By break of day, according to the 'Diary', the
Prince was at the rendezvous upon Edgehill. The rest of the horse were
there between 10 and 11 o'clock,[2] though according to Bulstrode, they
had orders to be there by 8 a.m. The Van of the Foot (Gerard's brigade,
and perhaps Belasyse's as well) 'came within an hour after, but the Rear
(which happened at that time to be the Lord-Lieutenant General's
Regiment) with the Artillery, came not within 2 hours after'.[2]

This delay gave the Royalist generals plenty of time to observe the
dispositions of the enemy, and to quarrel about their own. Looking down
upon Kineton they could see 'the Rebels Army drawing out, and setting
themselves in Battalia; . . . '[2] The King himself 'with his prospective glass,
took view of Essex's army in the vale, about a mile distant'.[3] The main
groupings of the enemy must have been sufficiently clear to them. They
could make out dragoons and musketeers taking up positions in the
hedges and briars on Essex's flank. They could see plainly the very
considerable body of cavalry (24 troops under Ramsey) drawing up on a
slight eminence on the Parliamentarian left. Then came a brigade of foot,
of four regiments, drawn up in line eight deep like a wall. Whether they
could make out a second brigade in support is doubtful. Traversing the
hostile front yet another brigade could be discerned with three regiments
in the front line. Then there was a regiment of horse. There were other
troops, too, in second line, but the details were probably difficult to
discern. One thing was very clear. The Parliamentarians had far more
horse on their left wing than their right. This must have influenced
Rupert in the distribution of his cavalry. The Prince had probably made
a sketch of the Royalist Battle – the fair copy of which we have in
de Gomme's plan. He did the same thing at Marston Moor.

Beyond question the Prince was excessively touchy about any interference, real or imagined, with his powers as General of the Horse. On one occasion he had expostulated with Lord Falkland for bringing him orders from the King himself. Falkland had very properly pointed out that 'it was his office to signify what the King bad him; which he should always do; and that he in neglecting it neglected the King; . . .'[4] Lindsey was no less jealous of his prerogative as Lord General, and with some justice was displeased when the King took Rupert's advice as to 'the figure of the battle they resolved to fight in with the enemy' . . . Lindsey preferred 'the order he had learned under Prince Morrice and Prince Harry, with whom he had served at the same time when the earl of Essex and he had both regiments'.[5] Ironically enough Lindsey was in the right. The Dutch order, adopted, was much plainer than 'the Swedish Brigade'[6] advocated by Rupert and Ruthven. One would have supposed that Astley to whom, as Sergeant-Major-General, fell the command of the foot, would have supported Lindsey, for he too had been in the Dutch army. But Astley never said much, was a friend of the Queen of Bohemia, Rupert's mother, and had been the Prince's tutor. Ruthven's part in this affair was not unimportant though his position in the army was as yet vague. He was a far more experienced general than Lindsey, but he had only arrived at Shrewsbury a few days before the army advanced. He had been made field-marshal, but, according to Clarendon, 'kept wholly with the horse to assist Prince Rupert'.[6] Not unnaturally he preferred the tactics he had learned under Gustavus Adolphus, whose name was still one to conjure with though he had been in his grave these ten years. The boy Duke of York, one day to be King James II and no mean soldier whatever one may think of him as a king, witnessed the whole embarrassing scene as the Dutch and Swedish schools fought the first skirmish of Edgehill Fight. Long after he wrote:

'When all his Majesty's troops were come up to him, he march'd down the hill, and order'd Ruthven (who was then but Feild Marshall . . .) an experienced officer who had serv'd the King of Sweden in the quality of Major General, to draw up his Army in battell. But the Earle of Lindsey who was Generall, was so much displeas'd at this preference, that he said, Since his Majesty thought him not fitt to perform the officer of Commander in Chief, he would serve him as a Collonell, and immediately went and put himself at the head of his Regim' of foot, which he desir'd might be placed opposite to that of the Earle of Essex, hoping thereby that he might ingage him personally. The foot was drawn up that day much differing from the manner now in use, but according to the Swedish Brigade as they then called it; . . . '

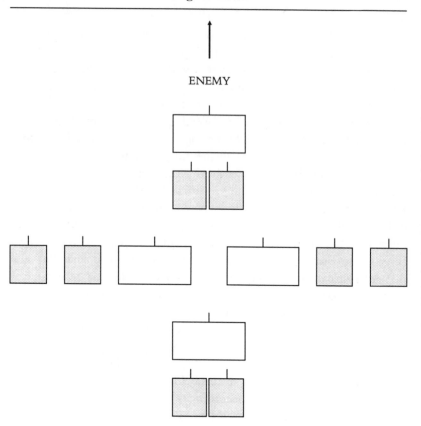

ENEMY

THE SWEDISH BRIGADE

LEGEND

Pikemen

Musketeers

Each of these brigades would number at least 2,000 men, and each body would be drawn up in six ranks, excluding officers, sergeants and drummers. In brigades, with more or less than four regiments, some of the bodies must have been formed by drawing out companies from the stronger regiments and amalgamating them. With each brigade there was a pair of light guns, but, unfortunately, de Gomme does not show us where they were planted, nor do we know whether they were manhandled forward when the army advanced.

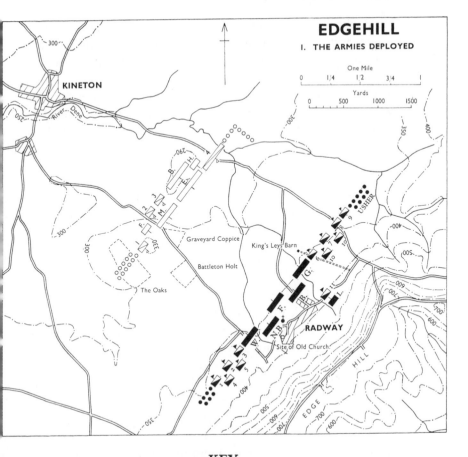

EDGEHILL

I. THE ARMIES DEPLOYED

KINETON

Graveyard Coppice

King's Leys Barn

Battleton Holt

The Oaks

RADWAY

Site of Old Church

EDGE HILL

One Mile
0   1/4   1/2   3/4   1

Yards
0   500   1000   1500

KEY

ROYALISTS

HORSE   FOOT   DRAGOONS   ARTILLERY

W. – Henry Wentworth
N.B. – Sir Nicholas Byron
F. – Richard Feilding
B. – John Belasyse
G. – Charles Gerard
L. –William Legge's Firelocks

1. Lord Wilmot's Regt.
2. Lord Grandison's Regt.
3. Earl of Carnarvon's Regt.
4. Lord Digby's Regt.
5. Sir Thomas Aston's Regt.
6. Prince Maurice's Regt.

7. Prince Rupert's Regt.
8. Prince of Wales' Regt.
9. King's Lifeguard
10. Sir John Byron's Regt.
11. Gentlemen Pensioners

PARLIAMENTARIANS

HORSE   FOOT   DRAGOONS OR MUSKETEERS   ARTILLERY

M. – Sir John Meldrum's Bde.
E. – Charles Essex's Bde.
B. – Thomas Ballard's Bde.

F. – Sir William Fairfax's Regt.
H. – Denzil Holles' Regt.
1. Lord Fielding's Regt.

2. Sir Philip Stapleton's Regt.
3. Sir William Balfour's Regt.
4. Sir James Ramsey's Wing

Modern copses shown: Modern Church shown:

No doubt this was an admirable formation for well-drilled veterans, designed, as it seems to be, for forming square, or diamond, to oppose hostile cavalry. For virtually raw levies one would suppose that the plainer order of the Dutch service would have been less confusing.

In 1642 Edgehill was a steep down virtually devoid of the trees which now mantle its northern slope. It was a formidable position, and it soon became obvious that Essex had not the least intention of storming it. The King and his generals, therefore, resolved to go down the hill and attack him.

> 'Whereupon great Preparations were made, and Precautions taken, for descending the Hill, which was very steep and long, and had been impracticable, if the Enemy had drawn nearer to the Bottom of it; but we saw by the Ranging their Army, that they intended to stay there for us, having a good Market Town by them, . . . '[7]

First Lt. Colonel Henry Washington, with Usher's Dragoons, descended the hill and took possession of some enclosures and briars on the Royalist right. Next a 'Forlorn Hope' of 600 horse went down as an advanced guard to the army.[7] These were followed by Dyve's Regiment of Charles Gerard's brigade. The 'Carriage Horses of the Cannon were put behind the Carriages, excepting a Horse or two before, and the Foot were ordered to descend as well as they could.'[7] By the time all this was done it was past 2 o'clock in the afternoon.[2]

Essex made no move while the Royalists drew up within cannon range of their front. Perhaps no more than half a mile now separated the armies.

> 'It was as fair a day as that season of the year could yield, the sun clear, no wind or cloud appearing.'[8]

★   ★   ★

FRONT LINE	SECOND LINE	THIRD LINE
Regiment/Colonel.	Regiment/Colonel.	

DRAGOONS

James Usher.

HORSE

Lifeguard. H. }		
(Lord Bernard Stuart)		
(Sir William Killigrew) }		
Prince Charles }		
(Sir Thomas Byron) }	Sir John Byron	
Prince Rupert		
Prince Maurice.		

FOOT

Charles Gerard		The Gentlemen Pensioners
Sir Lewis Dyve		(Sir William Howard)
Sir Ralph Dutton		'Colonel Leg's firelox'.
	Thomas Blagge	
	John Belasyse	
	Sir William Pennyman	
(Richard Feilding)		
Sir Thomas Lunsford		
Richard Bolle		
Sir Edward Fitton		
Sir Edward Stradling		
	Lifeguard F.	
	(Lord Willoughby d'Eresby)	
	Lord General	
	(Earl of Lindsey, K.G.)	
	Sir John Beaumont.	
Sir Gilbert Gerard		
Sir Thomas Salusbury		
Lord Molineux		

HORSE

Earl of Carnarvon		
	Lord Digby	
Lord Grandison		
	Sir Thomas Aston	
Lord Wilmot		

DRAGOONS

Sir Edward Duncombe	
Edward Grey	

THE ROYALIST HORSE

De Gomme's plan shows 2,500 Royalist horse divided into two precisely equal wings, each organized into nine squadrons. In each case the first line consists of seven equal squadrons and the second of two rather larger ones. The Gentlemen Pensioners are shown in reserve. From the number of standards shown by de Gomme one would suppose that the Royalists had 42 troops. Had every troop been up to strength the total should have been 2,940.

De Gomme's plan is a useful guide, but it may be misleading in three respects. In the first place 2,500 seems rather a conservative figure for the total strength of the Royalist horse. In the second it appears that they had at least 48 troops of horse, varying in strength from exceptionally small ones like Major Will. Legge's to some very big ones, including the Lifeguard, Newcastle's, Rupert's, Wilmot's and Northampton's. Thirdly, and more important, Rupert's wing was considerably stronger than Wilmot's.

At full strength 48 troops should have numbered, not 2,500, but 3,360. It is evident that the various Royalist units varied widely according to the wealth, influence, and powers of leadership of their commanders. This must have made it rather difficult for Rupert to organize his command.

The relative strength of the two wings, it is suggested, may be summarized:

RIGHT	Prince Rupert		
Lifeguard		300	
Prince of Wales		500	First Line
Prince Rupert		465	
Prince Maurice		180	
Sir John Byron		250	Second Line
		1,695	
LEFT	Lord Wilmot		
Lord Wilmot		355	
Lord Grandison		200	First Line
Earl of Carnarvon		200	
Lord Digby		150	Second Line
Sir Thomas Aston		150	
		1,055	
		2,750	
Gentlemen Pensioners		50	2,800

These calculations are, of course, approximate. In the absence of strength returns, or similar administrative documents, this must be so. To add to our difficulties at least one troop commander, Henry Hastings, later Lord Loughborough, cannot be assigned with confidence to any regiment.

Notes on the formation of the various regiments will be found in Part Three, Section Three. The table that follows summarizes their probable organization.

RIGHT WING

FIRST LINE

	Estimated Strength
LIFEGUARD. Two Troops	
Lord Bernard Stuart	300
Sir William Killigrew: Servants	
PRINCE OF WALES. Eight Troops.	
Prince of Wales: Colonel Sir Thomas Byron	
Duke of York: Lord d'Aubigny	
Earl of Newcastle: Colonel Charles Cavendish 120	
Earl of Lindsey:	500
Earl of Northampton: 100 gentlemen	
Earl of Westmoreland:	
Captain Davison: Servants of the whole Regiment.	
Earl of Crawford:	
PRINCE RUPERT. Seven Troops	
Lifeguard Sir Richard Crane. 100	
Lt. Colonel Dan. O'Neale 70	
Major Will. Legge 15	
Sir Lewis Dyve } 140	465
Sir Thomas Dallison	
Lord Dillon } 140	
Sir William Pennyman	
PRINCE MAURICE. Four Troops	
Prince Maurice's lifeguard	
Lt. Colonel Guy Molesworth	180
Captain Thomas Sheldon	
Sir Ralph Dutton	

SECOND LINE

	Estimated Strength
SIR JOHN BYRON. Six Troops	
Colonel Sir John Byron	
Lt. Colonel Frank Butler	
Major Gilbert Byron	250
Captain Sir Richard Byron	
Captain Allen Apsley	
Captain Edward(?) St. John	

LEFT WING

LORD WILMOT. Six Troops
Lord Wilmot: Capt.-Lieut. Robert Walsh	90	
Lt. Colonel Edward Feilding ⎱	85	
Major Paul Smyth ⎰		355
Captain John Harvey	70	
Captain Price	40	
Captain John Frescheville's under Lieutenant Jammot	70	

LORD GRANDISON. Four Troops
Lord Grandison: Capt.-Lieut. Edward Gerard
Major Sir Richard Willys   200
Lord John Stuart
Captain Francis Bertie

EARL OF CARNARVON. Four or five Troops
Earl of Carnarvon:
Lt. Colonel Sir Charles Lucas
Major (?) Richard Neville   200
Captain Alex. Standish
  . . .

LORD DIGBY. Three or four Troops
Lord Digby: Capt.-Lieut. Henry Harris
Thomas Weston   150
Richard Herbert(?)
John Lane

SIR THOMAS ASTON. Three Troops
Colonel Sir Thomas Aston
Lt. Colonel Sir James Bridgeman   150
Captain Flemming

REAR

GENTLEMEN PENSIONERS. One Troop
Lieutenant Sir William Howard. K.B.   50

HORSE[9]

General	Prince Rupert
Lieutenant-General	Vacant, but Wilmot was promoted lieutenant-general before 25 December 1642.
Commissary-General	Lord Wilmot
Quartermaster-General	. . .
Adjutant-General	Colonel David Scrymgeour
Provost-Marshal	. . .
Scout-Master-General	Sir William Neale?

THE ROYALIST FOOT

De Gomme shows the Royalist foot drawn up in five tertias or brigades. These five brigades included, according to de Gomme, 16 regiments. The army certainly included three others and there is evidence that at least one of these was actually present at the battle. Two pay warrants which have survived (16 and 24 November) show that the Royalist foot regiments varied greatly in strength. They differed also in armament and even in battle experience.

A regiment was supposed to have two musketeers to every pikeman. De Gomme's plan indicates, however, that the pikemen were equal in number to the musketeers. Moreover, as we have seen, there were three or four hundred men armed only with cudgels, pitchforks and such bucolic weapons. There is evidence that the regiments varied in the number of companies they had, as well as in the number of muskets they had contrived to obtain.

The table that follows attempts to show the relative strength of the five brigades. Their commanders seem to have been:

> Colonel Charles Gerard
> Colonel John Belasyse
> Colonel Richard Feilding
> Colonel Sir Nicholas Byron
> Colonel Henry Wentworth

The first three were regimental commanders; the last two named had no other command than their tertias.

Gerard's, Feilding's and Wentworth's brigades were in the first line: Belasyse's and Byron's in the second.

	Estimated strength on 16 November 1642
CHARLES GERARD	
Charles Gerard	600
Sir Lewis Dyve	212
Sir Ralph Dutton	637
	1,449
JOHN BELASYSE	
Thomas Blagge	700
John Belasyse	438
Sir William Pennyman	651
	1,789

RICHARD FEILDING

Richard Feilding	449
Sir Thomas Lunsford	330
Richard Bolle	534
Sir Edward Fitton	420
Sir Edward Stradling	723
	2,456

SIR NICHOLAS BYRON

Lifeguard	600
Lord General	866
Sir John Beaumont	300
	1,766

HENRY WENTWORTH

Sir Gilbert Gerard	509
Sir Thomas Salusbury	861
Lord Molineux	273
	1,643

In addition posted in rear of the Gentlemen Pensioners was the body de Gomme describes as 'Coll; Legs firelox', designed no doubt to guard the Train of Artillery.

It may be that recruits came in in good numbers in the weeks following Edgehill. On the other hand it may be that they did little more than replace casualties. It does not seem over bold to suggest that the average strength of brigades at Edgehill was 2,000 but that Feilding's was probably not much less than 2,500. If this is so de Gomme's figure (10,000) may be somewhat conservative. On the other hand he may omit the officers, in which case the total would not be less than 10 per cent. higher.

THE DRAGOONS

As we have seen the King had 800 dragoons as early as 12 September. When he was at Shrewsbury, Clarendon vaguely describes them as 'two or three regiments' numbering 'not above eight hundred or a thousand at the most'. Godfrey Davis asserts[10] that the Royalists had 1,200–1,500 dragoons at Edgehill, but as he quotes no source it seems unwise to credit them with more than 1,000. De Gomme does not help matters by omitting them from his plan altogether. It is however certain that there were three regiments, though in the absence of accurate information as to their strength, we can only suppose that the two regiments on the left wing outnumbered the single one on the right.

RIGHT
  Colonel James Usher
  Lt. Colonel Henry Washington
  Major . . . Hutchinson[11]

LEFT
  Sir Arthur Aston
  Colonel Edward Grey
  Lt. Colonel . . .
  Major Raphe Hebburne

  Colonel Sir Edmond Duncombe[12]
  Lt. Colonel . . .
  Major . . .

This last regiment was part of the Lifeguard.

According to Bulstrode (Lt.) Colonel George Lisle and Lt. Colonel (John) Ennis were on the left wing, but which regiments they were in does not appear.

THE TRAIN OF ARTILLERY[13]

Clarendon describes the Train of Artillery as 'a spunge that can never be filled or satisfied' and goes on to tell us that at the time when the King was at Shrewsbury it 'was destitute of all things which were necessary for motion, nor was there any hope that it could march till a good sum of money were assigned to it. Some carriage-horses and waggons which were prepared for the service of Ireland, and lay ready at Chester . . . were brought to Shrewsbury by his majesty's order for his own train . . .'[14] Fortunately the Royalists had, as Lieutenant-General of the Ordnance, a thoroughly competent officer, Sir John Heydon. Despite every disadvantage, especially lack of money, he organized a train of 20 guns, which was properly organized before the Royalists began their advance on London. This feat is certainly evidence of Heydon's administrative ability. Thanks to the zeal of one of his officers, Edward Sherburne, a number of the Royalist Ordnance Papers have survived and it is possible to tell precisely what cannon the King had at Edgehill.

	No.	Weight of shot in lbs.
Demi-cannons	2	27
Culverins	2	15
Demi-culverins	2	9
Fawcons	6	2½
Fawconetts	6	1½
Rabonetts	2	¾

These guns had been obtained from various sources. Some the Queen had sent from Holland in *The Providence*, which eluded the Parliamentarians and ran ashore near Bridlington (2 July) bringing 'about two hundred barrels of powder, and two or three thousand arms, with seven or eight field-pieces'.[15] Others belonged to noblemen such as Earl Rivers and Lord Strange, who were reported in mid-September to have five and 11 pieces of ordnance respectively. The two smallest pieces were probably Lord Paulet's two little brass drakes, mounted on carriages, which after being employed in the defence of Sherborne Castle, were shipped over in coal boats from Minehead to South Wales when the Cavaliers evacuated Somerset.[16]

At Edgehill, the infantry was drawn up in five brigades, and according to Joshua Moone, Colonel John Belasyse's secretary, 'before every body of foot were placed two pieces of cannon'.[17] Belasyse was one of the brigade commanders and so this statement cannot be ignored, though one would expect the guns to be in the intervals between the bodies of foot. Moone's statement accounts for 10 of the smaller pieces, the fawcons, fawconetts and rabonetts, of which there were 14 in all. One wonders where the other four were. There seem to be three possibilities. The first is that some of the infantry brigades had not two but three guns, and that therefore all the light pieces were well forward. The second is that four of the fawcons were in battery with the bigger guns, which seems extremely unlikely. The last is that four of the lightest guns were left with the force observing Banbury, if indeed such a force existed. The question must be left open.

A far more important problem is the siting of the six heavy pieces. Lt. Colonel A. H. Burne[18] placed them 'near the road for convenience and about Battleton Holt'. It is reasonable to suppose that heavy guns, drawn slowly along by great carthorses harnessed tandem, would not go into action very far from a road. The position of the firelocks on de Gomme's plan is a clue to the location of the battery, since their role would be to guard the train. They were stationed in rear of the right-hand infantry brigade – perhaps some 300 yards behind it. One would have expected the big guns to be behind the centre rather than the right-hand brigade. That they were not seems to argue some accident of terrain. The obvious solution is that the centre brigade had deployed in front of the village of Radway, and that had the guns been there they would, by reason of houses, enclosures and gardens, have had no proper field of fire. Working on that hypothesis one can understand a departure from a purely conventional layout. One thing is certain: the Royalist battery was on the lower slopes of Edgehill for a Royalist account describing the preliminary bombardment states that 'the King had so great an advantage of the hill that it turned to his disadvantage, for being so much upon the descent his cannon either shot over or if short it would not graze by reason of the ploughed lands . . . '[19]

1 Venn, p. 9.
2 R.O.A.
3 Warburton, Vol. II, p. 12, quoting *Sanderson's History of Charles I.*
4 Clarendon, Vol. II, pp. 350, 351.
5 *Ibid.* Vol. V, p. 351.
6 *Ibid.* Vol. II, p. 348.
7 Bulstrode.
8 Clarendon, Vol. II, p. 352.
9 See Part Three, Section One, Document 21, which gives some idea of the staff of the Royalist horse. Rupert's staff, it will be observed, was not very different from Bedford's.
10 Davies, Edgehill, p. 32.
11 Shot at Cirencester, 2 Feb. 1643.
12 'Deserter'. He gives the strength of this unit as 500 which is probably too high.
13 *General.* See:
    Lt. Colonel P. Young, The Royalist Artillery at Edgehill, 23rd October, 1642, J.S.A.H.R., Vol. XXXV.
    Dr. Ian Roy, The Royalist Ordnance Papers, 1642–1646. Part I, Oxfordshire Record Society, 1964.
14 Clarendon, Vol. II, p. 337.
15 *Ibid*, Vol. II, p. 213.
16 Hopton, pp. 11, 13 & 18.
17 Moone. See Section Five.
18 Burne, Battlefields of England.
19 Anon. See Section Five, No. 14.

12

The Parliamentarian Order of Battle

> We 'presently marched forth into a great broad Field, under that Hill,
> called, The Vale of the Red Horse, and made a stand some half a Mile
> from the Foot of the Hill, and there drew into Battalia, . . . '
>
> Letter of six Parliamentarian commanders

ESSEX INTENDED, as we have seen, to march on 23 October to the relief
of his garrison in Banbury. He can no longer have doubted that the
Royalists lay between him and that place, and it was natural that he should
be concerned for the regiment he had posted there, for his most recent
information as to the King's intentions was that plans had been laid to
besiege Banbury. Certainly the Roundheads, if not already on the move,
must have been assembled in and around Kineton, when 'unexpectedly
an Alarme came about eight a clock in the morning that the Enemy was
advancing within two or three miles, which accordingly proved so; . . . '[1]
Adoniram Bifield, Chaplain to Cholmley's Regiment – 'the base blew
coats' of Wharton's letters – rode out and claims that 'it pleased God' to
make him 'the first Instrument of giving a certain discovery of it, by the
help of a prospective Glasse from the top of an Hill, . . . '[2] However that
may be, it cannot have been long before the Lord General too was aware
of the situation, for the Cavaliers on the summit of the hill were making
no secret of their position.

Clarendon praises Essex's performance at this juncture saying:

> ' . . . that the earl with great dexterity performed whatsoever could be
> expected from a wise general. He chose that ground which best liked him.
> There was between the hill and the town a fair *campania*, save that[2] near
> the town it was narrower, and on the right hand some hedges and
> inclosures; . . . '[3]

Essex could not see the details of the Royalist dispositions on the top
of the hill for it is so steep that only men on the very edge would be
visible. He had, not only from the political but from the tactical point of
view, the greatest reluctance to strike the first blow. If the Cavaliers

declined to attack him he could hope to be stronger next day by three regiments of foot, 11 troops of horse and not less than seven guns. It was for him to play a waiting game, and it suited his stolid nature to do so. Though the King was between him and London, he had Warwick Castle at his back in case of disaster. With the Royalists concentrating against his main army Banbury was no longer in any immediate danger. These must have been some of the considerations that ran through his mind as he marshalled his men in their defensive position, and gave his orders to his brigade commanders.

One of these, Sir James Ramsey, has left us a clear account of his dispositions:

'After I had Orders from his Excellency the Lord Generall of our Army, and others my Superiours, [Bedford and Balfour] for ordering and commanding the left Wing of the Cavallery, I did accordingly put them in Posture Defensive, and Offensive, interlining the Squadrons with a convenient number of Musqueteers.'

He placed 300 musketeers in a hedge

'which did Flanke the whole Front of the left Wing; Thereafter on the head of every Squadron exhorting them to magnanimity and resolution, showing them the worth of their Ancestors, desiring them to shew themselves worthy such Noble Progenitors, and putting before them the justness of the cause.'

The enemy, he told his troopers, were

'Papists, Atheists, and Irreligious persons for the most part; . . .'[4]

He had with him several Scots officers, Colonel John Middleton and Majors Baylie and Melvill, who attested on 5 November that Sir James had deployed his squadrons

'at best advantage for fight, and did place severall Rankes of Musqueteeres betwixt the Squadrons of Horse, and interlarded them so well for offending of the enemy, and for defending of themselves as could be desired, . . . '

They confirmed that he

'did also lay upon the left hand of the Horse in a hedge two or three hundred Musqueteers, for to Flanke the Front of our Horse, and give fire to the Enemies at their charging . . .'[4]

These musketeers were drawn out of Ballard's brigade which was in the second line, 400 being taken from Holles', and 200 from Ballard's own regiment. This interlarding of horse with musketeers was a common practice in the Swedish service where Ramsey had learned his trade.

Ramsey gives no further details of the way in which he drew up his wing, but as he had 24 troops it is reasonable to assume that he paired them to form 12 squadrons and that he drew them up in two lines, rather like this:

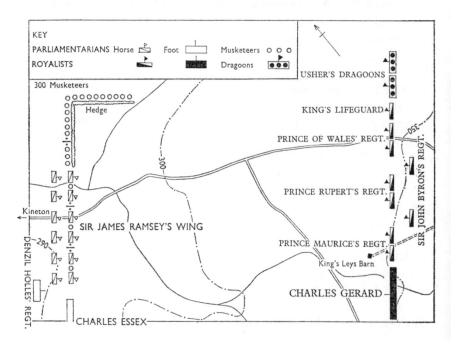

According to Bulstrode, Ramsey had three guns with him and it is not unlikely that one of these was in the hedge opposite the Prince of Wales' Regiment. Since 300 musketeers were in the hedges it would follow that the other 300 were in platoons of 60 between the squadrons of Ramsey's front line.

On Ramsey's right and somewhat to his rear were the four regiments of Charles Essex's brigade, deployed in a single line. The regiments probably fell in in eight ranks, which was the custom in the Dutch service whose tactics the Earl employed. Thus a regiment at full strength would occupy not less than 150 yards of front, and a brigade with its guns more than 600. It may be assumed that there were pairs of guns all along the front in the intervals between the regiments. Ballard's brigade was in rear of that of Charles Essex.[5]

On the right of the foot was Meldrum's brigade with three regiments in line, and one, that of Sir William Fairfax, in rear. This last unit was evidently 'refused' so as to protect Meldrum's right, which was rather 'in the air', for it had only the single cavalry regiment of Lord Feilding on that wing.

Where was the rest of Essex's cavalry? That is one of the mysteries of Edgehill, and all sorts of explanations, probable and improbable, have been advanced to explain Wilmot's failure to cross swords with them. It is not easy for two regiments, consisting of 12 troops, to vanish into thin air. We know that the Parliamentarians had Ballard's brigade of foot in second line supporting their left wing, Ramsey and Charles Essex. It is scarcely credible that Meldrum should have had only one regiment of foot to support him when the other wing had a whole brigade. We have the authority of James II for the assertion that part of Essex's cavalry 'was behind his foot', while Bulstrode says they put 'several Bodies of Foot with Retrenchments and Cannon before them', adding that 'all their Foot were lined with Horse behind them, with intervals betwixt each Body, for their Horse to enter, if need required'.[6]

If we place Stapleton and Balfour behind Meldrum much that followed in the battle falls into place. Having only three brigades of foot with him, Essex was compelled to support Meldrum with cavalry. We may assume that there were not less than two sizeable gaps on Meldrum's front, though, despite what Bulstrode says, there seems no reason why there should have been any in the part of the line occupied by Charles Essex[5].

On Meldrum's right was the single regiment of horse of Lord Feilding. This arrangement seems improbable, but there are still the two dragoon regiments to account for. If one of them was on the left there would scarcely have been any need to flank Ramsey's wing with Ballard's musketeers. It follows that Feilding's weakness was to some extent redressed by supporting his flank with some 700 dragoons 'in the bushes to make a shew,' as James II puts it.

With no plan, such as de Gomme's, to guide us, we cannot hope for positive certainty as to Essex's dispositions, but at least those here described do not violate any of the tactical ideas of his day.

The Parliamentarians had all the morning to marshal their army. According to Bulstrode, 'a little behind their left wing, was the Town of Keinton, which supplied them with provisions, and where their Baggage and Carriages were'.[6] But Ludlow for one had nothing to eat for 48 hours.[7]

Some of the cavalry and dragoons may have had the opportunity to get something to eat as they rode in from their outlying quarters. Folk memory in Tysoe preserves several tales. At a farm in Upper Tysoe, thought to be Dinsdale Farm, since demolished, the farmer's wife had just finished baking when a troop of horse appeared and took all her bread. The farmer quickly gathered up all his valuables and lowered them down a well. Middle Tysoe has its stories of troopers taking cheese, cider and beer, and Saddleton Street is said to owe its name to their saddling up there when they moved on.

In Temple or Lower Tysoe a farmer had the wit to hide his valuable cob in a barley rick, and the animal had the prudence not to neigh.

Lower Tysoe seems to have had a visitation from the other side, for legend has it that a youth leaning over a gate was asked by some troopers which side he was for. Taking them for Roundheads the cunning peasant said 'Parliament', whereupon a soldier sent a pistol shot past his ear. He vanished into the hills and was not seen again for some days.

For the infantry marshalled in the Vale of the Red Horse there were no such opportunities for marauding. The men must have been in position long before the last of the Royalist foot reached their rendezvous on the hill. Hour after hour they had to wait, something of an ordeal for men who for the most part had never been under fire. The autumn day was bright now, and the chaplains, Bifield for one, discharged their duty by passing from regiment to regiment and troop to troop to encourage the soldiery. But, except for a few provident individuals who may have had a crust in their 'snapsacks', the men had more sustenance for their souls than their stomachs. The hours dragged by. Noon came and went, and then the colours on the hill began to move. The Royalists, more numerous than anyone had expected, were coming down the hill.

THE HORSE

Colonel Ross, whose conclusions were accepted by S. R. Gardiner, reckoned that the Parliamentarians had 2,000 to 2,300 horse. The Parliamentarian troops, with two exceptions, had an establishment of 70 officers and men. The exceptions were the Lifeguard (100) and 'the General's Troop of 50 Carbines' under Captain Nathaniel Draper. It follows that the 42 troops should have mustered 2,990 horse. But many troops must have left for the front before they were complete, in consequence of the Ordinance of 28 September, and others had suffered casualties at Powick Bridge. It would seem, therefore, that Colonel Ross's[8] calculation is a reasonable one. For lack of exact strength returns it is assumed that the troops, with the exception of the Lifeguard (100), averaged 50 apiece, and that the total strength was 2,150.

Defective staff work must account for the absence of about eight troops which missed Edgehill. The trouble was that the small staff of eight general officers of the horse had to issue orders not only to eight regiments of horse and two of dragoons, but to a number of independent troops as well, a frustrating and inefficient process. The eight regiments which can be identified are:

> *Colonel*
> Earl of Bedford
> Sir William Balfour
> Sir Philip Stapleton ⎫
> The Lord General's Regiment ⎭
> Lord Feilding
> Lord Willoughby of Parham. With Hampden
> Sir William Waller
> Edwin Sandys
> Arthur Goodwin

Colonel Sandys had fallen at Powick Bridge but the remnants of his regiment were probably present with Ramsey.

At Edgehill the 18 troops on the Parliamentarian right were certainly organized in three regiments, those of the Lord General (the Earl of Essex), Balfour and Feilding. From this one might conclude that Ramsey's 24 troops on the Left were organized in four regiments each of six troops but, attractive though this theory is, it is almost certainly too tidy.

The staff of the Parliamentarian cavalry were:

OFFICERS GENERAL OF THE HORSE

Lord General of the Horse	Earl of Bedford
Lieutenant-General	Sir William Balfour
Commissary-General	Sir James Ramsey[9]
Adjutant-General	Major Gilbert Blare[9]
Quartermaster-General	Captain John Dalbier
Commissary for the Horse	Sir Edward Dodsworth
Commissary for the Provisions	John Ward
Provost-Marshal-General	John Baldwin

There is no reason to suppose that any of these were absent from the army.

RIGHT WING

	Estimated strength
LORD FEILDING. Six Troops	300
Colonel Lord Feilding	
Major Robert Burrill	
THE LORD GENERAL'S REGIMENT	
Seven Troops	400
Sir Philip Stapleton (100)	
Sergeant Major John Gunter	
Captain (Nathaniel) Draper (50)	
Lord Brooke	
Captain (James) Sheffield	
Captain Temple	
Captain (Oliver) Cromwell (arrived late)	

SIR WILLIAM BALFOUR. Six Troops   300
    Sir William Balfour
    Sergeant-Major John Urry
    Lord Grey of Groby
    Captain Nathaniel Fiennes
    Sir Arthur Hesilrige
    Captain Walter Longe

LEFT WING

COMMISSARY-GENERAL SIR JAMES RAMSEY.   1,200
SIR WILLIAM WALLER
    Sir William Waller
    Major Horatio Carew or
    Major Sir Faithfull Fortescue
    Captain Richard Grenvile?
ARTHUR GOODWIN
    Colonel Arthur Goodwin
    Major Gilbert Blare
    Captain Robert Vivers
    Captain Sir John Sanders

A list of 32 other captains and troops probably belonging to Essex's army, though not necessarily in the battle is:

	No.	Remarks
The Earl of Bedford	1	General of the Horse
Lord Grey of Groby	3	
Earl of Peterborough	4	
Lord Saye	5	
Lord Brooke	6	
Lord Hastings	7	Clarendon, Vol. II, p. 377.
Lord St. John	8	MW and PW. Probably on the left with Ramsey.
Lord Wharton	11	
Colonel Lord Willoughby of Parham	12	Joined on the evening of 23 Oct. (Whitelocke)
Lord Grey (of Wark)	13	
William Pretty	17	
John Neale	26	
Arthur Evelin	31	
Colonel Edwin Sandys' troop	33	MW Powick Bridge
Edward Kiteley (or Kightley)	35	Wrote an account of the battle
Edward Berry's troop	37	
Major Alex. Douglas's troop	38	K. Powick Bridge
Thomas Lidcott's troop	39	PW Powick Bridge
John Dalbier	41	Q.M.G.
Francis Fiennes	42	
Jo. Fleming	45	Casualty
Thomas Tyrrell	48	
George Austin's troop	52	PW Powick Bridge
Edward Wingate	55	
Henry Ireton	58	
John Fiennes	60	Arrived late

Francis Thompson	61	W.
Sir Robert Pye	63	At Oxford on 19 September
		(Wood, L. & T., p. 63)
Valentine Walton	73	PW
Sir Samuel Luke	–	
Rigby	–	

THE FOOT

Of the 20 regiments only 12 were in the line at Edgehill, though two more arrived near Kineton before nightfall. The nominal strength of each regiment being 1,310, including combatant officers, the 12 regiments present should have mustered 15,720.

Colonel Ross reckoned their strength at 11,000 and Godfrey Davies accepted his conclusions. The absence of 3,700 men through sickness and desertion seems excessive, and though Ballard's regiment was only 800 strong, we know that its case was exceptional. Brooke's had a detachment (probably one company) in Warwick Castle, but on the other hand Essex's Regiment with its higher establishment would have redressed these weaknesses. In the absence of strength returns an average of 1,000 per regiment, and a total of 12,000 seems the best estimate for the strength of the Parliamentarian foot.

The organization of brigades each about 4,000 strong on 23 October 1642 was:

SIR JOHN MELDRUM.   Right
    Lord Robartes
    Sir William Constable
    Sir John Meldrum (ex Lord Saye and Sele)
    Sir William Fairfax.   Rear
CHARLES ESSEX.   Left.
    Charles Essex
    Lord Wharton
    Lord Mandeville
    Sir Henry Cholmley
THOMAS BALLARD.   Rear towards the left.
    Earl of Essex
    Thomas Ballard
    Lord Brooke
    Denzil Holles

THE DRAGOONS

There were 700 dragoons with Essex at Edgehill. There were two regiments of dragoons in his army, their commanders being Colonel John Browne, who had been defeated at Powick Bridge, and Colonel James Wardlawe.

Each regiment seems to have had six troops, consisting, in theory, of 100 horse besides officers. In fact, it seems, the troops only averaged a strength of about 60. It is assumed, for reasons already given, that the whole body of dragoons was on the right wing.

The names of the troop commanders, predominantly Scots, were:

Colonel John Browne
Major Nathaniel Gordon
Captain Sir John Browne
Captain Rob. Mewer
Captain William Buchan
Captain Robert Marine
Colonel James Wardlawe
Lieutenant-Colonel George Dundas
Captain Alexander Nerne
Captain John Barne
Captain James Stenchion
Captain Archibald Hamilton

THE TRAIN OF ARTILLERY

If Essex's artillery was not particularly efficient it was not for lack of guns. Wharton saw 40 near Warwick on 21 September, and *Speciall Passages* reports that he had 46 at Worcester on 18 October. Even after he had lost seven guns at Edgehill, he was reported to have had 37 at Northampton on 2 November.[10] Hampden had at least seven guns with him on the day of the battle, but even so one can hardly credit the Earl with less than 30 guns on that day, and he may have had as many as 37.

For the rest singularly little is known about the Parliamentarians' artillery at Edgehill, for no complete list of their guns seems to be extant. Like their opponents, they had difficulty in obtaining draught horses, but, unlike them, they failed to solve the problem. The blame for the inefficiency of the artillery is generally laid at the door of the lieutenant-general of the Ordnance, a foreigner – probably French – named Philibert Emanuel du Boys.[11] His name (rendered as Philibert Eman. Duboyce) figures in the list of officers appointed by the Guildhall Committee, where he is described as controller of the ordnance and chief engineer. As the list was printed on 16 June one would think that he had had sufficient time to organize his command.

With the resources of the Tower of London at du Boys' command there was no shortage of field-pieces, and it is unlikely that he was starved for funds. Certainly his performance was far less impressive than that of the Royalist lieutenant-general, Sir John Heydon. The General of the Ordnance, the Earl of Peterborough, was evidently not expected to do the work of his office, for he received no criticism from his colleagues.

As to calibres, all we know for certain is that Essex had two 12 pdrs., one six pdr., and four 3 pdrs. Perhaps the guns were placed in pairs, as was the fashion throughout the war, and many of them between the bodies of foot in the front line. Ludlow tells us that the Parliamentarians planted the best of their field pieces on the right wing, and there was certainly one in the vicinity of Meldrum's brigade. There must have been another opposite the Royalist centre for the first Royalist casualty, hit in the preliminary bombardment when the armies would be outside musket-range, belonged to Feilding's brigade. There were also three cannon on the left wing. They may well have been behind the hedges for they scored a hit on the Duke of York's troop in the Prince of Wales' Regiment.

ORGANIZATION OF THE ARTILLERY

General of the Ordnance		Earl of Peterborough
Lt. General of the Ordnance		Philibert Emanuel du Boys★
Assistant to the Lieutenant-General of the Ordnance		Nicholas Cooke
Surveyor or Comptroller		Alexander Forboys (Forbes?)
Engineer		John Lyon
Engineer Assistants	6	Unnamed
Commissaries of the Ordnance, materials and ammunition	2	George Vernon
		John Phipps
Commissary to distribute victuals	1	Unnamed
Purveyor-General for munitions and all other necessaries belonging to the Ordnance		Captain Peter Cannon
Gentlemen of the Ordnance	18	Thomas Holyman
		Robert Barber
		Patrick Strelley
		Edward Wase
		Anthony Heyford
		Robert Bower
		Henry Edson
		James Francklin[12]
		Richard Honey
		Joshua Sing
		George Ransom
		Samuel Barry
		Daniell Barwick
		Thomas Rawson
		Thomas Sippence
		Thomas Crosse[12]
		Thomas Ayres
		William Hickson
Master of the carriages or Waggon Master		John Fowke
Principal Conductor for the draught-horses and ammunition		William Crawley★
Commissary for the draught-horses		Edward West★
Quartermaster		George Wentworth

600 Pioneers		Captain Edward Frodsham[13]
		Captain Henry Roe
		Captain John Dungan
		Lieut. Gerard Wright
		Lieut. Benjamin Hodson
		Lieut. Thomas Williams
Master Gunner		Lancelot Honiburne★
		(or Haniball)
Provost-Marshal		Christopher Troughton
Battery-Master		Edward Oakley★
Fireworkers and Petardiers	2	Joakim Hane
		William Roberts
Bridge-Master		Harman Browning
Assistant to the Bridge-Master		Jo. Herdine
100 Firelocks		
Captain		Lt. General du Boys★
Lieutenant		Richard Price
Surgeon		Mathew Broad

Those marked with an asterisk★ were enlisted before 16 June 1642 by the Committee at Guildhall, which was entertaining Reformado officers allegedly 'for the furtherance of the Service in Ireland.'

SUMMARY

	KING	ESSEX
HORSE	2,800	2,150
FOOT	10,500	12,000
DRAGOONS	1,000	720
GUNS	20	30–37
	14,300	14,870

1 A Worthy Divine.

2 The words 'about half a mile' are struck out.

3 Clarendon, Vol. II, p. 357.

4 The Vindication and Clearing of Sir James Ramsey, BM. Thomason Tracts, 669.f.6./184

5 P.O.A.

6 Bulstrode. See Section V, Document 2.

7 Ludlow. See Section VI, Document 2.

8 Colonel W. G. Ross, EHR, Vol. II, 1887.

9 Not in Peacock's list, but Blare's presence is known from SP 28.

10 England's Memorable Accidents, 3 November 1642.

11 P.O.A.

12 Peacock (p. 24) identifies these men with two captains of foot slain at Exeter and at the siege of Sherborne Castle. It seems very unlikely that this identification is correct.

13 Ensign in the Isle de Rhé expedition, 1627.

14 Surgeon to the train by 11 November 1642 (SP 28).

13

Edgehill Fight

'This only will we say, some of both sides did extreamly well, and others did as ill, and deserve to be hanged, for deserting and betraying, as much as lay in them, their Party;'

Letter of six Parliamentary commanders

'Tis observed that of all nations the English stick the closest to their Officers, and tis hardly seen that our common Soldiers will turn their backs, if they who commanded them do not first show them the bad example, or leave them unofficer'd by being kill'd themselves upon the place.'

King James II

IN ITS BROAD outlines the battle of Edgehill is not complicated. Having set to, some time was spent in last minute exhortations and instructions. There was a preliminary bombardment, and then the Royalists advanced. On the flanks their dragoons did their work well, then both wings of their horse not only routed their opponents, but pursued them eagerly for at least two miles, some slaughtering the runaways, some rounding up prisoners and others striving to capture enemy standards as trophies of their victory. Many reached Kineton and made spoil of the Parliamentarian baggage. Meanwhile the Royalist foot came to close quarters with the Parliamentarians, and were counter-attacked in turn by horse and foot, who broke two of the five brigades. The end of the day found both sides exhausted and the Royalists 'back on their start line', though still showing a bold front.

So bald a summary does but scant justice to the changing fortunes of a day that twice came near to putting an end to the war at a stroke.

For a variety of reasons it is extremely difficult to piece together the sequence of events in a battle that took place three centuries ago. The officers did not have watches, or, if they did, failed to synchronize them. Hardly anyone had a map and certainly not one of a scale to show tactical dispositions. Units did not keep War Diaries – not that those of the present day are as trustworthy as some Official Historians imagine. After a few vollies black powder smoke obscured the scene, and eyewitnesses tended to improve their personal observations with hearsay picked up afterwards around the camp-fire. Many regiments whose doings were of real importance have no chronicler. From the Royalist foot, for example, we have only Belasyse's secretary, who seems rather unreliable, and a vignette from Gervase Holles. One is left clutching at straws and the name of a fallen officer or the device on a captured colour may have real significance. Certainly the range of the guns in use, and the normal tactics of horse and foot afford many a clue.

If it has seemed worthwhile to reconstruct as far as possible the Order of Battle of each side, it is because one can only trace the movements of each side if one has a firm idea of how they were arrayed before the battle began.

Perhaps the Royalists were surprised that Essex allowed them to deploy, unmolested, at the foot of Edgehill. We do not know what eventually decided Essex to give the order for his guns to open fire. That the Parliamentarians opened fire first is well attested. Ludlow is precise upon the point. 'Our general having commanded to fire upon the enemy, it was done twice upon that part of the army wherein, as it was reported, the King was. The great shot was exchanged on both sides for the space of an hour or thereabouts.'

It was not difficult to pick out this target for Charles' entourage made a considerable body of horse. As the King rode down the line he was 'accompanied by the great Officers of the Army:' as well as the Prince of Wales and the Duke of York, the Duke of Richmond, the Earl of Dorset and others. His escort of 50 Gentlemen Pensioners increased the number and, 'that it might be known in what part of the Army the person of the King was, he had a scarlet cornet larger than ordinary carryd before him'.[1] Thus attended Charles 'rode to every Brigade of Horse, and to all the Tertias of Foot, to encourage them to their Duty' . . . and . . . 'spoke to them with great Courage and Chearfulness, which caused Huzza's thro' the whole Army'.[2]

It may be that it was this royal progress and the storm of cheering that provoked Essex to open fire. Captain Kightley says 'my Lord General did give the first charge, presenting them with pieces of ordnance, which killed many of their men, and then the enemy did shoot one to us, which fell 20 yards short in ploughed land and did no harm'.[3] If Lord Wharton is to be believed upon the point, the Royalist cannon did not kill 20 men,[4] while another Parliamentarian account[5] says 'wee gave them two shoots for one, and their ordinance blessed be the God of battels, did scarcely any hurt at all, whereas we scarcely discharged away a bullet in vaine . . . ' This has the ring of partisan enthusiasm, but with at least ten more guns than the Cavaliers the Parliamentarians should certainly have been able to get off more rounds. As has been remarked previously, the fire of the six big Royalist guns planted on the lower slopes of the hill, would plunge into the soft ground, and would get no riccochet effect.

Curiously enough the name of the first casualty is known. He was Lieutenant Francis Bowles of Feilding's Regiment,[6] which must have been near the centre of the Royalist line.

We do not know how long the preliminary bombardment lasted. Ludlow's estimate of an hour seems far too long for the artillery duel, for the Royalists, determined to attack, knew that they only had a few hours of daylight left.

The Royalist commanders now persuaded the King to withdraw somewhat.

'When our Army was drawn up at the Foot of the Hill, and ready to march, all the Generals went to the King (who intended to march with the Army) and desired he would retire to a rising Ground, some Distance from thence, on the Right, . . .'[2]

The traditional name 'Bullet Hill' marks this feature for us. There the King and his escort still presented a fair target for the bigger guns of his enemies.

What orders the Royalist cavalry generals gave to Sir John Byron and Lord Digby, who commanded the second line of each wing, we shall never know. If either was told that he was intended to act as a reserve he soon forgot it. In any case a second line should be regarded as a support rather than a reserve. The fact is that except for the 50 Pensioners there was no Royalist Reserve. This was a grave error, and one for which Lord Forth and Prince Rupert must bear the censure, for Lindsey, having been supplanted, cannot be held responsible, while the King himself as yet lacked experience in the Art of war.

In the normal way the 300 noblemen and gentlemen of the Lifeguard, the King's 'Volunteer-Guard', would have served as a reserve. But unhappily for Charles 'a vanity had possest that Troop, (upon a little provocation, or for a word of distaste the day before, or being called, *The Troop of Shew*) to desire this honour of being engaged in the first charge;'[7] and they were now drawn up in the post of honour on the right of Rupert's front line.

If the Prince can be faulted for not keeping a reserve he did not neglect to give his men last minute tactical instructions.

'Just before we began our March, Prince Rupert passed from one Wing
to the other, giving positive Orders to the Horse, to march as close as was
possible, keeping their Ranks with Sword in Hand, to receive the Enemy's
Shot, without firing either Carbin or Pistol, till we broke in amongst the
Enemy, and then to make use of our Fire-Arms as need should require;
which Order was punctually observed.'[8]

The Royalist commanders had 'perceived that the Rebels had placed
some Musqueteers under a Hedge that crost the Field, where the
Encounter was to be made, that flanked upon their left Wing'. Usher's
Dragoons were sent to beat them off 'which they very well performed'.[9]
Perhaps it was in this preliminary skirmish that Captain Gawdye received
the two bullets in his thigh.[10] On the other wing Sir Arthur Aston 'with
great courage and dexterity' beat off the Parliamentarian dragoons.[11]
There is no evidence that there was a prolonged resistance on either wing,
and since there seems to have been little disparity in numbers, the Royalist
dragoons deserved the praise their partisans bestowed upon them. The
musketeers on Ramsey's left could only fall back on foot, but the men
of Brown and Wardlawe's Regiments doubtless took horse and spurred
back to Kineton, where, if Captain Kightley is to be believed, they helped
themselves to their comrades' baggage.

One may imagine the uneasiness of the Parliamentarian horse on either
wing as they heard the musketry getting nearer their outer flank. Some
at least must have perceived dragoons and musketeers trickling away to
the rear. It was unnerving for nobody likes being outflanked. And on the
left some at least must have seen a solitary rider spur forward suddenly
and, tearing off his orange-tawny scarf, gallop up to the general sitting his
horse at the head of the Royalist cavalry. This was Lieutenant John van
der Gerish[12] of Sir Faithfull Fortescue's troop. He brought the news that
his troop commander intended to change sides and that the signal would
be his shooting his pistol into the ground.[13]

In the Prince's judgement the moment had now arrived to order the
advance. Even so he sent messengers to warn commanding officers of
Fortescue's intentions, but in the hurry of the moment nobody told either
Sir William Killigrew's or Sir John Byron's troops.

According to the Diary, Prince Rupert's regiments were given the
orders that 'when ye Cannon went off, then they should march'. Perhaps
this means that on a given signal all six big guns were to be fired
simultaneously. At best it was an unreliable arrangement since the fire of
Essex's artillery could confuse the issue. Certainly this signal must have
been reinforced by the trumpeters sounding a 'Tucquet'.[14] The Royalist
horse, three deep, began to move forward.

James II's little known description of this charge is worth quoting:

'But there was not the same equality of courage in the horse; for the Royalists march'd up with all the gallantry and resolution imaginable, especially the right wing led by Prince Rupert; tho while they advanced, the Enemy's cannon continually played upon them, as did the small divisions of their Foot which were placed in the intervals betwixt their squadrons, neither of which did in the least discompose them so much as to mend their pace. Thus they continued moving, till they came up close to the Enemy's Cavalry, which after having spent their first fire, immediately turn'd their backs, the Royalists pursuing them with great eagerness.'[15]

This is a picture of a steady well-controlled advance with the men getting up speed in the last 200 yards or so, when the trumpeters sounded the Charge.

On the extreme right Lord Bernard Stuart, at the head of the Lifeguard, found difficult going. 'They stood still all the while upon the hill expecting the charge so that we were fain to charge them uphill and leap over some 5 or 6 hedges and ditches.' Even his well-mounted gentlemen, many accustomed to the hunting field, must have found their ranks disordered by such an advance.

Further to the left the Prince of Wales' Regiment came under an ill-directed fire. Bulstrode, riding in the ranks of the Earl of Northampton's troop, recalled that when they 'came within Cannon Shot of the Enemy, they discharged at us three Pieces of Cannon from their left Wing, . . . which Cannon mounted over our Troops, without doing any Hurt, except that their second Shot killed a Quarter-Master in the Rear of the Duke of York's Troop'.

It may be that Rupert kept his men to a walk for the first hundred yards or so, but gradually the pace would quicken. Certainly the Cavaliers were not yet within effective range when the Roundhead cavalry discharged their carbines or 'long peeces afarre of(f), and without distance'.[16] These did as little harm as the cannon and the sight of the undismayed Royalists coming on sword in hand, was too much for Ramsey's troopers, though, no doubt, the last minute defection of Fortescue's troop[17] contributed to their panic. The Roundheads now wheeled about 'and ranne disorderly', leaving their musketeers to be cut to pieces by the Cavaliers. The officers led the way and Sir James Ramsey 'himself being engaged among the Squadrons of the Enemies Horse, was carryed violently out of the Field . . . ' This was the testimony of his friends. He himself described how he was 'carryed along, two miles at least' until being among the

Cavaliers in an enclosure he leapt a ditch where none could follow him and so escaped.[18] Colonel Sir William Waller was another to have a narrow escape, for his horse was killed under him.[19] According to Nathaniel Fiennes, Captain Robert Vivers' troop (Goodwin's Regiment) was one of the first that ran.

Thus after a brief resistance Rupert's furious charge had routed Ramsey's wing and left the Cavaliers 'Masters of their Cannon'.[20] No doubt, the victors of Powick Bridge had been confident of victory, but they can scarcely have expected it to be so sudden and complete. The enemy had looked solid enough standing on their hill. It had been a pleasant surprise when, during the advance, their roundshot had flown harmlessly overhead, and when their single premature volley had proved so harmless. It must have seemed too good to be true when instead of charging serried ranks they had galloped in to cut up little platoons of deserted musketeers, a few hapless cannoneers, and a mob of fleeing troopers. In the heat of the moment Sir William Killigrew's men fell upon some of Fortescue's troop, who had been slow to tear off their orange scarves. The rest of Rupert's men swept on in full cry, every man determined to seek out a victim or two.

There was but little resistance, though Lord St. John, despite Clarendon's allegations, may be credited with showing fight, for he was mortally hurt before he was taken. Bulstrode, no doubt charging on the same 'unruly horse' he bestrode at Powick Bridge, had overtaken his commanding officer – most improper – when some unknown Round-head turned on him and wounded him in the head with a poleaxe. The man was 'seconding his Blow' when Colonel Sir Thomas Byron came up and shot him dead with his pistol.

To the right, and a little way behind Ramsey's men stood Holles' Regiment whose colonel, having 400 of his men under Sir James' command, had a decided interest in the latter's fate. To his disgust he now saw this mass of cavalry, with the Royalist horse at their heels come rushing pell-mell down upon his regiment and break through it. Undaunted, he 'went and planted himself just in the way, and did what possibly he could do to make them stand; and at last prevailed with three Troops to wheel a little about, and rally; . . .'[21] It was no mean feat; indeed, Holles proved himself something of a leader on this day, for his Londoners, though ridden over by their own horse and their pursuers, rallied and, 'not dismaid', fought on.

Meanwhile the Royalist second line, Sir John Byron's men, 'seeing none of the enemy's horse left, thought there was nothing more to be done but to pursue those that fled, and could not be contained by their commanders, but with spurs and loose reins followed the chase . . .'[22]

Rupert, more effective than his subordinates, managed to stop three troops, but the rest of his wing swept on in great disorder to Kineton. No doubt on the way they performed good 'execution', as the term was, upon the runaways, but when they reached the town they found a new prey: the carts and waggons of Essex's army. All sorts of prizes came their way: Essex's coach, Sir Samuel Luke's commission, much baggage belonging to the six Parliamentarian commanders who composed their official account, Captain Kightley's waggon and money: and poor Robert Bennet, 'late waggoner of Exeter', lost his waggon and seven good horses worth at least £82.

It is absurd to suppose that men like the Earls of Dover and of Denbigh or Lord Capel, all of whom rode in the Lifeguard, coveted spoil of this sort. Nevertheless if Rupert's charge had driven the Roundhead left from the field, the Prince no longer had any substantial body of horse with which to exploit his success.

A notable casualty was Lord d'Aubigny, commander of the Duke of York's troop, who was mortally wounded. Lord Taafe (Prince Rupert's Lifeguard) was wounded in the mouth but recovered, and at least two of the Prince of Wales' troop were wounded, while Dr. John Nurse of Sir John Byron's Regiment was slain.

Wilmot had in one way a more difficult task than Rupert, for he had 'to charge in worse ground, amongst hedges, and through gaps and ditches, which were lined with musketeers'. Fortunately for him, however, Sir Arthur Aston and his dragoons had disposed of these gentry and so on the Royalist left wing the story, superficially, was much the same as upon the right. When Aston had done his work Wilmot led his men forward. It may be that his advance was synchronized with Rupert's by a sudden discharge of all six big guns. Perhaps he was able to see the right advancing and merely conformed.

Although Wilmot was much weaker than Rupert he must have outnumbered Feilding by nearly three to one. Rupert with something like 1,700 men had little enough trouble in disposing of Ramsey with 1,200 horse and those of the supporting musketeers who had not already been pushed back by Usher's Regiment. The unfortunate Feilding was swept from the field with, if anything, even less resistance than Ramsey's men. Sir William Fairfax's Regiment ran too, and none faster than Lieutenant Thomas Whitney, who found a horse and went post haste to London.[23] Whether Fairfax's men panicked when they saw Feilding routed, or were actually broken by the Royalist horse, is not quite clear.

Wilmot with less to do than Rupert might perhaps have controlled his men better. There is no evidence that he tried to stop them, and Lord

Digby, a young soldier compared with his opposite number, on the other wing, Sir John Byron, joined in the chase, his men eagerly rushing on to Kineton, killing waggoners and setting waggons on fire. But there were officers on Wilmot's wing who knew their work. Chief among these was Lt. Colonel Sir Charles Lucas (Carnarvon's Regiment).

Lucas with the help of others succeeded in halting and rallying some 200 men. No doubt this difficult task took time, but Lucas was a man who meant to be obeyed and even in the eyes of Clarendon, who disliked him, was 'a gallant man to look upon and to follow' in action.

With the aid of Lord Grandison, of Captain John Smith, who was acting as Lieutenant to Lord John Stuart's troop (Grandison's Regiment) and Wilmot's captain-lieutenant, Robert Walsh, Lucas managed to form up a body of horse drawn from at least three regiments. With these he determined to attack the right flank and rear of the Roundhead army, a manoeuvre he was to repeat on a grander scale some two years later at Marston Moor.

★ ★ ★

> O Lord! Thou knowest how busy I must be this day.
> If I forget Thee, do not Thou forget me.

With this soldierly prayer Sir Jacob Astley rose to his feet and crying out *March on Boys!* led forward the Royalist Foot. No doubt, he had waited his moment until he heard the signal salvo, or saw Rupert on the move. The foot advanced, as James II tells us, 'with a slow steady pace, and a very daring resolution'. The going was probably heavy from the autumn rains, and it was not easy for the soldiers, formed up six deep, to keep good order in their ranks. Probably their speed was not intended to be more than 70 paces to the minute, for good order, not speed, was the ideal.

The Parliamentarians were not unimpressed as the brigades of Belasyse and Sir Nicholas Byron came up into the gaps between the three front-line tertias, and the Royalists bore down on them.

> ' . . . their Foot, which appeared to us, divided into nine great bodies,
> came up all in Front, and after some playing with the Cannon on both
> sides, that part of it which was on their Left, and towards our Right Wing,
> came on very gallantly to the Charge.'[24]

This must mean that the brigades of Sir Nicholas Byron and Henry Wentworth came to close quarters but there seems to be no reason to suppose that all five tertias did not keep abreast of each other. Moone

Prince Rupert by Gerard Honthorst

Sir Charles Lucas by William Dobson
In his left hand he holds a wheel-lock
pistol and in his right a spanner for
winding it up

Charles I by David Des Granges

Prince Charles by William Dobson
The armour he wears is now in the
Armouries at the Tower of London

Robert Devereux,
third Earl of Essex

Sir William Waller

Henry Ireton by
Robert Walker

Nathaniel Fiennes by Mirevelt
His scarf was orange, the colours of the Earl of Essex, the armour painted black to prevent rust, and the left arm guard to protect the bridle-arm

Broughton Castle
The room at the top of the tower centre, is the Council Chamber where Lord Saye and his Parliamentarian confederates used to hatch their plots

Arlescote House, Warwickshire:
The quarters of the young princes

Prince Charles' signature, scratched
on a pane of glass is believed to be
genuine, though one wonders why
he omitted the letter 'P' after his
name. In 1642 the house belonged
to the Cooper family.

makes it quite clear that Belasyse's brigade as well as those on the left came to 'push of pike' and one cannot imagine that a fire-eater like Charles Gerard, who commanded the right hand tertia, was one pace behind him.

To the advancing Royalist infantry things must have seemed promising. They must have had some inkling of the success of the dragoons. Many on the outside of each phalanx would have seen the success of the cavalry, and word must have passed down the ranks that things were going well. Godfrey Davies puts it this way.

> 'As the royalist infantry advanced they must have thought the battle already nearly won. They might well have believed that Meldrum's brigade of foot was the only compact body left to fight.'[25]

It is a reasonable supposition, for the brigade of Charles Essex 'at the very first wholly disbanded and ran away, without ever striking stroke or so much as being charged by the enemy'.[24] It is probable that the shameful rout of Ramsey's horse broke their nerve. But it may be that they did not flee until the Royalist foot began to approach. 'Col. Charles Essex himself, and others, who Commanded these Regiments in Chief, did as much as Men could do to stay them; . . . '[24] Lord Mandeville's men would not stand 'though his Lordship beseeched them, yea cudgelled them' and Wharton's men, and all Cholmley's except some 80 'used their heeles'.[26] As if to confirm James II's view, Wharton declared that it was shrewdly suspected that there was treachery in the business 'for the Souldiers sweare that their Commanders ran first, and bid their souldiers run too, . . .'

The inhabitants of the capital found some confirmation of this when three officers came 'Post to London from the Army'. They were Captain Francis Wilson (Mandeville's Regiment), Lieutenant Thomas Whitney (Fairfax's) and 'one Shankes a Player' (Lieutenant Jo. Shanke of Cholmley's). These heroes

> '. . . in a very cowardly manner ran from their Companies at the beginning of the fight, and in a base and unworthy manner . . . possessed the people as they rode along with false rumours and untruths, telling of great losses, . . . and that there were not foure men of their companies escaped with life besides themselves, . . .'[27]

The brigade fled, but Essex's father, Sir William, stayed – to be taken by the foe and 'Captaine [Robert] Hunt though left all alone' was another who stood firm.[28] He was in Cholmley's Regiment and was one of those afterwards 'chiefly spoken of for their valour'.

Ballard's brigade, under its profane commander, saw Ramsey's men depart and Essex's follow them. Instead of quitting the field in flagrant rout this formation now marched up the hill to prolong the left flank of Meldrum's brigade. This was not the least wonderful event of that strange day, and is greatly to the credit of Ballard and his officers.

By this time Astley's brigades were at push of pike with the Parliamentarian foot. Now began the terrible struggle so well described by Clarendon.

> 'The foot of both sides stood their ground with great courage; and though many of the King's soldiers were unarmed and had only cudgels, they kept their ranks, and took up the arms their slaughtered neighbours left to them; and the execution was great on both sides, but much greater on the earl of Essex's party; and the King's general, in the head of his regiment on foot, was come within little more than pistol shot of that body where the earl of Essex was, (which was the thing he most desired in the world,) . . .'[29]

The seven remaining Parliamentarian regiments, Meldrum's brigade, now some 3,000 strong and Ballard's about 3,400, were in close combat with 10,500 Royalist foot.

The hedgehogs of pikemen, flanked by their supporting musketeers, now strove to bear the enemy back and break his line. In the heat of action the officers could not expect their musketeers to carry out with due ceremony all the numerous 'Postures of the Musquet, or Calliver', but had to content themselves with 'Make ready!' (pause), 'Present your Muskets!' (pause), 'Give Fire!', striving hard to get off a reasonably well-aimed volley once or twice a minute. Even at the closest range the bullets wandered in the smooth-bore barrels, but a body of foot six or eight deep was a mark hard to miss. With bullets weighing more than an ounce, terrible wounds were the rule rather than the exception.

Ballard, it seems, had marched up just in time, for the outnumbered Roundheads in their plain Dutch order, eight deep, held the 'Swedish brigades' of the Cavaliers at bay. But it was hot work for a time, too hot to last as James II tells us:

> 'The foot being thus ingaged in such warm and close service, it were reasonable to imagine that one side should run and be disorder'd; but it happen'd otherwise, for each as if by mutuall consent retired some few paces, and they stuck down their colours, continuing to fire at one another even till night; a thing so very extraordinary, that nothing less than so many witnesses as were there present could make it credible.'

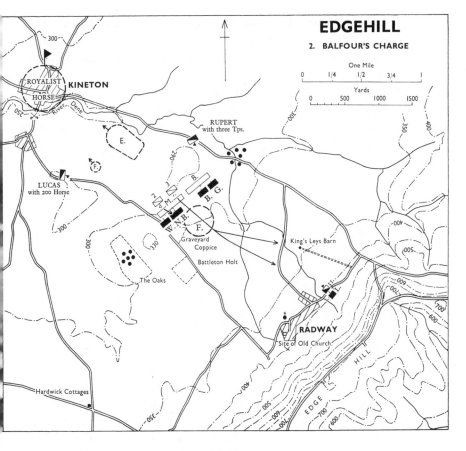

EDGEHILL
2. BALFOUR'S CHARGE

300

ROYALIST HORSE **KINETON**

River Dene

250

RUPERT
with three Tps.

E.

F.

LUCAS
with 200 Horse

300

B.

M.

W.N.B.

B. G.

F.

Graveyard
Coppice

Battleton Holt

The Oaks

300

330

King's Leys Barn

RADWAY

Site of Old Church

400

500

600

700

EDGE HILL

Hardwick Cottages

350

400

500

600

700

One Mile
0   1/4   1/2   3/4   1

Yards
0   500   1000   1500

300

350

400

KEY
ROYALISTS

HORSE	FOOT	DRAGOONS	ARTILLERY
		●●●●	·|· ·|· ·|·

W. – Henry Wentworth
N.B. – Sir Nicholas Byron
F. – Richard Feilding
B. – John Belasyse
G. – Charles Gerard
L. –William Legge's Firelocks

1. Lord Wilmot's Regt.
2. Lord Grandison's Regt.
3. Earl of Carnarvon's Regt.
4. Lord Digby's Regt.
5. Sir Thomas Aston's Regt.
6. Prince Maurice's Regt.

7. Prince Rupert's Regt.
8. Prince of Wales' Regt.
9. King's Lifeguard
10. Sir John Byron's Regt.
11. Gentlemen Pensioners

PARLIAMENTARIANS

HORSE	FOOT	DRAGOONS OR MUSKETEERS	ARTILLERY
		○○○○	·|· ·|· ·|·

M. – Sir John Meldrum's Bde.
E. – Charles Essex's Bde.
B. – Thomas Ballard's Bde.

F. – Sir William Fairfax's Regt.
H. – Denzil Holles' Regt.
1. Lord Fielding's Regt.

2. Sir Philip Stapleton's Regt.
3. Sir William Balfour's Regt.
4. Sir James Ramsey's Wing

Modern copses shown: ⌐ _ _ _ _ _ ¬   Modern Church shown: ⬥

It was now that the initiative passed to the Parliamentarian cavalry. Beyond question the credit for this goes to their lieutenant-general, Sir William Balfour, for Bedford, though praised for his courage,[30] was a general only in name.

Balfour had seen the Royalist horse rush furiously past both flanks of Essex's infantry and must have peered long and earnestly through the smoke-clouds to make out if indeed they had all gone. Satisfied upon this point he decided to attack simultaneously with the two regiments at his command, Stapleton's and his own. Out through the gaps in Meldrum's front he led them. Stapleton's being senior to his own was on Balfour's right.[31] It therefore fell to the former to attack the brigade of Sir Nicholas Byron, which even if the men were no better than the rest of the Royalist army, was probably the best armed. This charge, described by Ludlow, a participant, was repulsed with some loss.

> 'The enemy's body of foot, wherein the King's standard was, came on within musquet-shot of us; upon which we observing no horse to encounter withal, charged them with some loss from their pikes, tho very little from their shot; but not being able to break them, we retreated to our former station . . . '

This charge certainly gave Meldrum's men some respite but Balfour's own charge was far more successful. He struck the brigade of Colonel Richard Feilding, broke through a regiment that had green colours, 'beat them to their Cannon, where they threw down their Arms, and run away; . . . ' These cannot have been the Welshmen of Sir Edward Stradling's Regiment, for they had blue colours. But they also were shattered, Stradling being taken, Lt. Colonel William Herbert killed, and at least one colour captured. Most if not all of this brigade gave way, Feilding himself being captured as well as Colonel Sir Thomas Lunsford. The King on his eminence could now see his centre streaming back towards the hill with the Parliamentarians hot on their heels, cutting down the fugitives. The cavalry of his enemies inclining a little to their left began to make for the main Royalist battery.

All this while the King had been behind the foot. Now seeing the disorder they were in and observing that the Parliamentarian infantry were also advancing against them 'he resolved to march up to them himself to incourage them by his presence, and thereby to prevent their intire defeat; . . .'[32] But he had no intention of exposing the two young princes to the same danger. Turning to Richmond he ordered him to conduct them to the top of the hill. The Duke, however, excused himself whereupon Charles 'layd the same command on the Earle of Dorset, who answer'd him with an oath, "That he would not be thought a Coward for the sake of any King's Sons in Christendom" . . .'[32]

Sir William Howard, commander of the Pensioners, now received 'an absolute command' to go off with them, and then escorted only by Richmond, Dorset and some other gentlemen the King rode forward to his infantry. As he advanced one of his footmen was shot in the face just by his horse's side. This was danger enough, but it may be that he was in fact safer with the brigades of Gerard and Belasyse than with his 50 Pensioners.

Balfour and his men had pushed on and actually succeeded in getting among the guns, cutting up the cannoneers. It was here no doubt that Sir George Strode received his wound. Balfour laid his hand on a demi-cannon. 'Nails, nails', he shouted hoping to spike the guns, but there were none to be had, and he had to be content with cutting the 'ropes belonging to them'.[24]

Some at least of his regiment pushed on, for the Princes, accompanied by Mr Edward Hyde, had not gone a musket shot[32] towards the hill 'the evening now approaching',[33] when they saw a body of horse coming, 'from the left hand of the King's foot; . . . '[32] Thinking they must be Royalists, they rode towards them. Sir Richard Graham of Norton, Yorkshire, an equerry, 'rid very little before to know them' and was beaten off his horse, then stripped. He escaped by counterfeiting death.[33] The Princes and their escort now 'drew behind a little barn not far distant from them, which was incompassed by a hedge. In this barn severall of the King's wounded men were then dressing, . . . ' The Roundheads were now 'within half musket shott in a full body'. 'I fear them not!' cried Prince Charles, drawing a pistol from one of his holsters and 'spanning it'.[34] Sir John Hinton persuaded him not to charge as he intended to but 'to quitt the place, and ride from them, in some hast, . . . ' The Roundheads, evidently mistook a field hospital for a defended post, but one of them, excellently mounted, broke from the ranks, and careered down on the Prince. Hinton received his charge, they exchanged pistol shots, and the Cavalier dismounted his assailant, but as the man was armed *cap-à-pie*, he could not hurt him with his sword whereon one Miles Mathewes, a Pensioner, came up and proved the value of the pole-axe by settling the business. By this time the Princes had safely withdrawn.[34]

Though this prize had slipped through his fingers, Balfour had done a great deal of damage, and prudently withdrew whence he came.

Stapleton's Regiment, on falling back to its original position, had discovered that 'those who were appointed to guard the artillery were marched off' – or, to put it bluntly, had run away. They promised to stand by their colonel in defence of the guns, making one of their servants load and level one. For a single individual, probably quite ignorant of artillery work, this must have taken some time. Even trained cannoneers seem to have found it difficult with the clumsy equipment of those days to keep up a rate of fire of more than one round every 5–7 minutes.[35] According to Ludlow, the man had scarcely done loading when a body of horse appeared advancing from the direction of the Royalists. 'We fired at them with case-shot, but did no other mischief save only wounding one man through the hand, our gun being overloaded, and planted on high ground; . . . ' This was lucky because these were, of course, Balfour's men returning through the gap they had torn in the Royalist line, and the wounded man 'who was shot in the hand was giving us notice by holding it up; but we did not discern it'. By now it was getting dark.

Sir Nicholas Byron's brigade, having repulsed one cavalry charge, was still unbroken. Essex now ordered an attack by Lord Robartes' and Sir William Constable's Regiments of Foot. Presumably Meldrum's was engaging Wentworth's tertia. The charge was supported by the cavalry of Stapleton and Balfour 'who did it so home thrice together, that they forced all the Musqueteers, of two of their left Regiments to run in and shrowd themselves within their Pikes, not daring to shoot a shot, . . . '[24] Ludlow, writing long after, says that the Roundheads could not break Byron's brigade until Balfour charged them in rear and Stapleton 'marching down to take them in flank, they brake and ran away towards the hill'. The Official Account, written within a few days of the event, attributes this success to the arrival of Ballard with the Lord General's and Lord Brooke's Regiments, who 'forced that Stand of Pikes, and wholly broke those two Regiments, and slew and took almost every man of them; . . . ' It had been a desperate struggle. Lindsey fell and Lord Willoughby

' . . . in the heat of the Action hearing . . . that a blue riban[36] was fallen, and knowing it could be no other than the Earle of Lindsey his father, . . . hasten'd from the head of the Guards to his assistance, and found him lying in front of his own regiment with one leg broken by a musket-shott: Now this happening at that point of time when they received the charge of the Enemy's horse, so that it was impossible to carry him off, he stood undauntedly with his [half] pike in his hand bestriding his father, and in that posture wounded one of their Captains in the face, and almost push'd him off his horse; but his own men at the same time giving back, he was left ingaged in the midst of the Enemies', chusing rather to be taken with his father, that so he might be in a condition of rendering him what service was in his power, then to save himself by leaving him in that distress.'[32]

The Lifeguard meanwhile was locked in combat with Constable's Regiment. Sir Edmund Verney, the Knight Marshal, who bore the Banner Royal, 'killed two with his owne hands, whereof one had killed poore Jason [his servant], and brocke the poynt of his standard at push of pike before he fell, . . . ' He was wearing neither armour nor buff-coat for he seems to have had a premonition of death.[37] He was struck down by Ensign Arthur Young and the standard was snatched from his lifeless hand.

Though both the Lifeguard and the Lord General's Regiments were still strong when they rallied after the battle, their senior officers had suffered heavily. The brigade commander, Byron, was wounded, Lt. Colonel John Monro (Lord General) killed, and Lt. Colonel Sir William Vavasour (Lifeguard) taken.

Ludlow saw Lt. Colonel Middleton, a reformado, displaying the King's Standard. Essex, who himself when things looked their worst, had been fighting pike in hand like a private soldier, delivered the trophy to his secretary, Robert Chambers, who started for the rear with it.

Meanwhile Sir Charles Lucas had launched his 200 horse in a charge against Essex's rear. Fortunately for Meldrum and Ballard they ran into a mob of runaways. 'Sir Charles Lucas with some others and their troops . . . hath cut off four of their foot regiments, and taken a whole bag full of their foot colours.'[38] These no doubt belonged to Charles Essex's brigade and perhaps the regiment of Sir William Fairfax. It was a good success, but slaughtering fleeing troops was not so useful as an attack on the rear of the seven unbroken regiments would have been. With so many attractive trophies to be had – upwards of 50 ensigns were making for Kineton – it is no wonder that Lucas' 200 soon broke up and that his attack lost its momentum, though not before he had charged three times. In one of these onslaughts Captain Smith took a colour of Lord Wharton's Regiment, but then looking round he found he had only one man left with him. He started back towards the King's army, passing near six horsemen who were escorting a man on foot bearing what appeared to be one of the company colours of the Lifeguard. At this moment a boy called to him 'Captain Smith! Captain Smith, they are carrying away the Standard!' and not without difficulty convinced the Cavalier that it was indeed the great Banner Royal.

'They shall have me with it, if they carry it away!' said Smith, and, rapier in hand, rushed in crying, 'Traitor, deliver the Standard!' Though wounded himself he killed one Roundhead, hurt another and routed the rest, who fled leaving the Standard in his possession. It is said that it only remained in Parliamentarian hands for some six minutes. Not content with this success Smith later freed Colonel Richard Feilding.[39] He was knighted next day.

On the fringe of the fighting other cavalry had put in an appearance, Parliamentarians who had been quartered at a distance. Captain John Fiennes was one. Meeting Viver's men in full flight he 'tooke a great deale of pains' to make them and his own men stand and stop Ramsey's other runaways. In this he had some success.[40]

Captain Kightley, quartered five miles from the field, and knowing nothing of the fight until 1 p. m. hastened thither with his own troop and that of the late Major Alex. Douglas, overtaking another on the way. As he reached the battlefield a couple of hundred horse went by 'with all the speed they could . . . saying, that the King had the victory, and that every man cried for God and King Charles'. Kightley could see that fighting was still going on and that 'the Field was not lost, but no perswasions would serve'.

Turning, he found that the two other troops with him had bolted and that of his own not 36 remained. Douglas' men had evidently not got over their experiences at Powick Bridge.

He posted the remnants of his troop in a little field with a way through it, where his men took about 10 or 12 prisoners and disarmed 40 more, all of whom they could have slain. But he did not like the look of things sufficiently to approach nearer to the fight – 'the Armies were both in a confusion, and I could not fall to them without apparent losse of my selfe and those few which were with me, . . . '[41] Instead he joined up with John Fiennes, who had gathered 'a pretty body upon a hill together . . . ' Captain Oliver Cromwell's troop 'at length came to them also'.[40] Together they marched towards Kineton and hearing the Royalist horse were there they made a stand, and sent forth their scouts 'to give them intelligence of Colonell Hampdens Brigadoe that was coming another way to the Town, . . . ' They eventually succeeded in joining him.

It was only the arrival of Hampden's force that checked the ardour of the more eager Cavaliers, perhaps at the place now called Prince Rupert's Headland. The confusion in the area between Essex's line and Kineton was frightful. Adoniram Bifield 'at the latter end of the fight, not knowing what the issue of things might be, in the darksome Evening; while it was yet light,' rode to Warwick 'amongst hundreds of drawn swords, and yet was saved from the least touch of a blood thirsty hand'.[42] Mr Simon Ash, chaplain to Lord Mandeville's Regiment, had a narrow escape when four Cavaliers set upon him and 'one of them cut off his hat and raised his hair with his sword, but never touched his skin, . . .'[42]

Nor did the over-eager Royalist horse have an altogether carefree hack home. At the close of the day Stapleton fell upon a body of 5 troops of horse 'marching from our rear on the left of us under the hedges'. He charged them through a gap with his single troop and falling upon their rear, 'killed divers of them, and brought off some arms'. In this skirmish Ludlow was dismounted and 'being loaded with cuirassier's arms' had the greatest difficulty hoisting himself into the saddle again.[43]

The belated return of the Royalist horse came none too soon for the hard-pressed Royalist infantry. They now 'made up a kind of a Body again'.[24]

The right wing of the Royalist foot had never been put into disorder,[44] but by the confession of their enemies 'retired orderly, and at last made a stand; and having the Assistance of Cannon, and a Ditch before them, held us play very handsomly: . . . '[24] Perhaps it was during this fire-fight that Lieutenant William Holles (Dyve's Regiment) got his wound.

' . . . During the fight', wrote his uncle, Major Gervase Holles, 'he receaved a shot on the face and came up to me to the head of the brigade [Gerard's] bleeding very much. I bid him go and get himselfe drest; he replied he was not so ill shot as that he would leave the feild whilst I was in it, and so continued serving wth a great expression of courage and chearfulness notwithstanding the desease w[ch] his hurt conveyed him'.[45]

How much of the Royalist foot was still in action? On this point the account by Joshua Moone is of some help for he says that his master, Belasyse, 'only received a slight hurt upon his head, and had the good fortune to recover with Sir Jacob Ashley, the Major-General, and some others our foot upon the left wing; who never came to charge at all, so they stood entire.'[46] It looks as if this must refer to the tertia of Colonel Henry Wentworth, since there is absolutely no evidence that it was charged by Balfour or Stapleton, who indeed had enough to do to break the brigades of Byron and Feilding. There is a vague clue that Feilding's brigade was not entirely broken. The monumental inscription of Colonel Sir Edward Fitton implies that he commanded the Royalist artillery at Edgehill, which is certainly not the case. It is not impossible, however, that in the later stages of the battle his regiment was in the area of the main battery.[47]

The Parliamentarian advance was checked by a combination of all arms. The guns, for all that they had been overrun earlier in the day, certainly fired off 16 rounds of case-shot, a missile that would only be used at close range.[48] The foot of the right wing 'seeing some of the Cannon in danger to be lost, advanced again, and made the Place good; the Left hand of

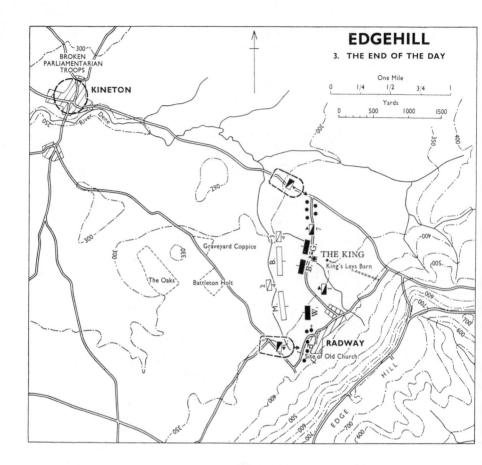

EDGEHILL

3. THE END OF THE DAY

BROKEN
PARLIAMENTARIAN
TROOPS

KINETON

River Dene

Graveyard Coppice

The Oaks

Battleton Holt

THE KING

King's Leys Barn

RADWAY

Site of Old Church

EDGE HILL

One Mile

0   1/4   1/2   3/4   1

Yards

0   500   1000   1500

KEY

ROYALISTS

HORSE	FOOT	DRAGOONS	ARTILLERY
	■	••••	·|· ·|· ·|·

W. – Henry Wentworth
N.B. – Sir Nicholas Byron
F. – Richard Feilding
B. – John Belasyse
G. – Charles Gerard
L. – William Legge's Firelocks

1. Lord Wilmot's Regt.
2. Lord Grandison's Regt.
3. Earl of Carnarvon's Regt.
4. Lord Digby's Regt.
5. Sir Thomas Aston's Regt.
6. Prince Maurice's Regt.

7. Prince Rupert's Regt.
8. Prince of Wales' Regt.
9. King's Lifeguard
10. Sir John Byron's Regt.
11. Gentlemen Pensioners

PARLIAMENTARIANS

HORSE	FOOT	DRAGOONS OR MUSKETEERS	ARTILLERY
		○○○○	·|· ·|· ·|·

M. – Sir John Meldrum's Bde.
E. – Charles Essex's Bde.
B. – Thomas Ballard's Bde.

F. – Sir William Fairfax's Regt.
H. – Denzil Holles' Regt.
1. Lord Fielding's Regt.

2. Sir Philip Stapleton's Regt.
3. Sir William Balfour's Regt.
4. Sir James Ramsey's Wing

Modern copses shown: L _ _ _ _ _ _ _ ┘   Modern Church shown:

Rebels Foot coming on apace to Charge them. By this time the Right
Wing of our Horse was returned from Chasing the Rebels, and were in
some Confusion, because they came from the Execution; but seeing our
Foot and Cannon in some danger to be lost . . . advanced in good Order
to Charge; ours made a stand, and soon rallied together having some
Dragooners with them gave them a Volly or two of Shot, which made
the Rebels instantly retire.'[44]

Clarendon, alias Mr Hyde, was now well to the rear of the Royalist
army, on top of the hill with the Princes, if indeed they had not already
retired to Edgecote. Nevertheless he criticises the Royalist horse for not
making another charge. His story that Lord Falkland pressed Wilmot to
charge Balfour only to be told 'My lord, we have got the day, and let us
live to enjoy the fruit thereof;' is perfectly credible. He goes on to say
that 'they who followed the enemy too far yet returned before it was
night, either the officers would not or could not rally so many of them
together as would charge that small reserve' under Balfour and Stapleton,
which he describes as moving about the field 'without standing in any
place to expect a charge'. It is not likely, however, that this cavalry –
officers without troops and troops without officers, and their horses
thoroughly blown – would have done much good. Under the circumstances the best thing was to form as best they could and support their
infantry. The Royalist Official Account states definitely that by the time
their dragoons – presumably Usher's Regiment – had repulsed the
Parliamentarian left 'it was grown so dark, that our Chief Commanders
durst not Charge for fear of mistaking Friends for Foes (though it was
certainly concluded by them all, that if we had had light enough, but to
have given one Charge more, we had totally routed all their Army;) . . . '

The Parliamentarians, not unnaturally, give a very different version:

'And by this time it grew so dark, and our Powder and Bullet so spent,
that it was not held fit we should Advance upon them; but there we stood
in very good Order; drew up all our Forces . . . and so stood all that Night
upon the place where the Enemy, before the Fight, had drawn into
Battalia, . . . '

In the crisis of the battle the King's presence had done much to steady
his infantry. Of their chief commanders Astley, Gerard, Belasyse and
Byron had all been hit, and Feilding taken, which made Charles' example
the more valuable. As darkness fell 'the foot appeared very thin . . . '[49]
and there were some who proposed that the King should rally as many
horse as he could and, leaving the foot and cannon to the enemy, hasten
into the West. This proposition received more support than it should

have done. But the gallant Sir John Culpeper, the Chancellor of the Exchequer, who had charged that day with Rupert, intervened most opportunely and 'with great warmth and passion', told Charles he was ruined if he harkened to it. On this the King who had already shown more than ordinary firmness that day, declared that he would not stir from the place until morning.

And so the two starved and bleeding armies, still within cannon-shot of one another, settled down to endure a night 'as cold as a very great frost and a sharp northerly wind could make it . . .'[49]

1 James II.
2 Bulstrode.
3 Kightley cannot have seen this with his own eyes. See his narrative in Section VI, Document 5.
4 Lord Wharton's Speech, (BM. Thomason Tracts, E.124/32.)
5 A True Copy of a letter.
6 See his petition. CSPD. 1659–1660. p. 434. He figures in 'A List of (Indigent) Officers'. 1663, in Lord Astley's Regiment. Astley took over Feilding's Regiment in 1643.
7 Warwick. He himself rode in the Lifeguard.
8 Bulstrode.
9 Royalist Official Account.
10 See Part III, p. 234.
11 Clarendon, Vol. II, p. 361.
12 Quartermaster, according to a document in SP 28. Clarendon says Fortescue was major to Sir William Waller, though the list in Peacock gives this appointment to Sir Horatio Carew (p. 48). Fortescue's conduct is explained by Clarendon (Vol. II, p. 360) who tells us that his 'fortune and interest being in Ireland, he had come out of that Kingdom to hasten supplies thither, and had a troop of horse raised for . . . that service; but as many other of those forces so his troop was disposed into that army, . . .'
13 Prince Rupert's Diary.
14 Venn, p. 9.
15 Godfrey Davies (Edgehill, p. 30) points out, for example, that S. R. Gardiner 'altogether ignored' these Memoirs, when writing his Great Civil War.
16 The Vindication . . . of Sir James Ramsey.
17 Fortescue 'with his whole troop advanced from the gross of their horse, and discharging all their pistols on the ground, within little more than carabine shot of his own body, presented himself and his troop to prince Rupert; and immediately with his highness charged the enemy,' (Clarendon, Vol. II, p. 360).
18 Vindication.
19 Vindication of Sir William Waller.
20 Thomas Scaife, a Yorkshireman, who first took up arms when the King set up his Standard at Nottingham, was wounded at Edgehill, and died in the service of Charles I. He left an orphan, Janie, who had not 'wherewith to mayntayne herself'. (BM. Add. MS. 15,858,f.235). Tobias Swinburne, Gent. (d. 1656), took up arms at York, was dangerously hurt at Edgehill. He returned home and was in York 'in the Leager

tyme' (1644). He laid down his arms after Edgehill and thereafter 'meddled not'. His estate was worth £15 per annum. He was buried in York Minster, 28 January 1656. (J. W. Clay, FSA, Yorkshire Royalist Composition Papers, Vol. I, pp. 140–142. Yorkshire Archaeological Society, Record Series, Vol. XV, 1893).

21 Parliamentary Official Account.
22 Clarendon, Vol. II, p. 361.
23 In September 1642 he came to London from Devonshire with his waggon laden with cloths and was there pressed into the Parliament's service in the train of artillery. He went with the army to Worcester and afterwards to Kineton, 'which service at the hazard of his life, he carefully performed' but lost his waggon and horses, 'being his whole livelihood'. On 26 May 1643 his petition for compensation was granted, and it was paid – in three instalments. (CSPD 1641–1643. p. 459.)
24 Parliamentary Official Account.
25 Godfrey Davies, Edgehill, p. 36.
26 Lord Wharton's Speech.
27 Speciall Passages
28 Lord Wharton's Speech.
29 Clarendon, Vol. II, p. 353.
30 Venn.
31 Stapleton commanded the Lord General's Regiment, and therefore his was the post of honour on the right.
32 James II.
33 Clarendon, Vol. II, p. 353.
34 Memoires by Sir John Hinton, Section V, Document 13.
35 The rate of fire during a bombardment at the siege of Pontefract Castle was one round every seven minutes. At the siege of Ostend (1602) the Spaniards on one occasion got off 11 rounds an hour per gun. (Venn, The Compleat Gunner, p. 85).
36 Lindsey was a Knight of the Garter.
37 Letter of Sir Edward Sydenham, quoted in *The Standard Bearer* by Major Peter Verney, p. 202, Part III, pp. 291–2.
38 Letter of Lord Bernard Stuart. Part III, pp. 280–1. [Document 12.
39 E(dward) W(alsingham) *Brittannecae Virtutis Imago*, 1644, Section V,
40 Captain Nathaniel Fiennes' Account, Section VI, Document 4.
41 Captain Edward Kightley's Account, Section VI, Document 5.
42 A Worthy Divine.
43 Ludlow and Parliamentarian Official Account.
44 Royalist Official Account.
45 Major Gervase Holles, Part III, pp. 286–8.
46 Joshua Moone, Part III, pp. 288–91.
47 His monument at Gawsworth, Cheshire.
48 Roy, Ordnance Papers, pp. 153 & 155. Compare Numbers 4 and 6.
49 Clarendon, Vol. II, p. 354.

14

Results of the Battle

' . . . both Sides pretended to the Victory; but since we retired up the Hill,
from whence we came down, and left the Champ de Battaile to the Enemy,
I think we had no great Reason to brag of a Victory:'

Sir Richard Bulstrode

We 'give you now a Narration of a blessed Victory which God hath given
us upon the Army of the Cavaliers, . . . '

Letter of six Parlimentarian commanders

'For all our great vycktorie I have had the greatest loss by the death of your
nobell father that ever anie freind did, . . . '

Sir Edward Sydenham to Ralph Verney, 28 October 1642

WHEN DARKNESS PUT an end to the fighting on 23 October neither side
had won the day. The Cavaliers, in consequence of their faulty initial
dispositions and the over-eagerness of much of their horse, had let slip a
real chance of decisive victory. The Parliament, crippled by the flight of
two regiments of dragoons, 30 troops of horse and five regiments of foot,
had fought back with admirable tenacity and in their turn had wrought
much havoc. But though they broke the Royalist centre, the return of
Rupert's cavalry put victory beyond their grasp. The armies had fought
themselves to a standstill but when night fell neither could claim that the
battle had been anything but a draw.

If the Royalists went back up the hillside it was not because they were
driven off the field but because they wanted to light fires and rally their
tired soldiers. Towards morning the King, who, his fortitude encouraged
by Culpeper's vehemence, had done so much to stiffen the resolution of
his commanders, took a few hours' rest in his coach.

Cold though the night was, evening had brought some relief to the
Earl of Essex, for Colonel John Hampden had arrived to reinforce him,
bringing with him two regiments of foot, Lord Willoughby of Parham's
Regiment of Horse,[1] besides several troops that had rallied on his brigade,

and a number of guns. It was a considerable reinforcement, and its commanders were full of fight.

The King for his part had few fresh troops at hand, though the small foot regiments of the Earl of Northampton and Earl Rivers may have been available.[2] On the other hand his cavalry, which had not lost 50 men, was practically intact, and so no doubt were his dragoons.

Neither side manifested much anxiety to renew the contest. Lack of food and the bitter night had cooled their ardour. Clarendon describes the Royalist array when day broke.

'Nor did the morning appear more auspicious; the troops of horse and foot appeared very thin; yet many, both officers and soldiers, who had sought warmer lodging in the cold night, returned in the morning to see what was become of their friends; and so the numbers increased. The ordnance were all safe, and though the field was covered with the dead, yet nobody could tell to what party they belonged; and that which composed the minds of the soldiers most was, that the enemy's troops appeared as thin, as broken, and as dispirited as they could wish; so that they who could longest endure the station they were in were like to remain masters of the field.'

It was suggested that 'one brisk charge' would settle the issue. But the cavalry officers pointed out that 'the bodies which were in view were rather an assembly of all the horse of the army than regiments or troops under their officers, and so they knew not how to draw them out, or to depend upon them'. The horses, it was alleged, were 'so weak that they would not be able to make a charge, . . . ' Presumably there had been little opportunity to water them. The men had had nothing to eat or drink for 24 hours. The officers had 'with much ado prevailed with them to keep the field', and had only succeeded because the King had continued there in person.[3]

The Parliamentarians were not in better case being 'almost starved with cold that bitter Night' and 'in extream want of Victuals'. When they saw that the Royalists had gone back up the hill they had retired 'to a warmer place near Kineton', but about 9 or 10 on the morning of the 24th they 'drew up again in Battalia, . . . '[4]

There followed a lull while the two armies stared at each other. The King took this opportunity to send Sir William Le Neve, Clarencieux King at Arms, with a proclamation of pardon to all those soldiers who would lay down their arms. Sir William, in 'his robe of office', went towards the Parliamentarian army, only to be met by troopers 'and charged upon his life, with pistols at his breast, neither to read any thing or to speak a word'. Led blindfold before the Earl of Essex he protested against 'the indignity and injury done to his office, contrary to the law of nations; which standers by laughed at; . . . ' He then began to read the proclamation, but it was snatched from him, with threats as to what would happen if he should let fall any of the printed copies. Essex asked Sir William whether the King and the Prince were in the field, and the herald told him that they 'had been exposed to the same danger with the rest'. The Earl said he knew the King was not there, and in Clarendon's opinion

> 'if he had not really thought so, he would never have asked the question in the hearing of so many who thereby were informed of what they had not before known or believed, for care had been taken that the soldiers should think that they fought against those malignants who kept the King from the Parliament, and that his majesty was not present in the field.'

Sir William was not permitted to stay long but 'blinded again, and conducted by a guard to the outmost limits of the army; . . . '[5]

The herald returned bringing news of the death of the Earl of Lindsey and though because of 'his sense of the danger he had passed' he had 'made little observation of the posture or numbers of the enemy' he did report that he had observed 'trouble and disorder' in the faces of Essex and his principal officers and dejection in the common soldiers who 'looked like men who had no farther ambition than to keep what they had left'.[6]

For three or four hours the armies watched each other, the King dining in the field upon a drumhead.[7] The only action that is recorded was the accidental capture of old Doctor Brian Duppa, Prince Charles' tutor. He owed his release to Sir John Hinton who persuaded Sir Thomas Aston to let him have a party of horse with which, 'after an hard dispute', he rescued him.

Neither side was eager to renew the battle and eventually the King ordered his men back to the quarters they had occupied before the battle, while Essex fell back to Warwick. If Hampden and Lord Willoughby, with their fresh regiments, wished to attack, Dalbier and others who had been in the battle advised against it.[8]

The Royalist Official Account asserts that the Earl, 'finding his Army extremely weakened and disheartened by the great Blow they had received by his Majesties Forces, withdrew himself to Warwick Castle; and the same Night the remainder of his Forces went also privately thither much distracted, . . . ' It seems, indeed, that this withdrawal was not conducted in very good order for on the morning of the 25th Rupert fell on the Roundhead's rear and took 25 waggons 'laden with Ammunition, Medicaments and other Baggage,' bringing some back and burning the rest.[9] Four carts with powder were blown up.[10] According to 'Prince

Rupert's Diary' if the Earl of Carnarvon's Regiment had come to the rendezvous in time to have gone with the Prince, 'they had routed ye enemy in probability'. Further pursuit was hindered by a heavy mist. Among the spoils of this excursion were Essex's plate and his cabinet of letters, which showed that a certain Blake, who was with the King, for a salary of £50 a week, had been betraying his counsels. He was hanged soon after.[11]

The withdrawal to Warwick was not the act of a general who thought he had won. Despite the timely reinforcements he had received Essex evidently found his men much shaken by their rude experience, and though the fighting on the 23rd had really ended in a draw, he now abandoned the field and its spoils to his enemies. 'My Lord of Essex', wrote Sydenham, 'is retired in great disorder to Warwick for the next morninge he suffired his cannon to be taken away within muskett shott of his armie, and never offired to hinder them; . . . '[12]

The most important trophies were the seven guns which fell into the hands of the Royalists. These were a valuable addition to the 20 guns belonging to the Train of Artillery for they included two 12 pdrs.; a 6 pdr. and four 3 pdrs. Only six of the guns the Cavaliers had previously were of heavier calibre than these.

Two days after the battle Sir John Heydon's clerks drew up 'a perfect state of the remaininge Magazine'. At the end of this document is a memorandum that 'There are some Musketts, Pikes & Armo' for the Foote w[ch]: wee gathered vp before & aft': the Battaile, but in regarde of the confusion thereof the number is not yett perfectly knowne the most of them being vnserviceable'.[13] Perhaps the Royalists were now able to arm the soldiers who previously had had nothing better than cudgels and pitchforks.

A great number of standards and colours were taken. Writing on 28 October the Knight Marshal, Sydenham, says: 'Ther is delivered to me fyftie two cornets and colors which was taken; I beleeve ther be manie more'. Rupert's Diary and the Official Account agree that 70 was the final score. The Royalists admitted a loss of 16 ensigns but not a single standard.[14]

It is not easy to estimate the number of casualties since the partisans of either side allowed free rein to their imaginations.

The 'battell was bloody on your syde,' Sir Edward Sydenham tells the son of the fallen Knight Marshal, 'for your hoorss rann awaye at the first charge, and our men had the execution of them for three miles; . . . ' The 30 troops that fled no doubt suffered heavily in deserters as well as in killed and wounded, but Sir Edward is clearly indulging in a little propaganda when he reports that 'it is sayd ther was killed and run away

since, eaygtt thowsand of his [Essex's] armie'. Something like 1,500 horse
and 5,000 foot fled at the beginning of the battle and many of these must
have fallen an easy prey to their pursuers, being either slaughtered or
taken. But many soldiers who vanished from the field must eventually
have rejoined the army. Sir Henry Cholmley's Regiment which had
numbered 1,200 on 1 October had only 552 men late in November.
These heavy losses – over 50% – must in the main have been due to
casualties, and desertions at Edgehill. It would perhaps be unwise to
assume that the other four foot regiments that fled were equally reduced,
but it must be remembered that if anything they did even worse than
Cholmley's men, a handful of whom stood their ground. The cavalry,
being mounted, had, of course, a better opportunity to get away.

Ballard's Regiment, which had fought bravely, suffered less heavily
than Cholmley's that ran. Even so the 776 men he had on 17 October
had fallen to 439 by 11 November, a loss of 337. Many of these would
have come from among the 200 musketeers left to their fate when
Ramsey's men broke. Holles' Regiment, which had 400 musketeers
detached, and was ridden over by both sides, must have suffered one
would think, even worse.

On the other side the heaviest casualties would obviously come from
the brigades of Sir Nicholas Byron and Colonel Richard Feilding because
they were broken. Ludlow, who fought against Byron's men, says that
he saw 'threescore lie within the compass of threescore yards upon the
ground whereon that brigade fought in which the King's standard was'.
Supposing that none of these were Parliamentarians, it still does not argue
particularly heavy casualties, and the regiments of the Lifeguard and the
Lord General were still strong in November. By the time they broke, the
two cavalry regiments of Balfour and Stapleton had already charged two
or three times, and were perhaps somewhat tired. It may be, too, that
their prudent commanders preferred to rally them rather than pursue the
broken Royalist infantry.

The 'Deserter',[15] whose work, unhappily, is far from trustworthy,
asserts that the five Royalist regiments which suffered worst were Lord
General's, Dutton's, Bolle's and Dyve's. But it is much more likely that
the list of the heaviest sufferers should be Lord General, Lifeguard,
Beaumont's, Feilding's, Lunsford's, Stradling's, Bolle's and Fitton's.

Estimates of the killed on both sides vary. Whitelock, who, though his
Memorials are full of interest, is not notably accurate, says: 'On both sides
were lost between 5000 and 6000 men'. There were less than 30,000
men engaged in the battle and losses of the sort Whitelocke suggests
would argue a loss of 20 per cent, which is highly improbable. A far more
sober estimate is to be found in the Life of Sir William Dugdale,[16] who

in February 1643 had a map made of the battlefield and took the trouble to find out 'the certain number wch lay buryed in each grave'. He tells us that it 'did not amount to full one thousand, though the report of the vulgar made them no less than five thousand'. If 1000 were killed it may be that another 2000 were more or less severely wounded. Perhaps James II's estimate of 1,500 killed, is the most probable.

Parliamentarian pamphleteers, writing for the delectation of the London public, did not scruple to assert that the Royalists lost 3,000 and the Parliamentarians 300. The absurdity of such propaganda needs no comment. Without the help of complete strength returns it is not easy to estimate the relative losses of each side. If the better-armed Parliamentarians may be supposed to have caused more casualties in the fire-fight, the Royalist horse must certainly have killed many of their enemies in the chase. And if the heavy losses in Ballard's Regiment were due to battle casualties, those of Cholmley's Regiment may have been due in part to desertion for, as Clarendon writes, 'of those who ran away in the beginning more stayed [away] than returned.'[17]

It is dangerous to come to any conclusions from such inadequate evidence. It is suggested, however, that the losses fell more heavily on the Parliamentarians than the Royalists, if only because great numbers of runaways lost heart and were never rallied again. Of the casualties whose names are known the majority are Royalists. This does not prove that they lost more officers or men, but that their casualties were men of greater social standing than their opponents.

The coldness of the night following the battle, and the inhumanity of those who stripped the wounded, saved a number of lives. One officer who might have bled to death was Captain Sir Gervase Scrope (Lord General's), who survived no less than 16 wounds. His son, Adrian, borrowed one of the King's coaches and carried him to safety the next morning. Sir Gervase recovered, though he always wore one arm in a sling thereafter.[18]

Lieutenant William Holles on the other hand had the 'extremity of the anguish increase by the sharpness of the season and want of present application shut up both his eyes, and swelled his face some days to a strange deformity'.[19]

Ludlow, like a young soldier, had given his cloak to his servant instead of strapping it to the back of his saddle. Consequently he was compelled to spend the whole of the night after the battle stamping up and down in his cuirassier's 'suite of iron' in an effort to keep warm.

Unaccustomed to campaigning, the mere struggle for existence taxed the ingenuity of most of the combatants on either side. Essex, though reinforced, was far from improving his situation during the days that followed. By the 25th he had permitted the Royalists to take the spoil of the field, and had made his disorderly withdrawal to Warwick harried by the superior cavalry of his opponents under their active and enterprising commander.

By withdrawing the Earl conceded a tactical and moral victory to his enemies. It remained to be seen whether the King would reap the strategic advantages now offered to him.

1 Whitelocke, p. 187.
2 They were with the army, but are not in de Gomme's plan. It seems not unlikely that they had been detached to observe the Parliamentarian garrison of Banbury.
3 Clarendon, Vol. II, p. 355.
4 Parliamentarian Official Account.
5 Clarendon, Vol. II, pp. 355 & 356.
6 *Ibid*, Vol. II, p. 365.
7 British Museum. Harleian MS. 3783,f.61.
8 Whitelocke, p. 187.
9 Royalist Official Account.
10 Lord Bernard Stuart.
11 Warburton, Vol. II, p. 35.
12 Sir Edward Sydenham's letter.
13 Roy, Ordnance Papers, p. 156.
14 See Dr. Williams' Library. MS Modern folio, 7, for some of Essex' trophies.
15 'A Most True Relation of the Present State of His Majesties Army.'
16 The Life of Sir William Dugdale, ed. William Hamper, F.S.A., pp. 20–21.
17 Clarendon, Vol. II, p. 375.
18 Bulstrode.
19 Memorials of the Holles Family.

CHRONOLOGY

1642

23 Oct.	Battle of Edgehill.
24 Oct.	Death of the Earl of Lindsey.
27 Oct.	Royalists capture Banbury. The King sends a Proclamation of pardon to Westminster.
28 Oct.	Rupert takes Broughton.
29 Oct.	Royalists enter Oxford. Peace negotiations proposed in the House of Lords.
31 Oct.	Edmund Waller urges the Commons to negotiate for peace. Parliamentarian Army at Northampton.
2 Nov.	The Commons consent to negotiations. Essex marches from Northampton to Olney.
4 Nov.	Royalists occupy Reading. Essex at Woburn.
5 Nov.	Essex at St. Albans.
7 Nov.	Essex re-enters London. Rupert summons Windsor Castle. Parliament invites the Scots to enter England and suppress Newcastle's army.
8 Nov.	Guildhall. The Houses appeal to the City for support.
9 Nov.	Charles at Colnbrook. The Commons decide to send a petition to the King. Essex ordered to take the field.
10 Nov.	Guildhall. Pym explains the peace overtures.
11 Nov.	Essex advances to Hammersmith.
12 Nov.	The Royalists storm Brentford
13 Nov.	Turnham Green. Essex concentrates his army. Royalists occupy Kingston. The City protests against an accommodation.
15 Nov.	The City offers to maintain an additional 4,000 horse and dragoons.
19 Nov.	Charles withdraws to Reading.
22 Nov.	Warwick resigns command of the London forces.
5 Dec.	Wilmot storms Marlborough.
9 Dec.	The Royalists allot their army its Winter Quarters.

15

The Campaign Concluded

Captain, or Colonel, or Knight in arms,
Whose chance on these defenceless doors may seize,
If deed of honour did thee ever please,
Guard them; and him within protect from harms.'

John Milton

IT IS UNCERTAIN whether the Poet was convinced that an assault on the City of London was intended in very earnest. One thing is certain: only by taking London could the King end the war. By retreating from Edgehill, Essex had conceded him victory. The chief result of the battle was, therefore, that it gave Charles the best opportunity he was ever to have of retaking his capital. The situation was in fact a very simple one. If the King could get to London before Essex he had a good chance of winning the war, for the people of the capital were by no means unanimous supporters of Pym and his party. It was a situation that demanded speed and decision. Every day that slipped by made it less likely that the Royalists would exploit their hard-won strategic success.

In this crisis the Royalists' movements, though brilliant by comparison with those of their enemies, were of a leaden slowness. Not until 27 October did they take Banbury, where, it seems, the captured garrison changed sides.[1] Not until the 29th did the King make a triumphal entry into Oxford.

Meanwhile Essex lingered at Warwick 'repairing his broken regiments and troops, which every day lessened, . . . '[2]

The captive Earl of Lindsey, before he died of his wound, had reproached friend and foe alike, declaring that he would never fight in a field with boys again. Before he expired he revealed to his captors that the Royal army numbered 14,000. It was a good deal more than the Parliamentarian commanders had expected. Their own army, reinforced though it was, scarcely equalled the King's while the superiority of the Royalist cavalry, already demonstrated at Powick Bridge, made the issue of any fresh encounter extremely doubtful.

Many officers and men were still missing, the most notable being Sir James Ramsey, who, though Essex did not yet know it, had actually reached London.

If Essex ever wrote a despatch describing Edgehill it has not been preserved. Nevertheless he was anxious to give his masters news of their army. The brief account by his chaplain, Steven Marshall, was written because the Lord General had not time. More important was the mission of Lord Wharton and William Strode, one of the Five Members, who were sent by the Lord General to address the Houses, who he knew 'could not but be full of great expectations'.

Wharton, who according to Royalist lampoons had concealed himself in a saw-pit during the fight, gave a frank and lucid account. He made no bones about the fact that a number of regiments, including his own, 'fairely ran away'. This was balanced to some extent by the news that other regiments had done well. It was music in the ears of the Londoners when they heard of Holles' redcoats, 'every one fighting like a Lion, . . . ' It was encouraging to hear that certain commanders had distinguished themselves: Bedford, Balfour, Meldrum, Stapleton, Hesilrige, Luke, Urry and Captain (Robert) Hunt, being 'chiefly spoken of for their valour'.

A study of the speeches shows that no extravagant claims of victory were made. Rather the message was one of impending crisis. As Lord Saye put it: 'Up and be doing, and the Lord will be with you'. It was obvious to everyone that the King was now nearer to the capital than was the army under the Earl of Essex. Men of the London Trained Bands, under 'the truculent London M.P. John Venn',[3] were sent to secure Windsor Castle, which had already been occupied by the militia of Berkshire and of Surrey. It was a timely move, for, when Rupert appeared on 7 November, Venn defied his summons. It was decided to raise a new army for the defence of London under a popular champion, the sailor Earl of Warwick.

Slow though they were the Royalists were the first to get on the move again. After the capture of Banbury (27 October) Prince Rupert proposed the formation of a flying column, of 3,000 horse and foot. With this he intended to march on Westminster and take the Parliament House, for he knew that he could get there before Essex. This suggestion did not appeal to the Council of War, the old Earl of Bristol rudely declaring that the Prince was a young man and would set the town on fire.[4] Since the London Trained Bands could muster 8,000 men it may be that Rupert's plan was over-optimistic. On the other hand his sudden appearance on the heels of Essex' messengers, with their excited accounts of panic, flight and dogged resistance, might have raised the London Royalists and stricken terror into the hearts of the waverers. The great merit of Rupert's plan was that it demanded speedy and decisive action.

The occupation of Oxford was of major importance to the Royalists for it was to be their capital and chief fortress for nearly four years. At first sight it looks strange that Essex should have garrisoned a relatively insignificant post like Banbury Castle while neglecting so important a city. It was not, however, his decision. Bulstrode Whitelocke, who is to be trusted when he is reporting his own experiences, tells us that he himself had been named as a fit person to be the governor, and that 'divers of the neighbours offered to bring 1,000 men at any time within a day's warning, . . . ' to be under his command. The townsmen too were 'very forward to engage', but Lord Saye would have none of it 'pretending favour to the university and country, and the improbability, in his opinion, that the king would settle there; . . . '[5] It is obvious that had it been possible to occupy Oxford without weakening Essex' field army, it would have been very much to the advantage of the Parliamentarians to do so.

The King's advance from Shrewsbury had undoubtedly thrown London into a state of great agitation. The first news of Edgehill had been brought by fugitives, some of whom were actually put under arrest for their cowardice and treachery. A Peace-party sprang up in the Lords and Commons, but a generation that recalls 1940 will not be surprised to learn that imminent danger awoke the resolution of the Londoners. They may not have wished to rebel against their Sovereign, but they had no intention of seeing their shops and houses sacked by the Royalist soldiery.

As the campaign progressed the Cavaliers were acquiring a taste for pillage. Broughton Castle and Fawley Court,[6] the homes of Lord Saye and Bulstrode Whitelocke, were both plundered with something approaching the heartlessness which Wharton's companions had shown to malignants and papists. When Prince Rupert's brigade was quartered at Henley, Sir John Byron's Regiment was at Fawley Court. Byron and his brothers 'gave order that they should commit no insolence to my house, nor plunder my goods; but soldiers are not easily governed against their plunder, . . . ' Whitelocke alleges that there was

> ' . . . no insolence or outrage usually committed by common soldiers on a reputed enemy which was omitted by these brutish fellows at my house. There they had their whores with them, they spent and consumed 100 load of corn and hay, littered their horses with sheaves of good wheat, and gave them all sorts of corn in the straw: divers writings of consequence, and books which were left in my study, some of them they tore in pieces,

others they burnt to light their tobacco, and some carried away with them, . . . '

Not content with that they killed his deer, and presented a tame young stag and his 'extraordinary good' hounds to Prince Rupert. They ate and drank 'all that the house could afford', broke open all his trunks and chests, stole his linen, let the feathers out of the beds, carried away his coach, and four good horses, and all his saddle-horses, 'and did all the mischief and spoil that malice and enmity could provoke barbarous mercenaries to commit . . . '

It was not, of course, to be expected that either side would spare the victuals or the horses of their enemies, but it is clear that Byron was no great disciplinarian. News of this sort of conduct travels fast and loses nothing in the telling. Small wonder if the Londoners were determined to avert a similar fate.

It is evident that neither side had much confidence in the success of the peace overtures that passed between them during the first half of November, and after Essex, moving at no great pace, had brought the battered remnants of his army into London (8 November) there was little reason for the Parliamentarians to dread the outcome of the King's tardy advance.

On the same day that Parliament sent Commissioners to wait upon the King, Essex was ordered to take the field once more. When (11 November) Charles received the petition of the Houses he expressly omitted to arrange for a cessation of arms, and that night he ordered Rupert to seize Brentford.

At dawn on the 12th the Prince fell upon the detachment at Brentford, but if the destruction of the regiments of Holles and Lord Brooke scored a tactical point, the chance of strategic success already lay in the past. The news of the Royalist onslaught provoked a swift reaction. The City trained bands came pouring out to join the army which Essex was concentrating on Turnham Green. Soon 24,000 men barred the King's farther progress. The Royalists were able to seize Sion House and to sink some barges full of men moving downstream from Kingston, which place they also occupied, but these tactical successes counted for little. All that mattered was that the King's triumphant advance had been halted. S. R. Gardiner sums up the situation admirably: 'Turnham Green was the Valmy of the English Civil war'.[7]

By his failure to push on after Edgehill the King had condemned his followers to a long war. With the resources of the City of London behind them the Parliament were in a far better position to wage a protracted struggle than were the Cavaliers. Falling back, unmolested, to Reading, and then to his new capital at Oxford, the King settled his army into winter quarters, establishing his field army within a ring of fortresses in the upper Thames Valley.

King Charles had won his first battle, but it was the Earl of Essex who had won the campaign.

1 Whitelocke, King's War, p. 188.
2 Clarendon, Vol. I, p. 375.
3 Wedgwood, p. 141.
4 Prince Rupert's Diary.
5 Whitelocke, p. 183.
6 Gardiner, Vol. I, p. 56.
7 *Ibid*, p. 60.

16

Of Veterans

'These are to certifie whome it may concerne that the bearer hereof Jasper Weintworth, faithfullie served his late Majestie of blessed memorie, from the first beginninge of these unfortunate warrs, untill the full dispersinge of his said Majesties Army. Witnes our hands this two and Twentieth day of August in the year of our Lord god one thowsand, six hundred and Sixtie'.

George Goldsbrough

Will. Leighton

Charles Molneux

Tho: Goldsmith[1]

THE STRUGGLE, whose issue the battle of Edgehill left undecided, had nearly eighteen years to run until the day when King Charles II was restored to his father's throne. Many indeed of the contestants were not to see that day, for the chances of war soon carried off members of either side. For both parties, for the prominent and the obscure alike, the future held a fair share of the triumphs and disasters incidental to the career of arms.

ROYALIST
KILLED IN ACTION OR DIED OF WOUNDS

Name	Place	Date
	1642	
Lieut. Thomas Daniell	Brentford	12 Nov.
	1643	
Lieut. Noland	Cirencester	2 Feb.
Lieut. William St. John	Cirencester	2 Feb.
Earl of Northampton	Hopton Heath	19 Mar.
Earl of Denbigh	Birmingham	3 Apr.
Col. James Usher	Lichfield	20 Apr.
Lt. Col. Richard d'Ewes	Reading	Apr.
Major Thomas Sheldon	Lansdown	6 July[2]
Nicholas Busy, cannoneer	Bristol	25 July[3]
Col.-Gen. Lord Grandison	Bristol	26 July
Col. Henry Lunsford	Bristol	26 July
Lt. Col. Nathaniel Moyle	Bristol	26 July
Capt. Nevile	Bristol	26 July
Capt. John Ashton	Bristol	26 July
Capt. Richard Nowell	Bristol	26 July
Capt.-Lieut. Davenport	Bristol	26 July

General Charles Cavendish	Gainsborough	27 July
Capt.? Peter Daniell	Gloucester	Aug–Sept.
Capt. James Chamberlain	Nr. Towcester	4 Aug.
Earl of Carnarvon	Newbury	20 Sept.
Lt. Col. Edward Feilding	Newbury	20 Sept.
Capt. Francis Bertie	Newbury	20 Sept.
Lord Falkland	Newbury	20 Sept.
Earl of Sunderland	Newbury	20 Sept.
Col. Richard Bolle	Alton	13 Dec.
	1644	
Capt. William Holles	Muskham Bridge	6 Mar.
Lt. Gen. Lord John Stuart	Cheriton	29 Mar.
Maj. Gen. Sir John Smith	Cheriton	29 Mar.
Col. John Godfrey	Tewkesbury	4 June
Capt. Mathew Radcliff	Greenland House	July
	1645	
Major Bunnington	Leicester	30 May
Sir William Crofts	Stokesay	9 June
Col. Richard Bagot	Naseby	14 June
Lt. Col. Sir Thomas Dallison	Naseby	14 June
Lt. Col. Edward Littleton	Naseby	14 June
Lt. Col. Francis Lawson	Naseby	14 June
Major Thomas Norwood		
(1618–1645?)	Taunton	
Capt. Sir Richard Crane	Bristol	23 Aug.
Earl of Lichfield (Lord Bernard Stuart)	Rowton Heath	24 Sept.
Capt. Lieut. Sir Troilus		Nov.?[4]
Turbervile		
	1646	
Col. Sir Thomas Aston, Bart.	Stafford	24 Mar.
1649		
Sir Arthur Aston	Drogheda	11 Sept.
1651		
Col. Sir Thomas Tyldesley	Wigan Lane	25 Aug.
	1658 or 1659	
Sir William Vavasour	Copenhagen[5]	

Several suffered execution for various reasons:

1645

Lt? Col. Francis Windebanke

1648

Sir Charles Lucas
Col. Sir George Lisle
Lord Capel

1649

King Charles I.

Lucas, Lisle and Capel were executed for their part in the defence of Colchester during the Second Civil War. They deserved a better fate.

Colonel Francis Windebanke was shot by his own side for the surrender of Bletchingdon House (1645). His bravery at Cheriton is well attested and his failure at Bletchingdon is attributed to the presence of his young wife, whom he did not wish to expose to the hazards of a siege.

A number of Royalist leaders died during the war from more or less natural causes.

	1643	
Capt. Hugh Haughton	Oxford	Bd. 25 May
Capt. Low	Oxford	Bd. 18 June
Col. Sir Thomas Salusbury		
Capt. Thomas Gylburte	Radley	Bd. 5 July
Capt. John Allen	Radley	Bd. 8 July
Capt. Lawson	Oxford. Plague	Bd. 29 July
Col. Sir William Pennyman, Bart. (1607–1643)	Oxford. Fever.	22 Aug.
Col. Robert Arden	Oxford. Smallpox.	22 Aug.
Col. Sir Edward Fitton, Bart. (1603–1643)	Bristol	Aug.
	1644	
Col. Sir Thomas Byron	Oxford Bd.	9 Feb.
Col. Sir Gilbert Gerard	Worcester	
Col. David Scrymgeour	Oxford Bd.	2 Dec.
Lt. Col. Sir Anthony Greene	Oxford Bd.	24 Dec.
	1645?	
Col. Sir George Boncle	In prison	

The valiant Sir Thomas Byron, having survived a dangerous wound at Hopton Heath, was the victim of a murderous assault by a brother officer, Captain Hurst, who was shot for his crime at Oxford.

Colonel Sir George Boncle, taken at Naseby, died in prison of 'hard usage'.[6]

Honours and awards, as well as hard knocks, came the way of a number of Royalist leaders – some even before the fighting began!

PEERAGES

Prince Rupert (1619–1682)	Earl of Holderness and Duke of Cumberland. Jan. 1644.
Earl of Forth (1573?–1651)	Earl of Brentford, 1644
Lord Bernard Stuart (1623?–1645)	Earl of Lichfield, 1645.

BARONS

Sir John Byron K.B. (d. 1652)	1643 Of Rochdale
Sir Jacob Astley (1579–1652)	1644
John Belasyse (1614–1689)	1645
Charles Gerard (d. 1694)	1645 Of Brandon

KNIGHTHOODS

1642

Name	Place	Date	Remarks
James, Duke of York	York	18 Apr.	Captain, H.
Earl of Carnarvon	York	18 Apr.	Colonel, H.
Lord d'Aubigny	York	18 Apr.	Captain, H.
Lord John Stuart	York	18 Apr.	Captain, H.
Lord Bernard Stuart	York	18 Apr.	Captain, H.
Brian Palmes	York	21 Apr.	Ordnance Commissioner. Later Governor of Belvoir Castle.
James Pennyman	York	24 Apr.	Lt. Colone, F.
Edmond Duncombe	York	27 June	Colonel, D.
John Digby	Newark	12 July	Later Colonel, F.
Robert Stapleton	Nottingham	13 Sept.	Distinguished himself at Edgehill.[7]
Capt. Richard Crane	Chester	26 Sept.	Rupert's Lifeguard. For bringing the news of Powick Bridge.
Col. Thomas Byron	Shrewsbury	27 Sept.	Prince Charles, H.
Arnold de Lille	Shrewsbury	29 Sept.	Prince Charles, H, later Lt. Colonel.
Major Richard Wyllis	Shrewsbury	1 Oct.	Lord Grandison, H.
Richard Byron	Shrewsbury	1 Oct.	Captain? H. Sir John Byron.
Anthony Morgan	Southam	21 Oct.	Later troop commander.
Richard Shuckburgh	Edgecote	22 Oct.	
Lieut. John Smith	Edgehill	23 Oct.	Lord Grandison, H.
Capt.-Lieut. Robert Welch (Walsh)	Edgehill	23 Oct.	Wilmot, H.
Wingfield Bodenham	Reading	7 Nov.	Later Colonel, H.
Edward Sydenham	Reading	9 Nov.	Knight Marshal.
Thomas Blackwell	Oxford	27 Dec.	Later Colonel, F.

1643

Name	Place	Date	Remarks
Lt. Col. Henry Huncks	Oxford	1 Jan.	Northampton, F.
Capt. William Mallory	Oxford	1 Feb.	Pennyman, F.
Sir William Neale	Oxford	3 Feb.	Scoutmaster-General, H. For bringing the news of Cirencester.
Edward Hyde	Oxford	22 Feb.	Chancellor of the Exchequer.
Henry Hunloke	Oxford	2 Mar.	Wilmot, H. Later troop commander, Frescheville, H.
Lewis Kirke	Oxford	23 Apr.	Gentleman Pensioner.
Col. John Urry	Oxford	18 June	Roundhead at Edgehill. For bringing news of Chalgrove Field.
Col. Sir Thomas Tyldesley		c.2 July	For the storming of Burton-on-Trent.
Lt. Col. Francis Butler	Oxford	15 July	Sir John Byron, H. For bringing the news of Roundway Down.
Lt. Col. Charles Compton	Oxford	12 Dec.	Northampton's troop.

Major William Compton	Oxford	12 Dec.	Captain, Northampton, F.
Capt. Spencer Compton	Oxford	12 Dec.	Captain, Northampton, F.

1644

Col. John Knotsford	Evesham	June	Gent. Vol. Northampton's troop.
Sgt. Maj.-Gen. Joseph Wagstaff	Crediton	30 July	Parliamentarian in 1642, Lt. Colonel, John Hampden, F. Later Major-General to Prince Maurice's army.
?Captain Thomas Prestwich	Cornwall	1 Sept.	Sir Thomas Aston, H.
?Captain William Ratcliff	Cornwall	1 Sept.	Sir Thomas Aston, H.
Lt. Col. John Boys	Nr. Newbury	22 Oct.	Rivers, F. For defence of Donnington Castle.
Lt. Col. Anthony Greene	Oxford	3 Nov. ⎫	Northampton, F. For defence of Banbury Castle.
Capt. Anthony Waldron	Oxford	3 Nov. ⎬	
James Croft	Oxford	18 Dec.	Gentleman Pensioner.

1645

Lord Capel	Oxford	17 Jan.	In Lifeguard, H. at Edgehill.
Lt. Col. Henry Chichley	Oxford	23 Jan.	Sir Richard Wyllis, H. Captain, F., Charles Gerard at Edgehill.
Major Richard Hatton	Oxford	27 Jan.	Gent. Volunteer. Sir Richard Wyllis, H.
Lt. Col. George Boncle	Oxford	30 Jan.	Sir Arthur Aston, H. Lt. Governor of Oxford. Major Sir Thomas Salusbury, F. at Edgehill.
Edward Walker	Oxford	2 Feb.	Garter King-at-Arms.
Col. Stephen Hawkins	Oxford	3 Feb.	Lt. Colonel, Sir Ralph Dutton, F. at Edgehill.
Charles Cotterell	Oxford	6 Mar.	Master of the Ceremonies. Captain, later Major Charles Gerard, F.
Bartholomew La Roche	Oxford	5 May	Principal fireworker.
Col. Richard Page	Leicester	2 June ⎫	Captains in Pennyman F. at Edgehill. Knighted for the storming of Leicester.
Major William Bridges	Leicester	2 June ⎬	
Col. Herbert Lunsford	Monmouth	6 July	Governor of Monmouth. Major, Lord General, F. At Edgehill.
Cornet John Walpole	Cardiff Castle	31 July	Lifeguard, H.
Lt. Col. William Leighton	Hereford	5 Sept.	Lifeguard, F.
Col. Barnaby Scudamore	Hereford	5 Sept.	Possibly Major to Blagge, F., at Edgehill.
Henry Wroth	Hereford	16 Sept.	Gentleman Pensioner.

Col. Theophilus Gilby	Newark	27 Oct.	Major, Belasyse, F. at Edgehill.
Edward Cooper	Oxford	20 Dec.	Gentleman Pensioner.
Col. George Lisle	Oxford	21 Dec.	Lt. Colonel, D. at Edgehill.
Capt. Charles Lee (Leigh)	Oxford	25 Dec.	Charles Gerard, F.

1646

Lt. Col. Thomas Shirley	Oxford	25 Feb.	Dyve, F.
Major William Byron	Oxford	25 Feb.	Sir John Byron, H.
Lt. Col. James Bridgeman	Oxford	8 Apr.	Sir Thomas Aston, H.

The King left Oxford on 27 April 1646

| Henry Talbot | | Oct. | Wilmot's Troop, H. Knighted at Kilkenny by the Marquis of Ormonde. |

A few of the leading Royalist officers, rather surprisingly, did *not* receive the honour of knighthood:

Lt. Colonel Dan. O'Neale	Prince Rupert, H.
Colonel Henry Washington	Governor of Worcester.
Colonel Thomas Blagge	Governor of Wallingford.

O'Neale fell out with the Prince and there is some evidence that Blagge incurred the King's displeasure, but there seems to be no good reason why Washington's services should have been overlooked.

HONORARY DEGREES

Between 1 November and the following February no less than 140 M.A.s, and a number of other honorary degrees of Oxford University, were created at the King's instance. It was convenient and inexpensive for the monarch to bestow the rewards of Minerva upon the followers of Mars. This 'Caroline Creation' eventually drew a protest from the loyal University which ventured to petition the King (21 February 1643) on the grounds that no fees were received from the recipients and that promiscuous conferment of these degrees, *honoris causa*, lowered their standing. His Majesty, while graciously promising satisfaction, continued from time to time to call upon Convocation to confer degrees 'by the King's letters'.

Among the recipients were Prince Charles, the Duke of York, Sir John Byron and his brother William, Sir William Killigrew and Major Degory Collins. Others were Thomas Colebrand and John Rivers.

Another form of honour sometimes given to distinguished officers was a grant of arms. Colonel Sir George Boncle and Sir Richard Page were both granted arms in 1645. The former, who had 'from his youth applyed himselfe to y[e] knowledge of Armes', came of a Scots family, as the Earl of Brentford testified, though the latter is said to have been 'humbly born'.[8] He died in great poverty at The Hague in 1657.

Medals were as yet rare, though, as Bulstrode tells us, both Sir John Smyth and Sir Robert Walsh had them for Edgehill. Sir John wore his 'in a large green watered Ribband, cross his shoulders'.[9] The portrait of Sir Thomas Tyldesley, in the National Portrait Gallery, shows a medal though it is not clear what this is.

The silver Medal for the Forlorn Hope, established thanks to the initiative of Thomas Bushell, was doubtless highly prized. How many of these were issued is unknown. Perhaps it was comparable to the Distinguished Conduct Medal or the Military Medal at the present day.

An Armorial Augmentation was another form of reward. Edward Lake, who received 16 wounds and was taken at Edgehill, received 'a Coat of Augmentation to be borne before his own: In a field gules, a right arm arm'd, carrying upon a sword a banner argent, charged with a cross betwixt sixteen shields, four in each quarter of the first and in the umbelique point one of our own lions of England. And for a Crest to the same Coat of Augmentation: A chevalier in a fighting posture, his left arm hanging down useless, and holding a bridle in his teeth, his scarf red, his sword, face, armes, and horse cruentated'.[10]

Lake was not only made a baronet, but was given the making of another. The King was particularly pleased with Lake because he was 'a professed lawyer' who had thrown off his gown and fought so heartily. Moreover the Doctor now recovered of his hurts had been sufficiently well advised to appear in the presence chamber at Christ Church, Oxford, and kiss the King's hand on the anniversary of the day when he had lost so much blood for him.

Lake was not the only man to receive an astonishing number of wounds at Edgehill.

Captain Henry Bellingham, 'of an ancient extraction in Sussex, and the only son of his father', must have got in the way of a hedgehog of pikes. On Wednesday 26 October he was 'found amongst the dead, and brought off by his friend, with twenty wounds; who, after ten days, died at Oxford, by the negligence of his surgeons, who left a wound in his thigh, of itself not dangerous, undiscerned, and so by festering destroyed a body very hopefully recovered of those which were only thought mortal'.[11]

Captain Sir Gervase Scrope (Lord General, F.) who had raised a company among his Lincolnshire tenants, owed his life to his spendthrift son, Adrian, to whom he had been reconciled just before the battle began. Laid low, according to Clarendon about 3 o'clock on the Sunday with 16 wounds in his body and head, and . . . lain stripped among the dead', he was not discovered until the Tuesday evening, 'for it was so late before his son found him; whom with great piety he carried to a warm lodging, and afterwards in the March to Oxford, where he wonderfully recovered'.[11] Clarendon tells us that the surgeons thought these gentlemen 'owed their lives to the inhumanity of those who stripped them, and to the coldness of the nights, which stopped their blood better than all their skill and medicaments could have done; and that, if they had been brought off within any reasonable distance of time after their wounds, they had undoubtedly perished'.

Lieutenant Francis Bowles, the first man struck at Edgehill, having his arm and shoulder shattered, was in action again, although he had lost the use of an arm, at Bristol and Naseby and lived to see the Restoration. Though stripped and left for dead he was found alive on 24 October, and taken to Oxford, where the King himself ordered that great care should be taken of him.[12]

Richard Pierce, Gent. (1620–1714), who, received a wound through the body as he was loyally defending King and Country', survived to the ripe old age of 94, being buried at Cowfold, Sussex, where his tombstone may be seen to this day.

Jasper Edmond, a Montgomeryshire man in Captain Floyd's company and Charles Gerard's Regiment, was shot through the knee and, surviving amputation, was recommended in 1644 to the Treasurer of the county of Oxfordshire, for relief 'as by statute is provided'.

Although there were well-known doctors with the Royalist army, notably William Harvey (1578–1657) the discoverer of the circulation of the blood, there was no proper hospital or ambulance service. It is rather surprising that men so seriously hurt as those named above should have survived. Perhaps the best Royalist surgeon was Richard Wiseman (1622?–1676), a noted and thoroughly practical author and later principal surgeon to King Charles II. He served in the West (1644–1645) and at Worcester (1651), but does not seem to have been at Edgehill. *En passant* there seems to be little evidence for Aubrey's story that the young princes were in Harvey's care at Edgehill.

A number of Royalist officers survived the Restoration and, claimed to part of the £60,000 granted by King Charles II 'for the Relief of His Truly-Loyal and Indigent Party'. Naturally many had been promoted and had served other colonels since 1642.

		Listed under	Rank and Regiment in 1642, if different
Stafford	Capt. Rob. Fleetwood ⎫	Beaumont, F.	
	Capt. Anthony Dormer ⎭		
L & W	Capt. Will. Woolverston ⎫		
Lincoln	Capt. Thomas Booth ⎭	Belasyse, F.	
L & W	Lt. Col. Sir Bartholomew Pell	Sir Theophilus Gilby, F.	Capt. Belasyse, F.
Lincoln	Capt. Martin Frobisher		Subaltern?
Stafford Q.M.	Hugh Grainger	⎧ Earl (of) Bristoll Digby, H.	
		⎩ Col. John Lane	
Lincoln	Capt. Thomas Cardinall	Dutton, F.	Lieutenant?
L & W	Capt. Thomas Hull ⎫		
Berks	Lieut. Sam. Hull ⎭		
Kent	Capt. George Grimes		Lieutenant.
L & W	Maj. Charles Kirk ⎫	Hawkins, F.	Capt. Dutton, F.
?L & W	Ensign Edward Jordan ⎭		
Bedford	Ensign John Halley	⎧ Feilding, F.	
		⎨ Capt. Peter	
		⎩ Walthall	
L & W	Major Charles Norword	Feilding, F.	
Hereford	Lt. Col. Thomas Coningsby ⎫	Lord Astley F.	Capt. ⎫
L & W	Lieut. Francis Bowles ⎭		Lieut. ⎭
L & W	Lt. Col. Urian Leigh	Fitton, F.	Major.
Chester	Capt. Thomas Green		
?Chester	Lieut. Will. Littler	Capt. Will. Davenport	
Chester	Capt. Peter Leigh	Thelwall, F.	One a capt. Fitton, F. and
Chester	Capt. Charles Leigh		subaltern?
Montgom.	Cornet Meredith Floyd		Lord Grandison, H. Major Sir Richard Willy(s)
Northum.	Lieut. Edmond Roddam	Grey. D.	
Wilts.	Q.M. Thomas Rutter	Lord Bernard Stuart	Lifeguard, H.
L & W	Lt. Col. Sir William Leighton	Earl (of) Lindsy	Major. Lifeguard, F.
?Berks	Capt. John Beeton		Subaltern?
L & W	Capt. Nicholas Berty		Subaltern?
L & W	Capt. Charles Fox		Subaltern?
Chester Lieut.	Edward Mackworth	⎧ Lord Willoughby (d'Eresby)	
		⎨ Capt. (Peter)	
		⎩ Walthall	
L & W	Lt. Col. Will. St. Clare	Lord Gen. Ruth(v)en	Capt. Lord General F.
Norfolk	Capt. Thomas Draper		
L & W	Lieut. Thomas Cordwayne	⎧ Earl (of) Lyndsy	
		⎩ Capt. Tho. Draper	
York	Capt. Francis Bateson★	Sir James Pennyman	Sir William Pennyman, F.
York	Capt. John Jackson		
York	Capt. Anthony Norton★		

(A large bracket labelled "Feilding, F." spans the Feilding / Lord Astley entries on the right.)

York	Capt. John Sympson*		Ensign. Capt. Will. Wyvell.
Durham	Lieut. John Eggleston*	Capt. ((Sir) William) Mallory	
Durham	Ens. James Corpes	Lt. Col. George Symms.	
York	Lieut. James Storre	{ Sir William Pennyman / Capt. Blakeston	
L & W	Lieut. Anthony Tatham	Capt. Humphry Elmes	
L & W	Lieut. Allen Sartan*		
Salop	Ens. James Read	Capt. (Francis) Lawson	
L & W	Col. Sir Horatio Cary	Prince Rupert, H. Major? Sir William Waller, H. Changed sides, 1643.	
L & W	Capt. & QMG Clement Martin		Lieut.
?Wilts	Q.M. Rob. Thatcham	Capt. Clement Martin	
?Southam	Cornet Edmond Hooke or	} Sir Thomas Dallison	
York	Cornet Jeremy Bower		
?L & W	Q.M. Will. Montgomery	Lifeguard	
?L & W	Q.M. John Field	Col. Will. Legge	
Denbigh	Capt. Nanny Floyd	Sir Thomas Salusbury, F.	
Denbigh	Lieut. Matthew Broughton		
?Oxon.	Lieut. Matthew Jones		
Denbigh	Ensign Hugh Daulben	Capt. Daulben	
?Glam.	Lieut. Thomas Thomas	{ Sir Edward Stradling / Maj. Carne	Edward Stradling, F.
Carm.	Lieut. John Read	Capt. Hopkins Dawkins	
Carm.	Lieut. Rob. Mansel	{ John Stradling / Lt. Col. Thomas Stradling	
Carm	Lieut. Edw. Mansel	Maj. Thomas Bushy	
L & W	Capt. Theod. Humphreys	Usher, D.	
?L & W	Lieut. Nicholas Watson	{ Henry Washington / Maj. Morrison	[Grandison, H.
Middlesex	Lieut. John Trussell	{ Sir Richard Willys, H. / Maj. (Richard) / Hatton	[Gent. Volunteer.
L & W	Lt. Col. Paul Smith	Wilmot, H.	Major
L & W	Capt. Edward Panton		Lieut. Lt. Col. Edward Feilding.
?L & W	Major John Beversham	Frescheville, H.	Gent. Volunteer Frescheville's troop. [Wilmot, H.
L & W	Col. Sir. Robert Walsh	Prince Rupert, H. Capt.-Lieut.	

A List of [*Indigent*] *Officers,* 1663, contains the names of some 7,000 Royalist officers, and it cannot be claimed that all those who fought at Edgehill have been included here. On the other hand those mentioned elsewhere in this work obviously were present. The only others included are those whose presence may be deduced from such clues as the counties where they resided and the commanders with whom they were associated. *A List of* [*Indigent*] *Officers* has to be used with some caution, since officers claiming naturally used the highest rank they attained, but often appear in the list under their *first* commanding officer. The officers of *both* Earls of Lindsey are listed together, there being no separate lists for the Lifeguard, F., and the Lord General's, F. But despite the pitfalls the list is a most valuable guide to the regimental history of the Royalist army, and is particularly useful because it indicates the territorial connections of the various regiments. It is interesting, for example, to see that Pennyman's Regiment, which Symonds and Clarendon tell us came from Yorkshire, had a number of officers from Durham.

Indigence was all too commonly the lot of the old Cavalier, but it was not universal. A number of former Royalist officers found employment in the army of King Charles II. The establishment of 1661 was very small and Royalist officers were glad enough to serve as troopers in the Lifeguard or to trail a pike in the Foot Guards.[14]

An inspection of the Army Lists of King Charles II and King James II shows the names of a number of Edgehill men:

The Duke of York.	Governor of Portsmouth.	1661.
Prince Rupert	Admiral of the White.	1665.
	Constable of Windsor Castle.	1668.
	Vice-Admiral of England.	1672.
	Colonel, Barbados Regiment, D.	1672.
	Colonel, Marine Regiment, F.	1672.
	General on Sea and Land.	1673.
	First Lord of the Admiralty.	1673–79.
Lord Charles Gerard	Captain. Lifeguard.	1661.
	Captain, H.	1666.
	Colonel, H.	1678.
Lord Belasyse	Governor of Hull and the Block Houses.	1661.
	Colonel, F.	1673.
Earl of Northampton (1622–1681)	Captain, H.	1666.
Maj.-Gen. Randolph Egerton	Lieutenant, Lifeguard.	1661.
	Captain, H.	1666.
	Still Lieut. and Lt. Col. in Lifeguard	1679.

ROYALIST COLONELS

John Frescheville	Captain, Royal Regiment, H. (The Blues)	1661.
John Russell	Colonel, H.M. Own Regiment. (F) (Grenadier Guards)	1661.

Henry Washington	Major (Grenadier Guards)	1661.
Edward Grey	Captain (Grenadier Guards)	1661.
Will. Legge	Captain, Tower of London	1661.
(?) Sir Francis Cobbe	Captain, Hull	1661.
Edward Villiers (d. 1689)	Governor of Tynmouth Castle	1661.
	Lt. Colonel, Earl of Ogle, F.	1667.
	Colonel, F.	1678.
	Lieut. and Lt. Colonel, King's own Troop of Guards.	1679.
William Pretty	Lieutenant, H. Colonel Charles Wheeler's Troop.	1666.
Lord Byron (1605–1679)	Captain, H.	1666.
Earl of Lindsey (1608–1666)	Captain, H.	1666.
Sir Theophilus Gilby	Major, Earl of Chesterfield, F.	1667.
Sir Allen Apsley, (d. 1683)	Colonel, F.	1667.
John Lane (d. 1667)	Colonel, F.	1667.
Roger Whitley (1618–1697)	Quartermaster-General	1667.
Sir Herbert Lunsford	Captain, Holland Regt. F. (Plymouth)	1670.
Ralph Hebberne	Captain, Barbados, D.	1672.
	Lt. Colonel, Prince Rupert, D.	1678.

ROYALIST LT. COLONELS

Daniel O'Neale	Captain, His Majesty's Own Troop.	
	Royal Regiment, H.	1661.
Sir Charles Compton	Captain, Royal Regiment, H.	1661.
Thomas Daniel	Captain, H.M. Own Regiment, F.	1661.
Sir William Compton	Captain, F. Tower of London	1661.
Sir Adrian Scroope	Captain, Earl of Cleveland, H	1662.
Henry Norwood	Lt. Colonel, Lord Rutherford, F. Dunkirk	1662.
	Colonel, F. Tangier 1664.	
	Lt. Governor, Tangier 1666.	
Sir William Leighton	Captain, H.M. Own Regiment, F.	1664–1665
Sir Paul Smith	Lieutenant, Duke of Richmond's Troop, H.	1666.
Alex. Standish	Lieutenant, Earl of Peterborough's Troop, H.	1666.
Guy Molesworth	Major, Lord Alington, F.	1667.
Thomas Coningsby	Major, Lord Vaughan's Regt. F.	1673.
	Lt. Colonel, Sir Lionel Walden's Regt. F.	1678.
Thomas Stradling	Colonel, F.	1678.

ROYALIST MAJORS

Timothy Blencow	Lieut. Captain, Robert Legge's Company, Portsmouth	1661.
Flamock Colborne	Q.M., Sir Charles Compton's Troop,	
	Royal Regiment, H.	1661★
Robert Walters	Captain, King's Regt. of Guards, Dunkirk	1661.
Philip Honywood	Captain, H.M. Own Regt. F.	1661.

ROYALIST CAPTAINS

Valentine Pine (1603–1677)	Lieut. Capt., Will. Legge's Company,	
	Tower of London	1661.
Martin Frobisher	Ensign, Hull	1661.
Sir William Killigrew (1605–1695)	Colonel, F.	1662.
William Sheldon	Captain, Sir William Killigrew's Regiment, F.	1662.
Thomas Willoughby	Lieut., Earl of Northampton's Troop	1666.

Charles Fox	Captain, Lord Morpeth's Regt. F.	1678.
Sir Bernard de Gomme		
(1620–1685)	QMG., H.	1672.
	Surveyor General, Ordnance	1685.

GENTLEMAN PENSIONER

Sir Henry Wroth	Captain, Royal Regiment, H.	1661.

GENTLEMAN VOLUNTEER

Robert Dongan	Lieut., Duke of York's Life Guard	1661.

CHAPLAIN

Dr. Matthew Smallwood, D.D.	H.M. Own Life Guard	1661.

SURGEON

Thomas Woodall	H.M. Own Life Guard	1661[15]

In 1660 the Gentlemen Pensioners consisted largely of former Cavaliers. In October of that year 25 of them 'who did personally and really attend' the King at Oxford and elsewhere, signed a petition to King Charles II. They included Lord Grandison, brother of the man who commanded a regiment at Edgehill. He had been a captain in Rupert's Regiment of Horse at Newark (1644) and it is most unlikely that he was not in the Royalist army from the outset. Sir John Walpole, Cornet of Charles I's Lifeguard, was another. He was Standard Bearer of the Pensioners in 1669. Captain Clement Martin, who led the patrol on the eve of Edgehill, and Miles Mathews, who had distinguished himself in the battle, were also signatories; and so was Philip Honywood (Grandison's Regiment). Sir Lewis Kirke was another who was almost certainly with the King in 1642.[16]

According to John Aubrey, Sir William Neale (1609–1691), whom he describes as being a great plunderer but dying penitent, was the last surviving field officer of King Charles I's army; but he is certainly mistaken. Sir Henry Newton (alias Puckering) (1618–1701), who was in the Lifeguard, H, at Edgehill outlived Neale by 10 years. He was Lieutenant-Colonel successively to Lord Capel, Marcus Trevor, and the Prince of Wales. William Beaw, major and later a bishop, did not die until 1705.

Perhaps the last survivor of the battle was William Hasland, who, at the age of 111, was granted a Chelsea pension of a shilling a day on 15 February 1731. He had not only fought at Edgehill, but with King William III in Flanders! According to the *London Daily Post* of 19 July 1736, an old Cavalier aged 123 was still living at Ribchester, Lancashire. He had had two horses shot under him at Edgehill, and had been wounded in the arm. Unfortunately his name is not given in this account

but it would seem to be William Walker of Alston. He was buried at
Ribchester on 16 January 1736, aged 122. There is a painting of Walker
in Tabley Hall, Cheshire, which shows him wearing 'his own hair; large
beard; great coat; with a walking stick in his left hand'. (*History of Ribchester*
by Tom C. Smith and Rev. J. Shorlt, 1890.)[17]

THE PARLIAMENTARIANS

From 1642 to 1644 the Earl of Essex's was the main Parliamentarian army.
Several of his regiments did not survive very long. Mandeville's and
Wharton's were soon disbanded perhaps because of their misconduct at
Edgehill, though others that did as badly served on. St. John's was lost at
Banbury, and Holles' at Brentford. Stamford's remained in the West,
where Merrick's soon went also. Fairfax's was sent to join Lord Fairfax
in Yorkshire (December 1642), Lord Brooke's went with its commander
to besiege Lichfield, and disappears soon after the death of its commander
in March 1643.

The formation of the army of the Eastern Association under the Earl
of Manchester (formerly Lord Mandeville) robbed Essex of some of his
best cavalrymen: Cromwell, Ireton, Fleetwood, Whalley, Desborough
and Berry. It is true that they were as yet young soldiers, but all were
soon to make their mark. By March 1643 Lord Willoughby of Parham
was commanding the Parliamentarian forces in Lincolnshire.

Waller took other officers of note, among them Sir Arthur Hesilrige;
Robert Burrill, who was to become a colonel; Horatio Carew; Edward
Kightley and Edmund Ludlow, who was soon to become a major and to
distinguish himself by his stubborn defence of Wardour Castle.

The Royalist cavalry had already shown their superiority. It is to the
credit of Sir William Balfour that, despite such losses as these, he was
eventually able to get some good work out of Essex's cavalry, notably at
Cheriton and in the escape from Lostwithiel (1644). There was no
repetition of the panic flights of Powick Bridge and Edgehill. If the
Roundhead cavalry suffered at Chalgrove and I Newbury, it was not for
lack of fighting spirit.

The capture of Reading, the relief of Gloucester, the two battles of
Newbury, Cheriton[18] and Lostwithiel were the chief actions in which
Essex's army was engaged.

The New Model Army, formed early in 1645, was an amalgamation
of the armies of Essex, Manchester and Waller. Essex's army, reduced on
5 May, contributed enough cavalry to form Fairfax's Lifeguard under
Charles D'Oyley, and the three regiments of Richard Graves, Sir Robert
Pye (d. 1701), and Thomas Sheffield. It also contributed 3,048 foot for

the regiments of Edward Harley, Walter Lloyd (k. 1645), Richard Ingoldsby and Richard Fortescue.[19]

All these commanders had received fairly rapid advancement. Of those who came from Essex's army, Pye, Sheffield, Lloyd and Ingoldsby, had been captains, while Charles D'Oyley had been nothing more than a gentleman volunteer in Essex's Lifeguard. Five lieutenant-colonels and five majors from Essex's army went into the New Model. Of these only two of the former seem to have been officers in the Edgehill army. These were Robert Farringdon and Jo. Francis, captains under Hampden and Holles respectively. This is evidence of a heavy turnover of officers in the main Parliamentarian army, but it is difficult to say whether this should be attributed to battle casualties or other causes.

Morbus campestris, a pestilential fever, perhaps typhus or typhoid fever, ravaged Essex's army in the summer of 1643, but this is thought to have afflicted the rank and file, crowded together in filthy quarters, rather than the officers.

Records of Parliamentarian losses are woefully defective. Among those killed or mortally wounded in action were:

	1642	
Lt. Colonel James Quarles	Brentford	12 Nov.
Captain Richard Lacey	Brentford	12 Nov.
	1643	
Colonel Lord Brooke	Lichfield	2 Mar.
Captain Edward Kightley	Chewton Mendip	10 June
Colonel John Hampden	Chalgrove Field	18 June
Major John Gunter	Chalgrove Field	18 June
Captain James Harcus	Gloucester	15 Aug.
Lt. Col. John Bamfield	I Newbury	20 Sept.
	1644	
Captain Valentine Walton[21]	Marston Moor	2 July
Colonel Sir William Fairfax	Montgomery Castle	27 Oct.
Lt. Col. Theodore Palaeologus	II Newbury	27 Oct.
	1645	
Colonel Walter Lloyd	Taunton	May
Sir John Meldrum	Scarborough Castle	21 July

A number of the officers of Essex's army changed sides, including:

The Earl of Bedford
The Earl of Peterborough
Lt. Colonel Sir Faithfull Fortescue
Lt. Colonel Edward Massey
Lt. Colonel Joseph Wagstaffe
Major Owen Parry
Major John Urry (three times!)

Major Horatio Carew
Captain (Major?) William Pretty
Lieut. Jo. Balstone

Massey, Wagstaffe and Urry were all major-generals in the Royalist army; Fortescue, Carew and Pretty became colonels; Parry was a lieutenant-colonel and Balstone, a major. Massey did not change sides until his impeachment by the army in 1647.

Several were dismissed for their failures in action, whether real or imagined.

Philibert Emanuel Du Boys, was quickly dismissed for his inefficiency in organizing Essex's Train of Artillery. Ballard's services were dispensed with soon after his repulse at Newark (1643). Nathaniel Fiennes, promoted colonel and made Governor of Bristol, was condemned to death for surrendering the city to Prince Rupert in July 1643. Captain Hercules Langrish, who had become Fiennes' major, was also held to have failed at Bristol.

The Self-Denying Ordinance put an end to the employment of Members of Parliament in the army, with the notable exception of Oliver Cromwell, who, having risen from captain to lieutenant-general in less than a year, remained as second-in-command to Sir Thomas Fairfax. This measure deprived Sir Samuel Luke and others of their commands, but was not, it seems, particularly unpopular.

The New Model put an end to the military career of Colonel Edward Aldrich. In 1642 he had been Lord Rochford's lieutenant-colonel. Essex praised his fidelity in rejecting Sir John Byron's overtures to betray Aylesbury to the Cavaliers (October 1643). He fought afterwards in Cornwall. On 28 March 1645 he wrote to Sir Thomas Fairfax objecting to changes in the list of officers he had nominated for his regiment in the New Model. 'I shall humbly desyre', he wrote, '(though my resolutions be to proceed) to desist rather then engage with dishonor, which of necessitie must followe.' This stand cost him his command.[22]

Charles D'Oyley took the wrong side in the struggle between army and Parliament (1647), and was dismissed. He set forth his services and misfortunes in a petition to the House of Commons (27 December 1647):

'Before these unhappy wars petitioner was a student at Oxford, but being obliged to fly thence, was plundered of his whole study of books, and other things of some value; since that time he has faithfully served Parliament in arms, and has been many times dangerously wounded, by which his health and constitution, formerly strong and sound, have been so greatly impaired, as to render him not only unfit for study, but for any hard service. He has himself suffered great cruelty as a prisoner of war, and has been plundered to his shirt. But in all his service no man can say that he has violated any man's estate or person, but he has been content with his pay, and most times without it; he has contributed his mite for Ireland, and would have gone there himself (though unfit) might he have had his regiment with him. The House formerly appointed him governor of Bristol, from which place he has, however, been suspended after having spent much in providing himself for it, so that, instead of being the better, he is two or three hundred pounds the worse.'[23]

There was already a rift in the Parliamentarian ranks by 1644. In Essex's army of 1642 the Presbyterians were probably a more influential group than the Independents. The latter, including notably Cromwell and Ireton, got the upper hand in Manchester's army. In the New Model of 1645 the Independents were all-powerful.

The gradual increase of Cromwell's power marked by such landmarks as Pride's Purge, the execution of the King, and the rule of the major-generals, left his government ever more narrow-based. There were Presbyterians who hated him as cordially as any Cavalier did. Much as he would like to have governed by democratic means, he was compelled to rule by force if only because his power lay in the army.

The men who were to be Cromwell's chief instruments were obscure enough in 1642. Henry Ireton (1611–1651), who became Cromwell's deputy in Ireland, was merely a captain at Edgehill. Cromwell's cousin, Edward Whalley (d. c. 1675) was a cornet, and his brother-in-law, the 'grim Gyant' John Desborough (1608–1680), was only his quartermaster at Edgehill, while John Berry was but a trooper. All three were to become major-generals.

Edmund Ludlow (1617?–1692) and Charles Fleetwood (d. 1692), both of whom were to be commander-in-chief in Ireland, were only gentlemen of Essex's Lifeguard in 1642. Rapid promotion came to others also. Quartermaster John Okey was a colonel of dragoons in the New Model. Horton, formerly Sir Arthur Hesilrige's falconer, was a colonel by 1643.

Of the 59 regicides, or commissioners who actually signed the death warrant of King Charles I, at least 15 had served in Essex's army of 1642, mostly as relatively junior officers:

Colonel Sir William Constable	(d. 1655)
Captain Richard Ingoldsby	(d. 1685)
Captain Lord Grey of Groby	(1623?–1657)
Captain James Temple	(d. 1668)
Captain John Alured	(1607–1659)
Captain Adrian Scroope	(1601–1660)
Captain Henry Ireton	(1611–1651)

Captain Oliver Cromwell	(1599–1658)
Captain Valentine Walton	(d. 1661)
Cornet Rob. Lilburne, Lord Brooke's troop	(1613–1665)
Cornet Thomas Horton, Hesilrige's troop	(d. 1649)
Cornet Edward Whalley, John Fiennes' troop	(d. c. 1675)
Quartermaster John Okey, Lord Brooke's troop	(d. 1662)
Edmund Ludlow, Gentleman Volunteer, Essex's Lifeguard	(1617?–1692)
Thomas Harrison	(c. 1618–1660)

In addition Colonel John Venn (1586–1650), the Governor of Windsor Castle, was a regicide. It is odd that with three exceptions this group had all served in the horse, which might be evidence that the mounted arm was officered by men more politically active than the foot, though the sample is too small to prove much.

At the Restoration Scroope, Harrison and Okey were executed, and Lilburne, condemned to lifelong imprisonment, ended his days in durance. Temple only escaped execution by producing evidence against his former colleagues. Whalley, Walton and Ludlow died in exile. Of Oliver's cousin, Richard Cromwell said to a group of officers in 1659: 'Here is Dick Ingoldsby, who can neither pray nor preach, and yet I will trust him before ye all'. Yet Colonel Ingoldsby was no simpleton. He suppressed Lambert's rising in 1659, and in 1661 not only obtained a pardon, but was created a K.B.!

A few of Essex's old officers found employment in the army of King Charles II, having changed sides during the war or helped to bring about the Restoration:

The Earl of Manchester (1602–1671)	Colonel, F., 1667.
The Earl of Peterborough	Governor of Tangier, 1662–3. Colonel, F., 1673. Colonel, H., 1678.
Earl of Denbigh (formerly Lord Feilding) (d. 1685)	Captain, H., 1667.
Captain William Pretty	Lieut. Sir Charles Wheeler's Troop, H., 1666.
Captain John Mill	Major, Col. Richard Norton, F., 1667.
Cornet (later Col.) Miles Morgan	Q.M. Duke of Richmond's troop, 1666.

If the Royalist army can claim the oldest named survivor of the battle, William Hasland, it seems that the only known female victim of the fight was a Parliamentarian. The Parish Register of Little Brickhill, not far from the route which Essex took on his march back from Warwick to London, includes under 30 November 1642: 'Agnes Potter, wounded at the battell of Edgehill was buryed.'[25] Perhaps she got her wound in the streets of Kineton when the Cavalier troopers were plundering the baggage train.

1 Wiltshire Quarter Sessions Records.

2 Sheldon's death was due to the accidental explosion of a Royalist ammunition waggon on the day after the battle of Lansdowne. The incident is described by Captain Richard Atkyns in his *Vindication*.

3 Busy, who was killed during the preliminary bombardment, is described as 'our skilful cannoneer,' . . . (Warburton, Vol. II, p. 246).

4 Killed when the royal army was on the march from Newark to Oxford (Dodd).

5 Vavasour was serving with the Swedish army when he was killed (Money, p. 76).

6 Lloyd.

7 Clay.

8 British Museum. Additional MSS. 14294.

9 Bulstrode.

10 The Camden Miscellany, Vol. IV, 1859. 'Sir Edward Lake's Interview with Charles I', p. 16.

11 Clarendon, Vol. II, p. 373.

12 Petition. The Hague, 8 May 1660. He begged for the mastership of tents, which his father and grandfather had for above 100 years. (SP. 29/2.f.175.1660). He appears in 'A List of [Indigent] Officers' as a Lieutenant to Captain Matthew Gore under Lord Astley, which means that at Edgehill he was in the regiment of Astley's predecessor, Richard Feilding.

13 PRO. 31/8/197,f.206.

14 Captain John Gwyn served as a gentleman trooper in the Lifeguard (Memoirs). Lieutenant Robert Wright (Northampton, F.) trailed a pike under Colonel John Russell in the regiment that is now the Grenadier Guards. (Middlesex QSR, 1676).

15 C. Dalton, English Army Lists and Commission Registers.

16 PRO. SP. 29/102,f.181. October 1660.
'The humble Peticon of such of yo[r] Maj[tie] Gentlemen Penconers in Ordinary who did personally and really attend your Maj[tie] at Oxford and elsewhere. Grandison, John Skrymshire, Charles Skrymshire, Henry Brownkard, Tho. Dorrill, [Sir] John Walpole, Edward Herbert, John Bennett, Ralph Clapham, Reginald Forster, Henry Gibbons, W[m]. Cony. [Sir] L[ewis] Kirke, C[lement] Martin, Bartholomew Jukes, Tho: Hales, Edward Brooke, Jo: Raymond, Thomas Rowe, John Cranfield, [Sir] Ellis Hickes, [Sir] Ed[ward] Brett, P[hilip] Honywood, Miles Mathews, William Sheldon.'

17 The Hon. J. W. Fortescue, A History of the British Army, Vol. II, p. 54, fn.

18 Some 2,000 of Essex's cavalry under Sir William Balfour reinforced Waller shortly before Cheriton.

19 See Godfrey Davies, Essex's Army, and Firth and Davies for these details.

20 Davies, Essex's Army, p. 43.

21 'A gallant young man, exceeding gracious', wrote Cromwell, and 'exceedingly beloved in the army of all that knew him,' . . . He died lamenting that God had not suffered him to be any more 'the executioner of his enemies,' . . .

22 Firth and Davies, Vol. I, p. 384.

23 *Ibid.*, p. 47.

24 It may be that we should add William Goffe (d. 1679?) to this list. Apprenticed to a London salter, he was imprisoned in 1642 by the Royalist Lord Mayor of London for promoting a petition in support of Parliament's claim to the militia. In 1645 he was a captain in Edward Harley's Regiment in the New Model Army, and we must, therefore, assume that his military career began some time earlier. As well as a regicide

he was major-general for Berkshire, Sussex and Hampshire. He escaped in 1660 and lived at Hadley, Massachusetts, with Whalley, who was his father-in-law. Tradition credits him with saving Hadley from an attack by Indians. Sallying forth from his hiding-place, the old Roundhead rallied the panic-stricken settlers and saved them from destruction (D.N.B.)

25 Lt. Colonel Wyness. Article on Little Brickhill in North Bucks Times, Sept.–Dec. 1933.

17

Of Apparitions

'Shall I strike at it with my partisan?'
William Shakespeare, Hamlet,
Prince of Denmark, Act I, Scene I

THREE MONTHS AFTER the battle of Edgehill, Thomas Jackson, a London printer, published a pamphlet entitled 'A Great Wonder in Heaven Shewing The Late Apparitions and prodigious noyes of War and Battels, seen on Edge-Hill near Keinton in Warwickshire.'[1]

This was followed within a few days by 'The New Yeares Wonder. Being A most certaine and true Relation of the disturbed inhabitants of Kenton . . . in which place is heard & seene fearfull and strange apparitions of spirits . . . '[2]

The first of these pamphlets, after pointing out that King John had fought a battle with his barons at Edgehill, describes how 'On Saturday – which was in Christmas time, between 12 and 1 o'clock in the morning', some shepherds, countrymen and travellers had heard 'First, the sound of drums afar off, and the noise of soldiers, as it were giving out their last groans;'. The spectres went on to re-fight the battle and 'the King's forces seemed at first to have the best, but afterwards they were put into apparant rout'. After three hours the 'poor men, glad that they were gone that had so long stayed them there against their wills, made with all haste to Kineton', where they knocked up William Wood, Esq., a J.P., who called up his neighbour Mr. Samuel Marshall the minister,[3] and related what they had seen, and 'averred it upon their oathes to be true'.

The next night, the Sunday before Christmas, Mr. Wood, Mr. Marshall and other substantial inhabitants of the neighbourhood went out and themselves saw the 'adverse armies, fighting with as much spite and spleen as formerly'. Terrified, they withdrew to their houses 'beseeching God to defend them from those hellish and prodigious enemies'. It was not until the next Saturday that the apparitions returned, fighting 'with far greater tumult . . . for four hours, or very near . . . '

Mr. Wood and others whose faith 'was not strong enough to carry them out against these delusions' now forsook their habitations. Mr.

Marshall, however, was made of sterner stuff and after observing the same phenomena the following Saturday and Sunday, went to Oxford and informed the King 'of all the aforesaid proceedings of the spirits'.[4]

'The New Yeares Wonder' tells of much the same apparitions adding the story of a troop of horse that came posting up to three countrymen full speed, and coming near them 'of a sudaine sunke into the earth which turned to their more greater feare and amaizement then at there first advancing'.

The pamphlet, with admirable precision, tells us that on 4 January (1642/3) some herdsmen who had seen these apparitions were jeered at in Kineton. But in the middle of the night the townsmen being abed were woken when 'the dolfull and hydious groanes of dying men were heard crying revenge and some againe to ease them of their paine by friendly killing them . . . ' The noise of drums and trumpets sounded a sudden alarm 'as if an enimye had entred in their towne to put them to a sudaine exicution and plunder all their estates'.

Some hid in corners, others 'lay sweating and halfe smothered in their beds, . . . ' The few bold enough to peer out of the windows saw 'armed horsemen riding one againe the other and so vanisht all'.

Many women miscarried and the stoutest hearted men confessed they had feared death.

Next night the townsmen set a strong watch, and once again a battle was seen in the sky.

It was suggested by some learned men that there might be carcasses as yet unburied, and, a diligent search being made, this was found to be so. The implication is that the apparitions ceased when these victims of the battle had received Christian burial.

The King, on hearing Mr. Marshall's story, sent Colonel Lewis Kirke, Captains Dudley and Wainman or Winman and three other gentlemen of credit, to investigate. They too saw the apparitions, recognizing divers of the slain, and by name, Sir Edmund Verney. 'A Great Wonder in Heaven' ends:

'What this doth portend, God only knoweth, and time perhaps will discover, but doubtless it is a sign of his wrath against this land, for these civil wars, which he in His good time finish, and send a sudden peace between His Majesty and Parliament.'

The 'New Yeares Wonder' is openly partisan in its conclusion . . .

' . . . the Lord in His mercy enlighten his Maiestys heart, that those eveill councelares which are about him may be put ever far from him and that wee may have peace. Amen.'

The Edgehill ghosts have not ceased to exercise their influence on succeeding generations of visitors to the battlefield. Miss B. M. Seaton, formerly matron at Uppingham School, relates that she had a very old uncle, born just after the Crimean War, who died aged 89. 'He always told us when we were children of the battle being fought again by the "ghosts".' When he was a boy (presumably in the 1860s or thereabouts), he went with a group of newspaper reporters to Edgehill. 'He said he stayed behind but several went towards the "ridge" . . . ' where the army could be seen on the sky line. Whatever upset them he did not know but *something* did, because they all returned – shaking & frightened & went off home as fast as they could . . . ' Her uncle said that one man told him that they had heard the 'clash of weapons'.[5]

In more recent times visitors have experienced the strange psychic aura of Edgehill. The international concert pianist, Michaeli, relates that since he was a child he had always cherished a strange longing to visit the site. His family, the Woollards of Suffolk, can trace their ancestry back to the 11th century, but apart from a sense of history natural in a family long established in one place, he is at a loss to account for this longing, beyond the fact that his father had told him that the battle was one of the outstanding events in British history. In June 1960 he visited the field with two close friends, one being a former Army officer. After lunching at Banbury they lost their way and

' . . . having no means of discovering precisely where we were, I asked my friends to stop for a few minutes. Getting out of the car I looked around me, and by some strange instinct, which seemed to come from the past, I was able to direct them to the site correctly, which then lay some two miles away from our stopping position.

As we went along the countryside, I became conscious of the fact that all the scenery was familiar to me, although I have never visited that part of the country before, and I mentioned this odd fact to my companions, who appeared to take it all with a "pinch of salt". Nevertheless, we arrived in due course, and I took myself off to a house on the site occupied by soldiers on guard. I would mention that I had no idea that I would find the site occupied by the military, having made no enquiries before I left London.

I explained briefly to the Officer in Charge that I had travelled from London to fulfil a life-time desire to visit the site, and having no permit, begged to be allowed to do so, which he most kindly allowed us to do. We were accompanied by two soldiers with tracker dogs.

As we approached a lane on the site, near to a place where Cavaliers and Roundheads are buried together, I became very disturbed, for I was aware that hundreds of unseen men were watching me. My agitation must have been quickly noted by my two friends who asked me why I looked so unwell and frightened, but all that I remember saying was that I wished to return home immediately.

On my return to my house in London that evening, unaccompanied by my companions, I was aware of a most terrifying fact, which was that I had brought back with me one of the dead from the battlefield.

At this point I would like to explain to the reader, that I am not an adherent of spiritualism, which I find most unnerving, and although as an artist, I may, like most, live on a somewhat tauter plane of emotion, these must be controlled to the maximum, particularly when performing in public.

This unseen but very evident visitor, was, I knew, beside me everywhere I went in my house, and remained with me for about a month after. In my mind I would see a man, clad in the period; and I would describe him as a Roundhead, for he wore armour, and had a small moustache, with deep piercing eyes, and carried a sword. His presence in my house, caused me such alarm, being as I was, alone, that I soon became highly nervous and unwell, and at night I left lights burning in all my rooms until morning came, when I felt less uneasy with the coming of daylight. This man, whoever he was, remained as I have said, for about a month, and then left me as suddenly as he had appeared, but the fact that I developed during his stay a highly nervous disposition is vouched for by those who knew me at that time.

I had heard of a society, namely The Society for Psychic Research, who dealt with such matters and I felt bound to write to them about my experiences, both on the battlefield, and in my home, seeking their help, and they kindly replied to the effect that although they had many records relating to psychic phenomena on Edgehill, they had no parallel in their records such as my own, and suggested that I should allow them to publish the facts which I had given them . . .

Were the events which I experienced a memory transmitted through my family generation by generation until it transplanted itself so firmly in my mind that I was forced to revisit an ancestor's battlefield, or is there such a thing as reincarnation? I do not know. All that I can state with truth, is that these events took place in my life, that I recognised the countryside and the site, was conscious of being watched by many hundreds of unseen eyes and that I brought back with me, one whose intentions were obviously unkind towards me. These things will remain with me as the most terrifying experience in my life, and will be remembered by me to the end of my days.'[6]

The present writer has visited Edgehill many times since the late '30s, without encountering a single spectre. Yet England has no more haunted battlefield than that which lies in the Vale of the Red Horse.

1 B.M. Thomason Tracts. E.85 (41).
2 *Ibid.* E.86 (23).
3 'The New Yeares Wonder' supplies their Christian names.
4 'The New Yeares Wonder'.
5 Letter of 4 November 1966 in the Author's possession.
6 Statement of 15 November 1966 by Michael Howard Romney-Woollard, in the Author's possession.

PART THREE

SECTION I

Documents Illustrating the Organization and Composition of the Royalist Army

1. ROMAN CATHOLIC OFFICERS

On 11 December 1640 a number of officers had been dismissed from the army raised against the Scots, because they were Roman Catholics:[1]

	Horse	Foot
Colonels	–	1
Lt. Colonels	–	2
Majors	1	2
Captains	2	10
Lieutenants	3	13
Cornets	6	–
Ensigns	–	13
Quartermasters	2	1
Sergeants	–	12
Corporals	3	–
	17	54

Of these 71 officers 26, if not more, seem to have served the King during the Civil Wars. These were:

Colonel Sir Arthur Aston,★	Sergeant-Major-General, D.
Lt. Colonel Thomas Howard	Colonel, H.
Major (Francis) Trafford	Colonel, H.
Major Sir John Beaumont★	Colonel, F.
Major Roger Powell (d.1644)	Lt. Colonel.
Captain Sir John Digby	Sergeant-Major-General, H.
Captain William Courtney★	Lt. Colonel, F. Possibly a knight and a colonel. Major to Sir John Beaumont at Edgehill.
Captain James Thomson	Possibly Lt. Colonel, F., to Sir Arthur Aston, H.
Captain Charles Gilmore	Major, F., 12 Jan. 1643, to Colonel Robert Ellice.
Captain Edward Drury	Colonel, D.
Captain Richard Poore or Power (k.1645)	Colonel Sir Richard Poore. Governor of Berkeley Castle.
Lieut. Troilus Turbervile★ (k.1645)	Captain-Lieutenant, Lifeguard, H. Knighted. Probably at Edgehill.

Lieutenant James Trist★	Dutch. Captain, Prince of Wales' Regiment, H. Probably at Edgehill. Rose to be a major.
Lieutenant Barnaby Bradford	Captain, Colonel Sir Henry Lingen, F. I.O. Hereford.
Lieutenant Thomas Throgmorton★	Probably captain, Colonel Richard Bolle, F.
Lieutenant William Molineux	Lieutenant in Colonel Sir Henry Lingen's Regiment, F. I.O. Hereford.
Lieutenant William Greene★	Rose to be Captain, Lifeguard, F. I.O. L & W
Lieutenant William Evers	A Captain and a Major Evers in the Royalist Army.
Lieutenant Edward Huddlestone	Major, F. to Colonel Edward Grey. In defence of Pontefract Castle.
Lieutenant Charles Kirke★	Captain, F. in Sir Ralph Dutton's Regiment and major to his successor, (Sir) Stephen Hawkins.
Ensign William Blunt	Two officers of this name, one being major of the Queen's Lifeguard, F., and the other a captain in the Prince of Wales', H.
Ensign Peregrine Tasberrowe (Tasburgh)	Captain, F., Marquis of Winchester. In garrison of Basing House. I.O. L & W., but really from Hampshire.
Ensign Thomas Crathorne	Captain, H., Sir Robert Clavering, and major to his successor, John Forcer, PW Malpas (26 Aug. 1644) and Sherburn-in-Elmet (15 Oct. 1645).
Ensign Francis Godfrey★	Captain, F., to John Belasyse, and later Lt. Colonel, F., to Sir Theophilus Gilby, his successor. P.W. Naseby.
Ensign Robert Skirrow★	Lieutenant, 30 Oct. 1642 in Colonel Richard Bolle's Regiment. Captain by 23 May 1643. P.W. Naseby Major at Colchester. 1648. P.W. I.O. L&W.
Ensign William Moore★	Probably the Captain William Moore who was buried at Oxford on 22 Feb. 1643.

Those marked with an asterisk★ were at Edgehill or belonged to regiments present there.

2. A TROOPER'S RATIONS

YORK. 4 AUGUST 1641. (Lt. General) Sir John Conyers to Captain John Mennes, commanding Commissary-General Henry Wilmot's Regiment of Horse. Orders a rendezvous to meet the King near Doncaster.

'It will be requisite, when they do march, that every trooper carry behind him in his oat sack three or four baits of oats or bread for his horse, and provision for himself, for some of them will be more than 24 hours from their quarters; and in the meantime let them feed their horses as well as they can, and put their equipage in good order that they may not be ashamed to be seen. And when they march let them have ammuntion delivered to them.'[2]

3. SUPPORT FOR THE KING

YORK. 20 JULY 1642. Secretary Nicholas to Sir Thomas Roe.

'The county of Lincoln has shewed itself beyond all expectation affectionate and ready to serve the King, in token whereof they will levy and defray 400 horse and horsemen, to be commanded as the King shall direct. They are upon raising of them, and the King has appointed four captains over them, gentlemen of the same county and estated therein.'

'The University of Oxford has voluntarily sent in 10,000L. to the King, and that of Cambridge a fair proportion also.'[3]

BEVERLEY. 27 JULY 1642. Secretary Nicholas to Sir Thomas Roe.

Nicholas describes the King's good reception by the gentry of Leicestershire the previous week.

'The (county) magazine, awhile since conveyed from Leicester by the Earl of Stamford to his house, was delivered up to the King on Monday, and then distributed into confidential hands.'

'Likewise a subscription of the county of Leicester to raise and maintain at their own charge six-score horse and horsemen, and sixscore more will be added by such gentlemen and others well-affected to his Majesty as could not be present at Leicester during his stay; . . .'[4]

NOTTINGHAM. 13 SEPTEMBER 1642. Sir Edward Nicholas to Sir Thomas Roe.

'The King is this day setting forth with his army, which marches to Derby this night and from thence by easy marches we shall go to Chester or Shrewsbury to join with 5,000 foot and 400 horse, which are raised for the King in Wales and the Borders. The King's army is much increased within these eight days, and near 2,000 arms have been hither brought in from this and adjacent counties. The Earl of Essex is at Northampton, where the soldiers mutiny every day and run away as fast as they can get out of town.'[5]

13 SEPTEMBER 1642. Sir Edward Nicholas to Sir William Boswell.

'Tuesday the King marched with his banner from Nottingham with 500 horse, five regiments of foot and 12 pieces of artillery. The trained bands met him at [Cavendish] Bridge about seven miles hence. 500 thereof offered themselves to attend the King . . . and the rest are disarmed . . . The King removes hence to-morrow to Uttoxeter, whither the artillery and train with 800 dragoons and some foot advanced yesternight . . .'[5]

4. SIDELIGHTS ON THE CAMPAIGN

The Lewn Book of Hatherton shows some of the expenses of a Staffordshire township.

14 Sept. 1642	For the trayned souldier and other nesesaryes.	£1
17 Sept. 1642	For the King carleiagis and other nessary.	£1
18 Sept. 1642	For the Kinge's carrage from Stafford to Welingtone.	£1
30 Oct. 1642	For his Majestie's army at Wolverhampton.	£1[6]

5. PRINCE RUPERT'S FORCE AT POWICK BRIDGE, 23 SEPTEMBER 1642

The troops may not yet have been regimented at this period. The regiments are those they served in at Edgehill, where known. Most of the troops were probably incomplete at this stage.

Troop Commander	Remarks	Regiment
Prince of Wales	Lieut. Thomas Daniel[7]	Prince of Wales
Earl of Northampton	Lieut. Robert Arden	Prince of Wales
Prince Rupert's Lifeguard	Captain Richard Crane[8]	Prince Rupert[9]
Sir Lewis Dyve	W., shoulder.	Prince Rupert
Sir William Pennyman	SP. 1660, Vol.II,f.5.	Prince Rupert
Prince Maurice	Two cuts in the head	Prince Maurice
Lord Wilmot	W. back	Lord Wilmot
Captain John Frescheville	Jack Jammot	Lord Wilmot
Sir Charles Lucas		Earl of Carnarvon
Lord John Stuart	John Smith	Lord Grandison
Lord Digby		Lord Digby
Lord Crauford		Prince of Wales
Henry Hastings		. . .
Captain Byron	W.[10]	Sir John Byron

6. THE QUARTERS OF THE ROYALIST ARMY, 12 OCTOBER 1642.[11]

The Guards of his Ma[tie] at Yerton Walson Oldbury & Morvell
Ld Generalls Guards at Badger
Ld Generalls Reg[t] at Rowton Ringleford and Ascott
Ea: Riuers at Stockton
Trayne of Artillery at Tashley
Col: ffieldings and Col: Bolles } at Wornhill
Col: Bellassis at Norton and Sutton
Col: ffitton and Col: Blagge } at Clauerley
Col: Salisbury at Swancourt Hockam Burcott
Col: Dieues & Col: Dutton } at Hawne
Col: Pennyman at Wicken
Ea Northampton at Bramley
His Ma[b] Guards of Dragoones at Wenlocke

7. CARTS, WAYNES AND HORSES

13 OCTOBER 1642

Charles R:

Order that noe	Our will, and pleasure is, and wee doe hereby
Carts, waynes,	streightly Charge, and Comaūnd all the Inhabitants of
horses taken vp	this o^r Countye of Shrewesbury or of any other
for the vse of the	Countye of this o^r Kingedome, whoe shall reciue
Artillery shall	warrants for the bringeing, or sendinge in any Carts
depte ye S^{r}vice	waynes, or Horses for the vse of o^r Trayne of Artillery
vpon payne of	that they, and every of them continue wth y^{er} Cartes
death	Waynes, and Horses in that o^r service, and not depart

from thence wthout o^r expresse pleasure declared therein vpon payne of death, of this wee require yo^u to giue them notice, that they may observe it accordingly. Giuen vnder o^r signe Manuel at o^r Court at Bridge north^2 this 13th of October. 1642.

To o^r trustye, and welbeloued S^r Jno. Heydon^3 kn^t. Lieutenñte gn'all o^r Ordeñnce, and to the comisšion^B for the same.
W.O. 55.457.60, fr.

8. A WARRANT FROM PRINCE RUPERT

19 OCTOBER 1642

These are to will & require you Forthwith vpon sight & receipt hereof to deliver to this Bearer for ye arming of mine owne Troope in his Ma^{tis}: present service. 30^{tie}: paire of your best holster and as many of your best spanners and as many of your best flaskes as also one hundred weight of pistoll shott (& 100^{11}: weight of carabine shott) of the most ordinary bore or gage (also 6 pouder baggs for Prince Maurice his Regiment) heerof you must not faile & for your soe doing This shall be your Warrant: Given at Packington heath^4 the 19th: of October 1642:

Rupert^5

To S^r: John Heydon knt Leietennant Generall [o]f his Ma^{tis}: Ordnance [a]nd to the Coṁissioners [a]ppointed for ye same
Received vpon this warrant Holsters 25p^r: shott 200^{11} waight pouder baggs Four

By mee James Eastland [Secretary to the Prince]
Endorsed: Prince Ruperts warr^t 1642 October
W.O. 55.423,f. 193

9. BYE TRAIN FOR BANBURY

22 OCTOBER 1642

Banburye. A Proporčon of Ordeñnce, Carriages, Powder, Shott, Match, &c to attend a Bye Trayne of 4 peeces of Ordeñnce, & 4000 ffoote. By warr' from his Matie vnder his Highn' signe Manuel. Bearing date the 22th of October 1642.viz.

Brasse Ordñnce mounted. viz.	{ Demi Cannons ----	2
	{ Culu'ings ---------	2
Rownd shott of yron	{ Demi Cannons ----	100
	{ Culu'ings ---------	100
Cases of tynn wth Muskett shott, or Cartouches, to ech round. 6.	-----------------	24
Powder for Th'ordñnce ---------------------------		10^c
Powder for 4000 Musketteeres ---------------------		3^Lasb.8.^c } 4^Lasb2^c.
Leade in shott -----------------------------------		4^tons.
Match ---		2^tons.

Materialls.

Wheele barrowes -------------------------------	
Hand barrowes ---------------------------------	All in ye ffields or Store
Shouells, & spades ----------------------------	
Pickaxes -------------------------------------	
Plancks -------------------------------------	50. or 60
Hand, & draught rope -------------------------	4^co. [coils]
Crowes of yron -------------------------------	12
Nayles of all sorts --------------------------	one barrell
Waggons, Carts, &c. --------------------------	57
Horsharneis { ffor the Thil ----------------	61
{ ffor the Trace --------------	349

Officers, Artificers, &c to attend the said Trayne. viz.

Cap^en. [Henry] Younger Comptroller.

Mounsieur Shebish Engenier.

Bradewynd de Hayne ffrizoon, worke base.

Mr George Cole	{ Clerks for the Municon
Mr Anthony Wharton	{ of ye Ordñnce, & ffoote.
Mr Henry Spe[ed]	Gentlemen of Th'ordennce
M^r W^m. Snedall	

Wm Betts to be chiefe Gonner, And 8 Gonners more, whereof Nicholas Busy to bee one.

The Mr Carpenter, & 6 other Carpenters

3 or 4 Wheelwrights

3 Coops.

A Ladlemaker.

A Smyth, & his S'vaunts.

Henry Elsey, and all the Matrozes.

All the Pyoneeres.

6 Conductors

A ffireworker.

All the aforesaid Officers, Artificers, &c are to bee selected and made Choice of by Cap^en Younger Comptroller.

M^dd. This Proporc̄on assigned for Banbury, but Countermaunded, in regard the whole Trayne the next morninge marched to Edgehill.[6]

W.O. 55. 457.60, ff. 1-2

10. FIELD OFFICERS, FOOT, 23 OCTOBER 1643

Colonels	*Lt. Colonels*	*Majors*
Charles Gerard	Edward Villiers	Francis Windebanke
Sir Lewis Dyve	Thomas Shirley	Gervase Holles
Sir Ralph Dutton	Stephen Hawkins	Degory Collins
Thomas Blagge	*William Lower*	*Barnaby Scudamore* or
		Robert Walters
John Belasyse	Sir Thomas Danby	Theophilus Gilby
Sir William Pennyman, Bt.	Sir James Pennyman	George Symms
Sir Thomas Lunsford	Henry Lunsford	Nathaniel Moyle
Richard Bolle	Richard d'Ewes	Edward Littleton
Sir Edward Fitton, Bt.	Anthony Thelwall	Urian Leigh
Sir Edward Stradling	William Herbert	John Stradling
Richard Feilding	Robert Conyngesbye	Peter Walthall
The Lifeguard		
Lord Willoughby d'Eresby	Sir William Vavasour	William Leighton
Lord General		
Earl of Lindsey, K.G.	John Monro	Herbert Lunsford
Sir John Beaumont	John Godfrey	William Courtney
Sir Gilbert Gerard	Ratcliffe Gerard	Richard Bishop
Sir Thomas Salusbury	John Royden	George Boncle
Lord Molyneux	*Roger Nowell*	Henry Byrom
Earl of Northampton	Henry Huncks	Anthony Greene
Earl Rivers	John Boys	*Francis*
		or } *Perkins*
		Robert

This list is a compilation from a variety of sources. A few who are somewhat doubtful are printed in italics.

11. MEMBERS OF THE LONG PARLIAMENT PRESENT AT EDGEHILL

	Member for:
John Ashburnham (1603–1671)	Hastings
Colonel John Belasyse (1615–1689)	Thirsk
James Lord Compton (1622–1681)	Warwickshire
Sir John Colepeper (1600–1660)	Kent
Lt. Colonel Sir Thomas Danby (1610–1660)	Richmond, Yorkshire
Viscount Falkland (1610?–1643)	Newport, I.O.W.
Thomas Fanshawe (1607–1652)	Lancaster
Lt. Colonel William Herbert (1609–1642)	Cardiff
Major Gervase Holles (1607–1675)	Grimsby
Edward Hyde (1609–1674)	Saltash
Sir John Pakington, Bart. (1620–1680)	Aylesbury

Colonel Sir William Pennyman, Bart. (1607–1643)	Richmond
Sir Richard Shuckburgh (1596–1656)	Warwickshire
Sir Edmund Verney (1590–1642)	Wycombe
Philip Warwick (1609–1683)	Radnor
Commissary General Henry Wilmot (1612–1658)	Tamworth

The Long Parliament seems to have been better represented in the King's Army than in Essex's – 16 to 13. Moreoever, this list of the Cavalier members present is probably incomplete. Others who may have been present were:

Orlando Bridgeman (1609–1674)	Wigan
Sir Richard Cave (k.1645)	Lichfield
Thomas Chicheley (1614–1699)	Cambridgeshire
Sir Frederick Cornwallis (1610–1662)	Eye
William Harrison (1619–1643)	Queenborough
Francis Newport (1620–1708)	Shrewsbury
Baptist Noel (1611–1682)	Rutland
John Russell (c.1620–1687)	Tavistock
Ferdinando Stanhope (c.1615–1643)	Tamworth

Of these six, Bridgeman, Chicheley, Compton, Cornwallis, Herbert and Pennyman, had early demonstrated their Royalist sympathies by voting against the attainder of Strafford. Wilmot had been expelled from the Commons on 9 December 1641, for his part in the Army Plot.

Stanhope became a colonel of horse in the army commanded by Henry Hastings, under whom he probably fought in 1642. Russell was a lieutenant-colonel at the storming of Cirencester (2 February 1643). Herbert and Verney fell at Edgehill. Harrison, Falkland and Stanhope were killed in 1643 and Cave at Naseby (1645).

No doubt Warwick was not the only M.P. serving among the gentlemen of the King's Lifeguard.

12. THE REMAINING STATE OF THE MAGAZINE

25 OCTOBER 1642

Wardington   25th day of October 1642.

M[r]: Newporte & M[r]: Parker are forthw[th] to draw vp a perfect state of the remaininge Magazine & out of it forthw[th] to supply the severall divisions allotted to the Ordñnce, Foote & horsse, according to the severall proporcōns formerly assigned.

And they are further to vse all dilligence in casting of as much Muskquett shott as wth any Industry may be procured & wth the first conveniency to cause a furth[r] proporcon of Carbine & Pistoll shott to be cast.

Jo: Heydon.

Wardington 25°:   The Remaininge State of his Maᵗ: Magazine in his
Octobᵉʳ: 1642.   Highnesse Traine of Artillerie

	Dj: Cannons ------	2.
	Culveringes -------	2.
	Dj: Culveringes ---	2. Iron cutts
	Mynions ----------	n.Ī
Brasse Ordñnce mō	Fawcons ----------	6. inde. 4. bastard
(vizˡ)	Fawconetts -------	6.
	Rabonetts ---------	2.
	12ˡˡ: bullett -------	2.
	6ˡˡ: bullett --------	1.
	3ˡˡ: bullett --------	4.

Mortʳ: peeces of brasse ------------------------	4	
Petards.	of Brasse ------------------------	
	of Iron ------------------------	

	Dj: Cannons --------------------	250.
	Cul ----------------------------	100.
Rounde	dj: Cul ------------------------	90.
shott of	Sakers -------------------------	50.
Iron for	Minions ------------------------	280.
	Fawcons ------------------------	670.
	Fawconetts ----------------------	670.
	3ˡˡ: bullett --------------------	14.

Granadoes for the Mortʳ: peeces ----------------	75.
Cases of Tynn for Cartouches ------------------	8.
Powder ------------------------------------	17ˡᵃˢᵗˢ:11ᶜ.
Match -------------------------------------	10ᵗᵒⁿⁿ.
Muskett shott ------------------------------	2ᵗᵒⁿⁿ.
Rests for musketts --------------------------	1200.
Leade in Pigges -----------------------------	10. pō.
Iron in Barrs -------------------------------	32. pō.
Bills ---------------------------------------	30.
Crowes of Iron ------------------------------	5.
Tents --------------------------------------	4.
Gynns --------------------------------------	one
Plankes ------------------------------------	30.
Tarr'd roapes -------------------------------	6. coyle.

Matterialls

Shovells & spades ---------------------------	500.
Pickaxes -----------------------------------	100.
Wheel barrows ------------------------------	10.
Hand barrowes ------------------------------	4.
Axes ---------------------------------------	100.
Smyths Tooles ------------------------------	
Carpentʳ: Tooles ----------------------------	

Memoᵣ: There are some Musketts, Pikes & Armoʳ for the Foote wᶜʰ: wee gathered vp before & aftʳ: the Battaile,[8] but in regarde of the confusion thereof the number is not yett perfectly knowne the most of them being vnserviceable.

W.O. 55. 457.62, ff. 3-4, and 60, ff. 3-4

13. BYE TRAIN FOR BANBURY

27 OCTOBER 1642

27⁰. October. 1642.

ffor Banburye. A Proporᶜon of Powder, Match, Shott &c to attend a Bye Trayne of 7 peeces of Brasse Ordeñnce, and an Armye of [blank] ffoote assigned for Banbury.viz̄.

Brasse Ordñnce mounted wᵗʰ theire Equipage. viz̄
- Demj Cannons ----- 2
- Culu'ings ---------- 2
- 12¹¹. bullett -------- 1
- 3¹¹. bullett ---------- 2

Rownd shott of yron. for
- Demj Cannons ----- 80
- Culu'ings ---------- 80
- Dj Culu'ings ------- 40
- ffawcons ----------- 80

Last C

Powder for the said Ordñnce ------------ 1. 7

More for the ffoote ---------------------- 1. 17.

Match ---------------------------------- one tonne.

Muskett shott -------------------------- 2ᵗᵒⁿˢ.

Materialls.

Shouells ----------------------
Spades -------------------------
Pickaxes ----------------------
Wheele barrowes -------------
} 2 Loades

Officers, Artificers, &c.

To ech Demj Cannon	Gonners. 3
	Matrozes 6.
To ech Culu'inge.	Gonners. 2.
	Matrozes. 4.
To yᵉ 12¹¹. bullett.	Gonners. 2.
	Matrozes. 4.

All the Pyoneers.

Gent of Th'ordñnce 3
- Mʳ [William] Stone
- Mʳ Snedall
- Mʳ Meritt

Clerks. 2
- George Cole
- Batcheloʳ.

	Mr Emerson.
	Mr Gold.
Conductors. 5.	Mr Sumpter.
	M^r [Cuthbert] Cartington.
	And another.

Carpenters.
Wheelewrights.
Coops.
One waggon wth Boudg barrells, Cartouches, & all Gonners ymplements.
Nayles of all sorts.

W.O. 55.457.60, f.5

14. THE ROYALIST FOOT, 31 OCTOBER 1642

On 31 October the King ordered Sir John Heydon and the Commissioners of the Ordnance to deliver out of the 'Store of Armes and amunition' under their command ' . . . the respective proportions, of Powder with Bullett and Match proportionable'. Receipts from officers of the regiments would be their 'discharge'.

		Receipt	
Regiment/Colonel	*lbs.*	*Date*	*Signatory*
Lieut. Generalls	200	1 Nov.	William Gamlyn Quar^{ter} (Master)
Regiment of Guards	(300)	5 Nov.	Tho Muckl(owe) Lieutenn^t
Col: (Sir Thomas) Lunsfords	050	1 Nov.	Henry Lunsford Lieutan^t Coll
Col: (Herbert) Price	050	1 Nov.	Tho: Springett quarter Master
the Earle Riuers	050	5 Nov.	Jo: Boys: leiu^t: Collonell
the Lord Molineux	050	5 Nov.	fran Saunders Sirgenmaior
Col: S^r G: Gerrard	100	2 Nov.	The m(ar)ke of Rich: Evans Serg^t. (to Captain) Edward Paynton
Sr Wm Pennyman	150	4 Nov.	John Denton sergeant
Col: (Thomas) Blagge	150	1 Nov.	Edward Evans Luietenant
Col: (Charles) Gerrard	050	7 Nov.	Ja: Hodgson Quarter M^r to Corll Gerard
Col: S^r L: Diue	080	1 Nov.	Gabriell Sauile (Captain)
Col: S^r R: Dutton	100	5 Nov.	Thomas Littellton quarter-master
Col: (Richard) ffieldinge	100	1 Nov.	Robt Ridley (Waggoner)
Col: (John) Bellassis	150	5 Nov.	Bartho: Pell. Captain
Col: (Sir Edward) ffitton	100	1 Nov.	Urian Legh Maior
Col: (Richard) Bolle	150	5 Nov.	Cap^m: Richard Bagot
Col: (Sir Thomas) Salusbury	100	1 Nov.	George Boncle (Major)
Earl of Northampton	90	1 Nov.	William Collett Quar.[12]

In a separate document (1 November) A:(ntony) Greene (Major) desires ammunition for the Earl of Northampton's Regiment 'for 180 musqueteers Ech man his bandiliers full'. This amounted to 90 lbs each of powder and match and 180 of bullet.

It will be noted that the regiments of Stradling and of Beaumont do not figure in this return.

One cannot assume that the return is a clear indication of the number of musketeers in each unit – except in the case of Northampton's Regiment – since we do not know that they had not still got a certain amount of ammunition which had not been expended in the recent battle. On the other hand the document probably does indicate which regiments had been most hotly engaged in the fire fight at Edgehill. This would seem to confirm that Sir Nicholas Byron's tertia (Lord General and Lifeguard) had done some heavy firing. On this hypothesis Belasyse's Brigade (Blagge, Belasyse and Pennyman) had also kept up a steady fire. Still, such theorizing can perhaps be pushed too far.

It is interesting to note the ranks of the officers collecting the ammunition.

Lieutenant-colonels	2
Majors	3
Captains	3
Lieutenants	2
Quartermasters	5
Waggoner	1
Sergeants	2
	18

In cases where one observes senior officers doing routine administrative work of this sort one suspects that all cannot have been well with the organization of the regiment. Lunsford, his brother being a prisoner, was actually the commanding officer. Had he no junior officer or quartermaster he could trust?

15. WALSALL CONTRIBUTES TO THE ROYALIST CAUSE

31 October 1642.

'The last of October 1642.

A note of money Recd and Paid by mee John Walton as followeth concerninge the Towne.

	£	s.	d.
Recd. of my sister Heynes for which Mr. Henry Sheapherd and my selfe have given Bond for it	30	0	0
Payd for Wyne and Bottles presented to Prince Roberte & otherwise for beere in all		17	0
Geven Prince Roberts Secretarie [James Eastland] .	2	2	0
Geven Prince Roberte in Gould, And a Purse withe it	20	0	0
Pd to my Sister Heynes for a nagge which was geven Prince Maurice	7	6	8
Pd for Charges at Hampton		3	6

Pd for Wyne and beere wch was spent on the			
Captines at Sherwyns		9	0
geven Captine Selbye	1	0	0
pd to Captine Major [Thomas] Button [D]	1	14	0
pd for beere att Henry Woods when Sir John			
Beomonte was there		6	0

'Sister Heynes' was Cicely Haynes, landlady of the Cock, Wolverhampton.*

16. A COMMISSION AS CAPTAIN OF HORSE

Charles R.
Charles by the grace of God King of Great Britayne ffraince & Ireland, defender of the faith &c To our trust & welbeloued *Roger Whitley*, Greeting, Wee doe hereby constitute and appoynt you to bee Captaine of one Troope of horse vnder the Regim^t of our trusty and welbeloved Colonell Charles Gerard, The which troope by vertue of this our Comission, you are forthwith to imprest and retayne of such as will willingly and voluntarily serue vs for our pay, and for the defence of our Royall person, the two houses of Parliam^t, ye Protestant religion, the law of the land, the liberty and propriety of the subject and priviledges of Parliam^t to bring them to our Royall standard, and to cause them to be duly exercised in Armes comanding all Inferior officers and souldiers of ye said Troope respectively you to obey as their Captayne according to this our Commission hereby given to you.

And you yor selfe Diligently to execute, and obserue such order and direccon as from tyme to tyme you shall receive from ourselfe, o^r Lieutenant Generall, Generall of our horse, yor Colonall, or any other yor superior officer, according to occasion and the discipline of warr. And in all things to gouerne yor selfe as vnto the duty and place of Captayne of a Troope doth of right apperteyne & belong. Given vnder our signe manuall at Our Court at Oxford the ffirst of November In the Eighteenth yeare of o^r Raigne 1642.[13]

17. PAY WARRANT OF 16 NOVEMBER 1642.

Charles R.
Our will and pleasure is, that out of such of our treasure as is in your custody you pay or cause to be paid by way of impress upon accompt these several sums hereunder expressed unto some chief officer of every regiment or their assignees for the use of the lieut[enant]s ensigns and other superior

---

* Gerald P. Mander, M.A., F.S.A., A History of Wolverhampton, edited and completed by Norman W. Tildesley, 1960.

officers of companies and also for the private soldiers of each regiment respectively defalking therefrom all such sums of money as by our commiss[ary] general of our victuals shall be charged upon any of them: and for your so doing this shall be your sufficient warrant. Dated at our Court at Oatlands the 16th day of November in the 18th year of our reign.

	£	s.	d.
To our lieutenant general's regiment	300	12	0
To colonel (Sir William) Pennyman's regiment	246	9	0
To colonel (Thomas) Blagge's regiment	248	17	0
To colonel (Sir Ralph) Dutton's regiment	242	5	0
To the regiment of the guards	208	16	0
To the lo(rd) of Northampton's regiment	114	12	0
To the lo(rd) Molineux his regiment	116	2	0
To the lo(rd) Rivers his regiment	140	11	0
To colonel (Richard) Feilding's regiment	166	13	0
To colonel (Sir Edward) Stradling's regiment	257	11	0
To colonel (Richard) Bolle's regiment	201	0	0
To colonel (John) Bellassys' regiment	182	11	0
To colonel (Sir Lewis) Dives his regiment	62	9	0
To colonel Gilbert Gerard's regiment	199	7	0
To colonel (Sir Edward) Fitton's regiment	166	19	0
To colonel (Sir Thomas) Salisburies regiment	245	17	0
To colonel (Sir Thomas) Lunsford's regiment	127	13	0
To colonel (Herbert) Prise's regiment	61	1	0
To colonel Charles Gerard's regiment			
To captain Buncle's company	17	9	0
To the regiment of guards more	30	0	0
More to colonel Dives his regiment	42	0	0
To colonel Salisburies regiment more	63	12	0

To our trusty and welbeloved Matthew Brodley, Esq., Paymaster General of the Army.[14]

18. PAY WARRANT OF 24 NOVEMBER 1642

(signature) CHARLES R.

Our will and Commande is That out of such of our Treasure as is in yo[r] Custody, you pay or Cause to be payd, by way of Imp[r]ess upon Accompt these severall Sommes hereunder exp[r]essed, unto some Cheife Officer of everie Reg[ment]; or their Assignes, for the use of the Lieut[nts], Ensignes, and other Inferior Officers of Companies, and also for the private Souldiers of each Reg[ment]. Respectively, defalking therefrom, all such/Sommes of money as by o[er] Commisary of ye Victualls, shall be charged upon any of them.

And for yo$^{(u)r}$ soe doeing,
this shall be yore sufficient Warrant: Dated at o^{re} Court at Redding the XXiiiith day of November in the 18th yeare of o$^{'re}$ Raigne.

To o^{re} Lieutenant Generall's Regim^t	300	12	0	ex^d
To Colo^{ll} Penyman's Regiment	246	9	0	ex^d
To Colo^{ll} Blagge's Regim^t	248	17	0	ex^d
To Colo^{ll} Dutton's Regim^t	242	5	0	ex^d
To y^e Regim^t of o^{ur} Guarde	223	16	0	cf:
To y^e Lo: of Northampton's Reg^t	172	4	0	cf:
To ye Lo: Molineux his Regim^t	116	2	0	cf:
To ye Lo: Rivers his Regim^t	140	11	0	ex^d
To Colo^{ll} Stradlings Regim^t	257	11	0	ex^d
To Colo^{ll} ffeldings Regim^t	200★	17	0	ex^d

2149-4-0

(End of recto of 1st leaf. A.L.)
(★217 corrected to 200. A.L.)
To Colonell

To Colo^{ll} Bolle's Regim^t	237	18	0	ex^d
To Colo^{ll} Belasys Regim^t	182	11	0	ex^d
To Colo^{ll} Dives Regim^t	183	9	0	cf
To Colo^{ll} ffitton's Regim^t	166	19	0	cf:
To Colo^{ll} Salisburies Regim^t	277	13	0	ex^d
To Colo^{ll} Lunsford's Regim^t	145	2	0	ex^d
To Colo^{ll} Prise his Regim^t	61	1	0	cf:
To Colo^{ll} Gilberte Gerrards Reg^t	200	0	0	ex^d
More to our^e Lieu^{tnt} Generalls Regiment for 40^{tie} new men added	12	0	0	ex^d
More to Sr Wm Penymans Regt. for 14 new men	4	4	0	ex^d

36330–14–0 [Rewritten] 3630–14–0
[corrected]

(Endorsed on verso of 2nd leaf:-
'Warrant^s to Impr^{rest} date
24to Novembris
1642'

The original warrant is in the collection of Anthony W. G. Lowther, Esq., to whom I am most grateful for permission to reproduce it.

19. THE CAPTURE OF MARLBOROUGH, 5/6 DECEMBER 1642

'On *Munday Dec. 5.* the Lord *Grandison* and Col. *Gray* appeared with their Troops on the North side of the Town, and about 12 a Clock some Regiments of Foot and Dragoons came up (in all making about 6000) together with their Ordnance, and then they began the Assault; but the

Town lying in a Valley between two Hills, their Cannon did no Execution; Col. *Blake* with his Regiment of Foot creeping behind the Hedges, and in some Ditches, got within Musket-shot, discharged upon the Town and next day my Lord *Rivers's* Regiment of Foot, and Col. *Gray's* Dragoons, with one Culverin, and one Demi-Culverin, Attacked them in two places at once, but were all warmly answered and obliged to Retreat, this Assault being made on the North-east side of the Town.

At the same time Sir *William Pennyman*, with a Regiment of Foot and some Dragoons, attempted the North-west-side, and especially their great Guns from thence plaid apace, but hurt neither Man, Woman or Child. And there were but 24 Men to oppose this whole Regiment in that place, yet they maintain'd the Fight near three hours, till at length some Granado's having fired an old thatcht Barn that stood near them, they were inforced to quit that Post: and the King's forces having afterwards fired a Dwelling House in another place, came resolutely on, and broke in through a great Inn, into the midst of the Town, shouting and crying out. *A Town! a Town! for King Charles, &c.* Then those in the Town began every one to shift for himself, but were for the most part taken Prisoners which way soever they flew; For the Lord *Digby* with his Regiment of Horse, and Capt. *Daniel Oneal* had beset the Town with Horse-men, from East to West on the South-side, and the Lord *Grandison* and the Lord *Wentworth* with their Troops, from West to East on the North-side, and their Scouts so kept the West and East passages, that none could escape without great hazard and difficulty. Having thus won the Town, they set fire to it in two other places so that there were four fires blazing at once, and the Soldiers fell to pillaging the houses and Shops, all the wearing Apparel, Plate and Money they took away, and all the Horses and Carts that were in the Town, which were the more, because those of the Country that came to the Market had been kept in. On the *Tuesday* they carried away the Prisoners, being in number between 100 and 120, marching on foot tied two and two together, before the Cannon, to *Oxford*; amongst whom the said Mr. *Franklin* and the two Scotch Commanders were the chief. There were 53 Houses burnt; and the Damage sustained by the Town (besides the value of those Houses) in Goods, Money and Ware, was computed to amount to near 50000 *l*. The chief Commanders on the King's side in this Action, were Commissary *Wilmot*, the Lord *Grandison*, the Lord *George Digby*, the Lord *Wentworth*, Sir *William Pennyman*, Col. *Gray*, Col. *Blake*, Col. *Washington*, &c. On the Town side, the two Scotch-men commanded, and they had but 140 men that fought, of whom there was not one kill'd, nor any in the whole Town, except two Country-men that were slain as they were running out of the Town, after it was taken.'[15]

From this we may deduce that the Royalist force was 3,300 strong and that it was commanded by Lord Wilmot, Commissary-General of the Horse. His force seems to have included:

1,000 HORSE

Lt Colonel Daniel O'Neal.   Prince Rupert, H.
Lord Wilmot, H.(?)
Lord Grandison, H.

600 DRAGOONS

Colonel Edward Grey.
Lt. Colonel Henry Washington.   James Usher, D.
Lord Wentworth's Company.

1,700 FOOT

Colonel Sir William Pennyman.
Colonel Thomas Blagge.
Colonel Earl Rivers.

ARTILLERY

One culverin.
One demi-culverin.

20. THE ROYALIST ARMY, 9 DECEMBER 1642

This table is based on the document entitled 'The Quarters of the Army thus settled the ninth of December 1642 at Oxford'.[16] The army is still virtually that which fought at Edgehill, except that two horse regiments – Sir Arthur Aston's and Lord Andover's – have joined, and the weak foot regiment of Sir John Beaumont has disappeared, probably into some garrison outside the orbit of the main 'Oxford Army'.

READING
   Richard Bolle, F.
   Richard Feilding, F.
   Sir Thomas Salusbury, F.   } 'Colonel ffielding's Tertia'[17]
   Edward Stradling, F.[18]
   Henry Lunsford, F.[18]
   Sir Edward Fitton, F.
   Sir Arthur Aston, H.[19]
   Sir Thomas Aston, H.
WALLINGFORD
   Lord Digby, H.
   Thomas Blagge, F.[19]
   Earl Rivers, F.
ABINGDON
   Prince Rupert, H.
   Lt.-General Lord Wilmot, H.
   Sir Lewis Dyve, F.[19]
EVESHAM
   Sir John Beaumont, F.
   later John Godfrey.
FARINGDON
   Prince Maurice, H.
   Sir Edmund Duncombe, D.
   Edward Grey, D.
OXFORD
   'The Regt. of the Guard',[18] F.
   Charles Gerard, F.
   Sir William Pennyman, F.[19]

Sir Ralph Dutton, F.
Lifeguard, H.[20]
WINCHESTER
Lord Grandison, H.[21]
BURFORD
Sir John Byron, H.[19]
James Usher, D.
BRILL
Sir Gilbert Gerard, F.[19]
Lord Molineux, F.
BANBURY
Earl of Northampton, F.[19]
John Belasyse, F.
Prince of Wales, H.
WOODSTOCK
The Lord Lt. General's, F.[22]
'his troop of horse on villages adjacent'.[22]
EYNSHAM(?)[23] 'EYNESTONE' now ENSTONE
Earl of Carnarvon, H.
ISLIP
Lord Andover, H.

21. STAFF OF THE HORSE AND GARRISON OF ABINGDON, 25 DECEMBER 1642[24]

	Men	Horses
The Quartermaster Generall	6	12
ffor the Cannon	30	36
Provost Marshal	. .	16
Adjacent (sic) Generall	6	10
Prince Rupert	16	52
The pticuler office^n of my lo: Wentworth & ye Lieu^t. Generall	30	65
The scout m̃ Generalls pticuler use	20	20
The foote officers of (Colonel) Sr Lewis Dive		
for maintennce of their horses	. .	50

Lord Wentworth was Sergeant-Major-General of the Horse, though exactly when he received this appointment is uncertain. The Adjutant-General of the Horse was Colonel David Scrymgeour, third son of the 1st Viscount Dudhope. He was a Scot. He distinguished himself at the storming of Cirencester (2 February 1643), leading the forlorn hope of Prince Rupert's Lifeguard into the town. He served in the Cornish campaign (1644)[25] and died at Oxford where he was buried on 2 December 1644.[26] In a document of 24 December 1642 he signs himself Dauid Scrymgoure' and is described as 'Agitant to ye Prince Rupert'.[27]

At Cirencester (2 February 1643) the Scout-Master General, who fought as a volunteer, was Sir William Neale.

22. ROYALIST CAVALRY QUARTERED IN OXFORDSHIRE, 11 JANUARY 1643

Colonel	Troops	Weekly Cost
Prince of Wales ⎫ Sir Thomas Byron ⎭	6	£252
Earl of Carnarvon	5 ⎫	£252
Lord Wentworth's company of Dragooners	1 ⎭	
Sir John Byron	6	£252
Lord Andover	3	£126
Colonel (Charles) Gerard	3	£126
Lord Digby	4	£168
		£1176

Thus a troop cost £42 per week to maintain.

Andover's and Gerard's regiments had been raised since Edgehill. It is probable that the other regiments were now more complete than in October 1642. It is obvious that they would not have had more troops in October 1642 than in January 1643.[28]

23. ROYALISTS PRESENT AT THE STORMING OF CIRENCESTER,
2 FEBRUARY 1643[29]

The Royalist army saw little action between Edgehill and the storming of Cirencester, which took place less than four months later.

Although a number of officers went home after the army went into winter quarters in December, most of those that fought at Cirencester probably fought at Edgehill. Prince Rupert's force consisted of six regiments of horse and his Lifeguard, a number of dragoons, some 'commanded' foot out of the garrison of Oxford under Colonel Lewis Kirke, and a bye train of artillery.

The six regiments of horse were:

Prince of Wales	:	Sir Thomas Byron
Prince Rupert	:	Lt. Colonel (Dan) O'Neale
Prince Maurice	:	
Sir John Byron	:	
Earl of Carnarvon	:	
Colonel Slater (Slaughter)	:	

Of these only the last was not an Edgehill regiment.

The dragoons were those of:
Lt. Colonel (Herbert?) Lunsford
Lord Wentworth
Earl of Northampton
(Colonel) Sir Edmund Duncomb
Lt. Colonel (Edward) Drury
Colonel (James) Usser (Usher).

Duncomb and Usher had commanded regiments at Edgehill, but the other units had probably been raised later.

The foot were drawn out of the four regiments at Oxford:

Lifeguard
Sir Ralph Dutton
Charles Gerard
Sir William Pennyman.
      The train consisted of:-
Demi-cannons (18 pdrs.)   2
Small drakes or field-pieces   4
Mortar 1
Monsieur (Bartholomew) la Roche was in charge of the mortar.

INDIVIDUALS

Lt. General Lord Wilmot
Lord Wentworth
Colonel Henry Wentworth
Colonel (David) Scrimsour (sic): 'generall adjutant', H.
Colonel (John) Innes: 'generall adjutant', H.
Sir William Neale: Scoutmaster-general.

HORSE

Sir Thomas Byron	:	Prince of Wales'
Sir Richard Crane	:	Prince Rupert's Lifeguard
Lt.Colonel (Dan) O'Neale	:	Prince Rupert's Regiment
Major (Will) Legge	}	
Lieut. Noland. K.		
(Captain) Lord Dillon		
Captain Curson		A new troop since Edgehill. Prince Rupert's Regiment.
Lt. Colonel Charles Lucus	:	Carnarvon's Regiment.

FOOT

Lt. Colonel (Will.) Layton (Leighton)	Lifeguard
Captain (Thomas) Min (Mynne)	Lifeguard
Lieut. (William) St. John	Lifeguard?
Captain (Mathew) Radcliffe	Dutton
Sergeant Major (Francis) Windebank	C. Gerard
Captain (Gilbert) Gerard	C. Gerard
Captain (Will.) Wivell (Wyvell)	Pennyman

DRAGOONS

Lt. Colonel (Henry) Washington	Usher
Major Hutchinson. W.	Usher
Captain (Francis) Morrison	Usher
Captain Vavasour	Usher?
Captain Alford	Duncombe
Lieut. (Humphrey) Wharton	Duncombe
Lt. Colonel (John) Russell	Lord Wentworth
Sergeant-Major (William?) Compton	Northampton

24. BUSHELL'S CONTRACT FOR CLOTHING

1642/3.[30]

'March the 6th 1642

Mr. [Thomas] Bushell made his proposition thus that he would procure for the King's Souldiers Cassocks, Breeches, Stockings & Capps at reasonable rates to be delivered at Oxford, and at the delivery to receyve readye money, or a bill of exchange to be payd at London, the choyce to be left to them who provide the clothes. And when one Loade of Clothes is brought, or in bringing, to go on with providing of a second Loade, and so from time to time till the Kings Army be all provided for, and payd for in such manner as before.

Ro: Heath.[31] Ri. Spencer.[32] Ni. Crisp.[33] Geo. Strode.'[34]

25. SURRENDER OF READING, APRIL 1643

The Articles were signed by:

	Colonel
Colonel Richard Feilding	
Colonel John Belasyse	
Colonel Richard Bolle	
Lt. Colonel Edward Villiers	C. Gerard
Lt. Colonel Anthony Thelwall	Fitton
Lt. Colonel Theophilus Gilby	Belasyse
Major George Boncle	Salusbury[35]

26. FIELD OFFICERS OF FOOT AT CULHAM CAMP, MAY 1643

Signatures	*Rank*	*Remarks*
J(ohn) Belasyse	Colonel	
Richard Bolle	Colonel	
John Owen	Colonel	Not at Edgehill.
Hen: Lunsford	Colonel	*Vice* Sir Thomas Lunsford
Rob'. Conyngesbye	Lt. Colonel	Richard Feilding then Sir Jacob Astley. Buried at Oxford 18 July 1643.
Antho: Thelwall	Lt. Colonel	Fitton, F.
Edward Tirwhitt	Lt. Colonel	Salusbury, F. but evidently not at Edgehill.
Tho. Shirley	Lt. Colonel	Dyve, F.
Theo: Gilby	Lt. Colonel	Belasyse, F. Major, at Edgehill.
Edward Littleton	Lt. Colonel	Bolle, F. Lt.Col. *vice* d'Ewes, K., Reading.
Toby Bowes	Major	Sir Jacob Astley.
Gervas Helwys	Major	Lord General.
Richard Bushoppe	Major	Sir Gilbert Gerard, F.
Ed: Williams	Major	Richard Herbert, F. Not at Edgehill.
William Compton	Major	Northampton, F., *vice* Anthony Green, promoted *vice* Sir Henry Huncks, dismissed.
ffrancis Saunders	Major	Lord Molyneux.[36]

27. A PROCLAMATION AGAINST OATHS AND PROPHANITY, 13 JULY 1643

Strictly forbids the use of unlawful oaths or scandalous acts, absence from sermons and morning and evening prayers. There has been a general liberty in the use of oaths and new coined execrations, prophanities, drunkenness and whoredom. Orders the articles of war dealing with these matters to be put in due execution in the army, so that we may expect a blessing from God. All chaplains of regiments are to attend their charges, and read divine service twice daily at the heads of their regiments, and preach to them every Sunday morning, with an extract from the Catechism in the Book of Common Prayer in the afternoon. Doctors Rives and Sherwood, the two chaplains general to the army, are to supervise this activity.

'Lastly because the confounding of Habites appertaining to both Sexes and the promiscuous vse of them is a thing wch Nature and Religion for-bid and our Soule abhors, and yet the prostitute Impudency of some women (If [the] same deceiue vs not) haue (wch we cannot thinke on but wth Iust Indignation) thus conuersed in our Armey therefor Lett no woman presume to Counterfeite her Sex by wearing mans apparell vnder payne of the Seuerest punishment wch Law and our displeasure shal Inflict;'

These orders to be published at the head of every regiment[37]

28. ATTESTATION OF THOMAS BUSHELL'S SERVICES

12 June 1643, Oxford.

Charles R.

Trustie and wellbeloved, wee greete you well; callinge to minds your vigilant eye of care upon all occasions, and the many true services you have actually done us in these times of trying a subjects loyalty: as in raiseing us the Derbyshire Minors for our Life Guard at our first entrance to this warr for our owne defence; when the Lord Lieutenant of that Countie refused to appear in the service: supplyinge us at Shrewsbury and Oxford with your Mint for the payment of our Armye, when all the Officers in the Mint of our Tower of London forsook their attendance, except Sr William Parkhurst; your changing the dollars with wch wee paid our Souldiers at six shillings a piece, when the malignant partee cried them down at ffive your stopping the Mutinie in Shropshire when the soldiers had left their arreares uppon the Countrye, and brought the associacion of the Gentrie to perfeccion; your providing us one hundred tonnes of lead shot for our Army without money, when we paid before twentie pounds per tonne; and your helpinge us to twenty six pieces of ordinance when wee were at a straight for supplying of Chester, Shrewsbury and other places; your cloathing our liefe Guard and three regiments more, with suites, stockings, shoes, and mounteroes when wee were readie to march in the ffield: your invention for our better knowinge and rewardinge the Forlorne Hope with Badges of Silver at your own charge when the soldiers were ready to run away through the instigation of some disafected persons: your contractinge with Merchants beyond the Seas, for providing good quantities of powder, pistoll, carabine, muskett and bullet, in exchange for your owne commodities, when wee were wantinge of such ammunicion: with divers other severall services which we hope our royall successors will never forget, and to assure you that wee shall beare them in our princelie remembrance, Wee hereby promise you, on the word of a Prince, to make those traitorous subjects Smyth, Wild and Stephenson for to restore those lands of Chawford Dene, Hampsteede and Euston which you sold them and to free you and your three Sureties Edmund Goodier, Charles Mordent, and the ladie Anne Wade of the debts you owe to such rebellious persons as shall be proved they have assisted the Parliament (either by their purse or power) against us, to the end that you maye enjoy your desires at Euston rocke and the rocks in Wales, which your own industrie and Gods providence hath helped you unto. Given under our signe manual at our Court at Oxford the twelfth daye of June 1643.

To our trusty and wellbeloved

Thomas Bushell Esq., Warden of

our Mint and Mr Worker of our

Mynes Royall.

This Attestacion was shewed unto Edward Panton and to Richard Sherwyn at their severall examynacions before mee.

C. Spelman.[38]

29. PRICES OF ARMS AND AMMUNITION

At the camp before Gloucester on 21 August 1643, Henry Percy, General of the Artillery, noted these ordinary prices:

Match	30s. per cwt.
Backs & breasts	15s. apiece.
Iron shot	£15 a ton.[39]

According to a contract between John Shaw, merchant of Antwerp, and Will. Sandys, a Royalist agent, the prices of firearms were:

A Musket	21s.
A pair of pistols	51s.
A carbine	31s.[40]

30. THE OXFORD ARMY, 1642–1646

It may be of interest to summarize the history of the Oxford Army during the rest of the war. Its main operations were:

1643		
16–27 Apr.	Defence of Reading	
25 Apr.	Action at Caversham Bridge	
26 Jul.	Storming of Bristol	
10 Aug.–5 Sept.	Siege of Gloucester	
20 Sept.	First Battle of Newbury	
1644		
29 Jun.	Battle of Cropredy Bridge	
Aug.	Cornish campaign	
27 Oct.	Second Battle of Newbury	
1645		
14 Jun.	Battle of Naseby	

1646
24 Jun.   Siege of Oxford

In the nature of things the composition of the Army varied as new regiments were added and old ones disappeared. This table only attempts to summarize the histories of those that served in the Edgehill campaign.

	Bristol	I Newbury	Cornwall	Naseby	
Charles Gerard	–	★	–	–	Garrison of Oxford 1642–4 To S. Wales early 1644
Sir Lewis Dyve	–	★	★	–	Garrison of Abingdon 1643 and of Sherborne Castle 1644–5
Sir Ralph Dutton & (Sir) Stephen Hawkins	★	★	–	–	Garrison of Oxford 1642–3 and 1644–6
Thomas Blagge	–	★	–	–	Garrison of Wallingford 1642–6
John Belasyse & (Sir) Theophilus Gilby	–	★	★	★	Destroyed at Naseby
Sir William Pennyman, Sir James Pennyman & (Sir) Richard Page	–	–	★	★	Garrison of Oxford 1642–3 Destroyed at Naseby
Richard Feilding & Sir Jacob Astley	★	★	★	★	Destroyed at Naseby in part
Sir Thomas Lunsford, Henry Lunsford & Prince Rupert	★	–	–	★	Fought at Marston Moor 2 July 1644. Destroyed at Naseby
Richard Bolle & (Sir) George Lisle	★	★	★	★	Destroyed at Naseby
Sir Edward Fitton Anthony Thelwall	★	★	★	–	Disappears after II Newbury
Lifeguard	–	★	★	★	Destroyed at Naseby
Lord General	★	★	★	–	Not at Naseby. Garrison of Woodstock?
Sir John Beaumont & John Godfrey	–	–	–	–	Destroyed at Tewkesbury, when Godfrey was killed 4 June 1644.
Sir Gilbert Gerard & Ratcliffe Gerard	★	★	–	★	Garrison of Worcester 1643–6. Main body destroyed at Naseby

Sir Thomas Salusbury &	★	★	★	–	Garrison of Devizes 1644–5.
Sir Charles Lloyd					Broken up after the surrender 23 Sept. 1645.
Lord Molineux	★	★	–	–	Returned to Lancashire after I Newbury?
Earl of Northampton	–	–	–	–	Garrison of Banbury 1642–6.
Earl Rivers	★	–	–	–	Garrison of Donnington Castle 1643–6.

31. MONUMENT TO MAJ.-GENERAL SIR THOMAS TYLDESLY IN WIGAN LANE

'An high act of gratitude erected this monument, which conveys the memory of Sir Thomas Tyldesley to posterity. Who served King Charles the First as lieutenant-colonel, at Edgehill Battle, after raising regiments of horse foot and dragoons. And for the desperate storming of Burton upon Trent [2 July 1643], over a bridge of 36 arches, received the honour of Knighthood. He afterwards served in all the war in great command; was governor of Lichfield; and followed the fortune of the Crown through the three kingdoms; and never compounded with the rebels though strongly invited. And on 25th August, was here slain, commanding as major general under the Earl of Derby. To whom the grateful Erector, Alexander Rigby, Esq was cornet. And when he was high sheriff of this county A.D. 1679, placed this high obligation on the whole family of the Tyldeslys.'

1 SP. 16.473, 52–53.
2 CSPD 1641-3. p. 72.
3 Op. cit., p. 359
4 Op. cit., p. 362
5 Op. cit., p. 389
6 Quoted in *Staffordshire and the Great Rebellion*, ed. by D. A. Johnson and D. G. Vaisey. Staffordshire County Council County Records Committee, 1964.
7 'Sr Thomas Daniell; wth ye P. of Wales'es Troop'.(Prince Rupert's Diary). He was not knighted until 1662, when he was a captain in the Foot Guards.
8 Knighted for taking the news of Powick Bridge to the King.
9 Early in 1643 the Lifeguard became independent of Prince Rupert's Regiment.
10 Colonel Sir John Byron and his six brothers all served the King. Three, Richard, Gilbert, and William, seem to have been in Sir John's Regiment, in 1642, while Sir Thomas commanded the Prince of Wales' Regiment at Edgehill. It is not clear which of these was wounded at Powick Bridge.
11 British Museum. Harleian MS. 6851,f.211. This document is endorsed in Sir Edward Walker's hand 'The Qrs of the Army 12 8ber'.
12 Roy, Ordnance Papers, pp.157–160.
13 The John Rylands Library. Mainwaring MSS., Letter A.10.
14 British Museum. Add. MS. 34713,f.1.

15 John Rushworth, Historical Collections, Part III, Volume II, pp.82–83. London, 1692.

16 British Museum. Harleian MS. 6851. Printed in my 'King Charles I's Army of 1642'. Journal of the Society for Army Historical Research, Vol. 17, 1938.

17 The regiments of Feilding's tertia are not named in the document, but there is no doubt as to which they were.

18 The colonels of these regiments were taken at Edgehill, but whereas Lunsford was replaced by his brother, Henry, Stradling and Lord Willoughby d'Eresby, now Earl of Lindsey, had their places kept vacant.

19 These colonels were also governors of the places where their regiments were quartered.

20 Omitted from the list of quarters.

21 Altered from Chipping Norton which is deleted in the list. In fact Grandison, H., and Grey, D., were both sent to Winchester, where they were captured by Sir William Waller on 13 December 1642. Clarendon (Vol. III, p. 405) puts Grandison's Regiment at 300 and Grey's at 200.

22 The Earl of Lindsey having died of wounds after Edgehill, Patrick Ruthven, Lord Forth, was made Lord Lt. General and inherited Lindsey's Regiment, F., and probably his troop, H., as well.

23 'Eynstone' in the list.

24 Belvoir Castle. MS.

25 Sir Edmund Walker's *Historical Discourses*, p. 61.

26 Wood's City of Oxford, Vol. III, p. 245.

27 Roy, Ordnance Papers, Vol. I, p. 185.

28 Compiled from *An Explanation of the Agreement . . . betwixt His Majesty and the Inhabitants of the County of Oxon*. Oxford, 16 January 1642/3.

29 *Bibliotheca Gloucestrensis*.

30 Ottley Papers, No.LXXXII.

31 Sir Robert Heath (1575–1649) was the Lord Chief Justice. It was he that tried Captain Lilburne at Oxford.

32 Richard Spencer of Orpington, Kent, raised a regiment, H., for the King. This may be the same person.

33 Sir Nicholas Crisp (1599–1666) was a great City merchant as well as a colonel H., and the owner of a number of ships.

34 Sir George Strode (1583–1663) was the officer of the Ordnance wounded at Edgehill, and was married to Crisp's daughter, Rebecca.

35 Rev. Ch. Coates, LL.B., *History and Antiquities of Reading*, 1802, p. 29. Coates gives Bolle as Bell and Boncle as Bond. The ranks of the signatories have been added.

36 British Museum. Harleian MS. 6804,f.55.

37 Ibid.f.75–6.

38 Sir Henry Ellis' 'Original Letters', 2nd Series, Vol. III, p. 309.

39 CSPD p. 479.

40 Bodleian Library. Rawlinson MS.D.395.(21),f.213.

SECTION 2

Documents Relating
to the Organization of the
Parliamentarian Army

1. THE AMMUNITION OF THE KINGDOM

On 1 December 1641 there were 278 lasts, 8 cwt., 60lbs., of gunpowder remaining in His Majesty's stores at the Tower, Portsmouth and Hull. Deducting 61 lasts required for 10,000 foot, and for a train of 30 pieces of artillery for Ireland, there remained in the stores 217 lasts, 8 cwt. 60 lbs.[1]

2. THE MUNITIONS OF THE KINGDOM, 2 FEBRUARY 1642

Memorial of the Officers of Ordnance to the Lords and other the Committees for 'muniting' of this kingdom, and for the affairs of Ireland. The Parliament, by instituting the first of those Committees some months since, manifested their provident care for securing the kingdom against all hostile attempts. The first foundation of 'muniting' the kingdom principally depends upon the judicious state, competent endowment, and continual support of a necessary magazine. The Officers of Ordnance, under whose charge the grand magazine of all provisions for sea and land service has remained for ages, out of a zealous and true sense of their duties, and in pursuance of a former remonstrance by them exhibited to that Committee, hold themselves bound and humbly crave leave to present to the consideration of that Grand Council the state of the magazine and office of the Ordnance. First, as it is the only standing and grand magazine for the munitions of war, it must have both a primary and secondary influence on the navy, forts, castles, and armies of this kingdom. Secondly, in its proper end and use, when it moves with a marching train of artillery or fleet, it has a continual influence on the respective members of the standing camp, here specified, and in the supplying of ammunition for renewing of all fights, and for timely supply after the fight. In all which, and many other respects, the necessity of the times and their peculiar duties, calling upon them, they have presumed to exhibit a short view of the most important defects of that magazine and office under the general heads here particularised, and then more fully analyzed.

1. The defect for the complete 'mounture' of the Navy with brass ordinance is 400 pieces; and the Parliament in 1624 provided 500 iron ordnance with their carriages and other equipage for the mounture of 50 colliers to attend his Majesty's fleet, which since have otherwise been disposed of, so that now none are remaining in the magazine for that service. But what time the casting of those 900 pieces would take, the founders will be best able to inform.

2. The proportion of powder for continual supply of the magazine has formerly been 20 lasts per month. But the saltpetreworks being suppressed, no powder has been delivered into the magazine these 13 months; and when all the proportions already ordered by sea and land shall be issued, there will remain but 4 lasts 9 cwts. of powder.

3. The present store of match is now but 40 tons, which ought to be equal at the least, if not double, to the yearly proportion of the powder; which, if but 221 tons according to the Parliament proportion, 1626, with the help of foreign supply, cannot be provided under six months at the least.

4. Before the 8,016 muskets (issued and to be issued for Ireland) can be again supplied with rests and bandoleers, six months time will be necessarily employed, The pistols, carbines, dragoons long pikes, swords, halberds, partisans, drums, saddles, &c. likewise issued and to be further issued for the Irish supply, will require four months to replace. *Endorsed*: A copy of the remonstrance to be exhibited to the Parliament, 12 Feb. 1641.[2]

3. THE EARL OF ESSEX'S COMMISSION, 12 JULY 1642

Abstract of the Commission from both Houses of Parliament, appointing the Earl of Essex (Captain General of the Parliamentary forces, &c.) The Earl shall have power to raise forces, &c. of all kinds meet for the war in all counties, and to lead them against all enemies, traitors, and rebels, and to employ the same for preserving the safety of his Majesty's person, defence of the Parliament, and conservation of this realm and the subjects thereof in peace and from all unlawful violence, oppression, and force, howsoever countenanced by any pretended commission or authority from his Majesty or otherwise. He shall have power to assign, &c., and shall be assisted by a provost-marshal for the execution of his commands according to this ordinance, also to command all forts, castles, and ships, and to give instructions for the punishment of all mutinies, tumults, and misdemeanours according to the customs of war. The Earl, commanders, and officers in the execution of the premises shall be saved harmless, and defended by the power and authority of both Houses of Parliament.[3]

4. MOUNTING MONEY, 28 JULY 1642

Warrant of the Committee of Lords and Commons for the safety of the kingdom to the Treasurers of money and plate for raising of horse and horsemen for the defence of King and Parliament. Whereas it is ordered that the several captains, lieutenants, cornets and quartermasters of each troop shall receive the sum of 280*l*., to be divided amongst them according to these proportions, viz., to every captain 140*l*., every lieutenant 60*l*., every cornet 50*l*., and every quartermaster 30*l*., for the instant preparing and furnishing themselves with horse, furniture, arms, and whatsoever else is necessary, according to their several places and offices which they hold in the troop; and these moneys to issue out of the 10,000*l*. appointed to be paid out by the Treasurers of money and plate brought into the Guildhall, London, for the raising of horse, horsemen, and arms for the defence of the King, Parliament, and kingdom It is therefore now further ordered that the said Treasurers do upon sight hereof deliver the sum of 280*l*. to Captain Thomas Lydcott, one of the captains appointed for this service, for furnishing himself and the officers of his troop as above specified.[4]

5. CLOTHING FOR THE FOOT REGIMENTS

On 6 August 1642 the Committee of Lords and Commons for the safety of the Kingdom ordered that the soldiers should have delivered unto them, at their first marching, coats, shoes, shirts, and caps to the total value of 17s. for every man. This order was signed by Essex, Nathaniel Fiennes, John Pym and Sir John Meyrick.

On the back of the document is a list of the foot regiments raised for this expedition:

> The Lord General (Earl of Essex)
> (Earl of) Peterborough
> (Lord) Say and Sele
> (Lord) Mandeville
> (Lord) St. John
> (Lord) Wharton
> (Earl of) Stamford
> (Lord) Rochford
> (Lord) Brooke
> (Lord) Robarts (sic)
> Sergeant Major Generals (Sir John Merrick)
> (Denzil) Holles
> (Sir Henry) Cholmley
> (Thomas) Grantham
> Sir William Fairfax

Sir Wm. Constable
(John) Hampden
(Thomas) Ballard
(Charles) Essex
(William) Bamfield.[5]

6. SCOTS OFFICERS

WESTMINSTER. 7 AUGUST 1642.
Sir John Danvers to (Sir Robert Foster).
'Sir William Balfour has at last accepted the place of Lieutenant-General of the Horse, under the Earl of Bedford, and, for want of others, many Scotchmen are entertained to assist the commanders of the Parliament forces.'[6]

7. COMPOSITION OF THE FOOT BEFORE 20 AUGUST 1642

This breakdown is abstracted from THE LIST OF THE ARMIE,[7] which can be dated before 20 August, when Lt. Colonel Henry Billingsley (Holles, F.) who appears in it, was cashiered.

	Colonel	Lt. Colonel	Major	Captain	Lieutenant	Ensign	Chirugion	Carriage-Master Waggon-Master	Chaplain	Provost-Marshall	Quartermaster
Earl of Essex–	1	1	1	7	9	8	1	1	1	–	–
Sir John Merrick★	1	1	1	7	–	–	1	–	1	1	–
Earl of Peterborough	1	1	1	7	10	10	–	–	–	–	–
Earl of Stamford	1	1	1	7	10	9	1	1	–	1	1
Lord Say and Sele (later Sir John Meldrum)	1	1	1	7	9	9	–	–	–	–	1
Lord Wharton	1	1	1	7	10	10	1	–	–	1	–
Lord Rochford	1	1	1	7	10	9	–	1	1	1	1
Lord St. John	1	1	1	7	10	10	1	1	1	1	1
Lord Brooke	1	1	1	7	10	10	1	1	–	1	1
Lord Mandeville	1	1	1	7	10	9	1	1	1	1	1
Lord Robartes	1	1	1	7	9	10	1	1	1	1	1
Sir Henry Cholmley	1	1	1	7	9	7	–	–	1	1	–
Denzil Holles	1	1	1	7	8	6	–	–	–	–	–
William Bamfield	1	1	1	7	10	10	1	1	1	1	1
Thomas Grantham	1	1	1	7	10	10	–	1	–	1	1
Sir William Constable	1	1	1	7	10	10	1	1	1	1	1
Thomas Ballard	1	1	1	7	9	10	1	1	–	1	1
Sir William Fairfax	1	1	1	7	10	10	1	1	–	1	1
Charles Essex	1	1	–	7	10	10	1	–	1	1	1
John Hampden★	1	1	1	7	3	2	–	–	1	–	–

★List of this regiment is obviously incomplete.

8. PAY FOR THE ARMY

There is among the State Papers a note by William Jessop (Deputy to Sir Gilbert Gerard) that on 29 September 1642 he sent from Guildhall in a waggon, eight chests of money, containing £10,000. This was received by Captain Francis Vernon, another of Sir Gilbert's deputies, at Worcester on 11 October.[8]

9. COLONEL JOHN BROWN'S FORCE AT POWICK BRIDGE, 23 SEPTEMBER, 1642

Brown commanded a regiment of dragoons. Whether the whole regiment was present is not clear. The regimenting of the Parliamentarian horse was as yet incomplete. There were ten troops of horse present.

		Troop*
Colonel Edwin Sandys	MW	33
Major Alex. Douglas	K	38
Captain Rob. Burrell	Reported K. but Colonel, 1643	18
Captain John Neale		26
Captain Edward Berry	K	37
Captain Thomas Lidcott	PW	39
Captain George Austin	PW	52
Captain John Fiennes		60
Captain Nathaniel Fiennes		. .
Captain Edward Wingate	PW	. .

*The numbers in the list printed by Peacock.

Of these the troops of Sandys, Douglas and Berry belonged to Sandys' Regiment; Burrell was major to Lord Feilding at Edgehill, while Nathaniel Fiennes served in Sir William Balfour's Regiment.

With the exception of Burrell's and Nathaniel Fiennes' troops those survivors of Powick Bridge who also fought at Edgehill must have been among Sir James Ramsey's 24 troops on the Parliamentarian left, facing Prince Rupert.

10. MEMBERS OF THE LONG PARLIAMENT IN ARMS IN 1642

	Member for:
Captain John Alured (1607–1659)*	Hedon
Captain Oliver Cromwell (1599–1658)*	Cambridge
Captain John Fiennes (c.1601–1674)	Oxfordshire
Captain Nathaniel Fiennes (1608–1669)	Banbury
Colonel Thomas Grantham (1612–1655/6)	Lincoln
Captain Thomas Lord Grey of Groby (1623?–1657)*	Leicester
Colonel John Hampden (1594–1643)	Buckinghamshire
Captain Sir Arthur Hesilrige (d.1661)	Leicestershire
Colonel Denzil Holles (1599–1680)	Dorchester
Captain Sir Samuel Luke (1603–1670)	Bedford
Sir John Meyrick (c.1600–1659)	Newcastle-under-Lyme

Charles Pym (c.1620–1671)	Beeralston
Colonel Sir Philip Stapleton (1603–1647)	Boroughbridge
Colonel John Venn (1586–1650)	London
Captain Valentine Walton (c.1594–1661)★	Huntingdonshire
Captain Edward Wingate (1606–1685)	St. Albans
Captain Thomas Hatcher (1589?–1677)	Stamford
	Not at Edgehill.

The regicides are marked with an asterisk.

11. OFFICERS CHARGED WITH THE EXAMINATION OF SIR JAMES RAMSEY

At St. Albans on 5 November 1642 a Committee met to examine the conduct of Sir James Ramsey at Edgehill, There were present:

> Sir John Merrick, President of the Council,
> Earl of Peterborough, General of the Ordnance,
> Sir William Balfour, Lieutenant-General of the Horse,
> Colonel Thomas Ballard, F.,
> Colonel Sir John Meldrum, F.,
> Colonel Lord Willoughby of Parham, H.,
> Colonel Sir Philip Stapleton, H.,
> Colonel Lord Rochford, F.,
> Colonel John Middleton, D.,
> Colonel Sir William Fairfax, F.

There were in attendance:

> Isaac Dorislaus, Advocate of the Army,
> Ro. Chambers, Secretary of the Army.[9]

Three officers were 'severally examined' and spoke in favour of Ramsey. They were: Colonel Middleton, Major Baylie and Major Melvill, all apparently Scots and probably some of those Ramsey had persuaded to join the Parliamentarians. It seems odd that Middleton, one of the witnesses, should also have been a member of the committee.[9]

Of the other members, Lord Willoughby of Parham and Lord Rochford had come up too late for the battle; Merrick had been at Worcester. Balfour, Ballard and Meldrum had all done well. Only Fairfax commanded a regiment that had run away.

12. 'THE STRATEGIC RESERVE'

The London Trained Bands.[10]

In the autumn of 1642 there were six regiments of London Trained Bands commanded by Major-General Philip Skippon (d. 1660), a veteran of the Dutch service, who was to distinguish himself throughout the war.

	Regiment	*Colours*	*Distinctions*	*Number of Companies*
1.	Red	Argent	Piles wavy	7
2.	White	Gules	Lozenges	7
3.	Yellow	Sable	Mullets	7
4.	Blue	Blue	Plates	7

| 5. | Green | Argent | Calthrops | 6 |
| 6. | Orange | Argent | Trefoils | 6 |

All the colonels were aldermen. The names of the field-officers were:

	Colonels	*Lt. Colonels*	*Sgt. Majors*
1.	Thomas Atkins	Marmaduke Rawden[11]	Randolph Manwaring
2.	Isaac Pennington	George Langham	Robert Davis
3.	Sir John Wollaston	John Venn	William Geere
4.	Thomas Adams	Edmund Foster	Samuel Carleton
5.	John Warner	Mathew Forster	Owen Rowe
6.	John Towse	Rowland Wilson	Thomas Buxton

13. A SHORTAGE OF SUTLERS' WAGGONS

22 November 1642.

Order of the Committee of the Lords and Commons for the Safety of the Kingdom. That 26 waggons be forthwith provided for sutlers for victualling 13 regiments. The Waggon-Master General now has only 14 serviceable waggons belonging to the State. He is forthwith to take up country waggons in and about London sufficient to make up 26. He is to cause them to be valued by the Commissaries appointed to value horses in London; upon whose certificate of their value the Treasurer of the Army shall satisfy it to the owners.[12]

1 CSPD 1641–3, p. 187.
2 *Ibid.*, p. 280–1.
3 *Ibid.*, p. 353.
4 *Ibid.*, p. 362–3.
5 *Ibid.*, p. 366.
6 *Ibid.*, p. 367.
7 Peacock, pp.25–46.
8 CSPD p. 395.
9 The Vindication of Sir James Ramsey.
10 British Museum. Thomason Tracts. 669.f.6.10.
11 Became a Royalist colonel and took part in the defence of Basing House and Faringdon Castle.
12 CSPD p. 408.

SECTION 3

Notes on the Royalist regiments

HORSE

THE LIFEGUARD

At Edgehill the two troops of the Lifeguard formed one squadron. Sir Philip Warwick, who describes himself, though a Member of Parliament, 'as one of the most inconsiderable Persons' in the Lifeguard, estimates the strength of the two troops at about 300 horse. He tells us that this 'Volunteer-Guard' was made up of Noblemen, Gentlemen and 'their attendance', and that they reckoned the value of their estates at £100,000 a year.

The officers of the King's troop were probably:

> Captain Lord Bernard Stuart.
> Capt.-Lieut. Sir Troilus Turbervile.
> Cornet John Walpole.
> Quartermaster Thomas Rutter.

Among the 'rank and file' were:

> The Earl of Denbigh.
> The Earl of Dover.
> Lord Capel.
> Sir Philip Warwick.
> Sir Henry Newton.
> Sir Thomas Corbett.
> Charles Cavendish.

The last-named showed such gallantry at Edgehill that he was given command of the Duke of York's troop, whose commander, Lord d'Aubigny, had been killed, and on 29 December he became a colonel.[1]

The Earls of Denbigh and Dover both had sons in Essex's army; Lords Feilding and Rochford.

The troop served throughout the war and particularly distinguished itself at Cropredy Bridge (1644).

PRINCE OF WALES

The history of this regiment, which had seven troops in 1642, has been traced in articles by the present writer.[2]

The Colonel was Sir Thomas Byron, who also commanded the Prince's troop. His Lieutenant, Thomas Daniel, of Beswick, Yorkshire, was major by 1643. The Prince's cornet was another Yorkshireman, a son of Sir Thomas Metham. Lord d'Aubigny, the commander of the Duke of York's troop, was a brother of the Duke of Richmond.

The Earl of Newcastle's troop was commanded, according to Bulstrode, 'by his brother Collonel Cavendish'. It had been raised, 120 strong, among his tenants and friends, and had been sent south as escort to a consignment of arms sent by the King from Holland. According to the Duchess of Newcastle 'it seems his Majesty liked the troop so well, that he was pleased to command their stay to recruit his own army'.[3]

According to Bulstrode Lord Willoughby d'Eresby commanded the troop of his father, the Earl of Lindsey. But in fact he fought at the head of the Lifeguard, F., and we do not know who the effective commander of the troop may have been. It seems not unlikely that it was some other member of the Bertie family, several of whom were in arms.

The Earls of Northampton and Westmorland 'commanded each their own Troop'.[4] The former was the head of a whole-heartedly Royalist family. Bulstrode began his service under him and writes:

'I was then with the Earl of Northampton [1601–1643], in his own Troop, which consisted of One Hundred Gentlemen of Quality. The Lord Compton, eldest Son to the Earl, was the Right-hand Man; Sir Charles Compton, his second Son, was Cornet; and Mr. [Robert] Arden, a Gentleman of one of the most ancient Families in Warwickshire, was Lieutenant to the Earl.'[5]

Northampton was commissioned as a colonel of horse on 25 November. As a veteran of Breda and Lemgo and a man of considerable wealth, he was an obvious choice for command of a regiment. With 100 gentlemen in his troop the Earl had not far to look for the 28 officers required for a regiment of 500 horse. It is not too bold, therefore, to suggest that his original officers had fought in his troop at Edgehill. These included:

Lord Compton.	Wounded as Lt. Colonel at Hopton Heath, and succeeded his father as Earl of Northampton.
Charles Compton.	Lt Colonel.
John Knotsford.	Wounded as a captain at Hopton Heath.
Harvey.	Captain. Killed at Hopton Heath 19 March 1643.
James Chamberlaine.	Youngest brother of Sir Thomas Chamberlaine, High Sheriff of Oxfordshire. Captain, K. near Towcester 4 Aug. 1643. Had fought at Powick Bridge, Edgehill and Brentford 'where his valour was eminently manifested'; and, probably, at Hopton Heath and Middleton Cheney.[6]

Herbert Jeffries.	Of Herefordshire. Lieutenant to James Chamberlaine. Nephew of Sir Herbert Price.[7]
George Chamberlaine.	Captain, vice Richard Bulstrode, of the troop originally raised by his brother, James Chamberlaine.[8]
Matthew Clarke.	Probably captain at Middleton Cheney (6 May 1643). His lieutenant, Daniell Kingsmill, PW I Newbury. PW himself at Compton House 9 June 1644.
Daniell Kingsmill.	Lieutenant to Clarke. PW I Newbury.
Sir William Farmer.	Captain by 19 December 1643.
Flamock Colborne.	Captain by 1645, later major.
Henry Browne.	Captain, or capt.-lieut. Buried Banbury 26 Oct. 1645.
Gyles Slany.	Captain in 1644.
. . . Middleton.	Captain or Lieutenant. K 22 Aug. 1644.
John Moore.	Captain in November 1644.
Reynold Wooton.	Captain in 1645.

Besides these William Tirwhitt lost an arm at Brentford in this troop, and being disabled for the horse service became a foot captain in the garrison of Banbury.[9]

It seems not unlikely that the captains of 1645 were the subalterns of 1643, chosen from among the gentlemen-volunteers of 1642.

Mildmay Fane, second Earl of Westmorland, K.B. (1602–1666), made his peace with the Parliament in 1644.

The seventh troop of the regiment was commanded by Captain Davison, 'an old experienced Low-Country Soldier, who was recommended for that Employ, by the old Earl of Northampton'.[10]

The regiment was being raised as early as June 1642, and had plenty of financial backing. It was probably the strongest cavalry regiment in the King's army at Edgehill, and though the troops were no doubt unequal in size, it is a reasonable assumption that the regiment was already at full strength, and could muster some 500 men.

PRINCE RUPERT

On 25 December 1642 the regiment was 465 strong with 630 horses. There were seven troops, including the Lifeguard. All the troop commanders were with the army before Edgehill, and since the unit had done no serious fighting during the two months since the battle, the December list is a fair guide to its strength on 23 October. The weakness of Legge's troop is accounted for by his being a prisoner of war between 23 August and about 4 October.

The organization of the regiment on 23 December was:

	Men	Horse
For the Prince	100	200
Lieuten[t] Colonell O Neale	70	80
Sergeant Major Legg	15	30

Sʳ Lewis Dive & Sʳ Tho: Dallison	140	160
My Lord Dillon and Sʳ Willm Pennyman	140	160
	465	630[11]

Other officers of the regiment included Sir Richard Crane, who commanded Prince Rupert's Lifeguard, which was soon to become independent of the regiment, Lieutenant Clement Martin and Legge's lieutenant, Noland, who was to be killed at Cirencester (2 February 1643).

Pennyman's troop did not remain long for by March 1643 he had a regiment of his own. But no others left and Rupert gradually increased his regiment until at the relief of Newark (21 March 1644) he had 10 troops as well as the Lifeguard.

The regiment was 500 strong at Marston Moor. When Will. Legge became Governor of Oxford (c. January 1645) the Prince seems to have given him at least four troops as a cadre for a new regiment, and in May 1645 Rupert's, now under Sir Thomas Dallison, Bart., consisted of 400 men in 8 troops. The Lifeguard, still under Sir Richard Crane, was 140 strong.[12]

The regiment, like its commander, was always in the thick of the fighting. Such was the Prince's magnetism that he was far more successful than any other Royalist commander in keeping his units up to strength, though he was far from being a wealthy man. Prince Rupert's troops were disbanded at Oxford on 24 April 1646.[13]

Rupert's officers included several professional soldiers. Crane had probably been at Lemgo (1638). O'Neale had been major to Sir John Conyers' Regiment in the Second Scots War; while Legge, though only a captain, had been lieutenant-general of the ordnance.[14] He was also master of the Royal Armoury. Clement Martin, a cornet in 1639, had been a lieutenant in Viscount Conway's Regiment of Horse in the Second Scots War. Dallison (1591–1645) had been in the Captain-General's Regiment in 1639.[15] His officers seem to have been play actors, who had been deprived of their livelihood when the Parliamentarians closed the theatres. These were Lieutenant Charles Hart, Cornet Nicholas Burt and Quartermaster Robert Shatterel. It seems likely that they served at Edgehill.

On 2 April 1644 Mr Robinson, who had ridden in Dallison's troop for two years, was recommended to the Prince for command of a foot company. Thomas Killigrew wrote: 'What metal he is I refer you to Sir Thomas Dallison', adding that this promotion would be a favour to 'Tom'. A man with two years service in April 1644 must have been a veteran of Edgehill. The letter is further evidence, were any needed, that the ranks of the Royalist cavalry were full of officer material.[16] Richard Grace, an Irishman who was a captain in the regiment in 1644 and therefore in all probability one of the original subalterns, had a remarkable career. He commanded Ormonde's Regiment of Foot in King Charles II's army raised in the Low Countries in 1656 and fought for the Spaniards at the battle of Dunkirk Dunes (1658). He was killed fighting for King James II when General Ginkell surprised Athlone in 1691. He must have had nearly 50 years military service.[17]

PRINCE MAURICE'S REGIMENT

This regiment had a good fighting record and rose to a strength of 400 in the summer of 1643.[18] At the Aldbourne Chase rendezvous (10 April 1644) the regiment was 300 strong and had seven troops with red standards.[19]

At Edgehill the regiment was probably incomplete for three of the early troop commanders had not yet received their commissions.[20]

It follows that there were not more than four troops at Edgehill. Undoubtedly these would include those of the field officers, Guy Molesworth and Thomas Sheldon, both of whom had been in the Second Scots War. Molesworth had been captain-lieutenant to Northumberland's Regiment, F., and Thomas Sheldon had been an ensign in Sir James Hamilton's, F.[21] The latter is mentioned by the 'Deserter', though wrongly assigned to the Prince of Wales' Regiment. He became major though probably not until the regiment was complete. Since Sir Ralph Dutton's Regiment of Foot was already with the army, it may be deduced that his troop, which served in Maurice's Regiment, was also present. He received a colonel's commission on 28 January 1643, but his regiment never seems to have been completed. To put the strength of the regiment at 180 is conservative. It may well have numbered 200 or even more.

Further details of the regiment's history may be found in the *Vindication of Richard Atkyns*.[22]

SIR JOHN BYRON'S REGIMENT

This, with the possible exception of the Prince of Wales', was the first completed for the Marquis of Worcester gave the colonel £5000 in gold for mounting money. Sir John's letter acknowledging the receipt of this money was dated from Leicester Abbey on 24 July 1642.[23]

At Roundway Down (13 July 1643) Francis Butler was Byron's lieutenant-colonel and there is no reason to suppose that he had not held this appointment since the beginning of the war. Three of Byron's brothers seem to have been in his regiment at Edgehill: Richard, Gilbert and William. Mrs Hutchinson says that Byron and his brothers had been bred in arms,[24] and this is certainly true of Gilbert who had been lieutenant to Major Dan O'Neale in Sir John Conyer's Regiment in the Second Scots War.[25] For this reason it seems likely that he rather than his elder brother, Richard, was major of the regiment. William, though major later in the war, does not seem to have had a troop at the outset. Perhaps he was captain-lieutenant or cornet to Sir John, Allen Apsley was certainly a captain as early as August.[26] St. John, one of the family from Lydiard Tregoze, Wiltshire, is first mentioned on 1 January 1643,[27] but since the Royalists lost very few cavalry officers in the 1642 campaign, there is no reason to suppose that he had not been a troop commander from the start. This was almost certainly Edward St. John (1617–1645), whose monument known as 'The Golden Cavalier' may be seen in the little church at Lydiard Tregoze. He was the fourth son of Sir John St. John and was related to Allen Apsley.

The regiment was 150 to 200 strong when it reached Oxford on 28 August, but was recruited by volunteers from the University and 250 seems a very modest estimate of its probable strength at Edgehill.

The regiment was to see a great deal of fighting, and particularly distinguished itself at Roundway Down (13 July 1643).

LORD WILMOT'S REGIMENT

Wilmot was raising his regiment by 5 August 1642[28] and by 25 December had 355 men and 450 horses.[29] Its strength at Edgehill was probably much the same.

The officers included several who had seen service. Lt. Colonel Edward Feilding had fought in the Low Countries.[30] Paul Smith had been a captain in the Marquis of Hamilton's Regiment, F., in the Second Scots War, and John Harvey had been a captain in the General of the Horse's Regiment in 1641.[31]

Wilmot's captain-lieutenant was Robert Walsh who played some part in rescuing the Banner Royal at Edgehill, and whose account of the battle appears on p. 292. He rose to be lieutenant-colonel, H., to Sir George Vaughan, the High Sheriff of Wiltshire (1643).

On 10 April 1644 Lord Wilmot's Regiment still had six troops and 250 men. The officers were:

> Lt. Colonel Paul Smyth
> Major Aymes Pollard
> { Captain John Harvey
> { Lieut. (Henry) Fitzwilliams
> { Cornet John Phillips, who was shot in the knee at Roundway Down
> Captain Duplant, a frenchman
> Captain Baskervile
> Capt.-Lieut. Wilmot

By this time Frescheville was a colonel, with Jack Jammot as his major, and his troop had left the regiment. The other officers, as likely as not, were Edgehill men, with the exception of Aymes Pollard who was with Hopton in the West in 1642.[32] Wilmot was dismissed in August 1644 and Pollard succeeded him as colonel.

At Edgehill Edward Feilding's lieutenant was Edward Panton.[33]

LORD GRANDISON'S REGIMENT

This was one of the oldest regiments for it was already being raised on 5 August 1642[34]. Assuming that Grandison was commissioned to raise six troops as was usual, he cannot have had more than four troops at Edgehill, for when Hopton began to assemble the Somersetshire Royalists he found two troops of Grandison's Regiment that had been levied there by commission from the King. Their commanders were Mr John Digby and Sir Francis Hawley and they remained with Hopton in the West.[35]

We can reconstruct Grandison's Regiment with some accuracy from the list of officers captured at Winchester in December[36] and from a list of prisoners sent from Portsmouth to Lambeth House.[37]

Troop Commanders	Lieutenants	Cornets
Colonel Lord Grandison	CaptLieut. Edward Gerard	John Bennett
Major Sir Richard Willys	Philip Honywood	. . . Savage
Captain Lord John Stuart[38]	Sir John Smith	. . .
Captain Francis Bertie[39]	Richard Williamson	George Booth

THE EARL OF CARNARVON'S REGIMENT

De Gomme seems to indicate that Carnarvon had four troops at Edgehill. The troop commanders would be the Earl and his lieutenant-colonel, Sir Charles Lucas; Richard Neville, who succeeded to the command when Carnarvon fell at I Newbury; and Alexander Standish, who was to be Neville's second-in-command.

Carnarvon had commanded a regiment in the second Scots War and Lucas, a professional soldier, had been trained in the Low Countries.

LORD DIGBY'S REGIMENT

On 11 January 1643 Digby's regiment had four troops. De Gomme's plan seems to imply that at Edgehill there were no more than three. The troop commanders would have included Digby himself, and his successor, Thomas Weston, a son of the first Earl of Portland, who was probably a field officer from the first.

A List of [Indigent] Officers includes Quartermaster Hugh Grainger (Staffordshire) who served under Colonel John Lane in this regiment.[40] By March 1643 Lane was a colonel and governor of Stafford. He can, therefore only have been a troop commander in Digby's regiment at the *beginning* of the war. He came from Wolverhampton, and was the elder brother of Jane Lane, who was instrumental in assisting the escape of King Charles II after Worcester (1651).

The fourth troop, only commissioned on 16 October 1642,[41] was possibly not present at Edgehill. Its commander, Richard Herbert (1600?–1655), was raising a regiment, F.,[42] which had not yet joined the army. Herbert had fought in the Scots War; he was M.P. for Montgomery (1640) and the eldest son of Lord Herbert of Cherbury.

Another officer of the regiment was (Captain?) Lieutenant Henry Harris, commissioned on 16 October 1642. He seems to have become lieutenant-colonel to Weston and was certainly still with the army in August 1644.[43]

The troopers included Henry Elkins of Kingswood, Wiltshire. A tailor by trade he had quite an impressive record. His petition of 1661 describes him as being:

' . . . a Souldier under the Comaund of the Right Ho[ble]: George Lord Digby in the service of his late Ma[tie] King Charles the first . . At Marlborough, Edghill, Newbery, Upton-upon-seavern, stow on the would, and at divers other places . . In w[ch] severall services yo[r] poore pet[r]. hath bin several times wounded & hurte . . . '

He had a wife and seven small children and in 1661 received a pension of 40 shillings a year.[44]

COLONEL SIR THOMAS ASTON

De Gomme seems to indicate that there were only three troops at Edgehill. The regiment was evidently raised in Cheshire and Lancashire and there is some evidence that the troops of Thomas Prestwich and William Radcliffe had been left there to assist Viscount Cholmondeley[45] in securing Cheshire, where Sir William Brereton was active for the Parliament.

Early in 1643 the regiment returned to Cheshire and was in the defeat at Middlewich (13 March 1643). A number of officers witnessed Sir Thomas Aston's account of the fight and probably belonged to the regiment. They were:

> Tho. Prestwich (Captain)
> Tho. Roston
> Tho. Holme. Major
> R(ichard) Wiltshire
> Jo. Wiltshire
> Fr. Aston

Wm. Ratcliffe (Captain)
Th. Roper
Nath. Naper (or Napper, Captain)[46]

Richard Wilshire had been Ensign to Captain Edward Villiers in Lord Grandison's Regiment, F., in 1641.[47] He rose to be lieutenant-colonel to Sir Thomas Prestwich, one of Sir Thomas Aston's successors in command of the regiment.[48] His presence at Edgehill is uncertain, but likely.

Francis Aston had been an ensign under Sir Arthur Aston in 1640[49]. Obviously a relative of his colonel's, he was probably his cornet at Edgehill.

The Cheshire Quarter Sessions Records cast a little light on the composition of this unit. The 'maimed soldiers' who petitioned for pensions after the Restoration include:

Corporal John Wright of Captain Flemming's troop, who served for four and a half years, and was wounded at Edgehill. William Holt or Hoult of Wade Green in Dutton Crewett, Lancashire, also served in Flemming's troop. His petition mentions his service at Edgehill, in Oxfordshire, at Brentford and in Cornwall (1644).

Thomas Jackson of Aston was in Sir James Bridgeman's troop at Edgehill. John Kettle of Over, who was also in Bridgeman's troop, fought at Edgehill, Brentford and Nantwich.

It looks therefore as if Aston had at least three troops at Edgehill.

Colonel Sir Thomas Aston
Lt. Colonel Sir James Bridgeman
Lieut. William Flemming

The regiment had an active career and was one of those disbanded in the West in 1646. Aston was succeeded as colonel in 1645 by Sir William Radcliffe, who was followed by Sir Thomas Prestwich.

THE GENTLEMEN PENSIONERS

Edgehill was the only battle of the Civil Wars in which the Gentlemen Pensioners appeared as a troop of horse. They were commanded by their lieutenant, Sir William Howard, K.B., of Tollesbury, Essex, and were some 50 strong. Miles Mathews, who was still a Pensioner in 1660, greatly distinguished himself in the defence of the young princes. It was probably then that Sir Henry Reeve was slain.

It is difficult to say who the other Pensioners present may have been. There is a list of 1636, but most of the names are Scots, and since few of them figure in the annals of the war, it seems likely that they were men who had been appointed by James VI and I and who in 1642 were rather elderly to bear arms. Those present probably included:

Road by
which
Royalist
right des-
cended
Edgehill
→

Probable
Royalist
'Start
Line'

→ to Radway

→ Radway

Edgehill
slope.

← Track
down
which
Royalist
left
would
have des-
cended
the hill

→ Radway

← Westcote
Manor

Ford of the Dene River

Here, according to Sanderson Miller, bodies and pieces of armour were dug up. The bridge is nineteenth century. The wide ford was at the left of the picture. Here Wilmot's men must have caught up with Parliamentarian runaways fleeing down the Tysoe–Kineton road. The first houses of Kineton can be seen in the background.

Mediaeval Round Tower on Beacon Hill

The news that a battle had been fought is said to have been signalled to London from this point. The church in the distance is Burton Dassett. The story that Cromwell watched the battle from this hill may be discounted.

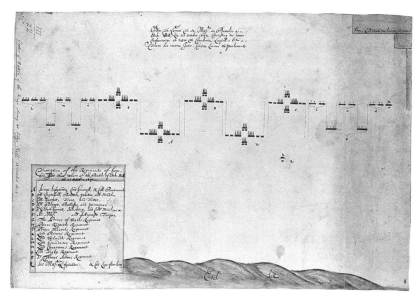
De Gomme's Plan

Edgehill: Then and Now
Taken from the left rear of Sir Arthur Aston's position. In 1642 the whole ridge must have resembled the bare down to the right of the picture. The 'hanging woods' were planted by Sanderson Miller, *c*. 1750.

The Monument at Edgehill
This stands by the B.4086 and is right on Sir James Ramsey's position.

. . . Bunnington. Killed at Leicester, 1645, as major of Prince Rupert's firelocks.
Edward Cooper. Knighted at Oxford in 1645.
James Croft. Became a lieutenant-colonel and compounded on Oxford articles.
Knighted during the winter of 1644/1645.
Sir Arnold Herbert. 1636 list and Oxford articles.
Sir Elias or Ellis Hickes. 1636 and 1660 lists.
Miles Mathews. See above. 1660 list.
William Painter. 1636 list. Compounded for his estate. May have become a captain.
Sir Henry Reeve. Killed at Edgehill.
Sir John Saltonstall. 1636 list. Oxford articles.
Sir Nicholas Selwyn. 1636 list. Later commanded the City of Oxford Regiment, F.
Humphrey Sydenham. A Pensioner by 1638. Major, H., to Colonel Edmond Wynd-
ham.
Francis Windham. 1636 list. May have been serving in the West.
Henry Wroth. 1636 list. Afterward served in the Lifeguard, H. Knighted 1645.
Sir John Wyndham. Was with the King at York.

After Edgehill some of the pensioners became commissioned officers.
It seems that others were merged into the Lifeguard of Horse.

FOOT

COLONEL CHARLES GERARD'S REGIMENT

Gerard's bluecoats, ten companies, were raised in Lancashire, Cheshire
and North Wales, including Flintshire and Montgomeryshire.

No list of the officers exists but one can be compiled, mainly from the
Royalist Ordnance Papers. At Edgehill the company commanders
probably included:

> Colonel Charles Gerard.
> Lt. Colonel Edward Villiers.
> Major Francis Windebanke.
> Captain Randle Egerton (d.1681).
> Captain Edward Hatton.
> Captain Gilbert Gerard.
> Captain Roger Whitley (1618–1697), Gerard's brother-in-law.
> Captain Floyd.
> Captain (Sir) Charles Leigh

Other officers were:

> Capt. Lieut. Charles (?) Sledd.
> Lieutenant Euble Lloyd, Windebanke's company.
> Lieutenant Richard Arter (sic), Gilbert Gerard's company.
> Quartermaster Ja: Hodgson.

William Hassell of Henkelow, Cheshire, served under Colonel Sir
Charles Vavasour,[50] and in 1642 became a sergeant in Captain Randle
Egerton's company and fought at Edgehill. When he petitioned he was
of St. Mary Magdalen parish, Oxford. Gerard's Regiment had been

garrisoned there from 1642 to 1646 and it would seem that the sergeant had made himself comfortable.[51]

Jasper Edmond, a soldier in Captain Floyd's company, was shot through the knee and lost his whole limb. Though he came from Montgomery, he was recommended (16 January 1644) to the Treasurer of the county of Oxfordshire for the relief provided by statute.[52]

Colonel Charles Gerard was the son of Sir Charles Gerard of Halsall, Lancashire. Windebanke's company was raised in Denbighshire.[53] Roger Whitley's father, Thomas, had been High Sheriff of Flint (1637), but after the Restoration he made a fortune farming the Post Office and bought Peel Hall, Cheshire, where he was to entertain King William III on his journey to Ireland.[54]

COLONEL SIR LEWIS DYVE'S REGIMENT

The commissions of Dyve's officers dated from 13 August 1642.[55] At Edgehill the company commanders of his regiment were:

> Colonel Sir Lewis Dyve.
> Lt. Colonel Thomas Shirley.
> Major Gervase Holles of Grimsby, Lincolnshire, Esq. (1607-1675)
> Capt. John Smyth of Somersby, Lincolnshire, Gent.
> Capt. Gabriell Savill of Wakefield, Yorkshire, Gent.
> Capt. Henry Peyton.
> Capt. Richard Nevill.
> Capt. Arthur Slingsby.[56]

By 23 May 1643 the original captains of Dyve's Regiment had all gone. Probably few, if any, were battle casualties, the major, Gervase Holles, was raising his own regiment of foot (Commissioned 7 December 1642[57]), while Richard Nevill is probably the man who was lieutenant-colonel, H., to Sir John Henderson, Governor of Newark.[58] Others also had probably returned to secure their own counties now that it was evident that the war would not be 'over by Christmas'.

On 23 May 1643 Dyve's captains, probably subalterns at Edgehill were:

> John Glassington
> Lawson
> Bolsworth
> Hamon
> Greenefeild[59]

Thomas Shirley (knighted 25 February 1646), who had been a captain in 1640, was still lieutenant-colonel, as he was throughout the regiment's existence. Glassington, who laid down his arms between 27 August 1644 and 28 April 1645,[60] was probably at Edgehill, and Hamon certainly was according to Sanderson, who, apparently mistakenly, refers to him as captain in his account of the battle. He was in Dyve's defence of

Sherborne Castle, 1645. Lawson died of the plague and was buried at Oxford on 29 July 1644.[61] Sanderson [62] says Hamon was a captain at Edgehill, and he may have been captain-lieutenant.

Dyve's quartermaster was John Audley.[63]

There is a good life of Sir Lewis Dyve by H. G. Tibbutt.[64]

COLONEL SIR RALPH DUTTON

Dutton's regiment of whitecoats had 10 companies.

The Duttons were an extremely wealthy family from Sherborne, Gloucestershire, and Sir Ralph probably raised many of his men in that county. His regiment, 800 strong, joined the King at Nottingham and he probably raised some of his men on the march, perhaps in Shropshire, which though a Royalist county produced no complete regiment for the Edgehill army.

On 23 May 1643 the company commanders were:

> Colonel Sir Ralph Dutton.
> Lt. Colonel Stephen Hawkins. Commissioned 28 July 1642 at Beverley.
> Major Degory Collins.
> Captain John Palmer.
> Captain Charles Kirke.
> Captain Will. Atkins
> Captain Matthew Radcliff.
> Captain Hopkins or Hoskins.
> Captain Thomas Hull.
> Captain Lou or Low (d.1643).

Dutton, perhaps because he was wealthy, had managed to collect officers of some experience. In 1640 Hawkins and Collins had been captains under Colonel Jerome Brett, F., and Palmer had been Hawkins' lieutenant. Kirke had been a lieutenant and Atkins had been an ensign.[65] It is likely that these 1640 officers were captains in 1642. Radcliffe was a captain at Cirencester and Hopkins at Edgehill, where Thomas Pritchard of his company was shot in the leg.[66]

Other officers included George Grimes, who was promoted to command Dutton's company (14 December 1643), soon after Hawkins took over the regiment, and Bradley who was a captain in the defence of Greenland House (1644). The Quartermaster was Thomas Littleton.

The career of one of Dutton's officers, Charles Kirke, may be reconstructed:

	1640	Lieutenant to Captain Henry Ventris in Colonel Sir William Ogle's Regiment.[67]
11 Dec.	1640	Discharged as a papist.[68]
(23 Oct.	1642	Battle of Edgehill.)
31 Jan.	1643	Captain by this date.[69]
(26 July	1643	Storming of Bristol.)
(20 Sept.	1643	First Battle of Newbury.)

6 Dec.	1643	Promoted major.
(Jun.–Jul.	1644	Defence of Greenland House.)
25 Oct.	1644	At the relief of Banbury.[70]
15 Nov.	1645	Sat on Lord Ogle's Court Martial at Oxford.[71]
	1663	Indigent officer. L & W.[72]

COLONEL THOMAS BLAGGE

Little is known about this regiment. Blagge was a Suffolk man and so were five out of his 12 indigent officers, but it would be strange if a Royalist regiment had been raised in the heart of the Eastern Association.

Blagge's lieutenant-colonel was (Sir) Will. Lower, who was probably with him from the first. 'Deserter', who is not altogether reliable, gives Barnaby Scudamore as his major in 1642. This is possible, though when Henry Hastings raised his regiment, H., Scudamore was his major.[73] In 1643 Robert Walters of Little Ouseburn, Yorkshire, was major to Blagge,[74] so he may have been one of the original captains.

Suffolk men can hardly have joined the regiment after 1642, since it would have been almost impossible for them to make their way through the Parliamentarian quarters. It seems likely, therefore, that Blagge's five Suffolk officers were with him from the first, though not necessarily with the rank given in *A List of [Indigent] Officers*. They were:

> Captain John Snelling
> Captain John Barber
> Lieutenant Jasper Brydon
> Lieutenant John Welham
> Lieutenant Thomas Loudell (Lowdall)

Another original officer was Lieutenant Edward Evans.[75]

Though never knighted, Blagge was a staunch Royalist and fought at Worcester (1651) and Dunkirk Dunes (1658).

COLONEL JOHN BELASYSE'S REGIMENT

This regiment of 10 companies was raised in Yorkshire and Nottinghamshire.

According to 'Deserter', the lieutenant-colonel was Sir Thomas Danby. This may well be correct. The major was Theophilus Gilby, who seems to have become lieutenant-colonel about May 1643, and eventually succeeded Belasyse as colonel.

At Edgehill the captains included Henry Bellingham, who was mortally wounded, and Bartholomew Pell, who was major by 23 May, and appears in *A List of [Indigent] Officers* as lieutenant-colonel to Sir Theophilus Gilby.

On 23 May 1643 the captains were:

> Francis Godfrey.
> John Woolverston, lieutenant in 1640.[76]

Henry Udall (Uvedale).
Baynes.
John Pollack.
Will. Booth, later major.
John Hilliard, later major.

All these must have been officers at Edgehill, but not necessarily as captains. Capt.-Lieut. Umphrey Baine, buried at Radley, Berkshire, 18 July 1643, would be another of the original officers.

The career of Lt. Colonel Francis Godfrey, a Norfolk man and a Catholic,[77] is worth recording.

(1638)	Ensign Godfrey is in the list of officers returned from foreign parts.
1640	Ensign Francis Godfrey was in Captain John Waldgrave's company in Colonel Sir Thomas Glenham's Regiment, F.[78]
11 December	Discharged as a papist.[79]
1642	(No doubt joined Colonel John Belasyse's Regt. F.) (The Battle of Edgehill.)
(1643 April	The defence of Reading.)
23 May	Captain Godfrey appears in the list of company commanders in Belasyse's Regiment at Culham Camp.[80]
(26 July	Storming of Bristol.)
(20 Sept.	First Battle of Newbury.)
Between 20 Sept. and April 1644	Promoted major to Colonel Sir Theophilus Gilby when Belasyse left the Regiment.
8 Aug. 1644	With the Royalist Army in Cornwall.[81]
(27 Oct.	Second Battle of Newbury.)
	Promoted Lt. Colonel *vice* Sir Bartholomew Pell.
1645. 14 June	Lt. Colonel Godfrey. PW at Naseby.[82]

COLONEL RICHARD FEILDING'S REGIMENT

The regiment had eight companies, and two at least, those of the Conyngsbys, were raised in Herefordshire.

The lieutenant-colonel was Robert Conyngsbye, who was buried at Oxford on 18 July 1643.

EDGEHILL, 23 October 1642.

Colonel Richard Feilding	
Lt. Col Robert Conyngsbye	
Major Peter Walthall	Gone by mid-May 1643
Capt. Toby Bowes	Major *vice* Walthall.
Capt. Thomas Conyngsbye	Major *vice* Bowes
Capt. Thomas La Warr, Leaward or Laward.	
Capt. Isaac Walley	PW Naseby
Capt Edward Jackson	PW Naseby

Reconstruction
PY: 5 March 1985.

On 23 May 1643 the captains were:

Jackson.	P.W. Naseby.
La Warr.	
Thomas Conyngsby, later lieutenant-colonel.	
Walley,	P.W. Naseby.
Robert Thimbleby.	Lieutenant in 1642.

By 4 July 1643 there was a captain Allen in the regiment, doubtless a subaltern in 1642.

Feilding had been a captain and Robert Conyngsbye a lieutenant-colonel in foreign parts. Five of the officers had served in the 1640 army:

Richard Feilding	Colonel, F.
Robert Conyngsbye	Major, F.
Peter Walthall	Captain, F.
Toby Bowes	Captain, F.
Thomas Conyngsbye	Lieutenant, F.

The regiment became Sir Jacob Astley's in about May 1643. Toby Bowes of Harraton, Durham, was his major, and commanded the regiment at Bristol (July 1643). It seems that Walthall was the original major. John Chantler, a Cheshire man, belonged to Major Peter Walthall's company, and served from Edgehill until the siege of Gloucester (Aug.–Sept. 1643), where he was killed. His widow, Anne, petitioned for a pension in 1662.[83]

COLONEL SIR THOMAS LUNSFORD'S REGIMENT

Lunsford raised his men in Somerset, and when Prince Rupert was colonel (1643–1645) it was a bluecoat regiment.

When the Marquis of Hertford and Sir Ralph Hopton reached Wells at the end of July they depended in part on the local trained bands

' . . . But that which conduced most to give the Marquesse some beginning of force was, that Lieut.-Colonell Henry Lunsford was come to him with Officers for a Foote Regiment and Commission from the King to raise for his Brother Sir Thomas Lunsford a Regiment of Foote in that County, in hope that hee should there recover the most part of his old Regiment which hee had there raysed for his Majesties service in the north, two yeares before; towards the arming of whom, a party was sent to Wincanton with caryages, that fetch'd from thence a magazeene of armes that had been deposited there a yeare or two before . . . '

A week later Lt. Colonel Lunsford's 'new leavyed men' were 'about twelve-score' strong.[84]

No list of the company commanders exists, but they certainly included:

Colonel Sir Thomas Lunsford
Lt. Colonel Henry Lunsford
Major Nathaniel Moyle
Captain Valentine Pyne

and probably Captains Thomas Gylburte and John Allen, who were buried at Radley, Berkshire, on 5 and 8 July 1643, respectively. A Captain Nevile slain at Bristol (July 1643) probably belonged to this regiment, as well as Captain Charles Ventris (1599–1643), whose death soon after is mentioned in a letter of Lt. Colonel John Russell to Prince Rupert (BM.Add.MS.18980,f.166), who had made the regiment his own after Colonel Henry Lunsford was mortally wounded at Bristol. Lunsford had commanded the foot in Rupert's Chalgrove Raid (17/18 June 1643) and it is evident that the Prince thought well of the regiment, for otherwise he would not have taken it over.

When Rupert was colonel, his field officers were John Russell and one (Dominic) Mitchell. The former was brought in from Lord Wentworth's Dragoons, but the latter may have been one of Lunsford's captains.

Sergeant William Stoakes of Shepton Mallet served throughout the war, and his petition shows

'That the peticon^r. hath allwayes beene a ffaithfull Constant and Loyall Subject. And a Souldier in his late Ma^{te} Souvrin^e Kinge Charles the ffirst of Blessed Memorie, wch is not unknowne to divers gentlemen Royalists who were eye Wittnesses to the same. Inn whch service yo' pet' through his courage and well affected disposicion towards the consideracon of his said Maties most just rights and previlidges was in severall fights seriously wounded in his body (vizt) att Babylon hill [7 Sept. 1642] neere Sherbourne under the Comand of Colonell Thomas Lunsford, afterwards the same Comand att Edgehill where the said Colonell was taken prisoner, from there under the Comand of Colonell Henry Lunsford att Brandford fight [12 Nov. 1642], then to Reading and there beseiged by [portion missing here] of Abington, next to the taking of Bristoll [July 1643] with Prince Rupert and from there by him Comanded to the Seige of Gloucester, a Sarjeant of foote, afterward under the Comand of Sr John Russell Leiutenant Colonell to Prince Rupert att the takinge of Boulton in Lancashire [27 May], to the takinge of Liverpool [7-11 June] and from there to Massey [Marston] Moore [2 July 1644] where yo' Pet' received many dangerous hurts. And afterwards taken prisoner att Naizeby fight [14 June 1645] & carryed to London where he lay languishing for the space of 12 or 14 weekes, . . . by the usurped and tyrannicall power yo' said pet' is brought into great want & misery beinge a very poore man with a wife and five small Children. Having lost the use of his lymbes is not any waye able to work for their mayntenance. And since it hath pleased God to restore his sacred Matie (whom God prosper) to the Throne of his late father's kingdome, yo' Pet' thereby hopeth that some comfort & refreshment will be provided for the mayntenance of himselfe and his poore family . . . '

He was ordered a pension of 40 shillings per annum.[85]

COLONEL RICHARD BOLLE'S REGIMENT

The regiment, eight companies, was raised in Staffordshire by William Lord Paget and assigned to Bolle. At Edgehill the company commanders seem to have been:

Colonel Richard Bolle.	K. Alton 13 Dec. 1643.
Lt. Colonel Richard d'Ewes.	MW Reading 1643.
Lt. John Roane	PW by 18 Sept. 1642.
Major Edward Littleton.	MW & PW Naseby as lt. colonel, 14 June 1645.
Captain Richard Bagot.	Colonel HF 1643 and Governor of Lichfield. MW Naseby.
Captain John Hanmer.	Commissioned York 8 Aug. 1642.
Captain Thomas Throckmorton.	
Captain Bevis Lloyd or Floyd.	PW Alton as captain, later major.
Captain Edward Fowler.	PW Naseby as major.

Bagot, Hanmer and Throckmorton had gone by 23 May 1643 when the company commanders included Captains Walden, Robert Skerrow and Hawkred, all no doubt subalterns in 1642. Skerrow's commission as lieutenant to Throckmorton is dated 30 October 1642. Perhaps his predecessor had fallen at Edgehill.

Ensign Edward Fowler of this regiment, who was buried at Yarnton on 12 August 1643, was doubtless related to the captain of that name.

Skerrow's career can be traced in some detail. The events in brackets are those in which the Regiment took part.

1640	Ensign F., colonel Sir Thomas Lunsford's Regiment.[86]
11 Dec. 1640	Discharged as a papist.[87]
(23 Oct. 1642	Battle of Edgehill.)
30 Oct. 1642	Commissioned as lieutenant in Captain (Thomas?) Throckmorton's company in Colonel Richard Bolle's Regiment.[88]
(Apr. 1643	Defence of Reading.)
	By 23 May 1643 captain.[89]
(20 Sept. 1643	First Battle of Newbury)
(29 Mar. 1644	Battle of Cheriton).
13 May 1644	Mentioned in a warrant of Colonel John Penruddock's.[90]
(Aug.-27 Oct.1644)	Cornish campaign and Second Battle of Newbury.
14 June 1645	P.W. at Naseby as captain in Colonel George Lisle's Regiment (ex. Bolle. F.)[91]
28 Aug. 1648	P.W. Colchester. Major to Colonel William Ayliffe.[92]

1663	Prisoner in Windsor Castle.[93]
	Indigent Officer. L & W.[94]

Bolle, a lieutenant-colonel in 1640, and Skerrow, seem to have been the only two Scots War officers in the regiment. The original company commanders were probably Staffordshire gentry rather than professional soldiers. This is certainly true of Captain Bagot and probably of Major Littleton. When Bolle was killed Lt. Colonel George Lisle, a soldier by trade and an excellent officer, was promoted to command the regiment.

COLONEL SIR EDWARD FITTON'S REGIMENT

A Cheshire regiment of eight companies. The field officers were Lt. Colonel Anthony Thelwall, who was to succeed Filton and Major Urian Legh. Thelwall had been a major in the 1640 Army and Captain Claver had served abroad, but the other officers seem to have been drawn from the Cheshire gentry.

On 23 May 1643 the captains were:

> Greene
> Claver
> Alcocks
> Lee (Legh)
> Will. Davenport.

The captain-lieutenant was Thomas Minshall, who evidently took over Alcock's company about 23 May 1643. His successor in Fitton's company was another of the Davenport family, who was killed at I Bristol.

Major Urian Legh (1600–1680) was a younger brother of Thomas Legh of Adlington (1593–1644), High Sheriff of Cheshire in 1629 and 1643. Thomas Legh had four sons, Thomas (1614–1687), Charles (b.1618), Peter (1620–1686) and Henry (1621–c.1686), all of whom fought for the King. Peter is said to have been taken prisoner at Naseby. Charles and Peter both appear as captains in *A List of [Indigent] Officers* under Thelwall. There is no evidence that Thomas, who became a lieutenant-colonel, served in Fitton's regiment, but Henry seems to have been a captain in it, for Samuel and John Platt were killed serving under him at I Newbury.[95]

Thelwall was not a Cheshire man. He came from a branch of the Thelwalls of Plas-y-ward near Ruthin, Denbighshire. He was a Catholic.

The Cheshire Quarter Sessions Records preserve the names of at least nine of Fitton's men though only one of their petitions mentions Edgehill. He was Sergeant Ralph Hassall of Minshull. A carpenter by trade, he was in Captain Thomas Minshall's[96] company, and fought at Edgehill, Brentford, and Bristol (July 1643.) His petition is certified by Thomas

Cholmondeley, Urian Legh,[97] Captain Peter Manwaring, Captain Peter Minsull and Matthew Smallwood, D.D., Chaplain in Ordinary to King Charles II and in Holy Orders before Edgehill. Later Bishop of Lickfield.

COLONEL SIR EDWARD STRADLING'S REGIMENT

The regiment was raised in South Wales, and had eight companies. A letter from the colonel casts some light on its early days.

> Honorable Sr.
> I send you by this bearer the copies of a letter and two orders that I received from his Matie: wch you should have had sooner but that I understood by Sr. Thomas Lewis that hee had given you information of the principall import thereof (the billetinge of 500 soldiers of my regiment in your county of Monm.) I have appointed my Seriant Maior, and my brother Capteyne Tho: Stradlinge to bee in or about Newport. I knowe they are both your obedient servants and my order unto them is that they be alwayes ready to obey your commands for the Kings, and the countreys service, I understand you have lately had a meeting with my lo: Herbert, who (I am sure) hath given you the accompt of the court, and the kings armies affayres; soe that I have nothing more to present unto you butt the assurance of all fidelity unto your noble self and family from
> Sr your most humble and affectionate servant
> Edw: Stradlinge
> St Donates Castle
> 17th Sep: 1642
> [OVER]
>
> for my noble and hon^d friend Sr. William Morgan Knt
> these the King's business at Tredegar[98]

The major referred to may have been John Stradling, soon to be colonel. At Edgehill the company commanders probably included:

> Colonel Sir Edward Stradling, P.W.
> Lt. Colonel William Herbert, M.P., K.
> Major John Stradling, later colonel.
> Captain Thomas Stradling, later lt. colonel
> Captain Henry Vaughan, W and resigned.
> Captain Howell, Gwynn, W, later colonel.

Gwynn was from Llanbrayn, Carmarthen, and although we are not told specifically which regiment he was in, he is likely to have been in the one raised in his part of the world.[99]

On 23 May 1643 the captains were:

Edward Carne of Ewenny, Glam, later major. Captain *vice* Vaughan, 30 or 31 Oct. 1642[100]
William Price.
Hopkins Dawkins.
. . . Morgan.
Thomas Bussey or Bushy, later major.

No doubt all these were at Edgehill, but probably not as company commanders.

The officers were country gentlemen rather than professional soldiers, though Carne had been a gentleman volunteer, H., in 1639. The rout of the regiment at Edgehill may perhaps be attributed to the lack of experienced officers to drill the new levies.

Stradling was confined in Warwick Castle until May 1644, when he was exchanged, arriving at Oxford on the 18th. He died there of fever on 20 June 1644, and was buried in the chapel of his college, Jesus.[101]

THE LIFEGUARD

The Lifeguard was raised in Lincolnshire, recruited with Derbyshire miners, and further reinforced by men from Cheshire. According to Warwick, it had 13 ensigns. Assuming that one of these was the Banner Royal, this means that the Regiment had 12 companies, instead of eight or ten.

At Edgehill the company commanders included:

> Colonel Lord Willoughby d'Eresby. P.W.
> Lt. Colonel Sir William Vavasour, P.W.
> Major William Leighton, W?, later lieut. colonel
> Captain Robert Markham, later major.
> Captain Sir Henry Radley, P.W.
> Captain Richard Walthall.
> Captain Walters
> Captain Thomas Cholmondeley
> Captain Thomas Leigh. Present on 22 Dec. 1642.[102]
> Captain Thomas Mynne. Fought at Cirencester.

Other officers included Lieutenant Thomas Mucklow and Quarter-master Ben. Stone.[103]

Lord Willoughby had been a captain in the Dutch service; Vavasour had been a colonel in the 1640 army, and Leighton had been a lieutenant in foreign parts. The other company commanders seem to have been country gentlemen.

The men wore red coats.

Sergeant Randle Whittacker, who was in Captain Richard Walthall's company, served all through the war 'from Edgehill until Stow'.

John Foxe of Kelsall was in Captain Watter's (Walter's) company at Edgehill, and left the Lifeguard for some reason, and was later in the garrison of Newark in Colonel Sir John Digby's Regiment.

William Pemberton and Randle Robinson were both in Captain Thomas Cholmondeley's company at Edgehill and after. Pemberton was captured at Naseby and taken to London, but, nothing daunted, turned out again in 1651 and fought for Charles II at Worcester.[104]

LORD GENERAL

This was another Lincolnshire regiment. It was about 1,000 strong and apparently had ten companies.

The company commanders included:

> Colonel the Earl of Lindsey, K.G.   M.W. & P.W.
> Lt. Colonel John Munro   K.
> Major Herbert Lunsford.
> Captain Marmaduke Constable   K.
> Captain Robert Townshend   K.
> Captain Sir Gervase Scrope   W.
> Captain Gervase Elwes or Helwys, later major.
> Captain Henry Hall. Captain by 2 November 1642.[105]
> Captain Thomas Draper.   I.O. Norfolk.

On 23 May 1643 the captains included:

> Henry Hall.
> Thomas Lund.
> William Sinclere, or St. Clare, later lt. colonel.
> Thomas Draper.
> Langden.

By this time there were only eight companies in the regiment. Other officers included Quartermaster William Gamlyn.

John Munro was the younger son of Hector Munro of Assynt (or Assint). He had been a captain in the Danish and a lieutenant-colonel in the Swedish service, and had distinguished himself by his gallantry at Oldenburg in 1627.[106]

The Regiment passed to Patrick Ruthven, Lord Forth, who became Lord General on the death of Lindsey.

COLONEL SIR JOHN BEAUMONT'S REGIMENT

Little is known of this regiment, which was evidently incomplete and only stayed a very short time with the main Royalist army. It was raised in Staffordshire. The officers included:

> Colonel Sir John Beaumont of Gracedieu.
> Lt. Colonel John Godfrey, Beaumont's successor.
> Major William Courtney or Courtenay, commissioned 7 Sept. 1642.
>   Later colonel?
> Captain Anthony Dormer. P.W.? I.O. Stafford.

Capt.-Lieut. Robert Fleetwood. Present 19 Jan. 1643.[107] I.O. Stafford
as captain.
Captain Raphiell Neale. Major to Godfrey at 28 Dec. 1643.

Several of the officers seem to have been Roman Catholics.

COLONEL SIR GILBERT GERARD'S REGIMENT

This was a Lancashire regiment, and had at least nine companies, whose
commanders included:

Colonel Sir Gilbert Gerard.
Lt. Colonel Ratcliffe Gerard, later colonel.
Major Richard Bishop, later lieut.-colonel.
Captain Edward Paynton.
Captain Edward Asheton.

On 23 May 1643 the captains were:

Pat. Gerard.
(William) Booth. P.W. Naseby.
Jo. Gerard. Second son of Lt. Colonel Ratcliffe Gerard. Fought at Edgehill.
(Hugh?) Houghton. Capt. Hugh Houghton was buried at Oxford on
      25 May 1643.[108]
Pat. Gerard, Jr.
Gilbert Houghton, later major.

Lt. Colonel Ratcliffe Gerard, his colonel's twin brother, had three sons,
Ratcliffe, John and Gilbert all of whom fought at Edgehill, though their
rank at that time is uncertain.[109]

John Bikerdyke (or Bykerdyk) of Salford was sent out in Captain
Edward Asheton's company in July 1642.[110] He was wounded at Edgehill,
but not very badly for he was in the fight at Brentford in November. He
was 'very sore wounded' at Brill on the Hill, which was successfully
defended by Sir Gilbert Gerard on 27 January 1643, when Colonel Arthur
Goodwin attempted to storm it.[111] Bikerdyke's services are attested by
Captain John Byrom (23 January 1661), probably a former officer of his
company.

COLONEL SIR THOMAS SALUSBURY'S REGIMENT

This seems to have been the largest regiment in the Royalist army, and
was raised in North Wales, especially Denbighshire and Flint. There were
probably men from Anglesey and perhaps a company from Cheshire.

On 6 August 1642 Salusbury wrote to Thomas Bulkeley at Baron Hill
(Anglesey), telling him that the gentry of Denbighshire and Flint had met
at Wrexham and agreed to levy £1500 to raise a regiment of foot in the
King's defence, of which regiment the writer was elected colonel. He
hoped to have the greater part of the men levied by the end of the week,
and many companies were already nearly full. He desired Bulkeley to

spare half a score of lusty fellows from his county as it fell to Salusbury to raise 350 – his own company, numbering 200, and that of his sergeant–major (Boncle) 'who is a stranger', another 150. Bulkeley was assured that if he would help in the matter he would be 'remembered by the King . . . '[112]

The company commanders included:

> Colonel Sir Thomas Salusbury, Bart. (d.1643) of Lleweni, Denbighshire, D.C.L. for Edgehill.[113]
> Lt. Colonel John Royden of Lloran Isa, Denbighshire (1574–1665). Captain of Chirkland light horse, 1639.[113]
> Major George Boncle. Later colonel, H.
> Captain William Broughton of Bersham, near Wrexham. A brother of Sir Edward; led Denbighshire levies to Selby in 1639.[113].
> Captain John Edwards, of Cristoinedd, later major.
> Captain Churlocke (Sherlocke of Ruthin probably).
> Captain William Robinson of Gwersyllt (d.1644)
> Captain Ravenscroft (of Bretton, Cheshire).

On 23 May 1643 the captains were:

> John Edwards
> (William?) Wynn
> William Robinson
> (Nanny?) Lloyd
> H. Salisbury
> Ravenscrofte
> Dyer

Robinson's lieutenant was Edward Hughes of Wrexham, a Low Country soldier, who fought at Edgehill, Brentford and Newbury.[114] Broughton was a Low Country officer and John Edwards was a captain in the 1640 army but on the whole the company commanders were country gentlemen. Major Boncle, however, had 'from his youth applyed himselfe to ye knowledge of Armes . . . '[115]

The Chaplain was the Rev. Jonathan Edwards M.A., B.D.[116]

Writing soon after Edgehill one Rob. Evans described Salusbury's men as 'twelve hundred poor Welsh vermin, the offscourings of this nation', but in fact they numbered some stout-hearted men among them, and there is no evidence that they broke at Edgehill.

In 1661 two old Welsh yeomen, both former corporals of this regiment were living at Devizes, where their regiment had been in garrison from 1644 to 1645.

> Robert Davyes of St. John the Baptist Parish states that: ' . . . haveinge a considerable estate in the place where he then lived, did in the beginning of the late warre leave his sayd estate where he contynued for the space of

three yeares & a halfe as a Corporall in one of the foote Companies in the Regiment of the then Collonell S[r] Thomas Salisbury & after in y[e] same Regiment under the Command of S[r] Charles Loyd as namely sometymes under y[e] Command of Capt. Robert Chaloner & sometymes under Cap[t] Roger Williams both captains in the said Regim[t] dureing w[ch] tyme your poor pet[r] not only lost all his goods & estate he then had, being taken away by y[e] then Parliam[ty] fforces But also received in the said service seaventeene sev'all wounds in his head fforebody Armes & hands, where amongst the rest he had parte of his Scull wasted & his head never since fully recou'ed & one of his armes made vselesse by y[e] sayd wounds, and further . . . that by reason of the sayd wounds & y[e] great losse of bloud . . . yo[r] pet[r] hath almost lost the sight of his eyes & allmost the use of both Armes whereby he is made unable to worke or use any bodily exercise for & towards the gayning of a livelihood & mayneteynance of himselfe wife & fouer children . . . '

Rowland Humfrey of the Parish of St. Mary had an even more distinguished record of service. His petition states that he

' . . . was long before the Battaile att Edgehill a foote Souldier in the service of the late Kings Mat[ie] Charles the first in the late Warrs in a Regim[t] under the Command of the then Coll. S[r] Thomas Salisbury untill his Deathe . . . & afterwards in the same Regiment under S[r] Charles Lloyd where yo[r] peticon[r] was made a Corporall & was sometymes in the foote Company of Capt. Robert Chaloner & sometymes of Capt. John Edwards in the same Regim[t] & so continued in the same service for the space of three yeares & upwards & untill after the Devizes Garrison was taken [1645] from the said S[r] Charles Lloyd shortly after w[ch] yo[r] pet[r] was forced to leave the same by reason of the Great Losse of bloud w[ch] he had susteyned to the greate weakeninge of his body through y[e] meanes of seaven sev'all woundes & w[ch] yo[r] pet[r] had before that tyme received in the said service vid[cet]:- one wound wth a sword in the head in y[e] ffight at Newbery; one shott through the hand in the same ffight; one shott through the Legg at Kidlington Greene betweene Oxford & Woodstocke, one wound wth a sword in the knee att Banbury, one wounde in the left Arme in Cornwall [1644] whereby he hath allmost lost the ves of it; one great Cutt wth a sword in the handrist att the taking [of] Bristoll [1643] for King Charles & alsoe a great blow with a muskett in the mouth w[ch] beate out allmost all his teeth before besides the cutting of his Lippes. att the sidge att Readinge, [1643] All w[ch] sd. woundes & blows . . . hath soe . . . decayed yo[r] pet[rs] body that he is thereby made almost unfitt for any bodily Labor & so unable to worke to gayne a Livelihood for himselfe & wife & two children, yo[r] pet[r] being growne poore & lost his estate he then had by reason of his being in the sd. service.'[117]

Davies was awarded a petition of 40 shillings per annum and Humfrey one of £3 per annum, to be paid quarterly.

Bartholomew Starky of Mouldsworth, Cheshire, belonged to the company of Captain Ravenscroft of Bretton. He was killed at Edgehill, and although the petition[118] of his widow, Elizabeth, does not mention his colonel's name, there is no doubt it was Salusbury. Captain Ravenscroft still commanded a company in Salusbury's Regiment on 23 May 1643.[119]

LORD MOLYNEUX'S REGIMENT

A Lancashire regiment which had seven companies. Its exact composition is obscure but the company commanders included:

> Colonel Richard, 2nd Viscount Molyneux of Maryborough. Died c.1651 without issue.
> Lt. Colonel Roger Nowell of Read, Lancashire.
> Major Henry Byrom of Byrom, Lancs., K.[120]
> Captain Francis Saunders. Major by 5 Nov 1642.
> Captain Robert Hesketh of Rufford?

On 23 May 1643 the captains were:

> Jo. Ashton of Curedall   } One or other of these was
> Jo. Ashton of Pinkey   } K. I Bristol.
> Henry Ogle of Prescot
> Prestidge.

Byrom's ensign, William Turner, was I.O. Lancashire.

Richard Olker, who was a soldier and officer for four or five years under Captain Robert Hesketh, was probably in this regiment. He fought at Edgehill, Brentford, Newbury and York (i.e. Marston Moor).[121]

THE EARL OF NORTHAMPTON'S REGIMENT

This regiment, eight companies, was raised in North Oxfordshire and Warwickshire and probably got some men from Buckinghamshire. It was with the Edgehill army, but de Gomme's plan does not show it in the actual order of battle. Since most of the officers had local knowledge, it may well have been masking the Parliamentarian garrison of Banbury.

At the beginning of August Dugdale attended Northampton in Warwickshire and tells us that 'many of the trayn'd-Band Souldiers, and other loyall persons came wᵗʰ Horse and Armes' to assist the Earl. At the skirmish at Southam, Warwickshire, on 23 August 1642 Northampton had already some 300 foot.[122]

The field officers of the regiment were:

Colonel Spencer Compton, 2nd Earl of Northampton, K.B. (1601–43).
Lt. Colonel Henry Huncks. Knighted 1 Jan. 1643.
     Dismissed May 1643.
Major Anthony Green. Lt. Colonel May 1643.

On 24 July 1643 a Council of War was held at Banbury. By that time the company commanders were:

Colonel: James, 3rd Earl of Northampton.
Lt. Colonel Anthony Green (d.1644).
Major William Compton (d.1663). Third son of the 2nd earl,
     lt. colonel, c.Dec. 1644.
Captain Spencer Compton.
Captain Hugh Vaughan. W siege of Banbury 1644.
Captain Charles Waldrond. Later major.
Captain Henry Rainsford.
Captain William Tirwhitt
Capt.-Lieut. Michael Poulteney.

Tirwhitt did not become a company commander until the loss of an arm at Brentford disabled him for the horse service.

Most of the others were probably captains in 1642 for the regiment, being in garrison at Banbury, saw but little action until their stubborn defence of the castle in the autumn of 1644.

Various other officers became captains later in the war and were probably with Northampton from the first.

They were:

	Captain by
Thomas Willoughby of Olney Park, Bucks.[123]	December 1643
George Ward.	
William Gannock.	30 January 1645
Robert Blencoe.	4 October 1645[124]

Northampton and his original lieutenant-colonel were both experienced soldiers. Huncks had been governor of Barbados (1639–1641). He was knighted on 1 January 1643, but fell under suspicion for corresponding with the rebels and was dismissed. He later served in the West and surrendered on Exeter Articles.[125] His mother, Katherine, was daughter of Sir John Conway.

Green had been a captain in the 1640 army and in Ireland.[126]

The quartermaster of the Regiment was William Collett.[127]

John ffloyd, who in 1661 described himself as 'now of Marston meysie in the County of Wilts, was between 6 and 7 yeares in the service of King Charles the first . . . ' under Northampton. The implication is that he joined at the very beginning of the war:

' . . . in which service he received severall desperate wounds and did undergoe many extreme hardships incident to soldiers and for his affection to his Royal Soveregne was plundered and robbed of a shop of ware of a considerable value, and now having lost and spent all his estate in his maiesties service, and being partly by wounds and hardships, which he then suffered, deprived of the naturall use of his Limbs is reduced to extreme necessity for his maintenance; . . . ,[128]

EARL RIVERS'[12] REGIMENT OF FOOT

There is no question that Earl Rivers' Regiment took part in the campaign, though if de Gomme's Plan is completely reliable it was not in the battle. The Cheshire Quarter Sessions Records give us the names of two petitioners who mention Edgehill in their record of services. They are: Drummer Ralph Dod of Tiverton, who was in Captain [Henry] Bennet's[130] company from Edgehill until the reduction of Donnington Castle [30 March 1646]; and William Adderton of Tarvin.

Rivers raised his men in Cheshire, at least in part.

The company commanders included:

> Colonel Earl Rivers.
> Lt. Colonel John Boys (1607–1664).
> Major Robert Perkins?
> Captain Peter Danyel of Over Tabley, Cheshire. MW Gloucester 1643.
> Captain (Henry) Bennet. Later major.

Lieutenant Thomas Daniell of Tabley and his captain (unnamed) were both killed at Brentford.

Boys had been a captain in 1640.[131] Knighted for his successful defence of Donnington Castle, he was considered 'one of the bravest and best officers' who served King Charles I.[132] At the Restoration he was made Receiver of Customs at Dover, and on 19 April 1662 he became Ormonde's deputy as commander and constable of the castle and fort of Duncannon.[133]

Other officers who served in the regiment were captains Edmond Done or Donne, Knight, Osborn and Gregory, but their rank in 1642 is unknown.

COLONEL WILLIAM PENNYMAN'S REGIMENT

This, the oldest regiment of the army, was raised in Yorkshire, though four of its indigent officers came from Durham. There is evidence that many of the men were volunteers from the trained bands.

The 1642 officers of this regiment, not necessarily in strict order of seniority, probably included:

Colonel Sir William Pennyman.	
Lt. Colonel Sir James Pennyman.	Colonel 1643.
Major George Symm of Marske.	Lt. Colonel 1643.
Captain Will. Wyvell	Major 1643.
Lieut. Robert Towers	Buried 23 Feb. 1643.
Ens. John Simpson	P.W. Naseby as captain. I.O. York.
Captain (Sir) William Mallory	Buried 22 July 1643.
Captain (Sir) Richard Page	P.W. Naseby as colonel.
Captain Henry Skipwith[134]	Captain c.Dec. 1643–June 1643.
Maud	
Blakeston	Captains in April 1643.
Humphrey Elmes	
Francis Lawson	P.W. Naseby as lieut. colonel
(Sir) William Bridges	and major, respectively.
Anthony Norton	Captain by April 1643. P.W. Naseby as captain. I.O. York.
Walker	Captain by June 1643.
Thomas Beverley of Smeyton	Captain. Buried 24 June 1644.
Francis Bateson I.O. York	Captains by 29 November 1644
John Jackson I.O. York	and senior to John Simpson,
George Etherington	ensign in 1642, but captain at
Robert Carrington	Naseby.
John Eggleston.	Lieutenant. I.O. Durham.
	Mallory's company. P.W. Naseby.
Lieut. Thomas Homewood	
Lieut. Rob. Howes.[135]	Later captain.
Quartermaster William Baty.[136]	

Page was a professional soldier, but the majority of the officers seem to have been Yorkshire gentry and trained band captains.

THE YEOMEN OF THE GUARD

A number of Yeomen Ushers and Yeomen of His Majesty's Great Chamber were with the King at Oxford. What part they played at Edgehill is uncertain. Perhaps some of them served in the Lifeguard, F.[137]

William Roberts (d.1644)
Edward Midwinter
John Herringman
James Montely
Edward Hill
Robert Hawkins
Richard Williames
John Teagg
Will. Harison
Nicholas Horne
Richard Hargrave
Henry Garrett
Daniel Lambert
John Morgan
John Bishop (d. 1643)
Nicholas Snow
Richard Barnes

DRAGOONS

There were three regiments of dragoons, totalling 800–1,000. One, Usher's, was on the right, and two Duncombe's and Grey's, were on the left. In December Grey's was about 200 strong. It may not be unreasonable to suggest that Usher's was about as strong as the other two put together.

COLONEL JAMES USHER'S REGIMENT

There is little to show where the regiment was raised. Its officers included:

Colonel James Usher	K. Lichfield April 1643.
Lt. Colonel Henry Washington.	Colonel 1643.
Lt. Colonel Henry Huddelston.	Lt. Col. 11 May 1643.
Major Henry Hutchinson.	W. Cirencester.
Captain Theod. Humphreys.	I.O. L & W.
Captain Francis Morrison.	Major, 1643.
Captain Nathaniel Gray	Major by Dec. 1643.
Captain (Francis?) Gawdye.	W. Edgehill.
Captain William Tuke.	Captain by 15 June 1643.[138]
Captain Henry Norwood.	Commissioned to raise[139] his company in Gloucestershire and Warwickshire, c.Dec. 1642.

When Usher fell, the regiment passed to Washington, who was Governor of Worcester during the seige of 1646.

Under 18 February 1643 the Journal of Sir Samuel Luke, the Parliamentarian Scoutmaster-General, records the interrogation of a Royalist officer, who had been wounded at Edgehill. It is of some interest as it illustrates the intelligence methods of the day.

'Major Gawdye. That he was a captaine of dragooners in the regiment of Collonell [James] Usher that hee was shott at Kenton with 2 shott in the thigh, that hee gave upp his commission 3 months since, but because hee was affraid hee should not gett home quietly hee saith hee was continually in the army where that regiment lay, and soe was a[t] Wantidge when wee were there and saith that wee might with great ease have taken them all.

He further saith that hee sent his man before through the contry with a brave horse and came thus meanely attended without spurrs or sword, because he would not be suspected. Hee further saith that hee knoweth his Majesties intencions were to have his horse to march to Norfolke and Suffolke and that about 3 weekes since his Majestie made him maior of a regiment of horse and gave him a troope of horse which were to be raysed in Norfolke by severall knights and gentlemen and they were to have 2 monethes pay aforehand, and to this purpose hee had his Majesties letters and commission to divers gentlemen whoe had sent word the horses were ready. Hee saith he beleeveth by the number of regiments every regiment consisting of 5 troopes that his Majestie hath 4000 horse and not above 6000 foote besides those of Newcastle. Hee further saith that the Lord Digby hath a regiment of horse and that his owne troope consists all of schollars, and that hee lyeth at Wheatley, noe other troope neare him, that they are very negligent in their troopes, and may easily be surprized, Digby himselfe being constantly there 3 tymes a weeke, but his wife and family live in one of the colledges.'[140]

A Francis Gaudy was a lieutenant in Lord Grandison's regiment, F., in 1640,[141] and may well be the same man.

COLONEL SIR EDWARD DUNCOMBE'S REGIMENT

This was a Yorkshire regiment. 'Deserter' says Duncombe had about 500 dragoons and that they were part of the Lifeguard. He probably overstates the numbers in the regiment. The history of the unit is obscure and it seems to have disappeared in 1643, though two indigent officers are listed, both from Yorkshire, Captain Will. Duncombe and Cornet Rob. Thompson.

The regiment was at the storming of Cirencester and Captain Alford and Lieutenant Humphrey Wharton are mentioned in the account.

Captain (or major?) Thomas Button, who had been a lieutenant in foreign parts, and a captain in 1640, and his brother (captain 30 Oct. 1642, Harleian MSS 6804/221) evidently belonged to this regiment. (See Roy, Ordnance Papers, p. 168.) Thomas Button was probably an Edgehill casualty.

COLONEL EDWARD GREY'S REGIMENT

This short-lived and incomplete unit seems to have been raised in the North. Along with Grandison's H., it was captured at Winchester on 12 December 1642. It was 200 strong.[142] The prisoners included:

> Major Ralph Heborne of Heborne, Northumberland. (1616–)
> Captain Robert Brandling of Leathley, Yorkshire (1620–1669).
> Captain John Wren, P.W. in Windsor Castle.
> Captain Booth.
> Captain Birkenhead.
> Lieutenant Edward Rodham, 'Hebberne's' troop, P.W. in Windsor Castle.
> Lieutenant Ralph Booth, Wren's troop. P.W. in Windsor Castle.
> Cornet Roger Brandling.

On 23 November the quartermaster was John Bath.[143]

Grey was a younger brother of Lord Grey of Werke, and later became a colonel, H., under Newcastle. He was from Northumberland.

In the 1640 army Wren had been a lieutenant, F., and Robert Brandling an ensign, F.

Lieutenant Edward Roddam (*sic*) is in *A List of* [*Indigent*] *Officers*. He also was from Northumberland.

THE TRAIN OF ARTILLERY

The Royalist Train of Artillery probably reached its greatest strength in the summer of 1643. On the arrival of Henry Percy, who succeeded the Earl of Newport as General, an establishment was laid down including:

General	
Secretary	
Lt. General	
Clerks	2
Comptroller	
Comptroller	
Clerk	
Commissary for the munition of the train	
Clerks	2
Commissary for the munition of the army	
Clerks	2
Assistant to the Commissaries	
Clerk	
Engineer	
Clerk	
Conductors	2
Engineer	
Clerk	
Conductors	2
Comptroller of the bye train	
Battery Master	
'Worke base'	
Gentlemen of the Ordnance	12
Chaplain	
Paymaster	
Clerk	
Commissary for the draught horses of the train	
Assistant	
Clerk	
Purveyor	
Messenger	
Quartermaster General	
Chirurgion	
Mates	2
Principal Conductor	
Conductors	44
Tentmaker	
Assistant	
Tentkeeper	
Servants	2
Gunfounders	9
Master Armourer	
Armourers	6
Master Gunner	

Mate	
Petardier	
Gunners	69
Matrosses	88
Captain of the Pioneers	
Lieutenant of the Pioneers	
Pioneers	200
Master Smith	
Farriers	2
Smiths	10
Master Carpenter	
Carpenters	11
Wheelwrights	12
Collarmakers	2
Master Cooper	
Servants	2
Gunsmith	
Gunstock Maker	
Turner	
Ladlemaker	
Wagonmaster to the Train	
Carters	43 (300)
Provost Marshal	
Servant	
Assistants	4
	575

This was a total of 575 officers, officials, and men, besides, it would seem, 257 carters who were not in constant pay. It is extremely unlikely that the Train was as strong as this in the autumn of 1642.[144]

ROYALIST ARTILLERY

Rates of Pay.   May–July 1643.

		Per diem.		
		£	s.	d.
General		4	0	0
Lt. General	c.	2	0	0
Engineer		0	12	0
Comptroller		0	10	0
Commissary for the munition of the train		0	10	0
Commissary for the munition of the army		0	10	0
Comptroller of the bye train		0	10	0
Commissary for the draught horses of the train		0	8	0
Secretary to the General		0	6	0
Assistant to the Commissaries		0	6	0
Provost Marshal & his servant		0	6	0
Battery Master		0	5	0
Purveyor		0	5	0
Quartermaster General		0	5	0
Principal Conductor		0	5	0
The Master Gunner		0	5	0
Petardier		0	5	0

Captain of the Pioneers	0	5	0
The Wagonmaster to the Train	0	5	0
Paymaster and his clerk	0	5	0
Clerk to the Lt. General	0	4	0 each
Gentleman of the Ordnance	0	4	0
The Chaplain	0	4	0
Assistant to the Commissary for the draught horses	0	4	0
The Chirurgion	0	4	0
The Master Smith	0	4	0
Clerk to the Commissary for the Munition of the train	0	3	0
Clerk to the Commissary for the Munition of the Army	0	3	0
'Worke base'	0	3	0
Messenger	0	3	0
Master Gunner's Mate	0	3	0
Master Carpenter	0	3	0
Clerk to a Comptroller	0	2	6
Clerk to the assistant to the Commissaries	0	2	6
Conductor to an Engineer	0	2	6
Clerk to the Commissary of the draught horses	0	2	6
Mate to the Chirurgion	0	2	6
Conductor	0	2	6
The Tentmaker	0	2	6
The Master Armourer	0	2	6
Lieutenant of the Pioneers	0	2	6
The Master Cooper	0	2	6
Assistant to the Tentmaker	0	2	0
Gunfounder	0	2	0
Gunner	0	2	0
Farrier	0	2	0
Ladlemaker	0	2	0
Assistant to the Provost Marshal	0	2	0
Tentkeeper	0	1	6
Servant to tentkeeper	0	1	6
Armourer	0	1	6
Smith	0	1	6
Carpenter	0	1	6
Wheelwright	0	1	6
Collarmaker	0	1	6
Servant to the Master Cooper	0	1	6
Gunsmith	0	1	6
Gunstock maker	0	1	6
Turner	0	1	6
Matross	0	1	4
Pioneer	0	1	0
Carter	0	1	0[145]

ROYALIST SOLDIERS BURIED AT YARNTON, OXFORDSHIRE

The village of Yarnton was set aside as a hospital in May 1643. The soldiers buried there may well have been men who had fought at Edgehill, the last named, Conductor Cuthbert Cartington, certainly had.

	Buried
Lord General's Regiment	
Ric. Meridick	11 May 1643
Thomas Franckye	15 June
Thomas Harris	21 Aug.
Colonel Richard Bolle's Regiment	
Benedict Bradly	
Richard Taylour }	15 June
Ralph Deane	17 June
Thomas Taylour	
Richard Gardiner }	20 June
Richard Farmer	23 June
John Breer	
Walter Mathews }	28 June
Willam Berry	8 July
John Latimer	10 July
Mr Edward Fowler, Ensigne	12 Aug.
Col. Sir Edward Fitton's Regiment	
Edward Hill	18 June
William Brodbyry	27 June
Robert Fitton	7 Aug.
Robt (blank)	9 Aug.
Colonel Henry[146] Lunsford's Regiment	
Richard Wood	10 Aug.
Humphrey Baker	12 Aug.
Train of Artillery	
Conductor Cuthbert Cartington[147]	31 Jan. 1644[148]

1 D.N.B.

2 Journal of the Society for Army Historical Research, Volumes 23–24 & 31.

3 Newcastle, pp.20 & 22.

4 Bulstrode, p. 76.

5 Bulstrode, p. 75.

6 *Mercurius Aulicus*, p. 432.

7 Bulstrode, p. 93.

8 Bulstrode, p. 94.

9 B.M. Add. MSS 29570,f.62.

10 Bulstrode, p. 76.

11 Belvoir Castle MSS.

12 Symond's Diary, pp.181 & 182.

13 F.J. Varley, The Siege of Oxford, p. 16.

14 Cottesloe MS Muster-Roll.

15 CSPD Add. 1625–1649, pp.606–7.

16 Catalogue of Morrison MSS, Volume III, p. 11.

17 Dalton, Vol. II, p. 567, Hertfordshire County Records. Volume I, p. 153 and Harl. MSS. 6804,f.169.

18 Hopton's *Bellum Civile*, pp.60 & 61.

19 Symond's Notebook. Harl. MS 986.

20 B.M. Harl. MSS 6852,f.1.

21 Peacock, pp.74, 75 & 88.

22 Military Memoirs: The Civil War. Richard Atkyns, edited by Brigadier Peter Young, John Gwyn, edited by Norman Tucker, F.R. Hist.S.

23 Warburton, Vol. III, pp.524 & 527.

24 Mrs Hutchinson, Vol. I, p. 174.

25 Cottesloe MS Muster-Roll.

26 Mrs Hutchinson, Volume I, p. 174.

27 *Mercurius Aulicus*, p. 1.

28 HMC. 5th Report, p. 191.

29 Belvoir Castle MSS.

30 Wood's City of Oxford, Volume III, p. 111.

31 Cottesloe MS Muster-Roll.

32 Hopton's *Bellum Civile*. p. 7.

33 C.C.C. p. 1070.

34 HMC. 5th Report, p. 191.

35 Hopton's *Bellum Civile*, p. 3.

36 Rev. G.N. Godwin, The Civil War in Hampshire, p. 44.

37 D. Gardiner, The Story of Lambeth Palace, p. 156.

38 Not taken at Winchester.

39 A son of the Earl of Lindsey.

40 Digby's officers are listed under 'Earl Bristoll', his later title.

41 B.M. Harl. MSS 6852,f.1.

42 Montgomery. 13 September 1642. R. Herbert to Sir Francis Ottley. Has been 'commanded to hasten ye levys of my Regm^t and to make Shrewsbury my Rendevous. Be advised if wth 500 men Itt be safe with the force and strength y^u have in y^r Towne, for me to strenthen and secure ye place. I have not yet beaten my Drums, but shall this weeke; and in honour Shropshire must assist in their contributions'. (Ottley Papers, No. XIII.)

43 'Hen. Harris' signed the petition of the officers of the Old Horse. c.8 August 1644. Warburton, Volume III, p. 17.

44 Wiltshire Q.S.R., Easter 1661.

45 B.M. Harl. MSS 6851,f.59.

46 J. Roland Phillips, Memoirs of the Civil War in Wales, Volume II, pp.56–61.

47 Cottesloe MS Muster-Roll.

48 *A List of [Indigent] Officers.*

49 Peacock, p. 79.

50 Vavasour's Regiment was in the Scots War (1640) and later went to Ireland, returning to England in the autumn of 1643.

51 Cheshire Q.S.R.

52 PRO. 31/8/197 f.206.

53 NLW. Crosse of Shaw Hill MSS 1123.

54 Norman Tucker, Royalist Officers of North Wales, 1642–1660, p.64.

55 Gervase Holles, Memorials of the Holles Family, p. 186. Camden Third Series, Volume LV.

56 Symond's Notebook. Harl. MSS 986.

57 Holles, op.cit. p. 188.

58 *A List of [Indigent] Officers.*

59 PRO. WO/55/1661. 'Arms delivery at the Camp at Culham.' 23 May 1643.

60 C.C.C., p. 92.

61 Wood, City of Oxford, Volume III, p. 245.

62 Sanderson.

63 Royalist Ordnance Papers.

64 Bedfordshire Historical Record Society, Volume XXVII (1948).
65 Peacock, pp.84, 85 & 89.
66 PRO. 31/8/197,f,355.
67 Peacock, p. 85.
68 SP. 16/473/52.
69 Roy, Ordnance Papers, p. 67.
70 *Mercurius Aulicus*, 1644, p. 1221.
71 Lord Ogle's Narrative. B.M. Add. MSS 27402.
72 *A List of [Indigent] Officers.*
73 Symond's Notebook. Harl. MSS 986.
74 BM. Harl. MSS 6804,f.197.
75 Roy, Ordnance Papers, p. 158.
76 Peacock, p. 85.
77 C.C.C., p. 116.
78 Peacock, p. 80.
79 SP. 16/473/52.
80 PRO. WO. 55/1661.
81 His signature appears in the Lords' Journals version of the letter of the Royalist commanders to the Earl of Essex.
82 Peacock, p. 99.
83 Cheshire Q.S.R., Trinity. Nantwich. 8 July 1662. The regiment had passed to Sir Jacob Astley before Chantler was slain, and at the siege of Bristol in July 1643 its major was not Walthall, but Toby Bowes.
84 Hopton's *Bellum Civile*, pp.2–3 & 9.
85 Somerset Q.S.R.
86 Peacock, p. 84.
87 SP 16/473/f.52.
88 B.M. Harl MSS 6804,f.221.
89 PRO WO 55/1661.
90 Warrant in the collection of Anthony W. G. Lowther,Esq., A.R.I.B.A., F.S.A.
91 Peacock, p. 97.
92 Philip Morant, The History and Antiquities of the County of Essex, Vol. I,p.70.
93 Name inscribed on the walls of the tower where Royalist prisoners were confined.
94 *A List of [Indigent] Officers.*
95 Cheshire Q.S.R.
96 Minshall was in fact Fitton's captain-lieutenant.
97 Major to Fitton and lieutenant-colonel to his successor, Anthony Thelwall.
98 NLW. Tredegar MSS. 911.
99 CAM, Volume II, p. 730.
100 B.M. Harl. MSS 6804,f.221.
101 Dugdale's Diary, pp.67 & 70.
102 Roy, Ordnance Papers, p. 183.
103 Royalist Ordnance Papers.
104 Cheshire Q.S.R.
105 Royalist Ordnance Papers.
106 Alex. Mackenzie, History of the Munros. pp.210, 471. See also Robert Munro His Expedition (1637) and John Mackay's Old Scots Brigade.
107 Royalist Ordnance Papers.

108   Wood, City of Oxford, Volume III, p. 243.

109   Walter Money, The Battles of Newbury, p. 79.

110   Lancashire Q.S.R.

111   *Mercurius Aulicus*, 1643, p. 52.

112   NLW. Calendar of Wynn Papers, p. 277.

113   Norman Tucker, Royalist Officers of North Wales, 1642–1660, p.19.

114   Denbighshire Q.S.R.

115   B.M. Add. MSS 14294. His commission as major was dated Woodstock 29 Oct. 1642, but he had clearly been acting as such from August onwards.

116   Ottley Papers, No. CCXXIX, p. 283.

117   Wiltshire Q.S.R.

118   Cheshire Q.S.R.

119   WO. 55/1661.

120   Chetham Society, Volume II, 1844, pp.336 *et seq*. Tracts relating to the Military Proceedings in Lancashire.

121   Lancashire Q.S.R. He was dead before 4 May 1663.

122   Colonel Cyril Field, Echoes of Old Wars, p. 29.

123   Son of Northampton's steward (C.C.C. p. 2096).

124   B.M. Add. MSS 29570, and papers preserved in the Northampton family throw much light on the composition of this regiment.

125   C.C.C. p. 1283

126   Peacock, p. 86.

127   Roy, Ordnance Papers, p. 110.

128   Wiltshire Q.S.R., Trinity 1661.

129   John Savage, second Earl Rivers (1603–1654).

130   Bennet was in fact major at the surrender of Donnington Castle (Walter Money, F.S.A., The Battles of Newbury, 1881, p. 160.)

131   John Boyes (Peacock, p. 77). His career is in D.N.B.

132   Colonel Joseph Bamfeild's Apologie. Holland(?) 1689. Copy in BM.

133   H.M.C. Ormonde, Vol. I, p. 239.

134   Roy, Ordnance Papers, p. 186.

135   SP. 29/13,f.45.

136   Roy, Ordnance Papers, p. 186.

137   Ottley Papers, No. CXXII and Calendar of Wynn Papers in the National Library of Wales, p. 284.

138   The Beating up of the Enemy's Quarters &c. Lichfield, Oxford, 1643.

139   B.M. Add. MSS 18980, f.10. Letter of Cornet Charles Cocks.

140   Edited by I.G. Philip, M.A., for the Oxfordshire Record Society, 1947.

141 Peacock, p. 77.

142   Clarendon, Volume II, p. 405.

143   Roy, Ordnance Papers, p. 167.

144   Bodleian Library. Rawlinson MS. D.395. (21) 208.

145   *Ibid*.

146   Lunsford had been killed at the storming of Bristol (July) and Prince Rupert took over his regiment.

147   Mr Cartington was one of the five conductors detailed for the Bye Train for Banbury on 22 October 1642 (Roy, p. 157).

148   Yarnton Parish Register.

NOTE

Three of the Royalist captains who fell at Edgehill cannot be assigned to any regiment.

Captain Alexander Gordoun, probably one of the Scots who joined the army with Ruthven. He was buried at Warmington.

Captain Henry Kingsmill of Sidmonton, Hants, whose monument is in Radway Church.

Captain Richard Sauner (Saunders?) of Worcestershire. He also was buried at Warmington.

From an inscription on Caesar's Tower, at Warwick Castle, we learn that 'Master John Smyth, Gunner to His Majestyes Highness: was a prisoner in this place in the year of our Lord, 1642, 2, 3, 4, 5'

SECTION 4

Notes on the Parliamentary regiments

These notes are based partly on Godfrey Davies' article, 'The Parliamentary Army Under The Earl of Essex, 1642–5', partly on Peacock and partly on the administrative papers preserved in the Public Record Office, State Papers 28. Where other sources have been used the references are given, but not otherwise.

The names of officers who are in the Reformado List of June 1642 are marked with an asterisk. Others may have served in the Scots Wars, or learned the rudiments of the military art with the Honourable Artillery Company, but in general Essex's captains seem to have lacked experience.

1. THE EARL OF ESSEX'S REGIMENT OF FOOT

This regiment, which wore orange coats, was raised in Essex and was 1,500 strong by 10 August 1642, when it received £1461 : 17 : 4 levy money. Probably, as in 1639, Essex had colours of 'orringe tawny and white.[1]

The company commanders were:

> Colonel the Earl of Essex.
> Lt. Colonel William Davies, later colonel of another regiment.
> Sergeant-Major Jo. Bamfield, later lieutenant-colonel, K. 1643.
> Captain Sir Anthony St. John.
> Captain Christopher Mathews, later major.
> Captain Jo. Skrimpshiere.
> Captain Thomas Skinner.
> Captain Roger Bettridge.
> Captain Thomas Ward.*
> Captain Edward Leventhorp.
> Captain-Lieutenant John Rainsford.
> The chaplain was Steven Marshall.

Davies had served as a captain in foreign parts and had been major to Sir John Merrick in 1640, while Captain Ward was a Reformado. St. John was to be wounded at the siege of Reading in April 1643, while Bamfield was killed at First Newbury.[2]

After Edgehill Captain Skinner paid a soldier 20/- for a George, which must have been taken from the mortally wounded Earl of Lindsey.

John Rainsford was possibly the author of the training manual called

'The Yong Soulldier', which was published in London in 1642.

Of the subalterns, Lieutenant Hugh Justice had been an ensign in 1640, and is a lieutenant in the list of Reformadoes (June 1642). Ensign William Bowen wrote an interesting account of Powick Bridge.[3]

The regiment served at the battles of Newbury and in Cornwall and was eventually merged into the New Model Army (5 April 1645). It seems to have been one of the better regiments of the Roundhead army.

2. COLONEL SIR JOHN MERRICK'S REGIMENT OF FOOT

The London greycoats were at Worcester during the battle of Edgehill, and later went into the West Country, where some broken companies took part in the battle at Launceston on 25 April 1643.[4]

The company commanders were:

> Colonel Sir John Merrick.
> Lt. Colonel Vincent Calmady.
> Sergeant-Major Will. Herbert.
> Captain . . . Tyer.
> Captain . . . Lower.
> Captain Francis Merrick.
> Captain Thomas Laugherne.
> Captain John Lloyd.
> Captain John Edwards.
> Captain John Baily.
> Capt.-Lieut . . .

Merrick, after serving as a major in foreign parts, had commanded a regiment in 1640, in which Herbert had been a captain, and Lloyd and Edwards, lieutenants. For the rest it seems Merrick had to be content with officers innocent of previous military training. Herbert rose to be a colonel and Governor of Plymouth.

3. THE EARL OF PETERBOROUGH'S REGIMENT OF FOOT

This regiment was not at Edgehill, but was taken at Banbury a few days later, when its strength is variously reported as 600 and 1,000. Nevertheless it seems to have survived until 25 April 1644, which perhaps means that it was deprived of its arms, and allowed to march away.

The company commanders were:

> Colonel the Earl of Peterborough.
> Lt. Colonel Sir Faithfull Fortescue.
> Sergeant-Major Francis Fairfax*, lieutenant-colonel *vice* Fortescue.
> Captain Sir Edward Payton.
> Captain Philip Dutton*.
> Captain Bevill Prideaux.
> Captain Robert Knightley.
> Captain John Butler or Botteler, later major.
> Captain Henry Lovell.

Captain George Blunt.
Capt.-Lieut. George Rowse.

The colonel and the lieutenant-colonel were both 'pluralists', the one being General of the Ordnance, and the other commander of a troop of horse. Both were at Edgehill, and while the former's doings have escaped record, the latter made himself notorious by changing sides. Presumably Francis Fairfax was left to command the regiment. He appears as a captain in the Reformado List, and had probably served on the continent for he was not in the 1640 army. Dutton was a Reformado captain-lieutenant, and lieutenant Jo. Balston or Balstone was another who had been 'entertained' for the service in Ireland. He was one of the few Reformadoes who had not got a step in rank, and it would seem that this did not please him. At any rate he returned to his allegiance, or deserted, and by 14 June 1643 – having taken a double step – was major in Sir Lewis Dyve's Regiment,[5] in which he was still serving during the defence of Sherborne Castle, 1645.

4. THE EARL OF STAMFORD'S REGIMENT OF FOOT

Stamford's bluecoats were in garrison at Hereford and so missed Edgehill. They afterwards became the garrison of Gloucester, where they greatly distinguished themselves.

The company commanders were:

Colonel the Earl of Stamford.
Lt. Colonel Edward Massey, afterwards colonel and Governor of Gloucester.
Sergeant Major Constance Ferrer.
Captain Thomas Savill.
Captain Edward Gray.
Captain Charles Blunt.
Captain Peter Crispe.
Captain Isaac Dobson.
Captain Arnold Cosbie.
Captain John Bird.
Captain-Lieutenant John Clifton*.

Edward Massey (1619?–1674?) was an excellent officer though at this time he does not seem to have had any military experience. His defence of Gloucester was a remarkable achievement. In 1651 he served as a Royalist general and was wounded shortly before the battle of Worcester at Upton on Severn.

Clifton and one of the lieutenants, Robert Hampson, were Reformadoes, but there is no evidence that the other officers were soldiers by trade. Captain Crispe, however, may have been in the Cadiz expedition (1625). Ferrer, Gray, Blunt and Crispe are all mentioned in the accounts of the siege of Gloucester, as are lieutenants William White and Robert

Mallery, both of whom became captains, and James Harcus, who was killed there, serving as Massey's captain-lieutenant.[6]

This must be rated as one of the most successful Parliamentarian regiments. It certainly owed much to Massey's energy and example.

5. THE REGIMENT OF FOOT OF LORD SAYE AND SELE AND SIR JOHN MELDRUM

Lord Saye's bluecoats were doubtless raised round his own home, Broughton in North Oxfordshire, an area where his power was challenged to some extent by his Royalist neighbour, the Earl of Northampton.

Before Edgehill Saye seems to have handed over his regiment to the Scots veteran Meldrum.

The company commanders were:

> Colonel Sir John Meldrum. Brigade commander.
> Lt. Colonel (George?) Hutchinson.
> Sergeant-Major Ja. Atchason or Acheson.
> Captain George Marrow.
> Captain Christopher Burgh, later lieutenant-colonel.
> Captain James Temple.*
> Captain Walter Lloyd, later lieutenant-colonel.
> Captain Morgan Tinne.
> Captain Robert Blowe.
> Captain Bussy Basset.
> Capt.-Lieut. John Rainsford.

Atchason may have been in the Cadiz expedition, Temple was a Reformado, and Rainsford was the author of 'The Yong Soulldier', but what other military experience there may have been in the regiment remains a mystery. Thanks perhaps to Meldrum's expert knowledge, the regiment acquitted itself well at Edgehill.

When Meldrum went north in 1643 command passed to Edward Aldrich from Lord Rochford's Regiment.

Symonds saw the regiment on 2 September 1644 when he witnessed the surrender near Lostwithiel and noted: 'Colonel Aldridge, blew colours with lions rampant or'.[7] This shows that the regiment had retained its original colours for the arms of Fiennes were three lions rampant or, on a field azure.

The regiment survived the disaster in Cornwall and was merged in the New Model Army in April 1645.

6. THE REGIMENT OF LORD WHARTON

Lord Wharton's regiment had a brief and inglorious career, for having fled at Edgehill it was disbanded in the following November. Despite

Royalist versifiers Wharton himself does not seem to have quitted the field with his men, probably he had been with his troop of horse.

In the summer of 1642 Wharton had been chosen Colonel-General of the Foot for the Irish Expedition, and officers had been chosen for it. He brought very many of them with him into Essex's army. Those marked with † in the following list were selected for the Irish Expedition.

Company Commanders	*Lieutenants*	*Ensigns*
Colonel Lord Wharton†	Charles Holcroft†	. . . Blake
Lt. Colonel Jeremy Horton†	Francis Fitzhugh★	Thomas Radford
Sergeant-Major Owen Parry†	Edward Browne†	Robert Hughes†
Robert Long†	Thomas Albany† or Allanby	Roger Moore†
Henry Carew†	William Browne	William Heydon†
Jude Leigh★	William Bridges	Edward Horton
Henry Skipwith†	George Usher	John Garret
Christopher Baily	William Emerson	Jer. Gardiner
. . . Gibbons	Anthony Masham★	Richard Bland†
Elias Struce† or Struice	Isaac Turney	Edward Horton
Provost-Marshal George Higham		
Chirurgion Jo. Broughton		

Thus a regiment designed for Ireland was almost entirely diverted into the Parliamentarian Army. This would seem to be evidence for the view that the Irish Expedition was unscrupulously used as a cover plan for the raising of forces against the King.

This may have caused some dissatisfaction. Owen Parry for one was to change sides, and to serve as lieutenant-colonel to Sir Henry Cary's Regiment of Foot in the West where he officered his company with his relations, Lieutenant William Parry and Ensign James Parry, from Herefordshire. Owen Parry, who had been a captain in 1640, lived to see the Restoration and to claim, along with his subalterns, part of the £60,000 set aside by King Charles II for loyal and indigent Cavaliers.

7. LORD ROCHFORD'S REGIMENT OF FOOT

This unit was at Coventry during the battle of Edgehill, but joined the main army late on the 24th.

The company commanders were:

> Colonel Lord Rochford.
> Lt. Colonel Edward Aldrich, later colonel of Meldrum's Regiment.
> Sergeant-Major Thomas Leighton.
> Captain Thomas Drake.
> Captain George Walsh.★
> Captain Philip Ballard.
> Captain Benjamin Hooke.
> Captain Francis Hudson.

Captain Jasper Brand.*
Captain George Willoughby.
Capt.-Lieut. Jo. Norship.

Aldrich had been a major in 1640; Leighton may have been in the Cadiz expedition, while, besides two of the company commanders, a lieutenant, Humphry Dimock, was a Reformado.

The Hertfordshire Quarter Sessions Records record the name of William Bygrave, of Ashwell, labourer, who claims to have served under Colonel Rochford at Edgehill, and Colonel Michell at Henley-upon-Thames.[8]

The regiment had been disbanded by 28 June 1643.

8. LORD ST. JOHN'S REGIMENT OF FOOT

At Oxford on the morning of 15 September 'a drumme went up and downe the towne, for volunters (sic) to serve the kinge and parliament under the lord St John's . . . '[9] though with what success we are not told. The regiment was at Worcester during the battle, which was nevertheless fatal to it, for its colonel, serving presumably with his troop of horse, received a fatal wound dying in the hands of his enemies. The regiment passed to Col. Sir Thomas Essex and went to Bristol.

Its company commanders were:

Colonel Lord St. John.
Lt. Colonel Thomas Essex.
Sergeant Major Edward Andrews, captain in 1640.
Captain Timo. Neale, later major to Colonel Denzil Holles (?).
Captain Oliver Beecher.
Captain Jo. Harvie.
Captain Lewis Pemberton*.
Captain Thomas Miles.
Captain John Hilderson*.
Captain Thomas Thorogood.
Capt.-Lieut. Theodore Palaeologus* of Landulph, Cornwall.

Palaeologus was already a captain-lieutenant in June 1642, but Pemberton and Hilderson had both advanced rapidly from the rank of ensign, evidence of the extreme difficulty the Roundheads had in finding officers with any experience.

Palaeologus fell at Second Newbury, serving as lieutenant-colonel to the regiment of Colonel Francis Thompson. He was buried in Westminster Abbey.

Another officer who continued to serve after the regiment disappeared, was Lieutenant Wendy Oxford, who was a captain in Sir Samuel Luke's garrison of Newport Pagnell in 1644.

9. LORD BROOKE'S REGIMENT OF FOOT

Raised in London, the regiment wore purple coats. When it entered Oxford on 27 September 'There were 8 or 10 auntients of them, of a purple cullour, with the arms of England and 7 starres in the feild. Every auntient had an hundred men under it, . . . '[1] It looks, therefore, as if the regiment was about 1,000 strong at this period. By mid–November, just before Brentford, it was down to 480, which even if officers are omitted, indicates heavy losses at Edgehill.

The company commanders were:

> Colonel Lord Brooke.
> Lt. Colonel Sir Edward Peto of Chesterton, Warwickshire.
> Sergeant-Major Walter Ailworth★.
> Captain Thomas Fitch.
> Captain John Lilburne.
> Captain Ralph Cotsforth.
> Captain Thomas Hickman.
> Captain Nicholas Warren.
> Captain . . . Sambridge.
> Captain John Bridges, Governor of Warwick Castle, later colonel.
> Capt.-Lieut. John Ashfield.

Except for Ailworth, a Reformado captain, the officers seem to have been without military experience, though Ashfield had been chosen as an ensign for the Irish Expedition.

Captain John Lilburne, 'Free-born John', the second captain, was certainly at Edgehill but all we know of his part in the battle is that the Earl of Warwick certified (11 November) that he was 'a man both faithfull, able and fit to be Captaine of a Troop of Horse (having shewed his valour at the battell of Kenton)'. It is reported that 'he kept the Field all Night'. He was taken prisoner at Brentford (12 November) after a brave resistance.[11]

Lord Brooke was killed at the siege of Lichfield in March 1643, and it is thought that his regiment did not long survive him.

10. LORD MANDEVILLE'S REGIMENT OF FOOT

Little is known of this regiment, which distinguished itself by the speed with which it quitted the field of Edgehill, and was disbanded about November 1642. Lord Mandeville became Earl of Manchester and had a regiment of foot in the Eastern Association (1643–1645). Its uniform was green coats lined with red, but there is no evidence that this had been the dress of his first regiment.

The company commanders were:

> Colonel Lord Mandeville.
> Lt. Colonel John Parkinson★.

Sergeant Major John Drake★.
Captain Francis Wilson★.
Captain Henry Samerster★ (or Somister).
Captain Edward Watts★.
Captain Robert Goodwin.
Captain Robert Palmer.
Captain Daniel Redman.
Captain Osborn Williams★.
Capt.-Lieut . . . Turkington.

Parkinson had been in the Cadiz as well as the Rhé expeditions,[12] and Drake had also served in foreign parts. Wilson, who is said to have set an ill example at Edgehill, Watts, Somister and Williams were all Reformadoes, the last three being recently promoted lieutenants. Watts had been in the 1640 army, but the others had probably soldiered abroad.

The chaplain of the regiment was the well-known preacher, Simon Ash.

11. LORD ROBARTES' REGIMENT OF FOOT

Robartes' redcoats went through all the campaigns of Essex's army and were merged into the New Model in April 1645. It was one of the regiments compelled to surrender at Lostwithiel on 2 September 1644.

The company commanders were:

Colonel Lord Robartes.
Lt. Colonel William Hunter.
Sergeant-Major Alex. Hurry.
Captain James Witcherly.
Captain Jo. Walker.
Captain Jo. Mercer.
Captain Mark Grimes, later lieutenant-colonel, F., to Colonel
        Edward Montague, in the Army of the Eastern Association 1644–1645.
Captain John Mill.
Captain Jonathan Elliot.
Captain James Fookes.
Capt.-Lieut. George Graden.

The chaplain was Dr. Calibut Downing, Rector of Hickford, Buckinghamshire, and West Ilsley, Berkshire. He was the father of the notorious Sir George Downing (1623?–1684), who treacherously procured the arrest of three of the regicides, Barkstead, Corbet and Okey at Delft in 1662.

Hurry, or Urry, was a Scot, and doubtless a soldier of fortune. He was captured at Second Newbury.[13] If there were any other professional officers in this regiment their previous careers are obscure.

12. COLONEL SIR HENRY CHOLMLEY'S REGIMENT OF FOOT

Though most of Cholmley's bluecoats fled at Edgehill, it seems there was no safety in flight, for of the 1,200 men it had on 1 October, only 552 remained on 23 November.

The company commanders were:

> Colonel Sir Henry Cholmley.
> Lt. Colonel Launce Alured.
> Sergeant–Major Thomas Southcot.
> Captain Henry Jenkins.
> Captain William Bateler (sic).
> Captain Henry Katcose.
> Captain Goddard Leigh.
> Captain Richard Jones*.
> Captain Robert Hunt.
> Captain John Bury.
> Capt.-Lieut. Michael Jobson.

The chaplain was Adoniram Byfield, the 'Worthy Divine' whose account appears as Document 3, Section Six.

The colonel was the second son of Sir Richard Cholmley of Whitby, Yorkshire.

Lieutenants George Fulwood and John Shanks were Reformadoes, but the latter's heart was not in his work.

The regiment disappeared before June 1643.

13. COLONEL DENZIL HOLLES' REGIMENT OF FOOT

Holles' Regiment of redcoats was raised in London, and its ranks were doubtless full of apprentices. The letters of Sergeant Nehemiah Wharton gave the impression that the men, while courageous and keen, were extremely undisciplined. If some took the field in the cause of Liberty and Religion, others were inspired by baser motives. Wharton gives his captain's name as Beacon but the company commanders listed in Peacock are:

> Colonel Denzil Holles.
> Lt. Colonel Henry Billingsley, cashiered 20 August 1642.
> Sergeant–Major James Quarles, Lt. Colonel *vice* Billingsley.
> Sergeant–Major Neale, *vice* Quarles. Probably Timo. Neale, who
> was 1st Captain to Lord St. John's Regiment.
> Captain Allen Povey, lieutenant 1640.
> Captain William Barke.
> Captain Richard Lacey.
> Captain George Harlock.
> Captain Jo. Francis.
> Captain William Burles.
> Captain . . . Bennet.
> Capt.-Lieut. Richard Parker, lieutenant 1640.

The chaplain of the regiment was a celebrated puritan divine, Obadiah Sedgwick (1601?–1658) MA. BD. Sedgwick had been chaplain to Lord

Vere in the Low Countries. Wharton tells us that the quartermaster, omitted from Peacock's list, was a Mr Egerton.

After distinguishing itself at Edgehill the regiment was cut up at Brentford and did not recover from the diaster. Quarles and Lacy were both driven into the Thames and drowned.[14]

Holles seems to have officered his regiment with civilians for only his unpopular lieutenant-colonel, Billingsley, and his captain-lieutenant, Richard Parker, appear in the Reformadoes list, though Captain Povey had been a lieutenant in 1640 and Quarles had been in the Cadiz and Rhé expeditions as a lieutenant.

14. COLONEL WILLIAM BAMFIELD'S REGIMENT

The absence of this regiment from Edgehill must be accounted for by its being in garrison, perhaps at Northampton.

The colonel and many of the officers† had originally been selected for a regiment in the Irish expedition, several of them obtaining a step in rank by remaining in England. Price, for example, was originally chosen as captain-lieutenant.

Company commanders	Lieutenants	Ensigns
Colonel William Bamfield†	Jo. Hart	Samson Manaton†
Lt. Colonel Sir Robert Wingfield*	Ambrose Cade	George Wingfield
Sergeant-Major Sam Price†	Ralph Garth†	Sym. Giggins
Captain Rob. Baker†	Thomas Durdo	Jo. Rose†
Captain Richard Benson†	Thomas Latimer†	Jo. Browne†
Captain Jo. Jessop	Hogan Rookwood	William Blake
Captain Jo. Minshaw†	Humphrey Burton†	Richard Jackson
Captain William Owen	Albion Derickbore	Jo. Price
Captain Thomas Stafferton	Henry Wray	Francis Barber
Captain . . . Pawlet	Andrew Ball	Thomas Hudson

Chaplain	Freeman
Chirurgion	Richard Searle
Quartermaster	Christopher Allanson
Carriage-master	He. Beecher
Provost-Marshal	Richard Gray

Of the rest Wingfield was a Reformado and Stafferton had been in the Ile de Rhé expedition.

The regiment seems to have been disbanded about March 1643.

15. THE REGIMENT OF COLONEL THOMAS GRANTHAM

This Regiment, as we have seen, was one of those a day behind the army on 23 October. It may be the regiment of russet coats which entered Oxford on 27 September, and fought a pitched battle in the streets with the bluecoats. Grantham had at least nine officers who had previous military experience and one would expect the regiment to have been rather better disciplined and trained than the rest.

The company commanders were:

> Colonel Thomas Grantham.
> Lt. Colonel Francis Clarke★.
> Major John Holman★.
> Captain Henry Ashley★.
> Captain Sir Thomas Pigot★.
> Captain Richard Gibbs.
> Captain Thomas Rogers★.
> Captain Francis Grantham.
> Captain George Slatford, lieutenant 1640.
> Captain Henry Blundell★.
> Capt.-Lieut. Francis Gray.

Reformadoes included Lieutenants Thomas Lee, Isaac Challys and Miles Hitchcock. Blundell, a junior ensign, is an example of quick promotion. Sir Thomas Pigot on the other hand had been a captain as early as the Rhé expedition and on 22 April 1627 solicited to be one of the ten captains to be retained.[15]

No Roundhead regiment seems to have had more professional officers, which did not prevent its disappearance early in 1643.

16.   COLONEL SIR WILLIAM CONSTABLE'S REGIMENT OF FOOT

Constable's bluecoats did well at Edgehill.

The company commanders were:

> Colonel Sir William Constable, Bart. (d.1655).
> Lt. Colonel Rob. Graeme.
> Sergeant-Major Henry Frodsham.
> Captain Thomas Eure.
> Captain James Breckham.
> Captain John Fenwick.
> Captain Simon Needham.
> Captain Ben. Cicill.
> Captain Humphrey Jones.
> Captain James Grey.
> Capt.-Lieut. Edmund or Edward Hackluyt, lieutenant 1640.

The chaplain was William Sedgwick, who, during the Commonwealth, was known for his zeal as 'the apostle of the isle of Ely'.

The colonel, who came from Flamborough, Yorkshire, had served under the second Earl of Essex, who had knighted him in Ireland as long ago as 1599. His lieutenant-colonel was probably a Scots soldier of fortune, while his major had been in both the Cadiz and Rhé expeditions.

Lieutenant Thomas Compton may have been the T.C. who wrote '*A more true and an exacter Relation*'. Certainly the regiment had no reason to be ashamed of its part at Edgehill. It was one of the ensigns, Arthur Young, later a captain, who had taken the Banner Royal. We do not know whether its casualities were heavy, but it is certain that the senior ensign, Joseph Smith of Shalbourne, Wiltshire, was a captain by the following spring, when he was wounded at the siege of Reading.[16] The rest went to Hull, August 1643.

17. COLONEL THOMAS BALLARD'S REGIMENT OF FOOT

This was one of the regiments originally designed, at least in theory, for Ireland. The list of his officers shows that the great majority were originally selected for the Irish Expedition.

Company commanders	Lieutenants	Ensigns
Thomas Ballard†	Leonard Moreton† or Morton	Henry Collingwood
Francis Martin †	Jo. Hughes	William Fowles† or Fowlis
Wil. Lower	Dan. Redman	Charles Parker†
Thomas Middleton†	John Lookar†	Robert Purpell
Francis Foukes, sen.†	Francis Fowke, jun.	Henry Higgins†
Edward Allen†	Francis Bowyer†	Thomas Axtell
Edward Primrose†	Edward Norbury†	Jo. Hardy†
Pet. Murford†	Robert Davies†	Edward Wett (West?)
Io. Browne★	Thomas Brandy	William Ogee
Robert Noyes† (Noyce)		William Garfoot†

Quartermaster	Io. Lamsdie	
Waggon-master	Jere. Burleigh	
Provost-Marshal	Ben. Ludlow	

†All these were chosen for Ballard's Regiment for the Irish Expedition.

Ballard's greycoats were raised in Buckinghamshire and on 17 October mustered 808 officers and men. Only 439 men (excluding officers) remained on 11 November. Some of the missing 337 may have been sick, but the greater part must have fallen on 23 October.

On 11 November some of the companies were very weak. Captain Murford only had 15 men and Captain Primrose only 19. Captains Browne and Noyes have disappeared, and it seems not unlikely that they were casualties of Edgehill. Their places were taken by two captains named Manby and Merricke from outside the regiment.

Ballard went north in the winter, leaving his regiment to Francis Martin, who commanded it until, about April 1644, it disappeared.

18. COLONEL SIR WILLIAM FAIRFAX'S REGIMENT

Although this regiment fled without striking a blow it survived the battle, and in December 1642 was sent to Yorkshire, where it continued its career in the army led by Lord Fairfax and his warlike son, Sir Thomas.

The company commanders, a fairly experienced group, were:

Colonel Sir William Fairfax (k. 1644).
Lt.-Colonel William Monings, captain 1640.
Sergeant-Major Jarvis Paine, captain 1640.
Captain Francis Rogers★, ensign 1640.
Captain Edward Odingsells.
Captain Thomas Rush, lieutenant 1640.
Captain Michael Bland, ensign 1640.
Captain Robert Wilshiere★, lieutenant 1640.
Captain Titus Leighton★, ensign 1640, later major (k. 1643).
Captain William Trunke.
Capt.-Lieut. David (or Daniel) Goldsmith, lieutenant 1640.
The chaplain was Mr. Thomas Crompton.

Monings, after serving as a subaltern in foreign parts, had been a captain in 1640 in the Marquis of Hamilton's Regiment as had Jarvis Paine. Rush and Bland had both served in Sir Nicholas Byron's regiment in that campaign. The Carriage-Master, Henry Ward, was a reformado lieutenant, as were Wilshiere and Leighton. Another lieutenant, Francis Bland, had been a Reformado ensign. Odingsells had been selected as a lieutenant for the Irish Expedition. One of the other lieutenants, Thomas Whitney, who had been an ensign in 1640, found himself in trouble after the battle for seeking safety in flight and spreading tales of woe.

19. COLONEL CHARLES ESSEX'S REGIMENT OF FOOT

Charles Essex was another colonel selected for the Irish Expedition.

Company commanders	Lieutenants	Ensigns
Colonel Charles Essex†	Francis Hall†	Jo. Shipman†
Lt. Colonel Adam Coning-ham† (or Cunningham)	Edward Barnewell†	Leonard Hawkins†
Sergeant-Major . . .	James Webb†	Jo. Wheeler
Captain William Roberts†	Ralph Williams	Jo. Watkins†
Captain John Jenkins†	Bartholomew Ellicot† or Elecot	Tracey Smart
Captain Francis Hall	William Hewet	Jo. Withers
Captain William Frederick	Christopher Crow	William Stratford
Captain Jo. Haselwood	Christopher Chidley	Thomas Fitz
Captain Samuel Loftus	James Burrell (or Barrell)	Rob. Shergoll
Captain Sir William Essex	Daniel Robinson	Richard Thornehill

Quartermaster	Roger Wase
Chaplain	Samuel Wells
Provost-Marshal	Martin Benthin
Chirurgion	Jo. Browne

Essex himself had been a captain in the Dutch service as early as 1634. His father, Captain Sir William Essex, lived at Lambourne in Berkshire. Both were unfortunate at Edgehill – the son killed and the father taken. An ensign, Robert Shergoll, also fell. Of the other officers Lieutenant Christopher Crowe had served in 1640.

Despite its poor start, the regiment survived. Watching the surrendered regiments pass (2 September 1644) Symonds noted 'Colonel Conyngham, green colours'.[17] The last colonel was Richard Fortescue who continued in command when the regiment was absorbed into the New Model Army.

20. COLONEL JOHN HAMPDEN'S REGIMENT OF FOOT

Hampden's greencoats were raised in Buckinghamshire. They are said to have had colours with the motto *Vestigia Nulla Retrorsum*. The regiment was a day behind the army at Edgehill and so had little opportunity to show its mettle.

The company commanders were:

> Colonel John Hampden (1594–1643).
> Lt. Colonel Joseph Wagstaffe.
> Sergeant-Major William Barriffe.
> Captain Richard Ingoldsby, of Lenthenborough, Buckinghamshire
>   (d.1685), later colonel.
> Captain . . . Nicholls.
> Captain . . . Arnett.
> Captain John Stiles.
> Captain John Raymont or Raymond, later major.
> Captain Robert Farrington.
> Captain . . . Morris.
> Capt.-Lieut. Henry Isham.
> The chaplain was William Spurstow.

The lieutenant-colonel was captured early in Jan. 1643, changed sides, and served with distinction in the Royalist army, being knighted. He had been a major in the French service. He was one of the leaders of Penruddock's rising in 1655.

Hampden's regiment was a strong one, though its numbers dwindled gradually in the early months of 1643. A strength of 893 on 21 January had fallen to 849 on 21 June.

When Hampden died of the wounds he received at Chalgrove Field (18 June 1643), another Buckinghamshire man took over. This was Thomas Tyrrell. He was succeeded by Richard Ingoldsby, the future regicide, who took the survivors into the New Model. This seems to have been one of the best Parliamentarian regiments.

HORSE AND DRAGOONS

Particulars of the Horse and Dragoon Regiments are given in Chapter Twelve. The regiments of Stapleton and Balfour were still in Essex's army in 1644.[18]

Colonel Arthur Goodwin was with the army at Turnham Green.

In November we find Colonel John Middleton commanding Lord Feilding's Regiment.[19] Whether the latter was thought to have failed at Edgehill cannot be said. Later in the war he was operating from Stafford, with his quartermaster of 1642, William Tovey, as one of his captains. It rather looks as if his military reputation survived Edgehill.

Lord Willoughby of Parham bore his black colours back to Lincolnshire, while Waller went to command in the West taking with him Feilding's major, Robert Burrill, who became a colonel.

 1 HMC. Rutland, Vol.I, p. 510.
 2 The Parliament Scout, 22–29 Sept. 1643. (BM.TT.E69)
 3 *True Relation of the Late Battell before Worcester.* (BM.TT.E119 (21))
 4 Burne & Young, p. 42.
 5 PRO. Royalist Ordnance Papers.
 6 See accounts of the siege of Gloucester in John Washbourne's *Bibliotheca Gloucestrensis*, two volumes, Gloucester, 1823.
 7 Symonds' Diary, p. 66.
 8 Hertfordshire County Records, p. 126.
 9 Wood's Life and Times, p. 61.
10 *Op. cit*, p. 66.
11 Pauline Gregg, Free-born John, p. 100. This is an excellent biography of a great-hearted militant Christian.
12 Acts of the Privy Council, p. 16.
13 *Mercurius Aulicus*, 1644, p. 1232.
14 Vicars, God in the Mount, p. 216.
15 CSPD 1627–8, p. 145.
16 Wiltshire Quarter Sessions Records.
17 Symonds' Diary, p. 66.
18 *Op. cit.*, p. 73.
19 SP 28/140.

SECTION 5

Royalist Accounts of the Battle

THE ROYALIST ACCOUNTS are fairly numerous and several of them give reasonably coherent descriptions of the battle. The best are the Royalist Official Account, Bulstrode's, James II's and the two by Clarendon. Of these only Clarendon's, which are easily accessible to the student, are not printed here.

1. THE ROYALIST OFFICIAL ACCOUNT

This account was clearly written by one of the King's entourage. It is not impossible that the author was (Sir) William Dugdale (1605–1686), who is known to have been diligent in collecting information about the battle. No doubt it was submitted to the Council of War before publication.

A Relation of the Battel fought between Keynton *and* Edgehill, *by His Majesty's Army and that of the Rebels; Printed by his Majesty's Command at* Oxford *by* Leonard Lichfield, *Printer to the University*, 1642.

UPon *Saturday* the 23rd of October, 1642, his Majesty had given Order for the Summoning of *Banbury*, and in Case of Refusal, the Besieging of it with 4000 Foot and four Pieces of Cannon; but that Evening Intelligence was brought that the Rebels had a Resolution to Relieve it; but it was not so certain, as to make any Change of the former Orders; yet upon *Sunday* at Three in the Morning, there came certain Intelligence, that the whole Army of the Rebels were Marching with all Expedition thither, and were quartered at *Keynton* 3 Miles from *Edgehill*; whereupon the King gave present Order for all his Army, both Horse and Foot, to March with all Expedition to *Edgehill*, being 4 Miles distant from his nearest Quarter. To which Rendezvous the King's Horse came between 10 and 11 a Clock in the Morning, and the Van of Foot came within an hour after, but the Rear (which happened at that time to be the Lord-Lieutenant-General's Regiment) with the Artillery, came not within 2 hours after. As soon as we came to the Top of *Edgehill*, which looks upon *Keynton*, we saw the Rebels Army drawing out, and setting themselves in Battalia; whereupon the King's Horse went down the Hill, and set themselves in order; the Foot likewise having Command to come down the Hill, and do the like;

but before that was done, and the King's Artillery came, it was past 2 in the Afternoon.

It being perceived that the Rebels had placed some Musqueteers under a Hedge that crost the Field, where the Encounter was to be made, that flanked upon their left Wing, there were some of the King's Dragooners sent to beat them off, which they very well performed; whereupon our whole Army advanced in very good Order, the Ordnance of both sides playing very fast, but that of the Rebels began first. The Charge began between the 2 Wings of Horse; those of the Rebels not standing our Charge a quarter of an hour before they fled, our Men having the Execution of them for 3 Miles together, the Horse of both our Wings routing their Foot as well as their Horse; and 2 whole Regiments of their Foot were absolutely cut off, by those of their left Wing, besides those put into Disorder by our Right. Whilst this was doing, the Bodies of the Foot met the King's Regiment of Guard, and the Earl of *Lindsey's* giving the first Charge, which was very well disputed a long time, until the Reserve of the Rebel's Horse (which had never been Charged) Charged our Foot upon the Flank, which our Foot resisted a good while, but at length not being seconded by our Reserve of Horse, which, contrary to our Order, thinking the Day was surely won, had followed the Execution of the Rebels so far, that they could not come in time to relieve them, they were put into some Disorder, in which the King's Standard (the Standard-Bearer being slain) and the Lord *Willoughby*, seeking to relieve his Father, who fell, being shot in the Leg, was, together with his Father, made Prisoner; but the Standard was soon relieved by the Lieutenant of the Lord *John Steward's* Troop (Capt. *Smith*) being newly returned from the Execution of the Rebels, the Left-side of our Foot being put into Disorder, all the rest gave way; yet those of the Right hand were never put into Disorder: But seeing some of the Cannon in danger to be lost, advanced again, and made the Place good; the Left hand of Rebels Foot coming on apace to Charge them. By this time the Right Wing of our Horse was returned from Chasing the Rebels, and were in some Confusion, because they came from the Execution; but seeing our Foot and Cannon in some danger to be lost, by reason that the Rebels Horse and Foot (those Horse which had never been Charged) advanced in good Order to Charge; ours made a stand and soon rallied together, having some Dragoons with them, and so advancing, made the Dragooners give them a Volley or two of Shot, which made the Rebels instantly retire. By this time it was grown so dark, that our Chief Commanders durst not Charge for fear of mistaking Friends for Foes (though it was certainly concluded by them all, that if we had had light enough, but to have given one Charge more, we had totally routed all their Army); whereupon both Armies retreated, ours in such Order, that we not only brought off our own Cannon, but 4 of the Rebels, we retiring to the Top of the Hill from whence we came; because of the advantage of the Place, and theirs to the Village where they had been quartere'd the Night before.

The King with the whole Body of the Horse, and those of the Foot which were not broken, quartered upon and on one side of the Hill, all that Night; and in the Morning, as soon as it was Day, drew half the Body of the Horse into Battalia, at the Foot of the Hill, and the rest of the Horse and the Foot on the Top of the Hill, where the Standard was placed; and having notice that 3 of the Rebels Cannon were left half way between us and their Quarter, sent out a Body of Horse, and drew them off, they not so much as offering to relieve them: So both Armies, facing one another all day, retired at Night to their former Quarters.

The Rebels in this Battel lost above 70 Colours of Cornets and Ensigns; we 16 Ensigns, but not one Cornet; but our Horse relieved not only the Standard, but divers of our Ensigns.

For the slain on both sides, the Number is uncertain; yet it is most certain that we killed five for one. It is true, that their Chief Officers having fleeter Horses than ours, not so many of their Foot, as ours, were slain and taken Prisoners, to our knowledge as yet; but we lost no Officer of Horse excepting the Lord *Aubigny*.

The next Day after the Battel, the Earl of *Essex* finding his Army extreamly weakned and disheartned by the great Blow they had received by his Majesties Forces, withdrew himself to *Warwick* Castle; and the same Night the remainder of his Forces went also privately thither much distracted, whereof Prince *Rupert* having Notice, the next Morning pursued them, but they were all got into *Warwick*, or dispersed before he could overtake them; but his Highness took 25 Wagons and Carriages of the Rebels, laden with Ammunition, Medicaments, and other Baggage, whereof he brought away part, and fired the rest.

This sudden returning back of the Rebels to *Warwick*, is not only a sure Argument of the weakness of their Army, but hath exceedingly disheartned all the Country which adhered to them, and were before (upon a false Rumor that the King's Forces were defeated) ready to have risen and fall'n upon his Majesty's Forces.

The 26th his Majesty by *Clarenceux* King of Arms, sent a Summons to *Banbury*, which being not thereupon yielded, his Majesty the next Day drew out part of his Army, with some Ordnance, against the said Town; upon the approach of which the Rebels Forces (being the Earl of *Peterborough's* Regiment which were in the Town, to the number of 600) came out, laid down their Arms, and asked his Majesty Pardon; and immediately the Town was rendred up. Upon which his Majesty sent out some of his Principal Officers to discover, and bring away, all such Arms and Ammunition as were found in the Town, and to take up, upon Tickets, all Woollen Cloth, Stockens, Shoes and Victuals, for the Accommodation of his Soldiers, forbidding all manner of Plundering, and permitting only one Regiment to enter and remain in the Town that Night.
Rushworth, III, II, pp.33–35.

2. SIR RICHARD BULSTRODE'S ACCOUNT

Sir Richard Bulstrode, whose *Memoirs and Reflections* were published in
1721, served at Edgehill in the Earl of Northampton's troop in the Prince
of Wales' Regiment of Horse. Despite a few inaccuracies, he gives one
of the best accounts for it hangs together well, and contains much detail
not found elsewhere. There is an analytical article by Sir Charles Firth in
E.H.R.,x., 1895, showing that the work is made up of genuine memoirs
with additions from Clarendon and Warwick.

> . . . The King came to *Nottingham* some Days before his Standard was set
> up, and hearing some Regiments, by Order from the Earl of *Essex*, were
> marching to *Coventry*, the King hastened thither with some Troops of
> Horse, well armed, and got thither the Day before the Parliament's Forces.
> However, the Gates were shut against him, and some of his Servants Kill'd
> from the Walls. The King had no Remedy for this Affront, but lodged
> that Night at *Stonely Abbey*, at Sir *Thomas Lee's*. The next Day the King's
> Body of Horse, being near the Enemy at *Southam* [23 August], who were
> not above Twelve Hundred Foot, with one Troop of Horse, in a free
> Campagne, yet they retired without being charged. Commissary *Wilmot*
> then commanded the King's Horse, and several Reflections were made
> upon his not charging them. About this time I was with the Earl of
> *Northampton* at *Warwick*, having left *Coventry* some Months before, where
> I resided with my Father, being then very young, and went with two
> Horses and one of his Men, to the Earl of *Northampton*, who was Lord
> Lieutenant of *Warwickshire*, with whom I was when he first put the
> Commission of Array in Execution at *Coleshill*, eight Miles from *Coventry*
> towards *Bermingham*. From thence we went to *Warwick*, in Hopes to have
> surprized that Castle; but [Lt.Colonel] Sir *Edward Peito* was gotten into it
> before, and had Orders to keep it for the Lord *Brook*, whose Castle it was,
> and his Lordship was then employed by the Parliament, to settle the Militia
> in *Warwickshire*. The Castle was strong, and well scituated, the River *Avon*
> running by it. Our Endeavours for taking it, were to little Purpose, for we
> had only two small Pieces of Cannon, which were brought from *Compton*
> *House*, belonging to the Earl of *Northampton*, and those were drawn up to
> the Top of the Church Steeple, and were discharged at the Castle, to which
> they could do no Hurt, but only frighted them within the Castle, who
> shot into the Street, and killed several of our Men. The King (as I said
> before) being repulsed from *Coventry*, hastened back towards *Nottingham*,
> and the Earl of *Essex* drawing near us with his Army, being then at *Southam*,
> my Lord of *Northampton*, with his Troop of Gentlemen, which were
> numerous, marched towards *Worcester*, where we met Prince *Rupert* with
> some Troops of Horse, with whom we joined and drew up in the Fields,
> not far from *Powyck* Bridge, upon the *Severn*, where we stood very quietly
> for some time, being informed that the Earl of *Essex* was marching after

us. We had not been long in this Posture, before some Troops of Horse, commanded by Collonel *Nathaniel Fiennes*, who lay on the other Side *Powyck* Bridge, expecting to meet the Vanguard of *Essex's* Army, passed the Bridge, and having passed the Defiles, he drew up his Troops not far from ours, which the Prince gave him Time to do; but then the Prince charged and routed them, and sent them back over the Bridge, in great Confusion and Disorder. In this Action we took several Prisoners, amongst whom was one Collonel [Edwin] *Sandys*, who was mortally wounded, and died some Hours after. Major [Alexander] *Douglass*, and several others, were killed upon the Place. This was the first Action I was ever in, and being upon an unruly Horse, he ran away with me amongst the Enemy, while we pursued them to the Bridge, in which Hurly I lost my Hat; by my Horse's Courage being somewhat abated, I stopp'd him before we came to the Bridge, and so returned with our own Troops. We retired that Evening into the City of *Worcester*, where being refreshed, we marched that Night towards *Ludlow*, where we stayed some time; and from thence we went to *Shrewsbury*, where we stay'd till the King came thither with his Army, which much increased in those Quarters, by several Regiments newly raised in those Parts for the King. The next Day after our leaving *Worcester*, the Earl of *Essex* came thither with his Army, and made that City his Headquarters for some time. The King stay'd at *Shrewsbury* till his Army was well recruited, and then Resolutions were taken to march towards *London*, in Hopes to get thither before the Earl of *Essex*, who was then, with the Parliament Army, about *Worcester* and *Warwick*.

While the King stay'd about *Shrewsbury*, his Army was modelled into several Regiments of Horse, Foot, and Dragoons, which, in all, made a considerable Body: The Horse were put into several Brigades, the Foot into Tertia's (as they were then called) and we had Three or Four Regiments of Dragoons: Our chief Want was Arms; for most of the Regiments, which were raised in *Wales*, were very ill armed. However, they were brave and resolute to serve their King, with such Arms as they had, or could get in their March, and our Army increased daily, by many coming to us from all Parts, as we marched. From *Shrewsbury* we marched thro' Part of *Staffordshire* and *Warwickshire*: . . .

We marched thro' a great Part of *Warwickshire*, and came under *Wormington* Hills, on *Saturday* in the Evening, the Twenty Second Day of *October*, 1642. The King lodged that Night, at Sir *William Chancie's*, at *Rattot* Bridge, and Prince *Rupert* at the Lord *Spencer's*, at *Wormleighton*. The Prince of *Wales's* Regiment in which we were, was quartered in two or three Villages under *Wormington* Hills, When it was dark, we saw several Fires not far from us, and sending out a Party to see, we were soon informed, that the Earl of *Essex* was there with his whole Army, and quartered at *Keinton*, a Market-Town. Whereupon our whole Regiment drew into the Fields, and had Provisions brought to us from the Villages, and we forthwith gave Notice to the King and Prince *Rupert*, and soon after we received Orders to be upon our Guard all Night, and to be the next Morning by Eight, at the Rendezvous upon *Wormington* Hills. The King, with the Prince of *Wales*, and Duke of *York*, came soon after, and Prince *Rupert*, who called a general Council of War, where it was debated, whether to march towards *London*, or to march back, and fight the Enemy, who we saw from the Hill, embattelling their Army in the Bottom near *Keinton*. To march from them was thought dishonourable, as if we feared them, and they would be sure to follow, and give us continual Trouble in our March, when we should not, perhaps find so good Occasion to fight them; and so it was resolved, that we should go down the Hill and attack them. Whereupon great Preparations were made, and Precautions taken, for descending the Hill, which was very steep and long, and had been impracticable, if the Enemy had drawn nearer to the Bottom of it; but we saw by the Ranging their Army, that they intended to stay there for us, having a good Market Town by them, and not far from *Warwick*. In the first Place, it was resolved, that [Lt.] Collonel [Henry] *Washington*, with his Regiment of Dragoons, should descend the Hill, and possess some Inclosures and Briars on the right Hand of our Army, and a forlorn Hope of Six Hundred Horse were ordered likewise to descend before the Army, and the Carriage Horses of the Cannon were put behind the Carriages, excepting a Horse or two before, and the Foot were ordered to descend as well as they could. The King was that Day in a black Velvet Coat lin'd with Ermin, and a Steel Cap covered with Velvet. He rode to every Brigade of Horse, and to all the Tertia's of Foot to encourage them to their Duty, being accompanied by the great Officers of the Army; His Majesty spoke to them with great Courage and Chearfulness, which caused Huzza's thro' the whole Army. I take the Liberty here to remember one Passage which was remarkable. It seems, that the very Morning, before the Army descended the Hill, the Duke of *Lenox* (being returned from his Travels) waited then upon the King, by whom his Grace was very well received and caressed. He brought with him one Mr *Scroop*, who had accompanied him. After this Gentleman had kissed the King's Hand, as also that of the Prince of *Wales* and Duke of *York*, the Duke of *Lenox* told the King, that the Gentleman's Father was [Captain] Sir *Gervase Scroop*, who had a good Estate, had raised a Foot Regiment [company] in *Lincolnshire*, to serve his Majesty, and was then in the Army, but very angry with his Son, and would not see him, or be reconciled to him, because he went with the Duke of *Lenox*, without his Father's Consent, and had spent much more Money than he allowed him. The Duke of *Lenox* therefore prayed the King to make them Friends. Whereupon the King sent for the Father, and told him, it was his Pleasure he should be reconciled to his Son, who being then present, demanded upon his Knees his Father's Blessing; whereupon the Father gave it him, and said thus to his Son: *I am now going down the Hill to serve the King, and if I be killed, I have left you, my Son, enough to Spend:*

And the Son presently answered; *And if I be killed, I shall leave you enough to pay for me.* And so the Father and Son went down the Hill together; and it so happened, that the Son saved the Father's Life, who having received many Wounds, was stript, and left for dead, and was brought off the next Morning by his Son, in one of the King's Coaches, who lived some Years after, always very kind to his Son, and left him a very good Estate. I have presumed to add this Particular, because I have had great Obligations to that Family; and upon King *Charles* II's Restoration, he was made Knight of the *Bath*, by the Name of Sir *Adrian Scroop*: And I was then one of the Gentlemen that brought him to the King, when his Majesty put the Red Ribband about him. But, leaving this Digression, let us turn again to the King's Army, which, about Ten in the Morning, began to descend the Hill, the Foot getting down several Ways which the Horse could not do, by reason of the Hill's Steepness. When the whole Army was down, and drawn into Order, the King desired the Earl of *Lindsey*, who was his Lieutenant General, that he would permit General *Ruthen* [Lord Forth], an old *Scotch* Officer, and who had long served under *Gustavus Adolphus*, the late King of *Sweden*, and had been a Lieutenant General in his Army, to draw up his Majesty's Army that Day, and to command it, being an old experienced General; to which the Earl of *Lindsey* (being wholly made of Obedience) willingly complied, and said he would serve the King that Day, as Collonel of the King's Royal Regiment of Foot[1] Guards, which he did, accompanied by his Son, the Lord *Willoughby of Eresby*. The Enemy had all the Morning to draw up their Army, in a great plain Field, which they did to their best Advantage, by putting several Bodies of Foot with Retrenchments and Cannon before them, and all their Foot were lined with Horse behind them, with Intervals betwixt each Body, for their Horse to enter, if need required and upon their right Wing were some Briars covered with Dragoons, and a little behind, on their left Wing, was the Town of *Keinton*, which supplied them with Provisions, and where their Baggage and Carriages were.

Our whole Army was drawn up in a Body, the Horse Three deep in each Wing, and the Foot in the Center Six deep. The Prince of *Wales's* Regiment was on the right Wing, which was commanded by Prince *Rupert*, and Collonel *Washington* was with his Dragoons upon our Right. In the Center was the Infantry, commanded in chief by General *Ruthen*, and under him, by Sir *Jacob Astley*. The Earl of *Lindsey* marched on Foot, in the Head of the Regiment of the Royal Foot Guards, with his Son, the Lord *Willoughby*, and Sir *Edmond Verney* carried the Royal Standard. The left Wing of our Horse was commanded by Commissary General *Wilmot*, with [Lieutenant-] Collonel [Edward] *Fielding* and some other principal Officers; and [Lieutenant-] Collonel *George Lisle*, with Lieutenant Collonel [John] *Ennis* were in the left Wing, with a Regiment of Dragoons, to defend the Briars on that Side, and we had a Body of Reserve, of Six Hundred Horse, commanded by the Earl of *Carnarvon*[2]. When our Army

was drawn up at the Foot of the Hill, and ready to march, all the Generals
went to the King (who intended to march with the Army) and desired he
would retire to a rising Ground, some Distance from thence, on the Right,
with the Prince of *Wales* and the Duke of *York* (having his Guard of
Pensioners on Horseback with him) from whence he might see the Issue
of the Battle, and be out of Danger, and that otherwise the Army would
not advance towards the Enemy: To which the King (very unwillingly)
was at last perswaded.

Just before we began our March, Prince *Rupert* passed from one Wing
to the other, giving positive Orders to the Horse, to march as close as was
possible, keeping their Ranks with Sword in Hand, to receive the Enemy's
Shot, without firing eit'ier Carbin or Pistol, till we broke in amongst the
Enemy, and then to make use of our Fire-Arms as need should require;
which Order was punctually observed. The Enemy stayed to receive us,
in the same Posture as was formerly declared; and when we came within
Cannon Shot of the Enemy, they discharged at us three Pieces of Cannon
from their left Wing, commanded by Sir *James Ramsey*; which Cannon
mounted over our Troops, without doing any Hurt, except that their
second Shot killed a Quarter-Master in the Rear of the Duke of *York's*
Troop. We soon after engaged each other, and our Dragoons on our Right
beat the Enemy from the Briars, and Prince *Rupert* led on our right Wing
so furiously, that, after a small Resistance, we forced their left Wing, and
were Masters of their Cannon; and the Prince being extreamly eager of
this Advantage (which he better knew how to take, than to keep) was not
content with their Cannon, and keeping their Ground, but eagerly pursued
the Enemy, who fled on the other side of *Keinton* towards *Warwick*: And
we of the Prince of *Wales's* Regiment, (who were all scattered) pursued
also, till we met with two Foot Regiments of *Hambden* and *Hollis*[3], and
with a Regiment of Horse coming from *Warwick* to their Army, which
made us hasten as fast back as we had pursued. In this Pursuit I was
wounded in the Head by a Person who turned upon me, and struck me
with his Pole-axe, and was seconding his Blow, when Sir *Thomas Byron*
being near, he shot him dead with his Pistol, by which Means I came back.
In fine, by meeting these three Regiments, we were obliged to return back
to our Army, and then found our great Error, in leaving our Foot naked
who were rudely handled by the Enemy's Horse and Foot together, in our
Absence, who fell principally upon the King's Royal Regiment of Foot
Guards, who lost Eleven of Thirteen Colours, the King's Standard-Bearer,
Sir *Edmond Verney*, killed, and the Royal Standard taken, which was
presently retaken by Captain *John Smith*, who was Knighted for it that
Night by the King, under the Standard Royal, and made a Baronet
[Banneret] with the usual Ceremonies; and had afterwards a large Medal
of Gold given him, with the King's Picture on the one Side, and the Banner
on the other, which he always wore to his dying Day, in a large green
watered Ribband, cross his Shoulders. He was afterwards killed at the

Battle of *Alresford* in *Hampshire*, in the Year 1644, which was called *Cheriton*
Fight, with the Lord *Bernard*[sic] *Stewart*, Brother to the Duke of *Richmond*,
and several others. [Captain-Lieutenant] Sir *Robert Walsh*, an *Irishman*; who
also pretended that he was very instrumental in regaining the Standard,
did also in the same Manner wear a green Ribband with a Medal; but
whether it was given him by Order, or how he came by it, I do not know,
tho' I have often seen him wear it. In this Battle of *Edgehill* (as it was always
called) during our Pursuit of the Enemy, the Earl of *Lindsey* was mortally
wounded, and taken Prisoner, with his Son the Lord *Willoughby*, who
killed the Man that wounded his Father, who died in the Earl of *Essex's*
Coach, as he was carrying to *Warwick*. Now, when we returned from
following the Enemy, the Night came soon upon us, whereas, in all
Probability, we had gained the Victory, and made an End of the War, if
we had only kept our Ground, after we had beaten the Enemy, and not
left our Foot naked to their Horse and Foot: And, to add to our Misfortune,
a careless Soldier, in fetching Powder (where a Magazin was) clapt his
Hand carelessly into a Barrel of Powder, with his Match lighted betwixt
his Fingers, whereby much Powder was blown up, and many kill'd. The
Night then soon parted both Armies, and both Sides pretended to the
Victory; but since we retired up the Hill, from whence we came down,
and left the *Champ de Battaile* to the Enemy, I think we had no great Reason
to brag of a Victory; For the King, with a great Part of the Army marched
that Night up to Wormington Hills, it being a hard Frost, and very cold.
But that which made us think we had the Victory, was that whereas the
Earl of *Essex* was commanded to hinder our getting to *London* before him,
by this Battle we were nearest *London*, and might have been there much
before the Earl of *Essex*, if we have taken right Measures: So that it may
be said of this Battle, *Victus uterque fuit, Victor uterque fuit.* There is always
great Difference in Relation of Battles, which do usually according to the
Interest of the Relators; when it is certain, that, in a Battle, the next Man
can hardly make a true Relation of the Actions of him that is next him;
for in such a Hurry and Smoke as in a set Field, a Man takes Notice of
nothing but what relates to his own Safety: So that no Man give a clear
Account of particular Passages.

On *Monday* Morning, being next after the Battle, several Parties were
sent down to view the Dead, the greatest Part of the Enemy, having retired
in the Night to the Town of *Keinton*, which was near them; and Mr *Adrian
Scroop* having seen his Father fall (being much wounded) desired the Duke
of *Lennox* to speak to the King, that one of his Coaches might go with
him, to bring up his Father's Body; which being granted, he found his
Father stript, with several very dangerous Wounds, and that he was alive.
Whereupon he lapt him up in his Cloak, and brought him in the Coach,
where he was presently dressed by the King's Chirurgeons, and by their
Care and Skill was cured, and lived many Years after, tho' he had seventeen
Wounds, and had died upon the Place, but that the Coldness of the

Weather stopp'd the Bleeding of his Wounds, which saved also several
other Mens Lives that were wounded. We rested all *Monday* upon the Hill,
to put our Army in Order; and seeing the Enemy (as we thought) were
preparing to retire, Prince *Rupert* was resolved, that Monday Night, to go
down the Hill, at a Place called *Sun-Rising*, a Mile on our left Hand, and
to fall upon the Enemy in their Retreat; and on *Tuesday* Morning very
early, the Prince, with a strong Detachment of Horse and Dragoons, fell
into *Keinton*, where he found all Houses full of wounded and sick Men,
with divers Officers, and several Waggons loaded with Muskets and Pikes,
and all Sorts of Ammunition, preparing to follow the Army, which was
marched towards *Warwick*. These Arms were extreamly wanting in our
Army, and were a very good Supply for some Hundreds of *Welchmen* were
so brave, that they had no Arms but Pitchforks, and such like Tools, and
many only with good Cudgels, yet they went down the Hill as eagerly to
fight, as the best armed Men among them. And indeed most of the Gentry
in North *Wales* most willingly ingaged for the King, and raised what Men
they possibly could for his Service, while the King stayed in *Shropshire*; and
the Gentry of that Country did in a most particular Manner shew their
Zeal for his Majesty's Service, there being scarce a Family of any
Consideration, in any of those Counties, that was not ingaged for the King;
as the *Salisburies*, the *Mostyns*, the *Trevors*, the *Thelwells*, and severall others
whose Families I have forgotten: But this I certainly knew, that none served
the King with greater Loyalty and Affection, than all the Gentry of North
Wales, wherein the Family of *Bulkeley* must not be forgotten, who were
always very eminent for the King's Service.

After this Battle of *Edgehill*, it was resolved the King should hasten to
London, and that if he could get thither before the Earl of *Essex*, with his
Army, the King would be certainly well received, and, in all Probability,
make an End of the War, of which the Parliament was in such Fear, that
several Expresses were sent to the Earl of *Essex*, to make all possible Haste
with Army to London, and prevent the King's Coming before him: But
our King trifled away his Time in taking *Banbury* and *Broughton House*,
which belonged to the Lord *Say*, Places of very little Consideration and
so marched very slowly towards London, where the Earl of *Essex* with his
Army arrived before him, tho' the King's Army was much nearer *London*,
after the Battle of *Edgehill*, if right Use had been made of it. By Judgment
of most, the Victory in this Battle was the King's, because he gain'd his
Point, a clear Passage for his Way to *London*; of which the Parliament was
so sensible, that not only reiterated Orders were sent to hasten the Earl of
Essex's March, but all the Shops, both in *London* and *Westminster*, were
shut up the next Day after the Battle, that the People might be in a better
Readiness to defend themselves and the Parliament.

But alas! the King retarded his March, of which the Earl of *Essex* taking
hold, got between the King and *London*; and in this our March towards
London, the Parliament sent a Petition to the King, in a much humbler

Strain than their former Messages to the King used to be; which Petition the King liked well, and resolved to reside at his Castle of *Windsor*, there to receive the Parliament's Propositions: But News being then brought to the King, that *Essex* was advanced towards him, and had possessed the Passes of *Windsor*, *Kingston*, and *Acton*, and that if *Essex* should also take *Brentford*, the King would be wholly surrounded, and deprived either of moving or subsisting: Whereupon a Council of War was called, and Resolutions taken, that the King's Army should advance to *Brentford*, where, at the first, we found considerable Opposition. The Prince of *Wales's* Regiment of Horse, where I was, being drawn up behind a great Hedge, where the Enemy had planted some Cannon, which we saw not, till they played so fast upon us, that we lost some Men, and were obliged to draw off and retire for our better Security; and upon our Foot's coming up, we beat the Regiments of *Hambden* and *Hollis* out of the Town, took several Prisoners and Arms, and sunk two great Barks in the River of *Thames*, with many Soldiers: And as two other Regiments came up to their Succour, they were also beaten, and we took some Colours and Cannon, and were intire Masters of *Brentford*, until the Night; but then finding the Earl of *Essex*, with his Army, was drawn out upon *Turnham Green*, with the Trained Bands of the City, and that the Enemy's Army was double to the King's, and that most of our Ammunition was spent; it was therefore thought fit by the Council, that the King should retreat. Whereupon the King retired that Night to the Lord *Cottington's* House, near *Hounslow*, and we marched the next Day by *Colebrook*, towards *Reading* and *Oxford*, the first of which Places was garrisoned, and *Oxford* was the King's Head Quarters, where he made his Residence. I can give this Relation with Certainty, being present in all that March, and in the Actions at *Brentford*, till the King's return to *Oxford*, and then the Earl of *Northampton* was commanded to *Banbury*, which was given him for Winter Quarters, with Orders to raise a Regiment of Horse.

1   Incorrect: Lindsey commanded his own Regiment, the Lieutenant-General's. Lord Willoughby d'Eresby commanded the Lifeguard.
2   Incorrect: Lord Digby commanded the reserve. Carnarvon was in Wilmot's front line.
3   Incorrect: It was Grantham's not Holles'.

3. KING JAMES II'S ACCOUNT

James, Duke of York, was only nine when he was present at Edgehill. He had, however, plenty of opportunity to discuss the battle with other eyewitnesses at Oxford during the war, and as a soldier – and a good one – he was well able to understand the events of that day.

The King sets
up his standard
at Nottingham.

With this supply of armes and ammunition being enabled to raise an Army his Majesty after having secur'd York, and left those parts in a good condition for his service, went attended with a considerable number of officers to Nottingham, and there first set up his Standard. Then it was that the zeal and affection of those Noblemen and Gentlemen who continued Loyall to him, appear'd in a most exemplary manner, shewing what might be perform'd, when men well born and rightly principled undertake to serve their Prince with diligence; For in a very little time, without any fund of mony but what themselves furnish'd, they rais'd so considerable an Army, that before the end of October the King was in a condition to fight a battell with the Rebells, tho they had begun to raise forces before him, and wanted neither mony, nor armes, nor ammunition, nor indeed any thing to make themselves as numerous and as well appointed, as they pleas'd; whereas his Majesty, notwithstanding the supply which he had received from Holland, was obliged as he passed along from York to Nottingham, and from thence to Shrewsbery, to disarm the train'd bands in all places, and to furnish his new rais'd forces with their armes; And yet after all those shifts and hardships, many of his men remain'd unarm'd.

His Majesty's Army being thus form'd, he departed from Shrewsbery about the middle of October, with a resolution to incounter the Army of the Rebells; and upon the 22 of the same month he came to Edgecot in Northamptonshire, not far from Bambury[sic], where having notice that the Enemy's forces under the command of the Earle of Essex were within a days march of him, he order'd his whole Army to meet him the next day at Edge Hill. He was no sooner arrived there with his first troop, than he saw the van of the Rebell's Army down in the bottom by Keynton, which soon after began to draw up in battell in the plain before that village, but advanced no further.

The Battell of
Edgehill
fought the 23
of October.

When all his Majesty's troops were come up to him, he march'd down the hill, and order'd Ruthven (who was then but Feild Marshall tho soon afterwards made Earle of Branford) an experienced officer who had serv'd the King of Sweden in the quality of Major General, to draw up his Army in battell. But the Earle of Lindsay who was Generall, was so much displeas'd

at this preference, that he said, Since his Majesty
thought him not fitt to perform the office of Commander in Chief, he would serve him as a Collonell,
and immediately went and put himself at the head of
his Regim[t] of foot, which he desir'd might be placed
opposite to that of the Earle of Essex, hoping thereby
that he might ingage him personally. The foot was
drawn up that day much differing from the manner now
in use, but according to the Swedish Brigade as they
then called it, and the horse in two wings; the right
commanded by Prince Rupert who was generall of it,
and the left by the Lord Wilmott his leiftenant generall.
Each wing had a second line or reserve, the one
composed of the Lord Digby's and Sir Thomas Aston's
regiment, with whom were some dragoons under the
command of Collonell Edward Gray, the other of the
Lord Biron's regiment, they themselves being at the
head of them; and on the right hand of the right wing,
were likewise some dragoons commanded by S[r] Arthur
Aston. According to the best relation of those who were
present and could best tell, his Majesty's Army consisted
of about eight thousand foot and two thousand five
hundred horse and ten piece of cannon; And the
Rebells had between ten and eleven thousand foot, and
they somewhat outnumber'd the Royall Army in horse
as allso in cannon. As for their order of Battell, they
made not their wing so equall as his Majesty's, for
knowing Prince Rupert was to command the King's
right wing, they put the greatest part of their best cavalry
into their left; as having lately felt the effects of his
courage and conduct near Worcester, where being
much inferiour in number to them, he routed a body
of their best horse: Besides this, to strengthen that wing,
they had small platoons of musquetiers betwixt every
squadron, and on their left hand some dragoons: As for
their right wing of horse, which were not all come up,
they drew that part of them which was present behind
their foot, seeing they were not strong enough to
encounter with the King's left wing, and lin'd the
bushes with some dragoons to make a shew. In this
posture they stood, expecting to be charg'd, without
advancing one step to meet the King's Army.

It was almost three of the clock in the afternoon
before his Majesty's Army was wholly drawn up in
Battell; at which time they march'd on with a slow

The fight of
Edgehill began
at 3 in the
afternoon, 23
October. The
King with the
Pce of W, and
the Duke
march'd
immediately
after the foot.

steady pace, and a very daring resolution. So soon as
they were within reach of cannon, the Rebells fir'd at
them, and their volly was made before the King's began
to play. His Majesty with the Prince of Wales and the
Duke of York, march'd immediately after the foot,
attended by several of the Lords whom he had
commanded to stay by him, and by the band of
pensioners on horseback led on by their leiftenant Sir
William Howard; and that it might be known in what
part of the Army the person of the King was, he had a
scarlet cornet larger than ordinary carryd before him.
When the Royall Army was advanced within musket
shot of the Enemy, the foot on both sides began to fire,
the King's still coming on, and the Rebell's continuing
only to keep their ground; so that they came so near to

The foot so
close to one
another that
they are within
push of pike.

one another that some of the batalions were at push of
pike, particularly the regiment of Guards commanded
by the Lord Willoughby and the Generall's regiment,
with some others; in so much that the Lord Willoughby
with his pike kill'd an officer of the Earle of Essex his
own regiment, and hurt another. The foot being thus
ingaged in such warm and close service, it were
reasonable to imagine that one side should run and be
disorder'd; but it happen'd otherwise, for each as if by

The Foot
continue till
night firing at
one another.

mutuall consent retired some few paces, and they stuck
down their coulours, continuing to fire at one another
even till night; a thing so very extraordinary, that
nothing less than so many witnesses as were there
present, could make it credible; nor can any other
reason be given for it, but the naturall courage of
English men, which prompted them to maintain their
ground, tho the rawnes and unexperience of both partys
had not furnished them with skill to make the best use
of their advantages. Tis observed that of all nations the
English stick the closest to their Officers, and tis hardly
seen that our common Soldiers will turn thair backs, if
they who commanded them do not first shew them the
bad example, or leave them unofficer'd by being kill'd
themselves upon the place.

The right wing
of the King's
horse led by
Pce. Rupert.

But there was not the same equality of courage in the
horse; for the Royalists march'd up with all the gallantry
and resolution imaginable, especially the right wing led
by Prince Rupert; the while they advanced, the
Enemy's cannon continually playd upon them, as did
the small divisions of their Foot which were placed in

the intervalls betwixt their squadrons, neither of which did in the least discompose them, or oblige them so much as to mend their pace. Thus they continued moving, till they came up close to the Enemy's Cavalery, which after having spent their first fire, immediately turn'd their backs, the Royalists pursuing them with great eagerness. One Ramsey who commanded that wing of the Enemy's, was it seems so thorowly frighted, that he never left running till he came to London.

The left wing of the Rebell's horse defeated by Pce. Rupert.

While this past, the left wing had not much to do, as having only some dragoons, and two or three regiments of foot before them, of which they made a quick dispatch; and then observing the Enemy's left wing intirely beaten, follow'd the chace of them in stead of falling into the flanck or reere of the Rebell's foot. The same errour was committed by the second lines of each wing; for in stead of staying by their foot, or charging the Enemy's foot, they also follow'd the chace of the routed horse, and continued the pursuit through Keynton, with such eagerness, that notwithstanding all the endeavours which were used by Prince Rupert, they were not to be rallied, till they met with two regiments of the Enemy's foot, who had with them some feild-pieces, and were coming up to joyn the rest of the Army: But the King's horse were then in so much disorder, that it was impossible for Prince Rupert to put them into a condition of doing any further service; it being almost dark before he could bring them back to the assistance of the foot whom he had left ingaged, and who while all this was passing, were reduced to great extremitys; for the Earle of Essex observing that all the King's horse were gone off in pursuit of his left wing, commanded that part of his cavalery which was behind his foot, to charge the King's and the general's regiments in the flanck, just at the time when they were so warmly ingaged at push of pike with his men. Tis true they were not broken with this charge, yet they were put into some disorder, which the Enemy's foot observing, advanced upon them, and drove them back as far as to their cannon; and to highten their success, at the same they took the King's Standard which was carry'd by Sir Edmond Verney, who was killed upon the place holding it in his hand: But the King's cannon playd upon them with such execution that it stopt their

The King's left wing having routed some foot and dragoons that were before them, follow the chace of the Rebell's left wing and leave their own foot ingaged. The same errour committed by the second lines of each wing Pce. Rupert endeavours in vain to rally them. The King's horse being all gone off, his foot is charged in the flanck by a part of the Enemy's horse wch. put them in disorder.

The King's
Standard taken
and Sr.
Edmond
Verney killed
holding it in
his hand.

further progress, and gave leisure to those regiments on the left hand which had given ground, to put themselves once more in good order, which the Enemy finding, advanced no further. At the same time the remnant of their foot were pressing vigourously on the King's, and had not the right hand Brigade commanded by Coll. Charles Gerard kept their order, and plyd those regiments which advanced upon them, with so great courage that they put the Enemy to a stand, the whole body of the King's foot had run great hazard of an absolute defeat; for had his Majesty's two wings given way, those in the main-battell could have made no long resistance. After this neither party press'd the other, but contented themselves to keep their ground, and continued fireing, till night put an end to the dispute.

A gallant
action of Lord
Willoughby.

And here deserues to be mention'd a gallant action perform'd by the Lord Willoughby, who in the heat of the Action hearing it reported that a blue riban was fallen, and knowing it could be no other than the Earle of Lindsay his father, he hasten'd from the head of the Guards to his assistance, and found him lying in front of his own regiment with one leg broken by a musket-shott; Now this happening at that point of time when they received the charge of the Enemy's horse, so that it was impossible to carry him off, he stood undauntedly with his pike in his hand bestriding his father, and in that posture wounded one of their Captains in the face, and almost push'd him off his horse; but his own men at the same time giving back, he was left ingaged in the midst of the Enemies', chusing rather to be taken with his father, that so he might be in a condition of rendering him what service was in his power, then to save himself by leaving him in that distress.

The King
perceiving his
foot in
disorder,
marcheth up to
them himself
to incourage
them.

All this while his Majesty was behind the foot; where perceiving the disorder they were in by the charge given them by the horse, and that at the same time the Enemy's foot advanced against them, he resolued to march up to them himself to incourage them by his presence, and therby to prevent their intire defeat; but judging it not fit to expose the Prince and the Duke of York to the same danger, he order'd the Duke of Richmond to carry them out of the battell, and conduct them to the top of the hill; who excusing himself from that imployment the King layd the same command on

The foot take new courage from his Majesty's presence and maintain their ground.

the Earle of Dorset, who answer'd him with an oath, That he would not be thought a Coward for the sake of any King's Sons in Christendom, and therefore humbly desir'd his Majesty to committ that charge to some other man; Thereupon the King layd an absolute command on S[r] Will. Howard, with his pensioners, which were about fifty, to go off with them. After which his Majesty with those who were remaining with him, pursuing his former resolution, marched directly

The Prince and the Duke are carryd out of the battell by the King's order.

to the foot, who, according to his expectation took new courage from his presence, and maintain'd their ground. As he advanced, one of his footmen was shott in the face just by his horse's side; after which he continued in the reer of the foot, till the battell was ended by the night. At the same time when the King was marching to the foot, S[r] Will. Howard went off with the Prince

The Prince, and the Duke escape narrowly from being taken prisoners at Edge Hill.

and Duke pursuant to his orders. and they had not gone above musket shott of[f] from the place, when they saw a body of horse advancing directly towards them from the left hand of the King's foot; upon which sending to see what they were, and finding them to be the Enemy, they drew behind a little barn not far distant from them, which was incompassed by a hedge. In this barn severall of the King's wounded men were then dressing, but the Enemy observing the King's men to be within the inclosure, drew immediately back without ingaging them, by which means the Prince and the Duke escaped the evident danger of being taken; for had they charged that small party they could not have fail'd of beating them, considering the vast advantage of their numbers. Upon their drawing back to joyn their foot, the small body which attended the Prince and the Duke were glad of the occasion to draw off further to the top of the hill towards the dusk of the evening, and as the darkness came on both Armys began to draw off, the Royalists to the browe of the hill, and the Enemy to Keynton; they left six pieces of their cannon behind them in the feild, and the King's Army some of theirs, without any soldiers to guard either. The next morning at break of day, his Ma[ty] seeing the cannon still remaining as they were left, sent five hundred horse, which brought off both his own and the Enemy's, in the face of their Army, who saw the action perform'd without once endeavouring to oppose it. It was then proposed to march down again, and fall upon them; but the King finding his foot much decreased in number, the greatest part of them being stragled into the neighbouring villages to get victuals, thought it not adviseable to undertake that action, and therfore about evening return'd to his former quarters at Edgcott; the enemy at the same time retreating towards Warwick.

About 1,500 men kill'd on both sides at the Battell of Edgehill.

And now it remains to give an account of what men were slain, the number of which was not so great as was commonly reported; for according to the best information, there were not above fifteen hundred bodys of both partys remaining on the feild of battell. Of persons of note on the King's side were slayn the Lord Aubigny, brother to the Duke of Richmond and captain of the Duke's troop, Monro a Scotchman, leiftenant collonell to the Generall's Regiment of foot, and some few days afterwards the Earle of Lindsey the Generall dyd of his wounds in Warwick Castle, whither he had been carry'd prisoner with his son. There were wounded the Lord Taff, Colonell Charles Gerard, Colonell Sir Nicholas Biron, Sir George Stroad an officer of the ordinance, Sir Richard Graham one of his Majesty's querryes, and Sir Gervase Scroop, who was left for dead upon the place and found next morning by his son with three and twenty wounds on him, strip'd of all his cloaths, unable to stirr, and lying amongst the dead bodys. It was the opinion of many chirurgions, that the frost which happen'd that night, occasion'd the saving of his life, by stopping of his blood. On the Rebell's side were slayn the Lord S\ John, Colonell Charles Essex, and other officers of inferiour quality.

The Royal Standard re-taken by a brother of the Lord Carington

The Royal Standard was once taken by the Enemy, but retaken by Captain John Smith, brother to the Lord Carington; who as he return'd from the pursuite of the Enemy's horse, happily fell upon that body of men which were carrying it away, for which seruice he was by his Majesty made Knight Banneret in the feild.

The day after the Battell, Prince Rupert proposed to his Majesty, that he might be immediately sent with the greatest part of the horse, and three thousand commanded foot to London; and undertook with them to possess himself of Whitehall and Westminster, and to drive out the rebellious part of the Parliament from thence, and to make good that part of the town 'till his Majesty should come up with the remainder of his Army; which might easily be effected, before the Earle

The King
instead of
marching
straight to
London is
perswaded to
take Banbyry,
and from
thence to
march to
Oxford.

of Essex with his shatter'd forces cou'd march thither
to oppose him: But this so seasonable a proposition was
first obstructed, and finally layd aside by the advice of
many in the Councill, who were affraid least his Majesty
shou'd return by conquest; one of them in plain terms
telling him, that it was too hazardous for him to send
Prince Rupert on that design, who being a young man,
and naturally passionate might possibly be urg'd in heat
of blood to fire the town. By these and such like
cautious remonstrances made and seconded by men of
the same principles, the King was first perswaded to go
and take in Banbury, which was commanded by
Colonell Fiennes for the Parliament; and that being
perform'd he was wrought on further, to march from
thence to Oxford; where staying some days, he delayd
his opportunity so long that he lost it and the Earle of
Essex got before him to the city, which oversight of his
Majesty was of fatall consequence to his affaires: For in
appearance had he marched directly thither, he had put
an end to the warr, and wholy extinguish'd the
rebellion. Because the factious party of the Parliament,
and all their adherents in the town, were under so great
a consternation that they wou'd certainly have gone out
at one end of it, whilst his Majesty was entring at the
other. But the Earle of Essex being return'd to them,
and the King's Army not appearing before they had
recover'd from their fright, they took heart again, gave
order to recruit their broken forces, and settled the
minds of their wavering freinds; as plainly appear'd,
when his Majesty aferwards too late advanced towards
them.

Life of James II . . . collected out of memoirs writ of his
own hand . . . Published from the original Stuart MSS.
in Carlton House, ed. by T.S. Clarke, 2 vols. 4to.
London, 1816, pp.9–18 inclusive.

*The next three accounts were all written by members of the King's Lifeguard of
Horse.*

4. LORD BERNARD STUART'S LETTER

A brief relation of the battle at Red horse field under Edgehill.
  We marched on Sunday morning from Edgcot to Edgehill which is 5
miles to fight with them there. After our men were put into battalia and

the cannon planted we gave fire with our cannon and then charged them with both wings of our horse. They stood still all the while upon the hill expecting the charge so that we were fain to charge them uphill and leap over some 5 or 6 hedges and ditches. Upon our approach they gave fire with their cannon lined amongst their horse, dragoneers, carabines and pistols, but finding that did nothing dismay the King's horse and that they came more roundly to them with all their fire reserved, just when our men charged they all began to turn head and we followed an execution upon them for 4 miles together. The left wing did the very same where Wilmot commanded. A great many of them saved their lives by getting our word For God and King Charles. Had our reserve of horse not mistaken but stood still in their place they were commanded, we have given them as absolute a defeat both of horse and foot as ever was given.

It was equally divided by these foot till night. A troop of their reserve did charge among our foot where they did a great deal of hurt, and took my Lord Lindsey prisoner (who is wounded) and my Lord Willoughby, [Lt.] Colonel [Sir William] Vavasor, Colonel [Sir Thomas] Lunsford, [Colonel] Sir Edward Stradling and [Captain] Sir H. Ridley, who are all prisoners in Warwick. But this loss [Lt. Colonel] Sir Charles Lucas with some others and their troops did suddenly redeem for he hath cut off four of their foot regiments, and taken a whole bag full of their foot colours. They have lost in all 58 colours horse and foot and we some 12 at most. We have taken 7 pieces of their cannon. Prince Rupert hath forced the E[arl] of Essex and his men to retire into Warwick with so much haste that the Prince hath 30 of his carriages, set fire on 4 carriages of powder. The rebels were more of horse and foot before the battle but now are reduced to a great deal less number by 10000; for what is killed and what is run away I am sure he hath lost so many. The K[ing] had 12000 foot before the battle. What is killed and run away I think is about 2500 and that is the most: he hath 10000 foot yet remaining and hath not lost 40 horse of his whole number he had before. They are reduced to 4000 and that is the most. The K[ing] hath taken Banbury yesterday and the castle which held within it both 1500 men and a troop of horse. This day he is gone for Woodstock and tomorrow for Oxford and marches straight for London &c. (28 October 1642)

Bernard Stuart
(Commander of the King's Lifeguard, H.)

British Museum, Harl. MS. 3783, fo.60. Printed in Godfrey Davies' The Battle of Edgehill. The spelling has been modernized.

5. SIR PHILIP WARWICK'S ACCOUNT

It was not long after he had obtained this victory upon Sandys, that he fought the great battell at Edge-hill, where the noble Earle of Lindsey, (a man of undaunted courage, and of a good experience in soldiery; for he and the Earle of Essex had bin Camarades and Commanders in foreign warrs, tho' they were now Generalls of opposite armies) was made a Generall, the King being Generalissimo himselfe; the old Generall Ruthen, a Scot, an experienc'd Commander, and a man of naturell courage, and purely a soldier, and of a most loyall heart, (which he had many occasions to shew, before the warr was ended, and which his Country-men remembred; for they used both him and his Widow, a Swedish Lady, with all extremity afterwards) was Ajutant in the command of the Horse; and Sir Jacob Ashley (who in every thing deserves Ruthen's character) was Major-Generall of the Army under the Earle of Lindsey; who, before the charge at the battell at Edge-hill, made a most excellent, pious, short and soldierly prayer: for he lifted up his eyes and hands to heaven, saying, *O Lord! though knowest, how busy I must be this day: if I forget thee, do not thou forget me.* And with that, rose up, crying out, *March on Boys!* for the King had given order, that untill the enemy should first have shot their cannon at our body of men, ours should not engage. In this battell Prince Rupert commanded the right wing of the Horse, and the Lord Wilmott the left; and the Lord Digby commanded one reserve of Horse and the Lord Byron the other.

But as if a fate had attended all we did, tho' Prince Rupert entirely routed the left wing of Essex's Horse, which being perceived, Wilmott had very little to do with the right: (for he that marks Wilmott's whole progress thro' this warr, shall find him much affected to be an umpire of peace; which had bin well done, if he had quitted the King's army, and gone into his Council, then a decider of the contest by the sword; tho' the Gentleman wanted no courage nor experience, nor, I hope, loyalty) but both reserves pursuing the chase, contrary to all discipline of warr, left the King and his Foot so alone, that it gave Essex a title unto the victory of that day; which might have bin his last day, if they had done their parts, and stood their ground. And it was the more strange, that the reserves would thus precipitately engage themselves, when they saw the King had given leave unto his own Volunteer-Guard of Noblemen and Gentlemen, who with their attendance made two such Troops, as that they consisted of about three hundred Horse: for a vanity had possest that Troop, (upon a little provocation, or for a word of distaste the day before, or being called, *The Troop of Shew*) to desire this honour of being engaged in the first charge; and I had the honour to be of the number, and to be one of the most inconsiderable Persons of it; and when wee valued the estates of the whole troop, wee reckoned there was 10000 *l. per ann.* in that Body, stak'd that day in that engagement against men of very disproportionable quality.

This was our first and great military misadventure; for Essex by his reserves of Horse falling on the King's Foot, prest on them so hard, that had not some of our Horse returned in some season unto the reliefe of our foot, we had certainly lost the day, which all circumstances considered, wee as certainly wonn. But the next day gave us the assurance of our victory; for the evening parting us, wee found the Lord of Essex was retreated with his army into Warwick town and castle: and wee advanced to the town of Banbury, which with its castle was garrisoned; and tho' Warwick was very nigh Banbury, yet wee took in the town and castle, and made prisoners the regiment quartered there; and so the King marched to Oxford, which he garrisoned. Whilst he refresht his men, Essex stole by other roads as many of his army to London, as he could; . . .

Sir Philip Warwick's Memoires, published 1702, pp. 228–232.

6. SIR HENRY NEWTON'S ACCOUNT

On 30 November 1685 H. Puckering, alias Sir Henry Newton, wrote from Warwick to the Duchess of Beaufort giving her an account of the exploits of her father, Arthur Capel, first Baron Capel of Hadham (1610?–1649) during the Civil Wars. Newton (1618–1701) changed his name to Puckering in 1654, when he inherited his uncle's estates. Only the part relating to 1642 is printed here.

In obedience, Madam, to your Grace's command, I have bethought myselfe of what I could most properly observe or remember of my dear Lord your father's military transactions in that time I had the honour to serve under him, whose worth and bravery would become and fill a volume to give him his due. In the beginning of that unfortunate war, I found my Lord at Nottingham, where in August 1642 the King set up his standard, and those horse and foote the King brought from the north encreased there dayly, and new commissions and leavys by that time he had marched through Derbyshire, Staffordshire, and Shropshire, with the addition out of Wales and Cheshire, made up a considerable army when the King came back from Chester unto Shrewsbury. The rise of this army was at York, where my Lord Capell first entered the list, and gave that good example by voluntary contributing pay for 100 horse* out of his own purse. For a great while when the army marched, my Lord, with many other Lords and Gentlemen of the best rank, put himself into the King's troope, commanded by my Lord Bernard Stuart, and quartered with it, which puts me in mind of one pleasant story and answer of my Lord's to the King, who coming to Bridgenorth, his troops were quartered out of towne at Sir William Whitmores, a fair large house, which would have given my Lord the accommodation with the other Lords of a good feather-bed. But my Lord went and tumbled in straw in the barne with – I think – 100 gentlemen and slept very sound, and comeing the next morning to Court, the King asked him 'my Lord how did you like your bed the last night?' 'Very well,' says my Lord, 'for since I came with your Matie from York, I never before met with a bed long enough for me.' At the battle at Kineton under Edge Hill, which was not long after, my Lord charged in that troop with a most undaunted courage. I remember Madam no other particular action of my Lords that winter, but observed him often called to Councill by his Matie when – possibly – he discovered so much ingenuity, togeather with a real integrity for the King's service, that some, who then had the ascendent, thought it best for their purpose to remove my Lord further from the King's care. And so he was sent away in the Spring, with a comission to command as Lieutenant Generall under the Prince of Wales, in the Counties of Worcester, Salop, Cheshire, and North Wales; but without ever a peny of money, or any other forces more than 80^{ty} horse, which he carried from Oxford – of which 14 were mine – haveing newly received a commission to serve under him . . .

★This is confirmed by the list printed in Peacock, p. 9.

The previous extract is taken from:

H.M.C., Twelfth Report, Appendix, Part IX. Calendar of the Manuscripts of the Duke of Beaufort, K.G., and others, p. 38.

7. 'PRINCE RUPERT'S DIARY'

Oct: 22 The day before Edge:hill we rendeyvouz'd; and my Lord of Bristol with a Party of 400 horse was to find out ye Enemy and brought word there was no Newes of ye Enemy.

The Prince came to Worm Layton, and just as his quart^r masters came there, the quarter mast^{ers} of ye Earle of Essex came also. and ye Ps Quarter Mast^r took them Prison^r, and brought them in by which meanes we had intelligence where ye Enemy was.

M^r [Clement] Martin one of ye Penson^r now to ye Kg was then a Lt and in ye Ps Regt.

Martin with 24 men went to Keinton, where ye Enemy was; and found them there; and then ye P: would have had us to fall on them: But others thought fit to send first to ye K.

ffrom thence, to Edge Hill. The P was there by break of day: but ye ffoot came after: and then the P: (being Gen^ll of ye horse) drew up ye Troops, and ord^r was given that when ye Cannon went off, then they should march.

Gen^ll Ruthen Mr de Gomez can give us the battle of Edge:hill.

The Enemyes horse quickly ran, and o^r ran after in disord^r.

Van Girish Lt to S^r ffaithfull ffortesque came over to ye Prince, and told him his Capt resolv'd to yield; and that the signall should be ye shooting off his pistol to ye Ground. The time was so short, ye Prince could not send notice of it to ye Ld *Birons*, and S^r Wm. Killigrews Troops. By which meanes sev^ll of them were hurt; by S^r Wm. Killigrews men. Ld Biron and others followd in great disord^r: which he should not have done; being ye Reserve. The Prince stopt three of ye Troops; but ye rest of o^r men follow'd ye enemy to Keinton Town.

In ye meantime Lord Willmott fell upon the Dragoons; and they ran away.

And here ye Kings Standard was taken, and re-taken, and ye Earle of Lindsey was killd.

70 of ye enemyes colours were taken, and 8 pieces of cannon.

At night ye P rally'd all ye horse again, and thought to have falln upon ye enemyes foot; but ye army, was in such disord^r that it could not be till morning; and then Essex was retir'd to Keinton, and ye K. to Edgcoate.

And that night ye Pr: with a party of horse followd Essex, and took all his plate, wth his Cabinett of Lett^{rs}, which shew'd that one *Blake* (who was with ye King) betrayd all his Ma^{tyes} Counsells, and he was afterwards hanged.

If he Ld Carnarvons Reg^t had come up to ye rendez vous, so as to have come alone wth ye Prince, they had routed ye enemy in probability. But etc.

Oct 27 Banbury was then taken, and ye Prince desir'd to have 3000 horse, musquetiers and a party of horse, and wth them he would march to Westm^r. who were then well dispos'd for ye K; and had intended to have taken ye Parl^t house and knowing well he might of got

thither before ye Ld of Essex. But some of ye Consell were ag^t it. Especially ye old Earle of Bristol. who sayd the Prince was a young man, and would set ye town a fire. And so that good Councell of ye Ps was rejected.[1]

On ye same day ye P took Ld Sayes house. [Broughton Castle].

The P: went from Egham to Colebrook, and told ye K: that at Branford [Brentford] were two Reg^{ts} of Hambens and Hollis and ye P desir'd of ye K some foot force to engage those two Reg^{ts} and that ye K would draw off ye army upon Hounslow-Heath.[2] Just as ye P was ready to fall on Ruthen came and took ye command, but ye P had ye Horse.

The enemy was beaten at Branford, and 2000 more came down from Kgstone by water. The P: commanded Col. Tho: Blake [Blagge] to take possession of Sion House fearing ye landing of force by water from Lond: and just as he possessed ye house the boats came with ye men from Kingston thinking to land there.

Our carts and Waggons filld ye lane beyond Branford

Out comes Essex wth ye London^n and ye Prince advising 500 musquet^n to be upon *Branford Bridge*. A retreat designed. And when we began to retreat ye P came to ye Bridge, and saw nobody there but Sr Jacob Ashly almost alone. There ye Pr: in ye water set his horse, till ye others marchd over ye Bridge, The enemy finding in how good ord^r ye army retir'd, forbore to follow.

1 Opposite this is written:-

. . . to have march'd with ye Horse and Dragoons, and 3000 foot to follow after as fast as they could. this Proposition was made after the Ld Sayes House was taken. The King himself did not disapprove of ye Proposition but 'twas so overprest by other importunityes, that he could not do it.

The P. in this only propounded the prosecuting of ye first design, which was to get London which was well affected, and without which in probability ye King could not subsist.

2 Opposite this is written:-

Essex's army lay then at Kingston, Acton, Branford, and thereabouts, and his Artillery at Knights Bridge.

'Prince Rupert's Diary', Wiltshire Records Office, Trowbridge. From internal evidence it is clear that the 'Diary' was not compiled earlier than 1662.

8. GERVASE HOLLES' MEMORIALS

Gervase Holles, major to Sir Lewis Dyve in 1642, tells us of the life of his young relative William (1621–1644).

Certainly if the times had continued calme, he was like to have proved a great example of literature. But the rebellion of England breaking out gave not only a stop to his studies but a period (too untimely a period) to his life. At the beginning of wch war whilst I was making my leavies he came to me to Newarke, and importuned me to put a pike into his hand that he might have the honour to serve his Souveraigne as his duty obliged him. But I (being both unwilling to divert him from y^t course in wch he had made so good a progresse and to expose him to the hazardes of war, he being all his father had living) would by no meanes yield to his importunity. Whereupon he returned and praevayled with his father to make it his request to me, wch he accordingly did at Nottingham after I had brought my company thither to the K^s standard. I was at the last overcome by them both, and he marched along wth me to Shrewsbury. There Captaine Jo. Smith being to leavy a foot company in the same regiment desired him of me and gave him his Partisan, for wch he received from the Earle of Lindsey this commission. [*Commission dated Aug. 13, 1642, constituting William Holles a Lieutenant in the Company of Captain Jo. Smith in Sir Lewis Dives' regiment.*]

This commission he receaved at Shrewsbury, as likewise his Captaine did his; but the Generall, having kindness for Capt. Smith (who had served under him before) permitted them to have their acts bearing date wth the rest of the regiment. In this capacity of Leiuetenant he served at the batayle of Kinton (comonly called Edge Hill) where, even at his first acquaintance wth danger, he exprest a great deale of courage and resolution. During the fight he receaved a shot on the face and came up to me to the head of the brigade bleeding very much. I bid him go and get himselfe drest; he replied he was not so ill shot as that he would leave the feild whilst I was in it, and so continued serving wth a great expression of courage and chearfulnes notwithstanding the desease wch his hurt conveyed him. The extremity of the anguish increast by the sharpnes of the season and want of present application shut up both his eyes, and swelled his face for some days to a strange deformity. The first time he opened his eyes was when his Matie attackt Banbury where (hearing y^t I was to command a forlorne of musquetiers wth orders to storme in case the enemy (then in parley) delivered not the towne) he forced open one of his eyes and came up to me desiring me to take him on in y^t service; but y^t by reason of his indisposition I refused him. Whilst the army quarter'd about Oxford he was thoroughly recovered, and marched in his command to Branford wher he shewed himself always diligent upon his duty. I remember having retreated from Branford, and the army divided, we had layne in leaguer some dayes at Marlow upon the Thames wth 5 regiments of foot, where receaving orders from the King to march away 2 of the regiments for Redding and the rest for Abingdon, we advanced to Netlebed, where receaving notice y^t the enemy, very strong both in horse and foot, persued us Colonell Hen. Wentworth (who commanded in cheife) order'd me (whose turne it was then to bring up the reare) to have the regiment ready to march so soone as the moone should rise, and to draw out a forlorne of 40 musquetiers to march musquet shot in the reare of the rest wth a good Leiuetenant to command them. Whilst I carefully executed theis orders and had all the souldiers at their collours by moone rise I found not one Leiuetenant present but my owne and Will Holles: wch I perticularly mention to testify his continuall vigilancy and diligence upon his duty. This was the last service he did me in y^t army: for his Matie had given me command a litle before to rayse him a regiment of foot, for wch I receaved my commission at Oxford, as Will Holles did this ensuing¹ for a company under me.

This young officer became a captain in the foot regiment of Gervase Holles 7 December 1642, and went with his colonel to Nottinghamshire where he 'designed' his levies. Captain William Holles afterwards served at the storming of Howley House (22 June), at the battle of Atherton (Aldwalton Moor, 30 June), at the siege of Bradford, and the recovery of

Gainsborough (30 July 1643.) He was mortally wounded at Muskham Bridge near Newark (6 March 1644).

1   Will. Holles' commission as captain is omitted.

Gervase Holles Memorials of the Holles Family, Camden Third Series, Volume LV, 1937, pp.186&187.

9. JOHN BELASYSE'S VERSION

Things being now to all extremity ill between the King and Parliament, many of the nobility and gentry who adhered to His Majesty being now repaired to York, that county raised a regiment of guards for his person under the command of the Earl of Cumberland, wherein my Lord had a troop listed for him. But after some ineffectaul attempts which the King made upon Hull, being resolved to declare a war and set up his royal standard, he quitted this troop of horse and raised a regiment of foot (at his father's charge), with which he advanced to the King at Nottingham, his being one of the first regiments that came into His Majesty's service, which was soon after armed and recruited to the number of 1,000 men from Nottingham. The first march was to Shrewsbury, where the King strengthened himself by supplies from Chester, Lancaster, and Wales, and during his stay there he had the command and guard of that city with his regiment.

His Majesty, having now a formidable army, and ready for service, advanced southwards towards the enemy, whose army, under the command of the Earl of Essex, drew downwards and flanked the King's in Warwickshire, at a place called Kenton, of which, so soon as His Majesty had intelligence, he gave order for all his troops to rendezvous at Edgehill. My Lord received his orders by a particular express from His Majesty having then at his quarters the charge of a whole brigade of foot, which he drew out at break of day, October the 23rd, 1642, and advanced to that place, where was met the whole army, and discovered in the valley below that of the Parliaments, standing in batallia. Ours then defended the hill and were drawn up in that order which had been formerly designed by General Ruthin, Sir Arthur Aston and Sir Jacob Ashley, which was into several brigades, after the Swedish way. His Majesty's General, the Earl of Lindsey, commanded the foot, divided into nine bodies, vitz.: five in front and four in reserve, which in the whole consisted of about 12,000. The right wing of horse was led by Prince Rupert, the General, and the left by my Lord Willmott, their Leiutenant-General, they being equally divided, about 1,200 in either wing. The King at the head of his Guards disposed himself as he saw occasion; before every body of foot were placed two pieces of cannon, and before them the dragoons, and 1,200 commanded musqueteers as Enfants Perdu[s]. That brigade which my Lord led up on foot was in the battalia or midst of the army.

The enemy's army, which consisted of about sixteen thousand foot and 3,000 horse, were drawn up in several bodies and reserves, much in the same manner of ours, but plainer order, the Earl of Essex leading the foot, and Sir William Balfour and Sir Philip Stapleton the horse.

His Majesty having now encouraged the soldiers (by what he said at the head of every regiment), gave order for the army to advance till they came within cannon shot, which began to play from both armies. Then our horse in both wings gave theirs the first charge, who immediately were routed and pursued by ours two or three miles, which thing alone occasioned the loss of an absolute victory to us, for tho' some regiments of their foot upon the left were broken, as well as their horse, yet all their right wing of foot stood fast and received our charge by the left wing of our foot (to which my Lord Lindsay [sic] commanded my Lord to join). We came after our shot was spent to push of pike and fought very gallantly, till having no manner of relief from our horse (who as I said before were all in pursuit of theirs), and a reserve of my Lord of Essex his guards of horse under the command of Sir Philip Stapleton (which had been undiscovered by us) falling upon our flanks and charging through whilst we were at a push of pike, we were at last broken, and upon the place our General, the Lord Lindsey, received a mortal wound, of which he died in three days. The standard bearer, Sir Edward Verney, also lost his life and the royal standard was taken, tho' afterwards recovered by Sir John Smith, with a party of horse, as he returned from following the chase. In this right wing of the King's foot, my Lord charged with his pike close by my Lord Lindsey, as also very many gallant officers, most of which were killed or taken. He only received a slight hurt upon his head, and had the good fortune to recover with Sir Jacob Ashley, the Major-General, and some others our foot upon the left wing; who never came to charge at all, so they stood entire. By this time the horse returned (but too late to our relief) and night approaching His Majesty gave order to retreat back to Edgehill. The loss on both sides was about equal, some 3,000 slain, amongst whom of quality, besides those named, was, on the King's part, my Lord Aubigny and others and my Lord Willoughby, Sir Edward Stradling, Colonel Lunsford and Colonel Stradling taken prisoners. And on the Parliament's the Lord St. Johns killed, but few taken. The only thing made them pretend to the victory was that our General was killed, and that their army kept the field that night. But we say they lost cannon, most of their colours, and the next morning quitted the field, so that the pillage remained to us; and yet Prince Rupert with the horse drew after the enemy till he had fixed them in Warwick. Then we marched still southward as we before designed, and took Banbury with a regiment of the Earl of Peterborough's newly raised by the Parliament, which the King gave my Lord. And then they marched to recruit those that had been killed of his at the battle, and then they marched on and possessed Oxford. His Majesty having their intelligence that my Lord of Essex was so shattered and dispersed at the battle, and that the City of London would declare for him if he approached, he did advance from Oxford as far as Windsor and Colebrooke where he received a message by the Earls of Northumberland and Pembroke from the Parliament for a treaty . . .

'A Brief Relation to the Life and Memoirs of John, Lord Belasyse: written and collected by his secretary, Joshua Moone.' Historical Manuscripts Commission. Calendar of the Manuscripts of the Marquess of Ormonde, K.P., preserved at Kilkenny Castle, New Series, Vol. II, 1903. The editor suggests that this narrative was probably written from Belasyse's dictation, but that it was written over a lengthened period, beginning in 1650. The editor has modernized the spelling.

10. SIR EDWARD SYDENHAM'S LETTER TO RALPH VERNEY

28 *October* 1642.   *Ano on the hill.*

For all our great vycktorie I have had the greatest loss by the death of your nobell father that ever anie freind did . . . he himself killed two with his owne hands, whereof one of them had killed poore Jason [Sir Edmund Verney's servant], and brocke the poynt of his standard at push of pike before he fell, which was the last account I could receave of anie of our owne syde of him. The next day the kinge sent a harald to offer mercie to all that would laye down armes, and to enquire for my Lord of Lynsee, my Lo Wyllowby and him; he brought word that my Lord of Lynsee was hurt, your father dead, my Lo Wyllowby only prysoner; he would nither put on armes or buff cote the day of battell, the reason I know not; the battell was bloody on your syde, for your hoorss rann awaye at the first charge, and our men had the execution of them for three miles; it began at 3 a clock and ended at syx. The kinge is a man of the least feare and the greatest mercie and resolution that I ever saw, and had he not bin in the fylde, we might have suffired. My Lord of Essex is retired in great disorder to Warwick, for the next morning he suffired his cannon to be taken away within muskett shott of his armie, and never offired to hindir them; it is sayd ther was killed and run away since, eaygtt thowsand of his armie. This day the kinge tooke in bamberie [Banbury]; our armie dayly increases; god in mercie send us peace and although your loss be as great as a sonn can loose in a father, yitt god's chyldren must beare with patience what afflycktion soever he shall please to laye upon them . . . My humbell sarvise to your sad wyfe. God of his infinite mercie cumfort you bothe which shall be the prayers of your freind and sarvant who shall ever be reddie to performe anie sarvise in the power of your Ed: Sydenham' and he adds as a postcript, 'Ther is delivered to me fyftie two cornets and colors which was taken; I beleeve ther be manie more.

Sir Edward Sydenham succeeded Sir Edmund Verney as Knight Marshal.

From *The Standard Bearer* by Major Peter Verney, p. 202.

11. SIR ROBERT WALSH'S ACCOUNT

Robert Walsh was captain-lieutenant to Lord Wilmot, H. He was the eldest son of Sir James Walsh, Bart., of Little Island and Ballygoner, Waterford. He died about 1690.

. . . The wars beginning then; truly I was offerd by the Houses of Parliament a considerable Imployment, my Tenent not leading me that way, I quietly got away, and went for *York* where my King was; and I in no ill equipage, and after kissing his hand, applyed my self unto the Lord *Henry Wilmot* late Earl of *Rochester* deceased, who left this Young Lord, I hope to inherit the Fathers Worth and Gallantry. The Lord *Wilmot* was then raising a Regiment of Horse for his Majesty, and as soon as I came to him, he did embrace me, bidding me welcome; not Alamode but in effect, telling me I should command his own Troop, then a raising, so I did, and in it a Hundred Valiant brave men, most Gentlemen of Estate and Quality, who not long after did so approve themselves; who could not choose but so to do, having such a General in the head of them as was his Lordship, what hath not he done to leave his Name Renowned.

Now give me leave Noble Readers, to give a relation of the first War betwixt King and Parliament, which truly is uncontradictable, for it shall carry nothing in it but a real Character of truth. At the Battle of Edge-hill, His Highness Prince *Rupert* that ever Renowned Person, Commanded the right Wing of our Horse, who put the Enemies into an absolute rout, and the Earl of *Brandford* the left, unto whose share it came to charge the Enemies right Wing, His Highness putting into a derout their left Wing, the Battle begun upon a Sunday Morning, and the Lord *Digby* commanded our reserve of Horse, who gave more Testimony of his Courage then of conduct, but that never to be buried in oblivion the deceased Earl of *Rochester*, this Lord being then Commissary General of the Horse, and in the head of our left Wing of Horse, and in the head of his one Troop, Commanded by Sir *Robert Walsh*, and his Lordships Troop consisting of at least a Hundred Brave and Noble Gentlemen, as Sir *John Dongan*, Sir *Brien O Neale*, Sir *Henry Talbot*, Sir *Walter Dongan, son* to Sir *John*, brave *Irish* Gentlemen, whose most Valiant deportment gave great Testimony of their Loyalty, as I may say did the whole Troop and his Regiment, as may witness that first service they were in, his Royal Majesty of Blessed Memory, and His now sacred Majesty, and his Royal Highness [the Duke of York], were not only there as witness of their Loyal subjects, but also hazardly and dangerously ingaged in the said Battle, to their great and ever Renowned Everlasting Glory. The Lord *Wilmot* having charged the right Wing of the Enemy, did beat them and put them so in disorder, as that they run confusedly into *Kington*, which was in the Rear of their Army, the reserve of our Horse unpremeditatedly follow the pursuit of the Enemy, which gave the advantage unto the reserve of the Enemies Horse, as also unto their main Body, that they fell upon that Renowned Most Honorable Earl of *Linzy* our General, and so furiously, as that His Majesties own Regiment was disordered, and divers of their standards taken at the same time, where the Noble Lord *Gerard* Commanding Three Regiments of Foot made a most manly stand, our Horse being for the most part mingled in the Enemies, and his Highness Prince *Ruperts* Horse pursuing, fortune proved so favourable unto Sir *Robert Walsh*, as to keep the Lord *Wilmots* Troop in a Body unscattered, so as he encountred some of the Horse that charged the Earl of *Linzy* in their return, this being in the rear of the Enemies Army towards the Town of *Kington*, Sir *Robert* with his Troop charged them and recovered the standards, which they took from the Kings Regiment, and also took some of the Enemies, and Sir *Robert* being then in the rear of the Enemies Army in the Town of *Kington*, did sieze upon Two Pieces of Cannon and a Waggon, brought them into the rear of His Majesties Army. His Glorious Majesty having lain that night upon the top of Edge-hill, his Army not then drawn from the Enemies, Sir *Robert* towards Morning brought the Two Pieces of Cannon and Waggon to the bottom of Edge-hill, and brought the standard of His Majesties, and some of the Enemies unto His Highness Prince *Rupert*, who immediately did present them, and Sir *Robert* unto His majesty, who was graciously pleased, there to Knight Sir *Robert* for the acceptable service he then did render.

From: *A True Narrative and Manifest*, 1679. Published for the Author (misspelt Walch), 35 pp., 1679. Printed in Holland (?). Copy in the British Museum.

12. EDWARD WALSINGHAM'S ACCOUNT OF THE DOINGS OF SIR JOHN SMITH

John Smith, a brother of Lord Carrington, was in Lord Grandison's Regiment. He rose to be major-general, H., to Lord Hopton and was killed at Cheriton.

. . . To this end he casts himself into the armes of the divine providence, and out of nothing begins to raise an Army for His owne defence; presently our *young Worthy* is sought for, and made Captain-Lieutenant *under the Lord Iohn Steuart* (brother to the *Duke of Richmond and Lenox*) a gentleman of wonderfull sweet and noble disposition.

This Troope was very eminent in respect of the Commander, upon whom the eyes of most men were fixt in extraordinary expectation, wherein whether they were deceived or no, let his succeeding actions declare. In the time of his Quartering at *Lincolne* there happened a passage worth noting. Not long before, there was a gentleman of quality in the Kings Army taken Prisoner by the *Proto Rebels* of *Kingston* upon *Hull*, and there in time of his durance was abused by one of the *Wrayes*, Heire to one of the chiefe Houses of that name in *Lincolnshire*, who like a Jay, cast a glasse of beere in contempt into the captive Gentlemans face. Whereof our *gallant Commander* hearing, was much incensed: determining to vindicate the wronged gentleman, if ever occasion were offered. Whilst he was at *Lincolne* this hotspur *Wray* comes to Towne, whereof he having notice, repaires to the house and enters the roome where *Wray* and divers others ill-affected to His Majesty were met; he demands of him whether he were the man who at such a time abused one of His Majesties Souldiers in *Hull?* the other peremptorily acknowledging the fact, he takes occasion with his cane to pay him his hire, and did it to the purpose, in such a manner, that the others present daunted with his courage, dared not once to stirre in *Wrayes* defence. This was an argument of his noble nature, and served the Souldiers and Townsmen to laugh at a long time after. The like he did since on a Knight of greater name and *bulk* in vindication of a noble Lord to whom that Knight had been too *ingratefull.* Indeed his disposition was such that he could better indure to see himselfe wronged, than any other ingenuous man, and would sooner vindicate anothers injury, then his owne.

He could not indure to see the insolence of Souldiers over the poore pesants and country people, neither ever would he tolerate it if it lay in his power either by foule or faire meanes to remedy. Which an Officer of the Army (who thought himselfe no meane man) experienced certainly at *Leicester.* This man usurpes power, upon I know not what authority, to presse, and dispose of Horses at his pleasure: which he performed with that insolence as was very grievous to the people. Wherefore they complained to this *generous Commander,* who immediately questioned the other about it, and finding him both very guilty, and peremptory in his offences: Layes him (although he were his name-sake) by the head and heeles in the stable, amongst the horses, and there lets him lie, *durante beneplacito,* till he was intreated to release him.

By this time the Cockatrice of this Rebellion was growne to some maturity, & amongst all that fought to lop the growing Monster our noble Captaine Smith gave one of the first blowes: the particulars whereof as they are related authentikely by the Herald [William Dugdale], (who extorted the relation from his owne mouth) I will here insert. In the beginning of *August.* 1642. He marcht with the Lord *Iohn Stuarts* Troope into *Warwickshire,* there to meet the noble Earle of *Northampton,* who was then in Armes for His Majesty. Captain *Bartue* [Francis Bertie] Troope marcht with him, and at *Rugby* on the edge of the aforesaid County he quartered the 8 of that moneth, where he understood that at *Kilsby* in *Northamptonshire,* about two miles distant, the Inhabitants had put themselves in Armes against His Majesties Proclamation; He therefore conceiving it fit to disarme them, did that night set a strong Guard in *Rugby* of about 30 Horse, to the end he might draw out of the Towne at any hower with the lesse noyse, or notice.

Before breake of day he marcht out, the morning being very wet, and before it was light, coming to *Kilsby* Towne side drew up his Horse in a body. As soone as it was cleare day he entred the towne, where presently he found the people gathering together, some with Muskets or other gunnes, others with Pitchforkes and Clubs, He asked them *what they meant, and told them he had no purpose to doe them harme, entreating them to deliver up their Armes for His Majesties service.* The unruly people no whit hearkned to his courteous desires, but furiously assaulted his Troop, (which could not be drawne up into a body in regard of the straightnesse of the passage) they wounded two or three of his men and some horses. Yet made he shift to disarme some of them, and then advances to the *Constables* house, where he finds more company; but comanded his men not to discharge a Pistoll upon pain of death, hoping yet by faire means to qualifie them. Immediately divers shot is made from the Windowes at him; whereupon, he commanded his men to give fire, and so presently dispatcht three or foure of them: which the rest seeing, ran away all except an old man that with his Pitchforke ran at Captain *Smith,* and twice stroke the tynes thereof against his brest, who by reason of his armes under a loose coate received no hurt, yet could not this old man by any intreaty be perswaded to forbeare, till a Pistoll quieted him. Here he took 40 Muskets, and the same day marcht towards the valiant Earle of *Northampton,* whom he met with [Lord] *Brookes* his *Ordnance,* about three miles from *Warwicke* and attended him thither. In this action if you consider the condition of those times, you will discover a great deale of discretion in the managery of it, and nothing favouring of rashnesse or vanity, some taint whereof you might well expect in a young Gentleman so spritefull, and over flowing with valour.

The next action remarkable that our fortunate gallant had a hand in, was that famous fight [Powick Bridge] *September* the 23. the same yeare, neare *Worcester:* where he charged with that bravery and discretion, that many confessed he did singularly promote the victory. Thus dayly he gained new honours, and his Laurell still flourished with more splendor than could be expected in his age.

To this at *Worcester* succeeds that memorable Battaile neere *Keinton* in *Warwickshire,* the particulars whereof following we owe to Mr. *Dugdale, Chester Heralds* carefull preservation. His Troope at this time being in the Lord *Grandisons* Regiment, was drawne up in the left wing of the Kings Army; This day his singular valour was most eminent for sundry notable actions, especially his rescue of His Majesties *Banner Royall,* vulgarly called the *Standard.* For after the Rebells left wing of Horse, and divers Regiments of Foot were routed, and execution followed by His Majesties Horse of both wings, through and beyond the Towne of *Keinton,* It happened that this prudent Commander saw some *eminent persons* of His Majesties Army, in pursuit of the flying *Rebells,* which he conceived had been appointed as a Reserve of Horse, for assistance of our foote: which much amazed him, hearing both Armies at that instant in sharpe fight, whereupon he presently seekes out the Lord *Grandison,* Sir *Charles Lucas,* and some other Officers of quality; and importuned their speedy rallying together of what horse in this confusion could be suddainly got, that so speedily they might returne to the assistance of our foot.

His excellent advice was very well resented by those noble Gentlemen, and accordingly they soone rallyed about 200 horse, and marched backe towards the Armies then in fight. In their passage they met with a great part of the Rebells of *Charles Essex* his Regiment, running confusedly towards *Keinton* Towne with their colours: those they presently charged, slew some, routed the rest and took all their Colours. This done these horse rallyed againe, and advanced, but they had not past farre before they met with about three Troopes of the Rebells horse, which were wheeled off from the reare of their foote, these also they charged, routed, and followed in execution so farre, that now this brave Commander could rally but fourteene men together to prosecute his returne: with which as he passed up still towards the reare of the Rebells Army, he met with a great part of the Lord *Whartons* Regiment that formerly were routed also, and now were with their Colours, confusedly hastening towards *Keinton* Towne; these with his fourteen horse he valiantly charg'd, and routing them tooke their Colours. The Majors Colours were taken by himselfe, which he delivered to one *Chichly* a groome of the *Duke of Richmond's*, who had taken a Colours of *Charles Essex* his Regiment.

But now of all his fourteen there was no more left but himselfe and *Chichley*: the rest following the pillage of the routed Rebells. As these two were passing on towards our Army, this *Mirrour of Chivalry* espies six men, three *Curiasiers* and three *Harquebusiers* on horsebacke, guarding a seaventh on foot, who was carrying off the Field a Colours rouled up which he conceived to be one of the ordinary Colours of His Majesties *Leife-guards*, and therefore seeing them so strong, intended to avoide them. Whil'st he was thus considering, a boy on horsebacke calls to him saying *Captaine Smith, Captaine Smith, they are carrying away the Standard*. He would not suddainly beleive the boy, till by great asserverations he had assured him it was the *Standard*, who forthwith said, *They shall have me with it, if they carry it away*; and desiring *Chichley* if he saw him much engag'd to throw down the other Colours & assist him; presently he charg'd in with his rapier at the footman that carried the Banner, (who was the Secretary to *Essex* the Rebells Generall) saying, *Traitor deliver the Standard*, and wounded him into the breast, whil'st he was bent forward to follow his thrust, one of those *Curiasiers* with a *pollax* wounded him in the necke through the Collar of his doublet, and the rest gave fire at him with their pistolls, but without any further hurt then blowing some pouder into his face.

No sooner was he recovered upright, but he made a thrust at the *Curiasier* that wounded him, and ran him in the belly, whereupon he presently fell, at which sight all the rest ran away. Then he caused a foot souldier that was neare at hand to reach him up the banner, which he brought away with the horse of that *Curiasier*. Immediately comes up a great body of His

Majesties horse which were rallyed together (according to his first advice) to charge the enemy againe, with whom he staid; delivering the *Standard* to Master *Robert Hatton*, a Gentleman of Sir *Richard Willyes* his Troope, to carry forthwith to his Majesty. So farr was he from prizing his owne action, or gaping after honour or reward. The day was now so farr spent that he had time left onely to rescue Colonell *Richard Feilding* who was taken Captive by the *Rebells*, and was leading away, whil'st in the interim our *Heroicke Commander* comes, and in despite of them sets him at liberty. Surely this daies worke deserves eternall memory, and concludes that he was borne this day to place a laurell garland on his Soveraignes head, and preserve the honour of His Nation; Many confesse that the preservation of our foot is due to his prudent foresight and advise. If his valour has afforded us nothing else but the *rescued Standard*, we could not sufficiently celebrate his praise. It had surely in the peoples eies beene a sad Omen of succeeding enterprizes, had we not by his fortunate and couragious atcheivement repaired so singular a losse; but this on the other side encourag'd them, who seeing the Standard so neare lost, yet happily regained, conceived hopes that though the *royall Diadem* was as deeply engag'd, yet by the fortunate endeavour of such *Noble Heroes* that also together with the Kingdome might be recovered.

The next morning *King* CHARLES sends for him to the top of *Edge Hill*, where His Majesty (though the modest Gentleman did what lay in him to avoid the honour) Knighted him for his singular valour. Immediately our worthy Knight (seeing the *Rebells* having gathered all the residue of their strength into a body, stood drawne up neare the side of *Keinton* Towne) signifies a great desire he had that our horse should charge them, but that being not resolved he craved liberty to have a small party assign'd him, with which he would endeavour to fetch off some of their *Canon*, which being granted he march't downe into *Keinton feild*, and of his party he drew out about 30 to approach neare the body of the Rebells, and face them whil'st horses were span'd in to draw off the peices: he commanded this party himselfe, facing their maine body within musket shot, but their horse were so aw'd with the former dayes worke, that they durst not adventure to charge him with that small party; with which he brought off three brasse peices of *Canon* that stood about the left wing of the Rebells army in the battaile; which action our whole Army stood looking on with wonder and applause. He concludes this dayes worke with the generous assistance he gave Sir *Gervase Scroopes* son [Adrian] in fetching off his valiant Father stript naked and almost dead, with the losse of so much bloud by nineteene wounds.

These valiant actions made him very eminent in His Majesties sight, so that the royall munificence gives him a troope of his owne, and the noble Lord *Grandison* elects him for *Major* to his Regiment: wherein he did singular service in divers places, exercising all parts of an excellent Commander; witnesse his gallant behaviour in the fight at *Brainceford*, and his beating up of the enemies quarters, with his souldierlike retreat, the same yeare in *December* neare *Winchester*. Where with a small party he dared to goe into the mouth of a powerfull army, to beat up their quarters, and afterwards when they came upon him when he had done great execution in the place, with such discretion to make his retreat scarce with the losse of a man in despite of them all.'

From: E(dward) W(alsingham), *Brittannicae Virtutis Imago*, Oxford, 1644.

13. SIR JOHN HINTON'S ACCOUNT

I went directly to your Royall father, of ever blessed memory, to York, and ioyneing with his Army, I marched with them to Beverley, and lay before Hull and in those parts.

Soone after his Majestie was pleased to take notice of mee, and the Royall Standard being set up at Nottingham, hee sent mee thither with letters and instructions to the Marquess of Hertford and the Lord Hopton, who thought fitt to make use of mee to ride into Wales, to Colonell Stradling and other gentlemen of quality there, in order to prepare their businesse and reception of the Army att Cardiff: which was accordingly don with good success and the Army being as complete as they could make itt, I marched with itt to Killingworth castle, and from thence to Edgehill.

Where on the 23rd of October, which was the first time your Majestie ever saw the enemy in a body, who were then under the command of the Earle of Essex, quartering at Keinton, his sacred Majestie of ever blessed memorie, being with his army near that place, and resolveing to fight them, marched downe the hill, which Essex percieveing, presently drawes out to engage the king, whose army being in batalia Prince Rupert commanding the right wing, the Lord Wilmott the left, and the maine battaile by the Earle of Lindsey, Generall of the feild, within a short time both armies engage, and after a sharp dispute (Prince Rupert routing Collonell Ramsay, and pursueing him towards Keinton, the Lord Wilmott being in the meane time forced from his ground by Sir William Balfour) the kings army destitute of both wings of horse, was both in front and flank attacqued by the enemies horse and foot, by which advantage Belfour disorders two regiments of foot, and forceth a way to the Royall Standard, where the Earle of Lindsey was mortally wounded and Sir Edmund Varney standard bearer slaine, and the standard itt self taken, but itt was soone after regained by Sir John Smith, for that action made knight; after which the kings foot quitting the field, retreated towards that side of the hill, from whence his Majestie first marched downe to engage; upon which retreat your Majestie was unhappily left behind in a large feild, att which time I had the honour to attend your person, and seeing the sudden and quick march of the Enemie towards you, I did with all earnestnesse, most humbly, but at last somewhat rudely, importune your Highnesse to avoid this present and apparent danger of being killed or taken prisoner, for their horse was by this time come up within half musket shott in full body, att which your Highnesse was pleased to tell mee, You feared them not, and drawing a pistoll out of one of your holsters, and spanning itt, resolved to charge them, but I did prevaile with your Highnesse to quitt the place, and ride from them, in some hast, but one of their troopers being excellently mounted, broke his rank, and coming full careere towards your Highnesse, I received his charge, and hauing spent a pistoll or two on each other, I dismounted him in the closeing, but being armed cap-a-pe, I could doe noe execution upon him with my sword, att which instant, one Mr Mathewes, a Gentleman Pensioner, rides in, and with a pole-axe immediately decides the businesse, and then overtaking your Highnesse, you gott safe to the Royall Army, and without this Providence you had undoubtedly miscarried att that time, which passage is related in a booke, entituled, 'Miraculum Basilicon,' printed in the yeare 1664.

The next day your Highnesse's Tutor, Doctor Duppa, was by accident taken prisoner, by a party, who were carryeing him away to the Enemie and haveing notice of itt, I presently applyed myself to Sir Thomas Aston, who with my self and a party, after a hard dispute, did rescue him.

From this Battle I marched with the Army to Banbury, and from thence to Oxford, where your Royall father was then gratiously pleased to giue mee the place of Physitian in Ordinary to your Person, being introduced by the Marquess of Hertford, and the Earle of Dorsett.

Memoirs of Sir John Hinton. Physitian in Ordinary to His Majesties Person, 1679.

14. A LONDON ROYALIST'S NEWSLETTER

From London.

On Saturday 22 of this month the quartermasters of the king's rear and those of the earl of Essex van met in one place near Banbury. On Saturday the king (contrary to the earl's expectation) did not march, so that the earl must either fight or hazard to retreat through such ways as would be dangerous to extremity. The king had so great an advantage of the hill that it turned to his disadvantage, for being so much upon the descent his cannon either shot over, or if short it would not graze by reason of the ploughed lands: whereas their cannon did some hurt having a mark they could not miss. Prince Rupert did not let them long dally with great shot, but by the general confession of his enemies did make lanes wherever he went. The left wing of the earl's army discharged at 40 yards distance, and then ran away all before they received or gave one blow in that wing where three regiments of foot besides the greatest part of the horse, so that the king's horse pursued them in execution till they came to the carriages which they fired that were with ammunition or plundered that were with goods, took the earl's coach, his privy purse with £2000 and, they say, very much of the public too. And doubtless had not the soldiers been too greedy and busy on the spoil, the earl's whole army had been routed. But in the meentime the battalia of the earl leads up to the king's, and by the courage of the apprentices (I mean butchers and dyers) with a very few others under the command of Hollis and Haslerigge a great impression was made in the king to the very standard, the bearer whereof, sir Edmund Varney, knight marshal, was slain and that taken, but in less than 6 minutes space recovered. In this action the earl of Lindsey received a shot in the thigh, which brake the bone. He was straight carried to a little village hard by and by some clowns discovered to the earl's commanders, and by them carried from thence to Warwick, where he died. His son is *dangerously hurt* and taken, my lord Aubigny slain. On the other side my lord St. John and *the lord Feilding*, but as yet we cannot know the certainty of prisoners or dead. Night made them sound a retreat, of both sides say the parliamentarians. I shall not contradict it. This I am sure that the king was master of the field where he dined *the next day* upon a drum head and stayed within 4 miles till the dead were buried. The same night of the battle he made great fires in his quarters. The earl made none. The king hath 9 of their cannon, all their carriages and 56 colours. Prince Rupert the next morning before day with some of his troop set upon some of the earl's troops in some villages and slew them. The king that day, Monday, appeared again in battalia, but the earl retreated to Warwick. The same day there came to the king an entire retiment of divers officers and pieces of companies from the adverse party.

Here are in this town sir James Ramsey, the commissary general of the earl's horse, the lord Hastings and divers others captains now in *prison* who came away believing they were the only surviving men. On Wednesday the lord Wharton and Mr Strowd, who are thought on the one side, but confidently reported on the other side to have run away, came into St. Margaret church and gave in the sermon a paper to the preaching Mr Case to give God thanks for the victory, being 3000 slain on the king's side and 300 on theirs. He did it an hour together, throwing such abominable dirt on private men and making such strong expressions to Almighty God that I tremble to think on them. After sermon the house sat and Mr Strowd had very many questions put to him, but he answered with so much distraction and so contradictorily that at last he desired my lord Wharton and he might confer together and that the next day he would give a better account. I must tell you some passages, though confusedly enough. Prince Rupert came to the king, and besought him to go out of the field protesting he would not else strike a stroke. The king did, but straight returned, and (I speak it on good ground) did charge gallantly, as forward in danger and in all things showing as much dexterity, presence of mind and personal courage as any man. He is said to be at Oxford last night for all the victory God was so bethanked. On Wednesday night late the children were carried from St. James into the city for the place's security, though the women with tears besought the contrary, the house not being aired, the children sickly and the night late. They fortify Westminster etc. but give God thanks and pray heartily.

This seems to be a Newsletter from a fairly well-informed Londoner of Royalist sympathies.

British Museum, Harl. MS. 3783, f. 61. Printed in Godfrey Davies' The Battle of Edgehill. The spelling has been modernized.

SECTION 6

Parliamentarian Accounts of the Battle

THE PARLIAMENTARIAN ACCOUNTS of the battle are very inadequate, which is perhaps an indication that the Roundheads felt they had little to boast of. Essex himself seems to have written no relation of the fight. Steven Marshall, chaplain to Essex's Regiment, F., wrote a letter to a Member of Parliament, published as 'A most true and succinct Relation of the late Battell neere Kineton in Warwick-Shire'. He specifically says that he wrote 'My Lord Generall not having time', but though he confirms that Essex had 12 regiments of foot and about 40 troops of horse, he gives us no details that are not to be found elsewhere.

The Parliamentary Official Account is full of useful detail, but its chronology suffers from its being compiled by six different people. It is perhaps the best of the relations from the Roundhead side. Ludlow's account, though probably written years later and mistaken as to the way the Banner Royal was recovered, is extremely valuable.

The Vindication . . . of Sir James Ramsey, useful though it is for the left wing of horse, tells us no more than has already been given in Chapter Thirteen, and is not worth printing in full.

Of several chaplains who wrote accounts of the battle, Mr Adoniram Bifield, the 'Worthy Divine', is far the best, and his letter is printed here. Captains Nathaniel Fiennes and Edward Kightley give us a certain amount of detail, which is not found elsewhere, though Kightley was not in the thick of the fighting, and Fiennes tell us nothing of his personal adventures.

The account in Special Passages is not to be trusted. It reports Colonel John Bellasis killed, when in fact he was only slightly wounded, and the Earl of Crawford (1606–1652?) as mortally wounded. Sir William Pennyman's Regiment is said to be at Bridgnorth, though De Gomme's plan shows that this was not so. It further states that Lord Taaffe was wounded in the mouth, that the House gave Essex £5000, and that Hampden's Regiment was 1200 strong. Lastly it reports that Sir Samuel Luke took 6 out of 26 colours taken.

1. THE PARLIAMENTARY OFFICIAL ACCOUNT

This account was compiled by Lt. General Sir William Balfour, Colonels John Meldrum, Thomas Ballard, Denzil Holles and Sir Philip Stapleton

and Charles Pym. The fact that they ventured to produce a semi-official
account of the battle may be taken as evidence that they considered
themselves among those who had borne the heat of the day.

The Account of the Battel at *Edgehill*, Oct. 23. 1642. as
publisht by Order of the Parliament.

SIR,

We should do our Army a great deal of wrong, and not discharge our Duty
of Thankfulness towards God, if we took not the first occasion to declare
his goodness, in giving so great a Blessing, as he hath now done to the
resolute and unwearied Endeavours of our Soldiers fighting for him in the
maintenance of his Truth, and for themselves and their Country, in the
defence of their Liberties and the Priviledges of Parliament; this makes us
give you now a Narration of a blessed Victory which God hath given us
upon the Army of the Cavaliers, and of those Evil Persons, who upon
Sunday the 23rd of this Instant, engaged his Majesty in a dangerous and
bloody Fight against his faithful Subjects, in the Army raised by Authority
of Parliament, for the preservation of his Crown and Kingdom. We
marched from *Worcester*, *Wednesday* the 19th, upon Intelligence that their
Army was removed from *Shrewsbury* and *Bridgnorth* and bending Southward, our Train of Artillery was so unready, through want of
Draught-Horses, and through other Omissions of Monsieur *Du-Boys*, that
we were forced to leave it behind to follow us, and with it the Regiments
of Col. *Hambden* and Col. *Grantham*; and staying for it, we could advance
no further than to a little Market Town called *Keynton*, in *Warwickshire*, 6
Miles from *Warwick*; whether we came the *Saturday* Night with 11
Regiments of Foot, 42 Troops of Horse, and about 700 Dragoons, in all
about 10000 Men; there we intended to rest the Sabbath-day, and the
rather, that our Artillery and the Forces left with it, might come up to us.
In the Morning, when we were going to Church, we had news brought
us that the Enemy was 2 Miles from us, upon a high Hill, called *Edgehill*;
whereupon we presently marched forth into a great broad Field, under
that Hill, called, *The Vale of the Red Horse*, and made a stand some half a
Mile from the Foot of the Hill, and there drew into Battalia, where we
saw their Forces come down the Hill; and drew likewise into Battel in the
Bottom; a great broad Company. Their Forces appeared to be much
greater than we could possibly have conceived them to be by the
Confession of the Prisoners we have taken; they that say least, say 14000,
which is the Earl of *Lindsey's Relation*, who was their General; but others
say 18000, and above 4000 Horse and Dragoons; the Wind was much for
their Advantage, and they endeavoured to get it more; which to prevent,
we were inforced to draw out our Left Wing to a great breadth, and by
that means, before the Battel was done, gained it wholly from them. In
our Right Wing were Three Regiments of Horse, the Lord General's,
Commanded by Sir *Philip Stapleton*, Sir *William Balford's* and the Lord

Fieldings; Sir *John Meldrum's* Brigade had the Van, Col. *Essex* was in the middle, and Col. *Ballard's* with the Lord General's Regiment, his own, the Lord *Brooks*, and Col. *Hollis* in the Rear. In the Left Wing were 24 Troops of Horse, Commanded by Sir *James Ramsey*, their Commissary-General. In this Posture we stood when the other Army advanced towards us; the strength of their Horse was on their Right Wing opposite to our Left; in their Left Wing they had but 10 Troops; but their Foot, which appeared to us, divided into nine great Bodies, came up all in Front, and after some playing with the Cannon on both sides, that part of it which was on their Left, and towards our Right Wing, came on very gallantly to the Charge, and were as gallantly received, and Charged by Sir *Philip Stapleton* and Sir *William Balford's* Regiment of Horse, assisted with the Lord *Robert's*, and Sir *William Constable's* Regiments of Foot, who did it so home thrice together, that they forced all the Musqueteers, of two of their left Regiments, to run in and shrowd themselves within their Pikes, not daring to shoot a shot, and so stood when our Rear came up; and then Charging altogether, especially that part of our Rear which was placed upon the Right hand, and so next unto them which was the Lord General's Regiment, and the Lord *Brook's*, led on by Col. *Ballard* who commanded that *Brigade*, forced that Stand of Pikes, and wholly broke those two Regiments, and slew and took almost every man of them; the Earl of *Lindsey*, his Son, the Lord *Willoughby*, and some other Persons of Note are Prisoners. Sir *Edmund Varney*, who carried the King's Standard, was slain by a Gentleman of the Lord General's Troop of Horse, who did much other good Service that Day, and the Standard taken; which was afterwards by the Lord General himself delivered unto his Secretary Mr [Robert] *Chambers*, with an intention to send it back the next day unto his Majesty; but the Secretary, after he had carried it long in his hand, suffered it to be taken away by some of our Troopers, and as yet we cannot learn where it is. The other two Regiments of our Rear, Col. *Hollis* and Col. *Ballard* Charged those which were before them, and then the whole Body of the King's Foot, except two other Regiments, ran away. By this time it grew so late and dark, and to say the truth, our Ammunition at this present was all spent, that we contented our selves to make good the Field, and gave them leave to retire up the Hill in the Night. But before we came to this, we will give you an Account of what passed in the other parts of our Army. Before our Rear came up to Charge, our Battalia at the very first wholly disbanded and ran away, without ever striking stroke, or so much as being Charged by the Enemy, though Col. *Essex* himself, and others, who Commanded these Regiments in Chief, did as much as Men could do to stay them; but Col. *Essex* being forsaken by his whole Brigade, went himself into the Van, where both by Direction and his own Execution, he did most gallant Service, till he received a shot in the Thigh, of which he is since dead. Now for our Rear, thus it was; before it, toward the outside of it, stood our Left Wing of Horse, advanced a little foward to the Top of a Hill, where they stood in a Battalia, lined with commanded Musqueteers, 400 out of Col. *Hollis's* Regiment, and 300 out of Col. *Ballard's*; but upon the first Charge of the Enemy, they wheeled about, abandoned their Musqueteers, and came running down with the Enemies Horse at their Heels, and amongst them pellmell, just upon Col. *Hollis's* Regiment, and brake through it, though Col. *Hollis* himself, when he saw them come running towards him, went and planted himself just in the way, and did what possibly he could do to make them stand; and at last prevailed with three Troops to wheel a little about, and rally; but the rest of our Horse of that Wing, and the Enemies Horse with them, brake through and ran to *Keynton*, where most of the Enemy left pursuing them, and fell to plundering our Wagons, by which many of us have received very great loss, and by Name your Servants that now write to you. Notwithstanding their breaking through Col. *Hollis's* Regiment, it was not dismaid, but, together with the other Regiments of that Brigade, marched up the Hill, and so made all the haste they could to come to fight, and got the Wind of the Enemy, and came on (if we may say it our selves, but we must do the Soldiers right) most gallantly, and Charged the Enemy, who were then in fight with our Van, and the Right Wing of our Horse, and (as it was said before) helpt to defeat the two Regiments afore-mentioned, and made all the rest run, but two other Regiments, which retired orderly, and at last made a stand; and having the Assistance of Cannon, and a Ditch before them, held us play very handsomely: And by this time it grew so dark, and our Powder and Bullet so spent, that it was not held fit we should Advance upon them; but there we stood in very good Order; drew up all our Forces, both Horse and Foot; and so stood all that Night upon the place where the Enemy, before the Fight, had drawn into Battalia, till toward Morning, that the Enemy was gone, and retired up the Hill, and then we returned also to a warmer place near *Keynton*, where we had Quarter the Night before; for we were almost starved with cold that bitter Night, our Army being in extream want of Victuals; and about 9 or 10 of the Clock drew out again into Battalia, and so stood 3 or 4 hours, till the Enemy was clean gone from the Hill, and then we drew again into our Quarter, and there have lain this Night, and purpose this Day, (God willing) after we have buried our Dead, to march to *Warwick* to refresh our Army, which is exceeding wearied with so many Nights watching, and so long a Fight, which held from Noon till dark Night. Two Particulars must not be omitted, one of Sir *William Balford*, who in the beginning of the Day broke a Regiment of Foot which had green Colours, beat them to their Cannon, where they threw down their Arms, and ran away; he laid his hand upon the Cannon, and called for Nails to nail them up, especially the two biggest, which were Demy-Cannon; but finding none, he cut the ropes belonging to them, and his Troopers killed the Canoneers; then he pursued the Fliers half a Mile upon Execution; and after returned to Sir *Philip Stapleton*, who in the mean time was Charging of the Red

Regiment, where the King's Standard was, and had Charged it home to push of Pike with his single Troop; and they then, together with the help of some of the Foot of our Rear, utterly broke it, as you had it before. The other Particular was of Sir *Philip Stapleton*, who, when Five Troops of the Enemies Horse returned from pursuit of our Left Wing, and from Plundering some of our Wagons, and passed by the outside of our Rear upon the Left hand, went and Charged them with his Troop, and made them run; but they finding a Gap in the Hedge, got away, and returned to the rest of their broken Troops, where they rallied and made up a kind of a Body again. If we had time, we could relate unto you many more observable Passages; but what you have here, shall serve you till we meet; This only will we say, some of both sides did extreamly well, and others did as ill, and deserve to be hanged, for deserting and betraying, as much as lay in them, their Party; but God alone is to be praised, who fought with us, and for us, and made it his own Work, to give the Victory unto his Servants. We have lost of note only Col. *Essex*, and we fear the Lord *St. John*, who was dangerously wounded. We here send you a *George*, found in the Field by a Common Soldier, and bought of him for Twenty shillings by one Capt. [Thomas] *Skinner*; we have promised him he shall have it again; we only sent it you as one of our Trophies, that you may see it. We believe you will hear of very many of great Quality slain on the other side; The King's Foot are either slain, or most of them run away, and are now very weak, and should have been pursued by us, but that we must of pure necessity, refresh our Men for 3 or 4 days, and then we shall (God willing) Address our selves to finish the Work. In the mean time, 'its very requisite Letters from the Committee should be writ into the Countries which are Southern, to stir them up, that they may rise and cut them off, or assist us at least against them; which hoping you will forthwith do, we Rest

Your faithful and humble Servants,

Denzell Hollis.	William Balford.
Ph. Stapleton.	Jo. Meldrum.
Tho. Ballard.	Charles Pym.

Our Lord General went last Night to *Warwick*, and is there very well, and had he been with us; we should not have presumed to have given you the first Advertisement; his Excellency did gallantly adventure himself that day in the Front against the enemy, exposing himself to more Danger than we could have wished.

Rushworth, III, II, pp.35-39.

2. EDMUND LUDLOW'S ACCOUNT

Ludlow served in Essex's Lifeguard, H.

. . . The night following [Powick Bridge] the enemy left Worcester, and retreated to Shrewsbury, where the King was; upon which the Earl of Essex advanced to Worcester, where he continued with the army for some time, expecting an answer to a message sent by him to the King from the Parliament, inviting him to return to London. This time the King improved to compleat and arm his men; which when he had effected, he began his march, the Earl of Essex attending him to observe his motions; and after a day or two, on Sunday morning, the 23rd of October, 1642, our scouts brought advice that the enemy appeared, and about nine o'clock some of their troops were discovered upon Edge-hill in Warwickshire. Upon this our forces, who had been order'd that morning to their quarteres to refresh themselves, having had but little rest for eight and forty hours, were immediately counter-manded. The enemy drew down the hill, and we went into the field near Keinton. The best of our field-pieces were planted upon our right wing, guarded by two regiments of foot, and some horse. Our general having commanded to fire upon the enemy, it was done twice upon that part of the army wherein, as it was reported, the King was. The great shot was exchanged on both sides for the space of an hour or thereabouts. By this time the foot began to engage, and a party of the enemy being sent to line some hedges on our right wing, thereby to beat us from our ground, were repulsed by our dragoons without any loss on our side. The enemy's body of foot, wherein the King's standard was, came on within musquet-shot of us; upon which we observing no horse to encounter withal, charged then with some loss from their pikes, tho very little from their shot; but not being able to break them, we retreated to our former station, whither we were no sooner come, but we perceived that those who were appointed to guard the artillery were marched off; and Sir Philip Stapylton, our captain, wishing for a regiment of foot to secure the cannon, we promised to stand by him in defence of them, causing one of our servants to load and level one of them, which he had scarce done, when a body of horse appeared advancing towards us from that side where the enemy was. We fired at them with case-shot, but did no other mischief save only wounding one man through the hand, our gun being overloaded, and planted on high ground; which fell out very happily, this body of horse being of our own army, and commanded by Sir William Balfour, who with great resolution had charged into the enemy's quarters, where he had nailed several pieces of their cannon, and was then retreating to his own party, of which the man who was shot in the hand was giving us notice by holding it up; but we did not discern it. The Earl of Essex order'd two regiments of foot to attack that body which we had charged before, where the King's standard was, which they did, but could not break them till Sir William Balfour at the head of a party of

horse charging them in the rear, and we marching down to take them in
the flank, they brake and ran away towards the hill. Many of them were
killed upon the place, amongst whom was Sir Edward [sic] Varney the
King's standard-bearer, who, as I have heard from a person of honour,
engaged on that side, not out of any good opinion of the cause, but from
the sense of duty which he thought lay upon him, in respect of his relation
to the King. Mr [William] Herbert of Glamorganshire, Lieutenant Colonel
to Sir Edward Stradling's regiment, was also killed, with many others that
fell in the pursuit. Many colours were taken, and I saw Lieutenant Colonel
Middleton, then a reformado in our army, displaying the King's standard
which he had taken; but a party of horse coming upon us, we were obliged
to retire with our standard; and having brought it to the Earl of Essex, he
delivered it to the custody of one Mr [Robert] Chambers, his secretary,
from whom it was taken by one Captain [John] Smith, who, with two
more, disguising themselves with orange-colour'd scarfs, (the Earl of
Essex's colour) and pretending it unfit that a penman should have the
honour to carry the standard, took it from him, and rode with it to the
King, for which action he was knighted. Retreating towards our army, I
fell in with a body of the King's foot, as I soon perceived; but having passed
by them undiscovered, I met with Sir William Balfour's troop, some of
whom who knew me not would have fired upon me, supposing me to be
an enemy, had they not been prevented, and assured of the contrary by
Mr Francis Russell, who with ten men well mounted and armed, which
he maintained, rode in the lifeguard, and in the heat of the pursuit had lost
sight of them, as I myself had also done.

I now perceived no other engagement on either side, only a few great
guns continued to fire upon us from the enemy: but towards the close of
the day we discovered a body of horse marching from our rear on the left
of us under the hedges, which the life-guard (whom I have then found)
having discovered to be the enemy, and resolving to charge them, sent to
some of our troops that stood within musquet-shot of us to second them;
which though they refused to do, and we had no way to come at them
but through a gap in the hedge, we advanced towards them, and falling
upon their rear, killed divers of them, and brought off some arms. In which
attempt being dismounted I could not without great difficulty recover on
horse-back again, being loaded with cuirassier's arms, as the rest of the
guard also were. This was the right wing of the King's horse commanded
by Prince Rupert, who, taking advantage of the disorder that our own
horse had put our foot into, who had opened their ranks to secure them
in their retreat, pressed upon them with such fury, that he put them to
flight. And if the time which he spent in pursueing them too far, and in
plundering the wagons, had been employed in taking such advantages as
offered themselves in the place where the fight was, it might have proved
more serviceable to the carrying on of the enemy's designs. The night after
the battle our army quartered upon the same ground that the enemy fought

on the day before. No man nor horse got any meat that night, and I had touched none since the Saturday before, neither could I find my servant who had my cloak, so that having nothing to keep me warm but a suite of iron, I was obliged to walk about all night, which proved very cold by reason of a sharp frost.

Towards morning our army having received a reinforcement of Colonel [John] Hampden's and several other regiments, to the number of about four thousand men, who had not been able to join us sooner, was drawn up; and about daylight we saw the enemy upon the top of the hill: so that we had time to bury our dead, and theirs too if we thought fit. That day was spent in sending trumpeters to enquire whether such as were missing on both sides were killed, or prisoners. Those of ours taken by the enemy were the Lord St. Johns, who was mortally wounded, and declared at his death a full satisfaction and cheerfulness to lay down his life in so good a cause; Colonel [Valentine] Walton, a member of Parliament, and Captain [George] Austin an eminent merchant in London; of whom the last died through the hard usage he received in the gaol at Oxford, to which he was committed. It was observed that the greatest slaughter on our side was of such as ran away, and on the enemy's side of those that stood; of whom I saw about threescore lie within the compass of threescore yards upon the ground whereon that brigade fought in which the King's standard was. We took prisoners the Earl of Lindsey, General of the King's army, who died of his wounds; [Colonel] Sir Edward Stradling, and Colonel [Sir Thomas] Lunsford, who were sent to Warwick-Castle. That night the country brought in some provisions; but when I got meat I could scarce eat it, my jaws for want of use having almost lost their natural faculty.

Our army was now refreshed, and masters of the field; and having received such a considerable addition of strength as I mentioned before, we hoped that we should have pursued the enemy, who were marching off as fast as they could, leaving only some troops to face us upon the top of the hill: but instead of that, for what reason I know not, we marched to Warwick; of which the enemy having notice, sent out a party of horse under Prince Rupert, who on Tuesday night fell into the town of Keinton, where our sick and wounded souldiers lay, and after they had cruelly murdered many of them, returned to their army. The King, as if master of the field, marched to Banbury, and summoned it; and tho about a thousand of our men were in the town, yet pretending it not to be sufficiently provided for a siege, they surrendered it to him. From thence the King went to Oxford, and our army after some refreshment at Warwick returned to London, not like men that had obtained a victory, but as if they had been beaten. The Parliament ordered them to be recruited; and about the same time [3 Nov.] sent to the King, who was advanced with part of his army to Maidenhead, or thereabouts, to assure him of their earnest desire to prevent the effusion of more blood, and to procure a right understanding between his Majesty and them. The King in his answer, which was brought by Sir Peter Killegrew, professed to desire nothing more, and that he would leave no means unattempted for the effecting thereof. Upon which answer the Parliament thought themselves secure, at least against any sudden attempt: but the very next day the King taking the advantage of a very thick mist, marched his army within half a mile of Brentford before he was discovered, designing to surprize our train of artillery, (which was then at Hammersmith) the Parliament, and City; which he had certainly done, if two regiments of foot and a small party of horse that lay at Brentford had not with unspeakable courage opposed his passage, and stopt the march of his army most part of the afternoon: during which time the army that lay quarter'd in and about London drew together; which some of them, and particularly the life-guard, had opportunity the sooner to do, being at that very time drawn into Chelsey-fields to muster, where they heard the vollies of shot that passed between the enemy and our little party; the dispute continued for some hours, till our men were encompassed quite round with horse and foot; and then being over-power'd with numbers on every side, many brave and gallant men having lost their lives upon the place, the rest chusing rather to commit themselves to the mercy of the water, than to those who were engaged in so treacherous a design, leap'd into the river, where many officers and private souldiers were drowned, and some taken prisoners. However the enemy's design was by this means defeated, and they discouraged from any farther attempt that night. The Parliament also were alarm'd in such a manner with the danger and treachery of this enterprize, that they used all possible diligence to bring their forces together, so that by eight of the clock the next morning we had a body of twenty thousand horse and foot drawn up upon Turnham-green, a mile on this side of Brentford: those of ours also that lay at Kingston were marching to us by the way of London. The enemy drew out a party of theirs towards the hill at Acton, which we attacked, and forced to retire in disorder to their main body. And here again, in the opinion of many judicious persons, we lost, as at Edge-hill before, a favourable opportunity of engaging the enemy with great advantage, our numbers exceeding theirs, and their reputation being utterly lost in the last attempt. But the Earl of Holland and others, pretending to encourage our army by their presence, made use of their time to disswade the Earl of Essex from fighting till the rest of our forces arrived; magnifying the power of the enemy to him, and thereby giving them an opportunity to draw off their forces and artillery towards Kingston, which they did as fast as they could, leaving only a body of horse to face us between the two Brentfords, the rest having secured themselves by a timely retreat: upon this party some of our great guns, guarded by a regiment of foot, were, towards the evening, ordered to be fired. The life-guard was drawn up in the highways to secure our foot from any attempt of horse that might be made upon them; which some great men, who pretended a resolution to fight in that troop, blamed, charging the advisers thereof with rashness, in hazarding them in such a pound, where they must inevitably be cut off, if the enemy should advance upon them. But I fear this great care was only counterfeit, and that those persons well knew the enemy to be in a flying, and not in a charging condition, as it quickly appeared; for our cannon no sooner began to play upon them, but they retired to the main body of their army, the rear of which had by that time recovered Hounslow-heath. The enemy took up their head-quarters at Kingston, where, by the advantage of the bridg over the Thames they hoped to be able, tho inferior in number, to defend themselves against a more numerous army, if they should be attacked, and to put in execution any design they might have upon the city or places adjacent. To prevent which our general caused a bridg of boats to be laid over the river between Putney and Battersey, which was no sooner finished but the enemy retired to Oxford by way of Reading, which place they fortified, and placed a garrison therein, a party of ours having quitted it upon their approach . . .

The Memoirs of Edmund Ludlow, 1625–1672, ed. C. H. Firth, M.A., pp.41–48.

3. ADONIRAM BIFIELD'S ACCOUNT

A
LETTER
Sent from
A Worthy Divine
[Mr. Bifeild in MS]
To the Right Honourable
The Lord Mayor of the City of
LONDON   [Isaac Pennington]
Being a true Relation of the battaile

(From Warwick Castle 24 Oct 1642
at 2 a clock a.m.)

London
Octob. 27 Printed for Robert Wood.
1642

Sir,
Yesterday, being the Lords
day, His Excellencie
intending to march from
Kinton a little Village in
Warwick-shire, towards
Banbury to relieve it, un-
expectedly an Alarme

came about eight a clock in the morning,
that the Enemy was advancing within two
or three miles, which accordingly proved so;
and it pleased God to make my self the first
Instrument of giving a certain discovery of
it, by the help of a prospective Glasse from
the top of an Hill, when the two Armies
were drawn into Battalia; about two a clock
in the afternoon, a very sore and fierce Battail
began, which continued about four houres in
mine own sight and hearing, much blood
was shed, and a gallant spirit expressed by
our Infantry, even to such a degree of Va-
liantnesse, as may crown every common soldier with the honour of a Commander. But
the left Wing of our Horse being charged
by the King's right Wing, was suddainly put
to flight so that the right Wing in which
your Son [Pennington] was placed, did the best service for
the Chevalry, Where your Sonne is (or any
of the rest of my Lords Guard) I know not,
I hope they are safe, because upon diligent
enquiry, I yet hear no hurt of any of them.

. . . we did beat the enemy out of the Field,
and gained four pee-ces of Ordnance.
This morning it is expected that 3. or 4. fresh
Regiments on our side, as namely Colonell
Hampdens, Colonell Granthams, Colonell Bark-
hams, and the Lord Rochfords Regiments
should joyn with the rest. The residue of our Army to fall on the remainder of the Kings
Forces, hoping for us glorious successe as before. Colonell Vavasor assures us, that the
King himself for some time was in the
Army, . . . Some say that Rupert is slain:
      A few of our Waggons were burned and
plundered by
the Enemy, who wheeled about into our
Rere, but our Musquetiers played bravely upon them in the mean time, and recovered our
Waggons again, and sixe pieces of Ordnance
which we had lost, our Enemy had the wind
more with them, but we had more of the
Hill, we had but twelve Regiments in the

Field, about fifty troops of Horse (I think)
at the most, and some 2. Regim. of Dragoons.
His Excell. maintained the fight most gallantly. And our Noble Lords, as the L. Wharton,
Willoughby of Parham, Roberts, &c. did us bravely. All this hath God enabled our Army to
perform, though from Wednesday till this
moment of my writing, the Common soldiers
have not come into a bed, but lodged in
the open field, in the wet and cold nights,
and most of them scarse eate or drank at all
for 24. hours together, may, I may say for 48.
except fresh water where they could get it;
Mr. [Simon] Ash was marvellously preserved from
the cruelty of four Cavaleers which set upon
him, one of them cut off his hat and raised
his hair with his sword, but never touched
his skin, God hath brought most of our Ministers this night to Warwick, Mr. [Simon] Ash
amongst the rest, and Mr. [Steven] Marshall, whose
danger was no lesse: For my own part, after
I had discharged my duty as far as I was enabled, by passing from Regiment to Regiment, and Troop to Troop to encourage
them, at the latter end of the fight, not knowing what the issue of things might be, in the
darksome Evening; while it was yet light, I
rid to Warwick amongst hundreds of drawn
swords, and yet was saved from the least
touch of blood thirst hand. The Cavaleers
some of them pursuing our Horsemen, which
as I said before, forsook their ground in the
left Wing of the Army, and fled to Warwick.

He sends this letter to
' . . . stop the mouth of false rumours: . . . '
and asks the Lord Mayor to let
' . . . my noble friend Sergeant-Major Skippon' read this 'news proper
for his element.'
He ends with his love to Mr Case & humble respect to
'your good Lady.'

B.M. Thomason Tracts E 124/21.

4. CAPTAIN NATHANIEL FIENNES' ACCOUNT, 36 TROOP, H

A most True and Exact Relation. Published in London, 9 *November* 1642.

He denies that his brother, John (60 troop) was the first to fly on the left wing, and tells us that none of Lord Saye's sons were on that wing. John Fiennes had been at Evesham before the battle.

He alleges that Captain Robert Vivers (65 troop) 'in one of Colonell Goodwin's Troops' was one of the first that ran. He goes on to say that Captain John Fiennes 'tooke a great deale of pains to make his own men and Captain Vivers men which were with him to stand, and to stop the Run-aways that came from the Army, and this he did, and made two or three stands, and at length gathered a pretty body upon a hill together, and with them (there being Captain [Edward] Keightlyes and Captain [Oliver] Cromwell's Troopes at length came to them also) he marched towards the Towne; and hearing the enemy was there (as indeed they were there with the greatest part of their horse) they made a stand, and sending forth their Scouts to give them intelligence of Colonell Hampdens Brigadoe that was coming another way to the town, and so joyning themselves unto them, they came to the Army together.'

Nathaniel Fiennes goes on to say that his brother John showed much courage at Worcester (Powick Bridge) and that all Lord Saye's three sons are safe.

British Museum, Thomason Tracts. E.126/38.

5. CAPTAIN EDWARD KIGHTLEY'S LETTER

Published at London, 4 *November* 1642. Kightley, or Kyghley, appears in the list of the Parliament Army as commander of 35 troop. He was killed at Chewton Mendip on 10 June 1643.

'... hee [the King] had the advantage of the ground and wind, and they did give a very brave charge, and did fight very valiantly; ...' He says that the Royalists had 15 regiments, F., and 60 regiments (troops), H. He gives the Parliamentarian strength as 11 regiments, F., and 40 regiments (troops) H. After stating that 600 Parliamentarian horse ran away he continues:

'I was quartered five miles from this place, and heard not any thing of it, untill one one of the Clocke in the afternoone, I hasted thither with Sergeant Major [Alex.] Duglis' troope [38 troope] and over-tooke one other troope, and when I was entring into the field, I thinke 200 horse came by me with all the speed they could out from the battell, saying, that the King had the victory, and that every man cried for God and King Charles. I entreated, prayed, and perswaded them to stay, and draw up in a body with our Troopes, for we saw them fighting, and the Field was not lost, but no perswasions would serve, and then I turning to our three troopes, two of them were runne away and of my Troope' I had not six and thirtie men left.

Staying in a little field with a way through, his troop took about 10 or 12 horse and disarmed 40. They could have killed them all. He goes on ' . . . the Armies were both in a confusion, and I could not fall to them without apparent losse of my selfe and those few which were with me, . . . '

Kightley mentions that Captain [Jo.] Fleming and his cornet [Ed. Fleming] were both killed or taken prisoner, and adds 'he had not one officer which was a souldier . . . '

The captain, who lost his waggon and money, gives his opinion that 'our foote and Dragooners were the greatest Pillagers'. According to him the Royal Standard was in Parliamentarian hands for an hour and a half. He estimates that Essex's army did not lose over 300 men.

1   Mortally wounded at Powick Bridge.

B.M., Thomason Tracts, E. 126/13.

6. SIR SAMUEL LUKE'S ACCOUNT

Luke was commissioned as captain, H., on 30 July 1642, and as Scoutmaster-General on 14 January 1643. In a letter to the Committee of Accounts of 13 November 1646 he explained his inability to produce his commissions:

' . . . that for my horse it bore date with the first but was lost at Edgehill and I canne not finde any record of it. There I lost my sumpture [sumpter] and many horses and had my waggon plundred but my officers and others are ready to testifie it uppon oath, for that for my scoute masters place it was lost at [First] Newbury where I lost both waggon and horses.'

I.G. Philip, Journal of Sir Samuel Luke, I., pp. v-vii. Oxfordshire Record Society, 1947.

Appendices

METEOROLOGICAL OBSERVATIONS
AT R.A.F. GAYDON (432FT) ON THURSDAY NOVEMBER 3RD, 1966

Time	Wind (Degs from True North)	Knots	Visibility (Statute miles or yards)	Temperature °C	Humidity %	M.S.L. Pressure (Millibars)	Remarks
0050	030	6	3 mls	--0.6	91	1024.6	Sky Clear. Frost.
0155	030	6	3 mls	--0.7	93	1023.8	1/8 4000' Frost.
0254	030	8	3 mls	+0.3	85	1023.3	7/8 5000' Frost.
0353	360	10	4 mls	+0.5	89	1022.3	7/8 5000' Frost.
0450	360	9	4 mls	+1.0	93	1022.2	7/8 4100' Frost.
0554	010	7	4 mls	+1.5	88	1021.7	7/8 4000' Frost.
0652	330	2	3 mls	+1.4	87	1021.5	1/8 4000' Frost.
0751	330	6	4 mls	+1.4	85	1021.0	1/8 4000' Frost.
0854	340	6	3800yd	+1.8	87	1020.6	1/8 4500' Frost. (Last traces cleared by 0900)
0953	360	7	4000yd	+3.5	86	1020.1	2/8 5000'
1054	010	9	21/2mls	+4.7	89	1019.7	2/8 4500' 1/8 15,000'
1153	350	8	23/4mls	+5.1	86	1018.6	3/8 4800' 1/8 12,000'
1252	350	10	3 mls	+6.5	84	1017.8	1/8 1700' 3/8 5000'
1353	360	10	3 mls	+6.4	80	1017.0	2/8 2200' 1/8 5000' 2/8 12,000'
1453	340	7	23/4mls	+6.4	78	1016.4	1/8 2000' 1/8 5000' 2/8 22,000'
1553	330	5	3 mls	+5.6	82	1015.6	1/8 4500' 1/8 25,000'
1653	310	4	3 mls	+4.3	85	1014.8	2/8 22,000'
1753	330	2	3 mls	+3.5	90	1014.6	2/8 22,000'
1852	330	5	4000yd	+3.5	88	1014.0	2/8 22,000' Dew forming
1952	Calm		3500yd	+1.2	92	1013.6	1/8 22,000' Frost
2051	Calm		3500yd	+1.2	96	1013.0	1/8 4000' 2/8 22,000' Frost
2120★	Calm		1100yd	--	--	--	3/8 22,000' Mist & Frost
2151	Calm		1000yd	--0.5	99	1012.2	3/8 22,000' Fog & Frost
2254	190	5	600yd	--0.4	99	1011.2	1/8 10.000' 3/8 22,000' Fog & Frost
2352	190	4	700yd	+0.5	98	1010.1	4/8 5000' 2/8 10,000' 3/8 22,000' Fog & Frost

★ Special observation due to reduction in Visibility.

Maximum temperature 0900–2100   +7.3°C
Minimum temperature 2100 (2nd)–0900 (3rd)   –1.1°C
Grass level minimum temperature   –4.1°C
Rainfall – Nil.

The poor visibilities during the day were due to industrial haze from the Midlands.

Sunrise 0700   Hours of Bright Sunshine 7¾ (estimated hourly since
Sunset 1630   no sunshine recorder at Gaydon)
Morning Nautical Twilight 0550   Evening Nautical Twilight 1750

A SIDELIGHT ON THE RAISING OF THE ROYALIST ARMY

The information contained in this appendix relates to Chapter VII. The documents upon which it is based were sent to the author in reply to a letter in *The Times Literary Supplement* and arrived too late to be used at the time of writing that chapter.

In 1702 William Beaw, (1615–1705) Bishop of Llandaff composed a short history of his long life★.

'In the beginning of the war between Charles I and the Parliament before the battle of Edgehill,' Beauw, who had been made a Fellow of New College, Oxford, in 1638, 'left his studies and advantages and went into the King's service, carrying with him of his Pupils and other scholars and gentlemen no less than 12 . . . '

The twelve were:

(1) Erasmus Sacheverell (1620–c.1647), eldest son of Ambrose Sacheverell, rector of Tadmorton, Oxfordshire. A scholar of Winchester in 1634, he matriculated from New College, 17 November 1637, aged 17, and took his B.A., 16 May 1641. Beaw describes him as 'Fellow of that College, his pupil and afterwards Major of Dragoons'. Sacheverell compounded (16 December 1646) admitting that he had been in arms, but asserting that he had come in on 20 April 1646 and enlisted under Captain Pile in a Parliamentarian troop of horse under Major-General (Richard) Browne and taken the National Covenant. The death of his father, a delinquent, had given him a sequestered estate, for which he was compounding. Sacheverell did not long survive as a turncoat for he was dead by 2 August 1647, when administration of his estate was granted at Oxford.

(2) Timothy Blencow (–1668), seventh son of John Blencow of Marston St. Lawrence, Northants. Beaw calls him 'Fellow of the same College his Pupil and afterwards Major of Foot'. Blencow had been a Fellow since 1638. He served under Colonel Edward Broughton and Colonel Richard Beard, and is probably the Major Blyncott (sic) taken prisoner at Colchester in 1648. He became B.C.L., 2 November 1647, was ejected from his fellowship by the Parliamentarian visitors in 1648 and restored in 1660. In 1661 he was lieutenant of Captain Robert Legge's company in the garrison of Portsmouth. He died unmarried.

(3) John Price (c.1621–1685) from Llanasaph, Flintshire, whom Beauw describes as 'Fellow of same College his Pupil and afterwards Captain of Horse'. Price had become a Fellow in 1641. According to Foster he was a major in Charles I's army. Expelled in 1648, he was restored in 1660. He was created M.A. on 12 February 1661, was Vicar of Mold, 1661–1663, and Rector of Hawarden,

Flintshire, 1666–1685, created B.D. and D.D. on 26 June 1669, he became a Canon of St. Asaph, 1682–1685. His monument is at Hawarden. Norman Tucker informs me that he was a younger brother of Colonel William Price of Rhiwlas (near Bala) and served in his regiment of foot.

(4) Thomas Rivers (c.1622–) fourth son of Sir John Rivers of Chafford in Penshurst, Kent, whom Beaw describes as 'Fellow of the same College and afterwards Cornet of Horse'. He had matriculated from St. Edmund Hall, 16 April 1641, aged 19, and became a Fellow of New College in 1643. Although he did not submit to the Parliamentary Visitors in 1648, it is uncertain whether he was expelled.

(5) John Rivers, third (?) son of Sir John Rivers, who Beaw tells us was Thomas' brother and 'afterward Captain of Horse'. He was created M.A. 1 November 1642 in the 'Caroline Creation', which is proof that he had served in the Edgehill army. Foster's tentative suggestion that this John Rivers was 'possibly student of Middle Temple 1644, as second son of Marcellus Rivers, barrister of that Society' is certainly erroneous.

(6) Robert Bainham (Baynham) (c.1617–1669) of Yate, Gloucestershire, 'Fellow of the same College afterwards Cornet of Horse'. Fellow of New College, 1644; B.A., 9 February 1647; expelled, 1648, and restored, 1660, he died, aged 52, on 8 December 1669. From the scrolled tablet with a cartouche of his arms in New College cloisters it is evident that he was a member of the armigerous family of Baynham of Westbury, Gloucestershire. Wood, recording his death, calls him a physician.

(7) William Ayliff (Ayliffe) (–1664). 'Fellow of the same, after Quarter-master to a Regiment of Horse'. He is not to be confused with Colonel William, son of Sir Benjamin Ayliffe, an officer who only fought in the second Civil War. The quartermaster was at Winchester College in 1632, became a Fellow of New College in 1640 and was created BCL, 11 December 1646. He was Headmaster of Thame School from 1647–1655 and Vicar of Ambrosden, near Bicester, Oxfordshire, from 1655–1664. Anthony Wood describes his end. He 'leaped naked out of his window belonging to the vicaridge of Amersden, & broke several parts of his body, and died soon after. He had married a yong rich widdow, lived high, and had severall children by her; but shee dying in the prime of her yeares, & leving him & the children little or nothing of her estate, & her joynture going away with her life, he grew exceedingly discontented thereupon, & made away with himself'. (Life & Times, II, p. 11.)

(8) Daniel Appleford (1616–1645), son of Daniel Appleford, of Michelmarsh, Hampshire, armiger. Another Wykehamist he matriculated from New College,

---

* Dated 23 April 1702 it came down through the Willis family to Bickham Sweet-Escott Esq., who kindly communicated its contents to the author.

6 November 1635, aged 16, was created B.A., 13 June 1639, and M.A. 12 April 1643. Beaw says he was a Fellow but Foster does not confirm this. His will was proved at Oxford, 5 August 1645.

(9) John Trussell, doubtless the second son of James Trussell of London, cloth-worker (Visitation of London, 1634). Beaw merely tells us that he was 'Brother to one of his pupils'. but Foster gives no Trussell who fits this description. He lived to see the Restoration for in *A List of [Indigent] Officers* we find 'Middlesex Trussell John Lieut. to Maj. [(Sir) Richard] Hatton' under Colonel Sir Richard Willys. From this we may suppose that in 1642 Trussell, like his future troop commander, was a volunteer in Willy's troop in Lord Grandison's Regiment.

(10) John Creech, gentleman, who is not mentioned by Foster, was not an indigent officer, and escaped the attentions of both the Parliamentarian Committees for Compounding and for the Advance of Money.

(11) John Cresswell (1611/2–1654) the son of Richard Cresswell of Purston, Northamptonshire. If he was a member of the University he is not mentioned by Foster. In 1645 he was Treasurer of Banbury garrison, which was the stronghold of the Earl of Northampton. His activities attracted the attention of the Committee for the Advance of Money (p. 966) which ordered that his estate be seized and secured (23 May 1649). Briefly the case against him was that he had been receiver under Sir William Compton of moneys for Banbury garrison, 'and a great gainer by these wars'. He was said to have a large estate at Purston and Charlton, let at £240 per annum, and stocked by himself. He had another estate at Lye, Aston Canes, Wiltshire, and this was let at £120. He had compounded for neither. His activities were described (25 April 1649) by William Dry and Richard Hall of Weedon, who alleged that 'six years since' – which seems to mean during the Edgehill campaign of 1642 – 'some of Prince Rupert's forces under Col. [Lewis] Kirk were in Helmedon, where Creswell (sic) willed them to plunder the town'. They took 86 horses, and plundered Dry of goods worth £80. Not content with this they tied him neck and heels and detained him two days and a night, on Cresswell's accusation that he was 'an enemy to the King'. Cresswell was evidently well-to-do. In 1652 the Committee was informed that he had a personal estate, value £3000 or £4000 in sheep, cattle &c. This had been seized in 1649, but discharged on false pretenses that they belonged to others! (CAM 966–8)

Cresswell married Elizebeth daughter and co-heir of Rowland Wilcox of Lilbourne, Northamptonshire, and had two sons and six daughters. He was killed in a duel on 21 May 1654 at the age of 42.

(12) Thomas Colebrand, 'gent, Commoner of Edmund Hall'. Thomas Colborne or Colebrond was created M.A. on 1 November 1642, another of those whose military services in the Edgehill campaign were recognized by an award in the 'Caroline creation'. Nothing else is known of him but it is tempting to suppose that he was related to Flamock Colborne of the Earl of Northampton's Regiment

of Horse. This leads to speculation as to when precisely Beaw and his band of twelve friends joined the King.

Had they still been at Oxford during Sir John Byron's visit (28 August–10 September) they would obviously have departed when, on the approach of Parliamentarian forces, he was compelled to withdraw. Fighting had begun in the Midlands when early in August the Earl of Northampton took some cannon from Lord Brooke. There had been quite a serious skirmish at Southam on 23 August. Cresswell was certainly a neighbour and supporter of the Earl, while Sacheverell, and Blencow, living as they did in Oxfordshire and Northampton-shire might be expected to join the nearest important Royalist commander. Willys was at Kenilworth in August (Dugdale, p. 18). and it may well be that Trussell joined him at that period. On the whole then I am inclined to the theory that Beaw and his party first joined the Earl of Northampton about the beginning of August, and were with the main Royalist army from the time that the Earl's forces were absorbed into it. In addition the M.A.s to John Rivers and Thomas Colborne may be looked upon as awards for their military service at Edgehill.

As to Beaw's own career. 'He himself served the King from a Pike to a Major of Horse★, was wounded in the service (and on that account still halts) and kept long a Prisoner of war, and at last turned out of his Fellowship and all that he had, and forced by his sword (which at first he never intended to draw but for his own Prince) to seek his bread in foreign parts, . . . ' He became a lieutenant-colonel of horse in the service of the Czar of Muscovy but left 'that honorable and profitable service to serve King Charles II in his affairs beyond the seas'. He undertook 'many journeys by sea and land, and endured many hardships and often ran the hazard of his life for the space of about 2 years together, and all this out of his own purse . . . ' 'and the poor remainder of his fortune spent, he was forced' to go into the army of King Charles X of Sweden 'whom he served in all his Polish wars and afterwards in the service of the King of Poland . . . ' At the Restoration he entered Holy Orders and was restored to his Fellowship 'by order of the King'. (30 August, 1660). He was presented to the New College living of Adderbury, North Oxfordshire, on 2 February 1661 and resigned his Fellowship on 26 August following. He was a single man and was quite well off. Adderbury brought him a yearly income of £330 and he had in addition 'no inconsiderable sum of money abroad in the hands of some friends'. He could afford to give his college £10 towards the New Buildings erected in the Garden Quadrangle in the 1660s.

A few years later he married Frances, daughter of Alexander Bourchier of Southampton who bore him eight children. In 1679 King Charles II rewarded him with the see of Llandaff, one of the poorest in the country. Its income amounted (c.1702) to no more than £420, though since he retained his living

---

★ His great-great-grandfather Guillaume Beau, is said to have been a colonel of foot at the siege of Boulogne (1544).

of Adderbury his sufferings cannot have been too grave. Encouraged by a typically vague promise from the monarch – 'My Lord, I do not intend that you shall die Bishop of Llandaff' – the old Cavalier set his thoughts, first on the see of Hereford, and then of St. Asaph. But he was a 'stranger at court' though Evelyn heard him preach there on 18 March 1683, and preferment did not come his way. He was a supporter of the Seven Bishops which may conceivably have stood in the way of his advancement. Despite a serious accident to his leg in 1683 he was still sufficiently vigorous to attend Queen Anne at her Coronation (1702) and 'walked all the way both forward and backward'.

In 1692 Beaw described himself as a good friend of Henry Compton, Bishop of London (1632–1713), who was the youngest of the six loyal sons of the Earl of Northampton who was so active for the King in 1642. One is tempted to hazard the guess that this was a friendship dating back to the days of the Civil Wars.

In compiling these notes on Beaw and this band of friends who joined the King in time for Edgehill I have had a great deal of assistance from Miss Margaret Toynbee and Bickham Sweet-Escott, Esq. The authorities consulted include Foster's *Alumni Oxonienses*, the Visitations of London (1643), of Oxfordshire (1634), and of Northamptonshire (1618 and 1681) as well as Wood's Life and Times.

THE NORWOODS

The four sons of Richard Norwood of Leckhampton (1574–1630) all served the King, and two of them fought at Edgehill. The four were:

Charles Norwood (1613–1692), who fought at Edgehill in the regiment of Colonel Richard Feilding and rose to the rank of major. He was Clark to the Virginia Assembly, 1654–1657.

Henry Norwood (1614–1689), who had a successful career, fought at Edgehill in Usher's Dragoons. He distinguished himself at I Bristol, and was with Henry Washington in his defence of Worcester (1646). In 1648 he and some friends, including his old comrade-in-arms, Major Francis Morrison, planned an expedition to Virginia, where Norwood's second cousin, Sir William Berkeley, was Governor. He sailed from Deal on 23 September 1649 abroad the *Virginia Merchant*.

In 1654 he was implicated in a plot for distributing arms in Worcestershire, Leicestershire, Staffordshire and Derbyshire, and the following year was arrested on suspicion of complicity in Gerard's Plot. Examined by Cromwell himself he 'proved a peremptory fellow and would not confess'. He spent five years in the Tower. In 1659 he and Sir John Boys, 'formerly great cavaliers', carried letters to King Charles II in Holland (Pepys' Diary, 21 April and 3 May 1659). On 24 March 1660 he was made an Esquire of the Body and the King presented him with a silver porringer. He was present at the coronation of King Charles II. His subsequent military career was remarkable.

Major	Lord Rutherford, F.	7 Sept. 1661.
	Garrison of Dunkirk.	
Lieut. Colonel	Garrison of Dunkirk.	10 March 1662.
Deputy Governor of Dunkirk		19 March 1662.
Lieut. Colonel	The (1st) Tangier Regt., F.	9 April 1663.
Colonel	The (2nd) Tangier Regt., F.	11 Aug. 1664.
Lieut. Governor Tangier		21 Feb. 1666.

He took part in the capture of New York and returned to England in 1669. He was J.P. for Gloucester (1670) and M.P. for that city (1675–1678).

William Norwood (1615–1703). No details of his military career are known. He emigrated to Virginia in 1648.

Thomas Norwood (1618–1645), probably missed Edgehill as he was taken when Sir John Byron's Regiment was attacked at Brackley on 28 August 1642. He became a captain and was killed at Taunton in 1645.

G. Marion Norwood Callam, The Norwoods. An Introduction to their History, Vol. I, and Dalton, Vol. I.

RELICS OF THE BATTLE

In July 1967 Miss M. Fell of 58 Keswick Walk, Wyken, Coventry, presented three lead musket balls to the author. These were picked up on the battlefield some 80 years ago by her grandfather, a Mr Hemming, a native of Kineton – of the family of John Hemming or Hemminge (d. 1630), actor and co-editor of the first folio of Shakespeare. Two of the bullets weigh 1 1/4 oz. and the other 1 1/8 oz. The line round the circumference caused by the bullet mould can be clearly seen on the two heavier bullets. The author has a bullet from Marston Moor which weighs just over an ounce, and five from Naseby, one of which weighs fractionally more than an oz., and the others just under. During a search of the Gravesend Copse area, using mine detectors, a leaden musket ball, weighing approximately 1 1/4 oz. was found (1967).

Another bullet, given to a Mr Prickett, and now in the possession of David Fisher, was weighed in the author's presence (6 August 1967) and found to be 2lb. 14 3/4oz. In theory a minion was a 4-pounder and a falcon a 2 1/4-pounder. This bullet would be too large for the latter, and would have made a very inaccurate projectile for the former; fitting the barrel very badly and therefore having altogether too much 'windage' it would wander in its flight. It was picked up at Moorlands Farm and must, therefore, have been discharged by the Parliamentarian artillery. A similar ball was found at Hornton by a Mr Yates.

On 5 August Mr T. Jeffes of Radway showed the author two cannon-balls given to him by a Mr Griffin in 1964. These came from the Thistleton Farm area and had been taken thence in about 1941, when the War Department took over. They weigh approximately 23 1/2 lbs. and 12lbs. respectively, from which one would conclude that they were fired by a demi-cannon and a culverin respectively. One would expect that balls found in the Thirstleton Farm area would be from the Royalist guns. Certainly they had two demi-cannon –

theoretically 27-pounders – and two culverins – theoretically 15-pounders. The Parliamentarians lost two 12-pounders in the battle, and it is not impossible that the second bullet was ammunition for one of them.

Mr Martin Jeffes showed the author a musket bullet similar to those sent him by Miss Fell. He had discovered this (c.1963) while ditching about a quarter of a mile NW of the present Radway Church. This could be a Parliamentarian bullet fired during the last phase of the battle.

A ball weighing 19 pounds and two others weighing only half a pound each, are in the possession of Lord Leyster Hospital, Warwick. They were found near Thistleton Farm and should therefore be Royalist missiles. The three small balls may be caseshot, but they could have been fired from a robinet, which was a 3/4 pounder.

During the construction of the Central Ammunition Depot, Kineton (1942), six or more cannon balls were found in the vicinity of the Graveyard. Their weight is said to have varied from 6 to 22 pounds, but it seems that their exact weight and precise location were not properly recorded and so this proves very little.

In 1922, during the construction of the Ironstone Railway from Edgehill to Kineton, some cannon-balls were found in a disused brick-kiln at a point described as 300 yards east along the Arlescote Road from the foot of Bullet Hill. These must have been some of the shots from Ramsey's wing which, as Bulstrode tell us, 'mounted over our Troops, without doing any Hurt, . . . '

Other relics of the battle include hand made nails, a seventeenth century horseshoe and part of the rim of a heavy vehicle found during the mine detector search of Great Grounds (1967), a spear (pike?) head found by Mr Yates of Hornton, and a pikehead found at Upland Farm in 1950, and now in the Banbury Museum. The same Museum possesses a sword found in Broughton Church yard, while Mr L. Todd of Manor Farm, Ratley, found another sword in 1950. Grimmer remains were found in about 1880 near the ford on the Little Kineton to Kineton road; the skeletons of several men, perhaps Parliamentarian runaways, or men detailed to escort the baggage train.

One is struck by the fact that a number of these cannon balls do not fit neatly into the various types of artillery used in 1642. One would expect to find 27 or 15 pound balls for demi-cannon and culverin, yet we find balls of 23 1/2, 22 and 19 pounds. It is evident that theory and practice did not go hand in hand. Yet this is not so surprising when we recall the charges of inefficiency levelled against the Parliamentarian artillery, and the difficulties of the Royalists in providing a train at all. Their troubles are illustrated by a petition recently found in the Public Record Office by Dr. Ian Roy:

When his late Matie: was to take the feilde, the firste Councell of war appointed Sr John Heydon Sr John Pennington Sr Bryan Palmes Sr George Strode and John Wandesforde to forme and conduct the traine of Artillery att Edge hill, Sr George received woundes which were helde mortall, and John Wandesforde alone brought of the trayne to Oxforde and his

Highenesse Prince Ruperte did Commaunde dragoones to dismounte and Imployed those in that Saruice. (S.P.29.66. No. 46)

One can only admire the Prince's talent for improvisation. The comments of the dragoons are best left to the readers' imagination.

Bibliography

(*Place of publication London, unless otherwise stated*)

A List of [Indigent] Officers: A List of Officers Claiming to the Sixty Thousand Pounds &c. Granted by His Sacred Majesty [King Charles II] for the Relief of his Truly-Loyal and Indigent Party, 1663.

T. ARNOLD: Note on the Battle of Edgehill. EHR. Vol. II, 1887.

Captain Richard ATKYNS: Military Memoirs. The Civil War. Richard Atkyns, ed. by Brigadier Peter Young. John Gwyn, ed. by Norman Tucker, 1967.

W. H. BLACK: Docquets of Letters Patent . . . of King Charles I at Oxford, 1837. (Printed but unpublished. There is a copy in the PRO, Round Room.)

D. BRUNTON and D. H. PENNINGTON: Members of the Long Parliament, 1954.

Sir Richard BULSTRODE: Memoirs . . . 1721. His account of the 1642 campaign is reprinted in Part III.

Lt. Colonel A. H. BURNE, DSO: Battlefields of England, 1950. Includes a chapter on Edgehill.

Lt. Colonel Alfred H. BURNE, DSO, FRHist.S., and Lt. Colonel Peter YOUNG: The Great Civil War, A Military History of the First Civil War, 1642–1646, 1959.

Rev. Adoniram BYFIELD: A Letter sent from a Worthy Divine. Printed in Part III.

CAM: Calendar of the Proceedings of the Committee for Advance of Money, 1642–1656, ed. M. A. E. Green, 3 vols., 1888.

CCC: Calendar of the Proceedings of the Committee for Compounding, &c., 1643–1660, ed. M. A. E. Green, 5 vols., 1889–92.

CSPD: Calendar of State Papers, Domestic. 1641–1643.

Earl of CLARENDON: The History of the Rebellion and Civil War in England (Ed. W. D. Macray.) Oxford, 1888. Six Vols. This is by far the best edition of Clarendon.

J. W. CLAY (ed.): Yorkshire Royalist Composition Papers, 3 Vols., Yorkshire Archaeological Society, Record Series, Vols., 15, 18, 20, 1893–6.

Charles DALTON (ed): English Army Lists and Commission Registers, 1661–1714, Vol. I (1661–1685), 1892.

Godfrey DAVIES: The Battle of Edgehill. EHR. Vol. 36, 1921.

Godfrey DAVIES: The Parliamentary Army under the Earl of Essex, 1642–5. EHR 1934.

Sir Bernard DE GOMME: 'Plane of the Battle of Etch Hill 1642.' Royal Library, Windsor Castle. 111/22.

'DESERTER': A Most True Relation of the Present State of His Majesties Army, &c. Printed for I. E. at the Eagle and Child in Paules Church, 1642. Received by Thomason on 3 December.

Sir William DUGDALE: The Life, Diary, and Correspondence of Sir William Dugdale, Knight . . . ed. William Hamper, 1827.

William ELDRED: The Gunner's Glasse, 1646. (B. M. Thomason Tracts, E. 371 (10)).

Sir Henry ELLIS (ed.): Original Letters . . . 2nd Series, Vol. III.

Captain Nathaniel FIENNES: His account of Edgehill is printed in Part III.

C. H. FIRTH and R. S. RAIT (ed.): Acts and Ordinances of the Interregnum, 1642–1660. 3 Vols., Vol. 1. (1642–1649), 1911.

Sir Charles FIRTH: Cromwell's Army. 3rd Edition, 1921.

C. H. FIRTH: The Journal of Prince Rupert's Marches, 5 Sept. 1642–4 July, 1646. EHR. Vol. 13, 1898.

Sir Charles FIRTH and Godfrey DAVIES: The Regimental History of Cromwell's Army. 2 Vols. Oxford, 1940.

G. K. FORTESCUE: Catalogue of the pamphlets . . . relating to the civil war . . . collected by George Thomason, 1640–1661. 1908. Thomason was a London bookseller, who collected the newspapers, tracts and broadsheets of his day as they appeared.

Samuel Rawson GARDINER: History of the Great Civil War, 1642–9. First published 1886–91. The 1903 edition (4 Vols.) has many corrections. Reprinted 1987 and 1988 The Windrush Press, Gloucestershire.

Captain John GWYN: See Captain Richard ATKYNS.

Sir John HINTON: Memoires . . . See Part III.

Major (later Colonel) Gervase HOLLES: Memorials of the Holles Family. Ed. A. C. Wood. Camden Society, Third Series, Vol. LV. 1937. The passage concerning Edgehill is printed in Part III.

Lord HOPTON: *Bellum Civile*. Somerset Record Society, 1902. Ed. Charles E. H. Chadwyck Healey, KC., FSA.

Mrs Lucy HUTCHINSON: The Life of Colonel Hutchinson. Ed. C. H. Firth. 2 Vols. 1885.

King JAMES II: Life of James II . . . collected out of memoirs writ of his own hand . . . (Ed. J. S. Clarke.) 1816. The King's valuable account of Edgehill is printed in Part III.

D.A. JOHNSON and D. G. VAISEY (ed.): Staffordshire and the Great Rebellion. Staffordshire County Council County Records Committee, 1964.

JOURNALS of the House of Commons.

Mary Frear KEELER: The Long Parliament, 1640–1641. A biographical study of its Members. Philadelphia, 1954.

Captain Edward KIGHTLEY: See Part III.

David LLOYD: Memoirs of the Lives . . . of those . . . personages that suffered . . . for the Protestant Religion and . . . allegiance to their Sovereign . . . 1637–1660. 1668.

Anthony W. G. LOWTHER, Esq., ARIBA, FSA: Ashtead, Surrey. MSS Collection. Royalist Paymaster-General's Warrant of 24 Nov. 1642.

Edmund LUDLOW: Memoirs of Edmund Ludlow. Oxford 1894. Ed. by C. H. Firth. Ludlow's eyewitness account of Edgehill will be found in Part III.

Sir Samuel LUKE: Journal of Sir Samuel Luke, ed. I. G. Philip, M.A., 3 Vols. Oxfordshire Record Society, 1947, 1950, and 1952–1953. The original is in the Bodleian Library.

Sir Samuel LUKE: The Letter Books, 1644–45. Ed. by H. G. Tibbutt, FSA. 1963. Joint publication of the Bedfordshire Historical Record Society and HMC.

MERCURIUS AULICUS: Ed. by Sir John Berkenhead. Oxford, 1643–1645. The Royalist weekly journal.

Rev. G. MILLER: Rambles Round the Edgehills, 1900. Reprinted by the Roundwood Press, 1967. Valuable for topographical information.

Walter MONEY: The First and Second Battles of Newbury and the Siege of Donnington Castle (1643–6). Edns. 1881 & 1884.

Joshua MOONE: A Briefe Relation of the Life and Memoires of John Lord Belasyse. HMC. Ormonde MSS. New Series, 1903. The account of Edgehill is printed in Part III.

Duchess of NEWCASTLE: The Life of . . . William Cavendish, Duke of Newcastle. 1886. Ed. by C. H. Firth.

The OTTLEY Papers: Original letters and papers of Sir Francis Ottley, Knight, Royalist Governor of Shrewsbury, 1642–1643. Ed. by William Phillips for The Transactions of the Shropshire Archaeological Society, 2nd Series, Vol. VI, Part I *et. seq.* 1893.

Edward PEACOCK. The Army Lists of the Roundeads and Cavaliers, Containing the Names of the officers in the Royal and Parliamentary Armies of 1642, ed. E. Peacock, 2nd edn., 1874.

D. H. PENNINGTON and I. A. ROOTS: The Committee at Stafford, 1642–1645. Manchester 1957.

J. R. PHILLIPS: Memoirs of the Civil War in Wales, 2 Vols. 1874.

POA: Parliamentarian Official Account. See Part III.

Sir James RAMSEY: The Vindication and Clearing of . . . BM. Thomason Tracts. 669. f. 6./184.

Basil N. RECKITT: Charles the First and Hull. 1639–1645. 1952.

ROA: Royalist Official Account. See Part III.

Colonel W. G. ROSS, RE: Note on the Battle of Edgehill. EHR. Vol. II, 1887.

Dr. Ian ROY: The Royalist Army in the First Civil War. Unpublished thesis. 1963.

Ian ROY: The Royalist Ordnance Papers, 1642–1646. Part I. Oxfordshire Record Society. 1964.

Ian ROY: The Royalist Council of War, 1642–6. Bulletin of the Institute of Historical Research. Vol. 35. 1962.

Prince RUPERT: 'Diary'. These notes, which from internal evidence, can be dated later than 1662, are preserved in the Wiltshire Record Office at Trowbridge. See Part III for the part relating to the Edgehill campaign.

John RUSHWORTH: Historical Collections . . . 1618–1649. 7 Vols. 1659–1701.

Sir William SANDERSON: A Compleat History of the Life and Raigne of King Charles from his Cradle to his Grave. 1658.

Colonel Sir Henry SLINGSBY: The Diary of . . . Extracts printed in the Autobiography of Captain John Hodgson. Edinburgh, 1806.

Joshua SPRIGGE, MA: *Anglia Rediviva*: England's Recovery: being the History of the Motions, Actions, and Successes of the Army under . . . Sir Thomas Fairfax, 1647.

Captain Henry STEVENS: The Papers of . . . Ed. Margaret Toynbee, MA, FSA., PhD. Oxfordshire Record Society, Vol. 42 (1961).

Lord Bernard STUART: Letter, See Part III.

Sir Edward SYDENHAM: Letter, See Part III.

Richard SYMONDS: The Diary of . . . Camden Society. Vol. 74. 1859. Ed. by C. E. Long.

Richard SYMONDS: Unpublished notebook. BM. Harleian MS. 986.

THOMASON TRACTS: E. 126 (39). Useful account of Powick Bridge by one of Captain Nathaniel Fiennes' troop.

H. G. TIBBUTT. The Life and Letters of Sir Lewis Dyve. Bedfordshire Historical Record Society, Vol. 22. 1948.

Norman TUCKER: Royalist Officers of North Wales, 1642–1660. A Provisional List. Colwyn Bay, 1961.

Jonathan TURMILE: MS Book of Standards and Colours. Dr. Williams' Library MS Modern, folio 7.

Major G. TYLDEN: Horses and Saddlery, 1965.

Captain Thomas VENN: Military and Maritime Discipline, 1672.

Major Peter VERNEY: The Standard Bearer. 1964.

J. VICARS: *Jehovah Jireh*. God in the Mount. (1641–Oct. 1642). Vol. 1 of England's Parliamentarie Chronicle. 3 Vols. 1643–6.

E. A. WALFORD: Edgehill: the Battle and Battlefield: together with some Notes on Banbury and thereabouts. Banbury, 1886. 2nd Ed. 1904.

Sir Edward WALKER: Historical Discourses, 1705.

Sir William WALLER: Vindication of the Character and conduct of . . . 1793.

Colonel Sir Robert WALSH: A true Narrative and Manifest. Holland? 1679. See Part III.

E(dward) W(ALSINGHAM): *Brittanicae Virtutis Imago or* . . . the life . . . of . . . Major-General Smith.' Oxford, 1644. (T.T.E. 53 (10)). The account of Edgehill is reprinted in Part III.

Eliot WARBURTON: Memoirs of Prince Rupert and the Cavaliers. 1849. Many of the original letters received by the Prince during the war are in the British Museum (Add. MSS).

Sir Philip WARWICK: Memoires of the Reign of King Charles I . . . 1702. Warwick's description is given in Part III.

J. WASHBOURNE: *Bibliotheca Gloucestrensis*: a collection of . . . tracts relating to the county and city of Gloucester during the civil war. Gloucester, 1825.

C. V. WEDGWOOD: The King's Peace. 1955.

C. V. WEDGWOOD: The Great Rebellion: The King's War, 1641–1647, 1958.

Colonel Lord WHARTON: Speech. BM. Thomason Tracts. E. 124. 32.

Sergeant Nehemiah WHARTON: Letters . . . Ed. by Sir Henry Ellis. *Archaeologia, Vol. XXV, 1853.*

Bulstrode WHITELOCKE: Memorials of the English Affairs. 1682. And Oxford, 1853.

WILTSHIRE: Quarter Sessions Records. The originals preserved in the Record Office at Trowbridge have been consulted. They were rather inadequately calendared in HMC. Various Collections.

Anthony WOOD: 'Survey of the Antiquities of the City of Oxford', composed in 1661–6. Ed. Andrew Clark, M.A., 3 Vols. Oxford 1899.

Anthony WOOD: The Life and Times of Anthony Wood, antiquary, of Oxford, 1632–1695, described by Himself. Ed. Andrew Clark, M.A., Vol. I. (1632–1663). Oxford, 1891.

G. WROTTESLEY: A History of the Bagot Family.

YARNTON (Oxfordshire): Parish Register.

Brig. Peter YOUNG: Oliver Cromwell and his Times. 1962.

Brig. Peter YOUNG and John ADAIR: From Hastings to Cullodon. 1964.

Peter YOUNG: King Charles I's Army of 1642. JSAHR. Vol. 17, 1938.

Peter YOUNG: King Charles I's Army of 1643–1645. JSAHR. Vol. 18, 1939.

Peter YOUNG: The Prince of Wales's Regiment of Horse, 1642–46, 3 Parts. JSAHR, Vols. 23–4, 1945–5, Vol. 31, 1953.

Peter YOUNG: The Royalist Army at Edgehill: A Seventeenth Century Plan. JSAHR, Vol. 31, 1953.

Peter YOUNG: The Royalist Artillery at Edgehill, 23rd October, 1642. JSAHR., Vol. 31, 1953.

Index

The names of all regiments and commanders are included, and all individuals given specific mention, together with all relevant place names. Battles, sieges and other engagements are italicised.

Compiled by Bruce Stevenson, FLA.

The Windrush Press

GREAT BATTLES SERIES

AGINCOURT
Christopher Hibbert
Paperback £9.99 Illustrated

HASTINGS
Peter Poyntz Wright
Paperback £9.99 Illustrated

MARSTON MOOR
Peter Young
Paperback £15.99 Illustrated

THE BOYNE AND AUGHRIM
John Kinross
Paperback £10.99 Illustrated

CORUNNA
Christopher Hibbert
Paperback £12.99 Illustrated

WELLINGTON'S PENINSULAR VICTORIES
Michael Glover
Paperback £12.99 Illustrated

TRAFALGAR: THE NELSON TOUCH
David Howarth
Paperback £12.99 Illustrated

WATERLOO: A NEAR RUN THING
David Howarth
Paperback £12.99 Illustrated

ARNHEM
Christopher Hibbert
Paperback £10.99 Illustrated

Order from THE WINDRUSH PRESS, LITTLE WINDOW, HIGH
STREET, MORETON-IN-MARSH, GLOS. GL56 0LL
MAJOR CREDIT CARDS ACCEPTED
TEL: 01608 652012 FAX: 01608 652125
£1 post and packing within the UK

The Windrush Press

MILITARY HISTORY BOOKS

A SOLDIER OF THE SEVENTY-FIRST
The Journal of a Soldier in the Peninsular War
Edited and Introduced by Christopher Hibbert
'His elegant style and his descriptive power take us with him at every step.'
The Sunday Telegraph
Paperback £9.99

THE DIARY OF A NAPOLEONIC FOOT SOLDIER
Jakob Walter
A conscript in the Grande Armée's account of the long march home
on the retreat from Moscow
Edited and Introduced by Mark Raeff
'One of the best memoirs of Napoleon's 1812 campaign'
The Guardian
Illustrated Paperback £9.99

THE RECOLLECTIONS OF RIFLEMAN HARRIS
One of the most popular military books of all time
Edited and Introduced by Christopher Hibbert
*'Describing narrow squeaks and terrible deprivations, Harris's account of fortitude and resilience
in Spain still bristles with a freshness and an invigorating spikiness.'*
Scotland on Sunday
Paperback £9.99

THE LETTERS OF PRIVATE WHEELER
An eyewitness account of the Battle of Waterloo
Edited and with a Foreword by B.H. Liddell Hart
'We have no more human account of the Peninsular War from a participant in all its battles'
The Daily Telegraph
Paperback £9.99

THE WHEATLEY DIARY
A Journal & Sketchbook from the Peninsular War &
The Waterloo Campaign
Edited and Introduced by Christopher Hibbert
Paperback £10.99 Illustrated in colour

THE RECOLLECTIONS OF SERGEANT MORRIS
A Cockney Soldier at Waterloo
Edited by John Selby
Paperback £9.99

Order from THE WINDRUSH PRESS, LITTLE WINDOW, HIGH STREET,
MORETON-IN-MARSH, GLOS. GL56 0LL
MAJOR CREDIT CARDS ACCEPTED
TEL: 01608 652012 FAX: 01608 652125
£1 p&p within the UK